Correspondence from the End of the Universe

Story & Art by Menota

1

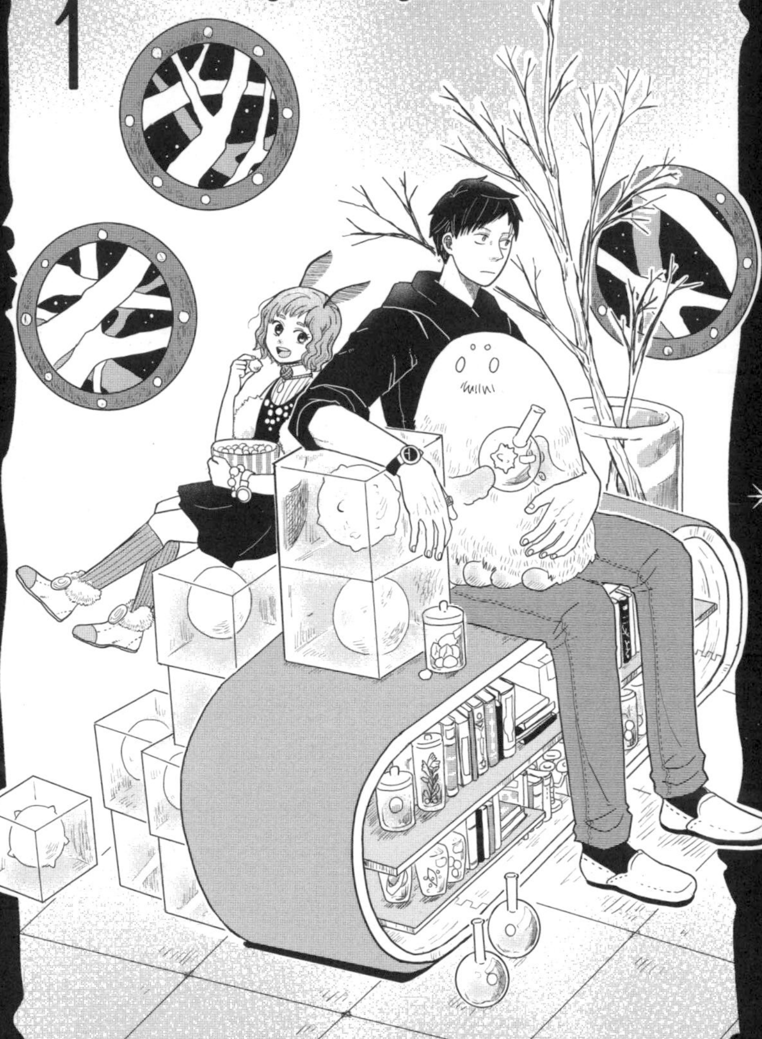

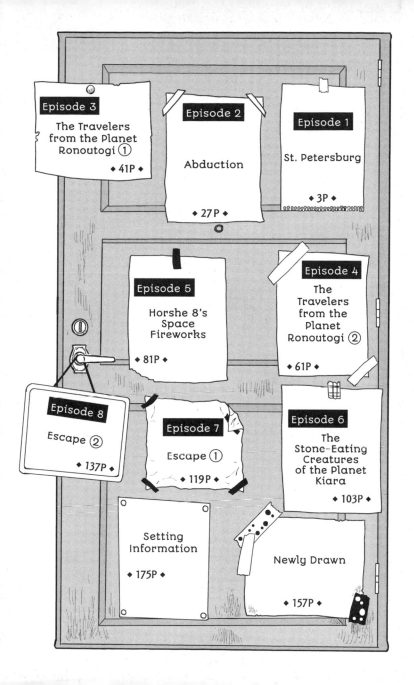

Episode 3
The Travelers from the Planet Ronoutogi ①
◆ 41P ◆

Episode 2
Abduction
◆ 27P ◆

Episode 1
St. Petersburg
◆ 3P ◆

Episode 5
Horshe 8's Space Fireworks
◆ 81P ◆

Episode 4
The Travelers from the Planet Ronoutogi ②
◆ 61P ◆

Episode 8
Escape ②
◆ 137P ◆

Episode 7
Escape ①
◆ 119P ◆

Episode 6
The Stone-Eating Creatures of the Planet Kiara
◆ 103P ◆

Setting Information
◆ 175P ◆

Newly Drawn
◆ 157P ◆

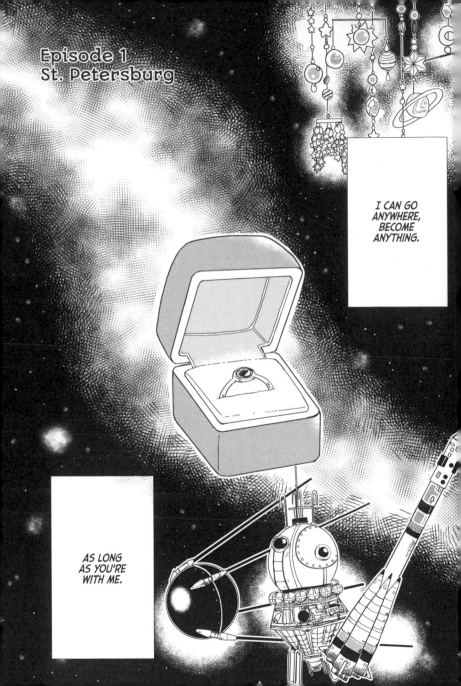

Episode 1
St. Petersburg

I CAN GO ANYWHERE, BECOME ANYTHING.

AS LONG AS YOU'RE WITH ME.

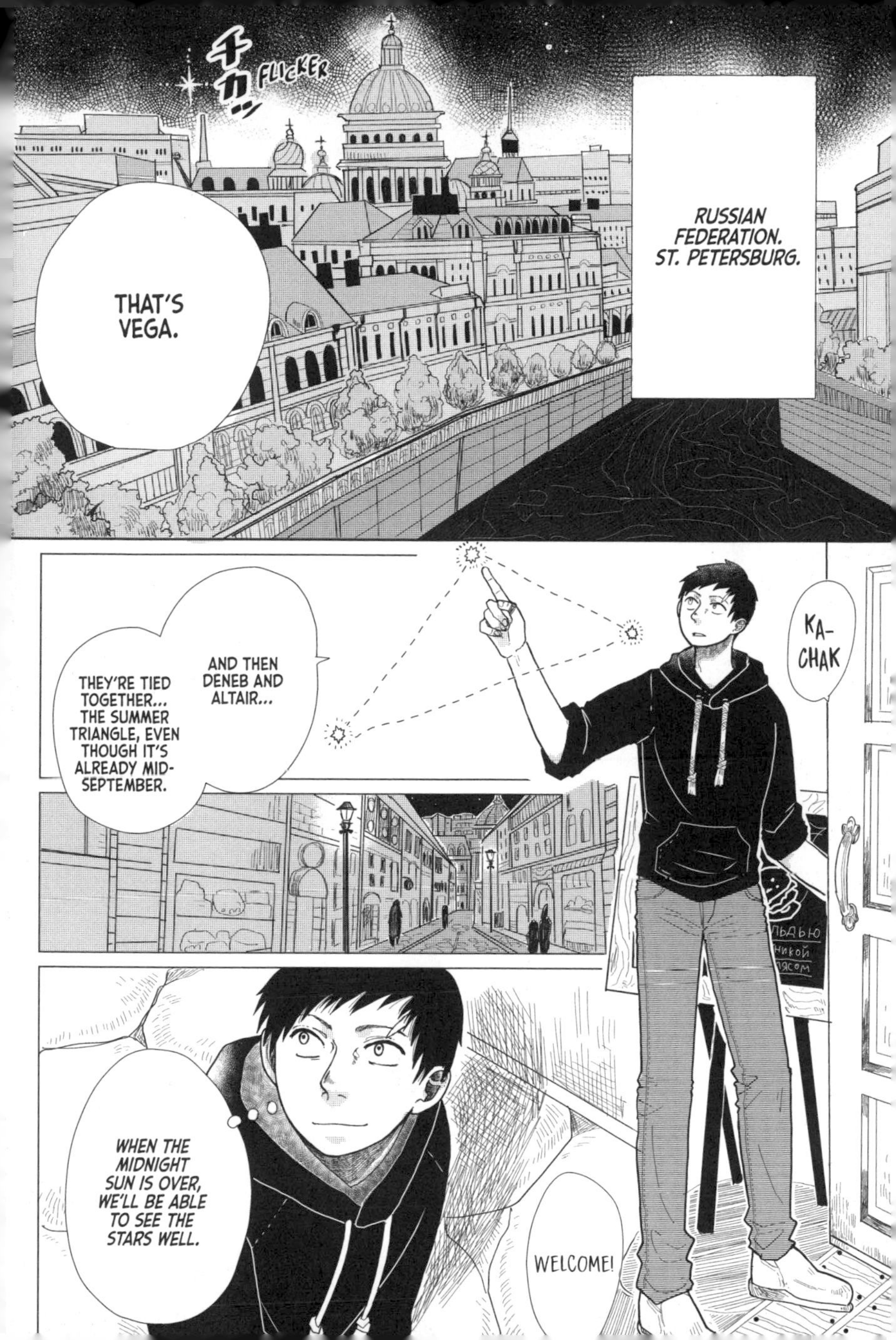
RUSSIAN FEDERATION. ST. PETERSBURG.
チカッ FLICKER
THAT'S VEGA.
KA-CHAK
AND THEN DENEB AND ALTAIR...
THEY'RE TIED TOGETHER... THE SUMMER TRIANGLE, EVEN THOUGH IT'S ALREADY MID-SEPTEMBER.
WHEN THE MIDNIGHT SUN IS OVER, WE'LL BE ABLE TO SEE THE STARS WELL.
WELCOME!

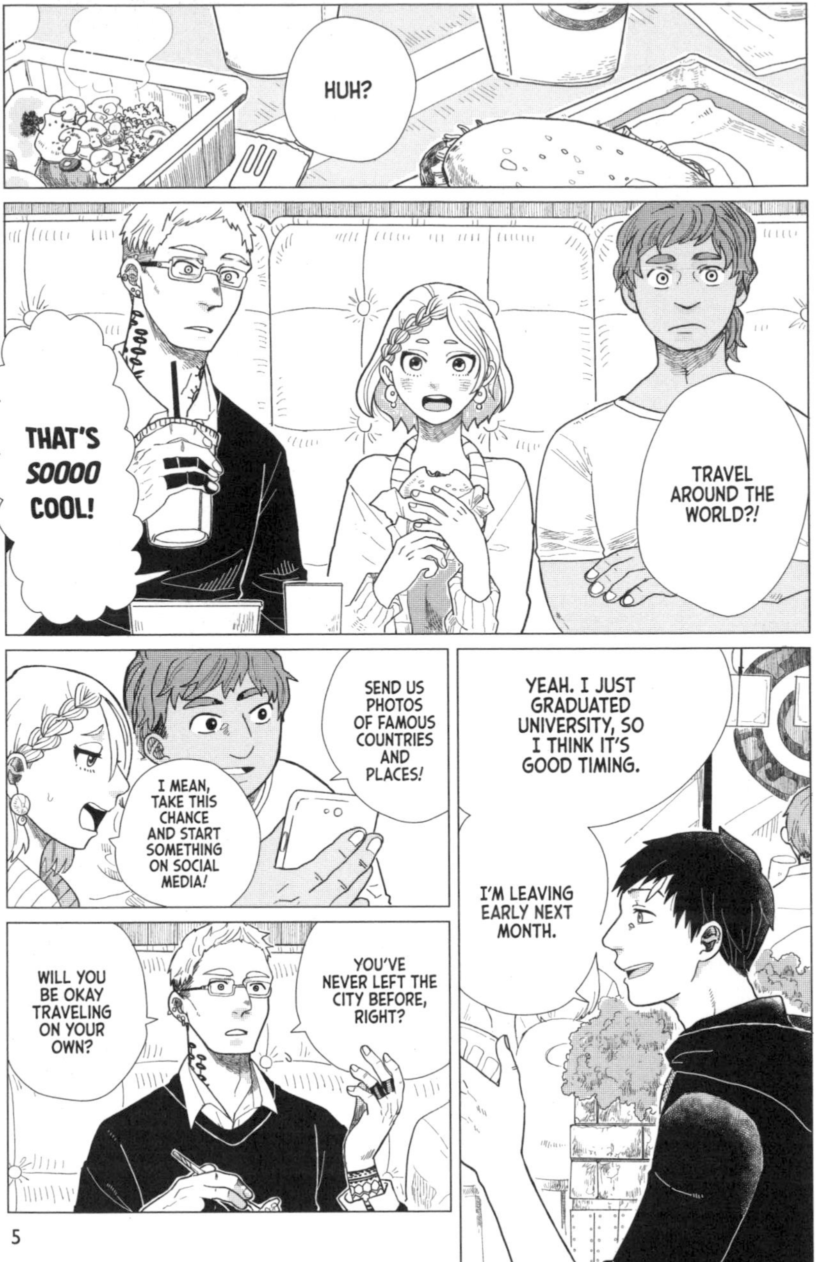
HUH?
TRAVEL AROUND THE WORLD?!
THAT'S SOOOO COOL!
YEAH. I JUST GRADUATED UNIVERSITY, SO I THINK IT'S GOOD TIMING.
I'M LEAVING EARLY NEXT MONTH.
SEND US PHOTOS OF FAMOUS COUNTRIES AND PLACES!
I MEAN, TAKE THIS CHANCE AND START SOMETHING ON SOCIAL MEDIA!
YOU'VE NEVER LEFT THE CITY BEFORE, RIGHT?
WILL YOU BE OKAY TRAVELING ON YOUR OWN?

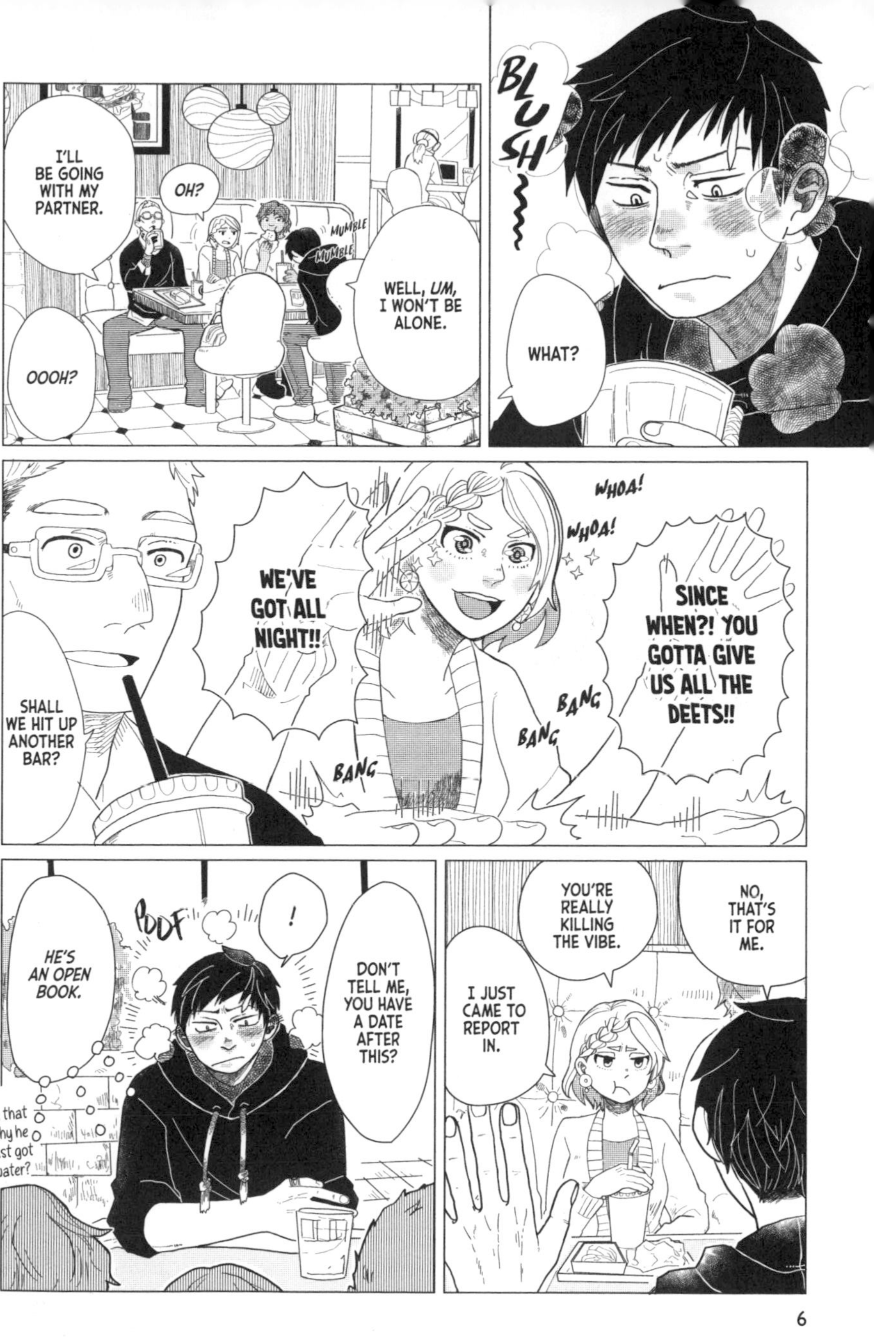
BLUSH~
WHAT?
WELL, UM, I WON'T BE ALONE.
MUMBLE MUMBLE
OH?
I'LL BE GOING WITH MY PARTNER.
OOOH?
WHOA! WHOA!
SINCE WHEN?! YOU GOTTA GIVE US ALL THE DEETS!!
BANG BANG
BANG
WE'VE GOT ALL NIGHT!!
SHALL WE HIT UP ANOTHER BAR?
NO, THAT'S IT FOR ME.
YOU'RE REALLY KILLING THE VIBE.
I JUST CAME TO REPORT IN.
DON'T TELL ME, YOU HAVE A DATE AFTER THIS?
!
POOF
HE'S AN OPEN BOOK.
Is that why he just got water?

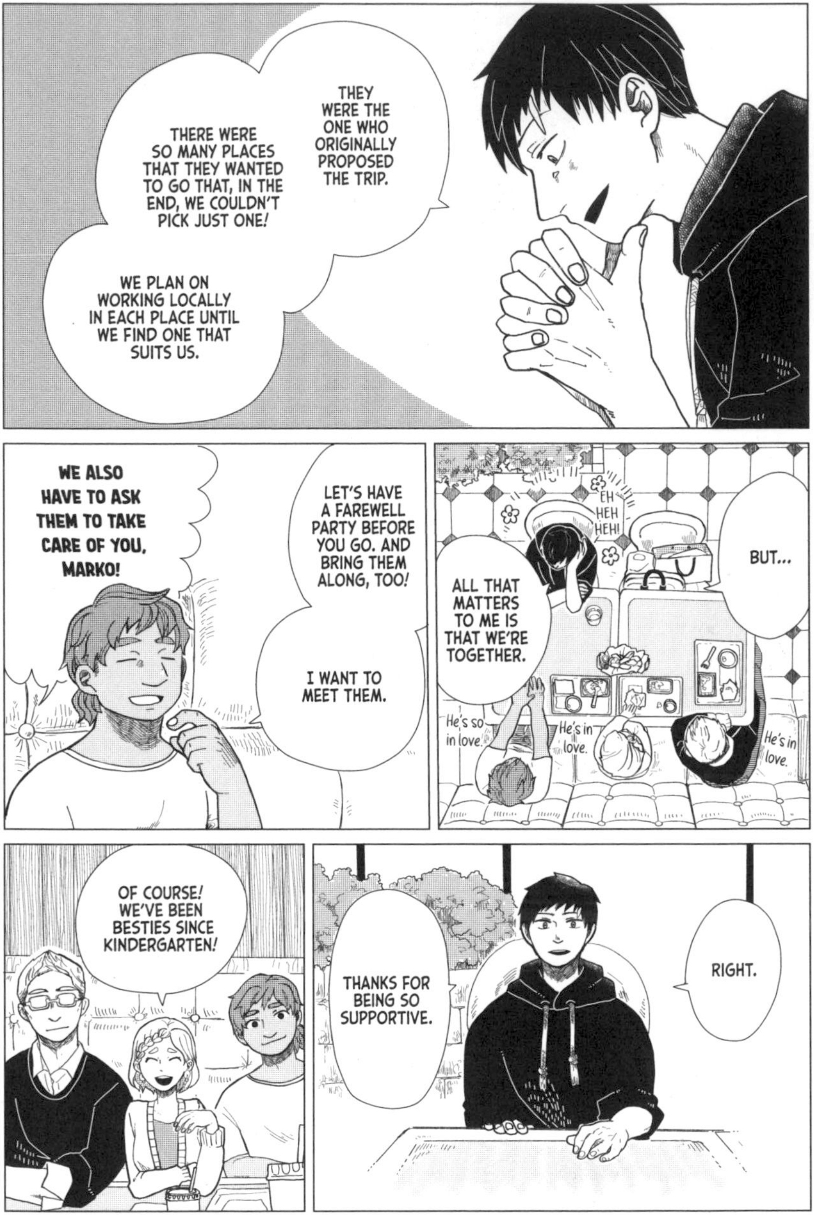
THEY WERE THE ONE WHO ORIGINALLY PROPOSED THE TRIP.
THERE WERE SO MANY PLACES THAT THEY WANTED TO GO THAT, IN THE END, WE COULDN'T PICK JUST ONE!
WE PLAN ON WORKING LOCALLY IN EACH PLACE UNTIL WE FIND ONE THAT SUITS US.
BUT...
EH HEH HEH!
ALL THAT MATTERS TO ME IS THAT WE'RE TOGETHER.
He's in love.
He's in love.
He's so in love.
LET'S HAVE A FAREWELL PARTY BEFORE YOU GO. AND BRING THEM ALONG, TOO!
I WANT TO MEET THEM.
WE ALSO HAVE TO ASK THEM TO TAKE CARE OF YOU, MARKO!
RIGHT.
THANKS FOR BEING SO SUPPORTIVE.
OF COURSE! WE'VE BEEN BESTIES SINCE KINDERGARTEN!

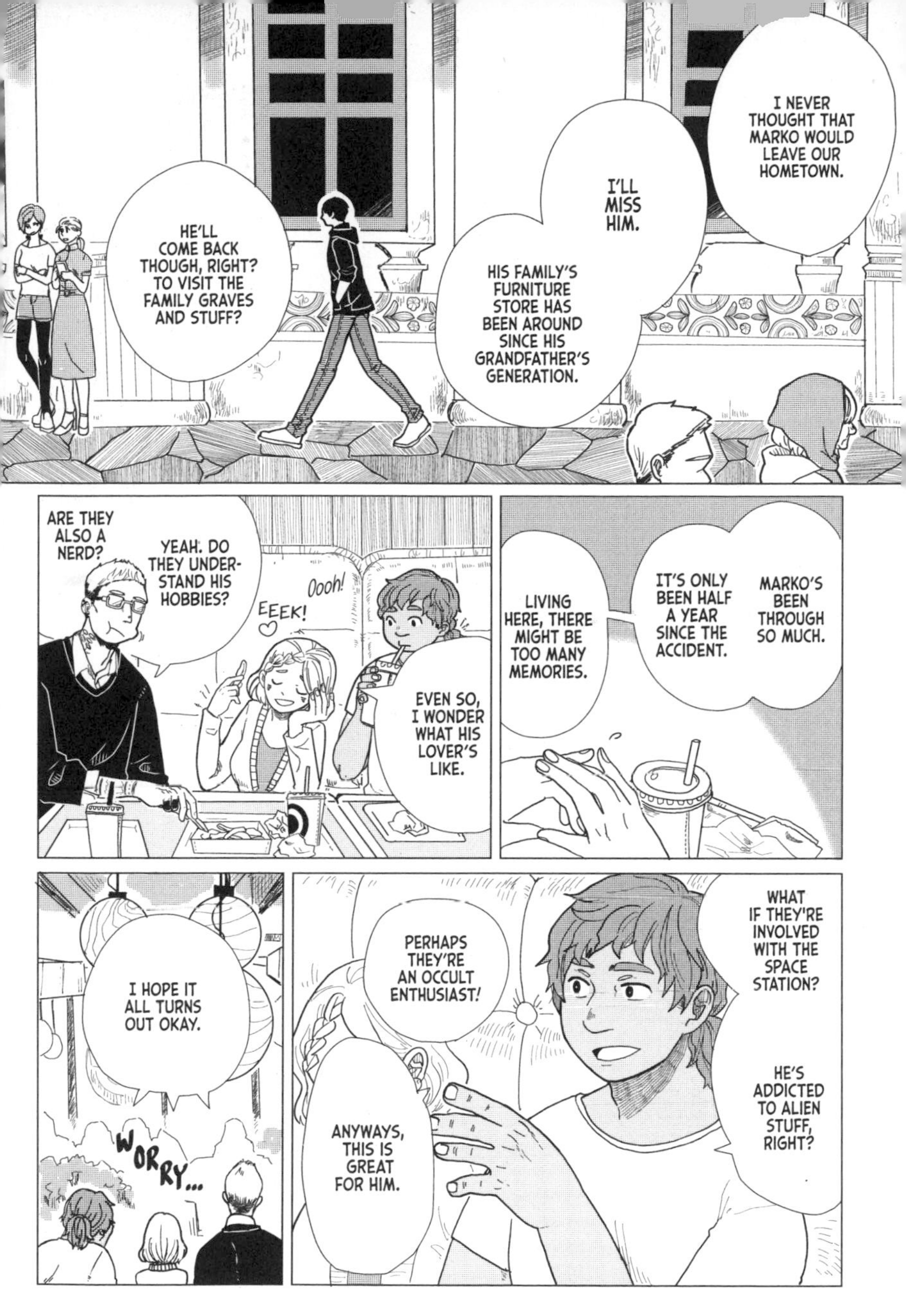
I NEVER THOUGHT THAT MARKO WOULD LEAVE OUR HOMETOWN.
I'LL MISS HIM.
HIS FAMILY'S FURNITURE STORE HAS BEEN AROUND SINCE HIS GRANDFATHER'S GENERATION.
HE'LL COME BACK THOUGH, RIGHT? TO VISIT THE FAMILY GRAVES AND STUFF?
MARKO'S BEEN THROUGH SO MUCH.
IT'S ONLY BEEN HALF A YEAR SINCE THE ACCIDENT.
LIVING HERE, THERE MIGHT BE TOO MANY MEMORIES.
EVEN SO, I WONDER WHAT HIS LOVER'S LIKE.
Oooh!
EEEK!
YEAH. DO THEY UNDER-STAND HIS HOBBIES?
ARE THEY ALSO A NERD?
WHAT IF THEY'RE INVOLVED WITH THE SPACE STATION?
PERHAPS THEY'RE AN OCCULT ENTHUSIAST!
HE'S ADDICTED TO ALIEN STUFF, RIGHT?
ANYWAYS, THIS IS GREAT FOR HIM.
I HOPE IT ALL TURNS OUT OKAY.
WORRY...

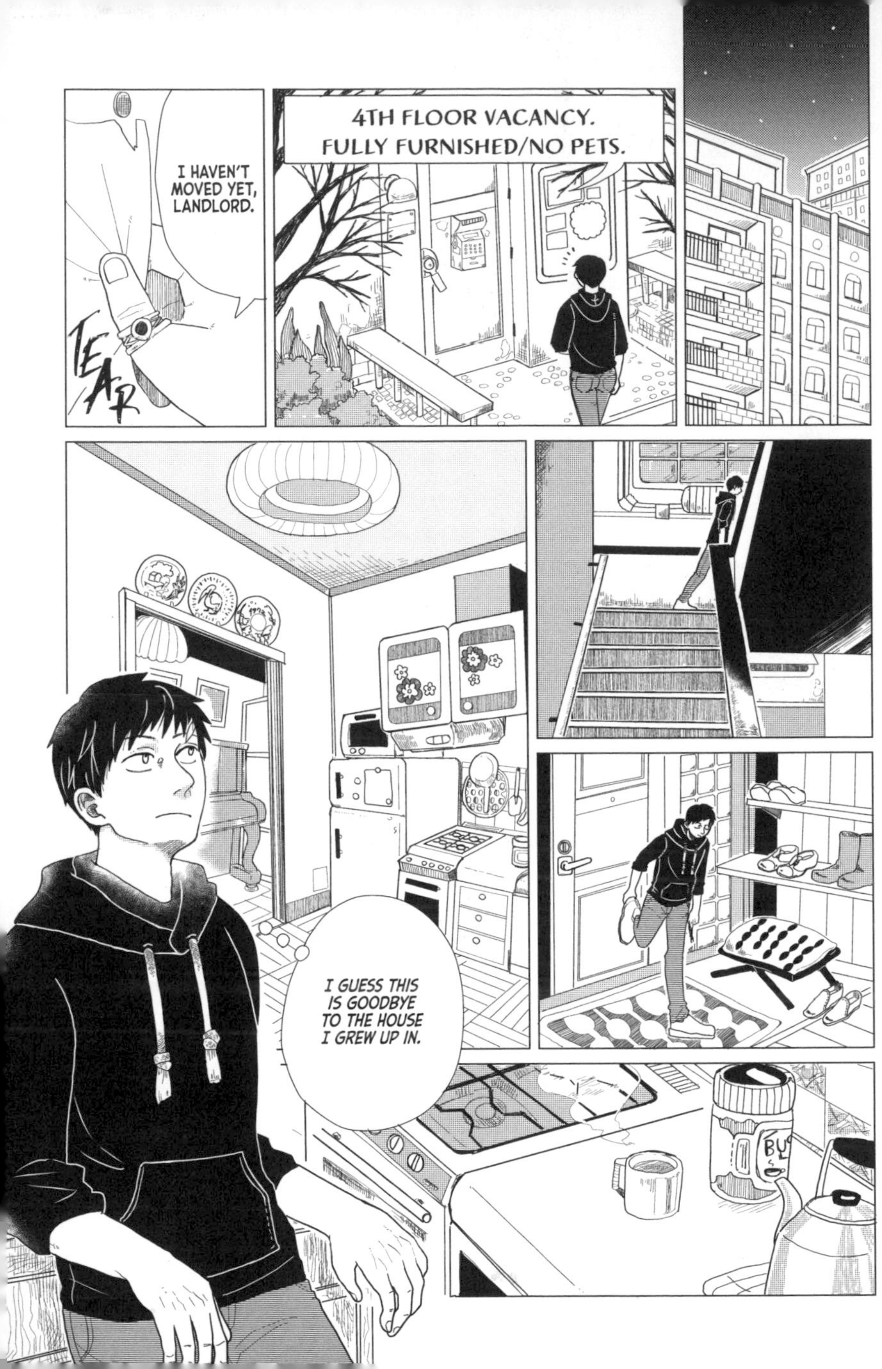
4TH FLOOR VACANCY.
FULLY FURNISHED/NO PETS.
I HAVEN'T MOVED YET, LANDLORD.
TEAR
I GUESS THIS IS GOODBYE TO THE HOUSE I GREW UP IN.

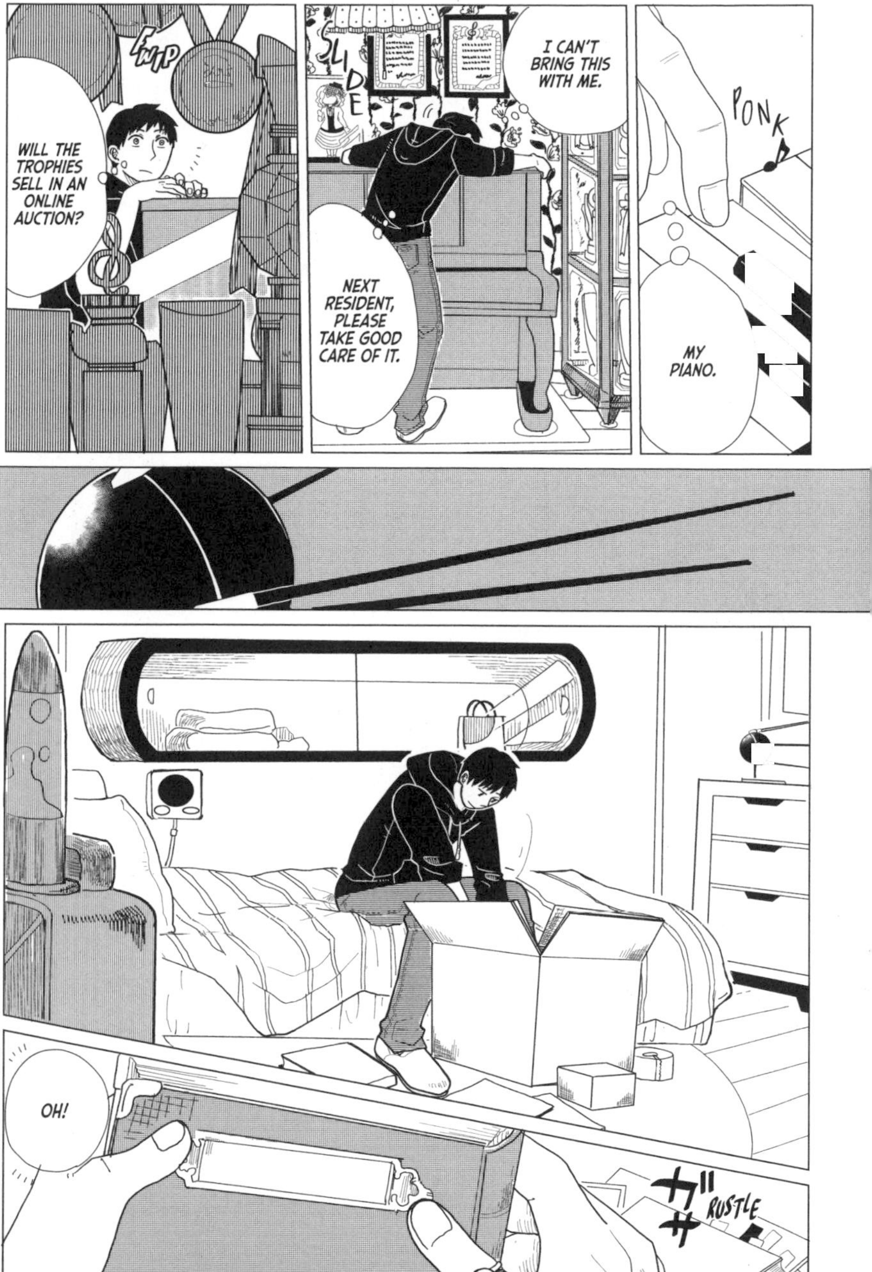
PONK
MY PIANO.
I CAN'T BRING THIS WITH ME.
SLIDE
NEXT RESIDENT, PLEASE TAKE GOOD CARE OF IT.
FWIP
WILL THE TROPHIES SELL IN AN ONLINE AUCTION?
ガサ
RUSTLE
OH!

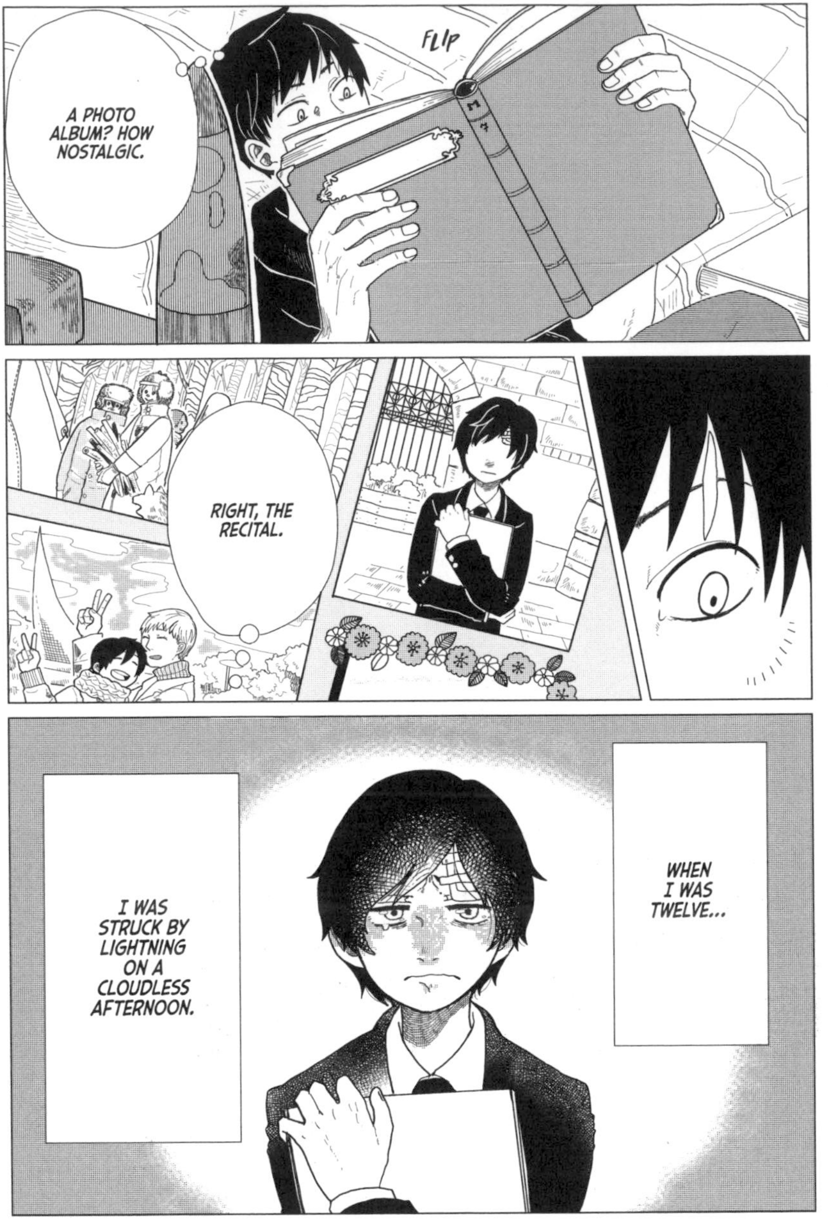
FLIP
A PHOTO ALBUM? HOW NOSTALGIC.
RIGHT, THE RECITAL.
WHEN I WAS TWELVE...
I WAS STRUCK BY LIGHTNING ON A CLOUDLESS AFTERNOON.

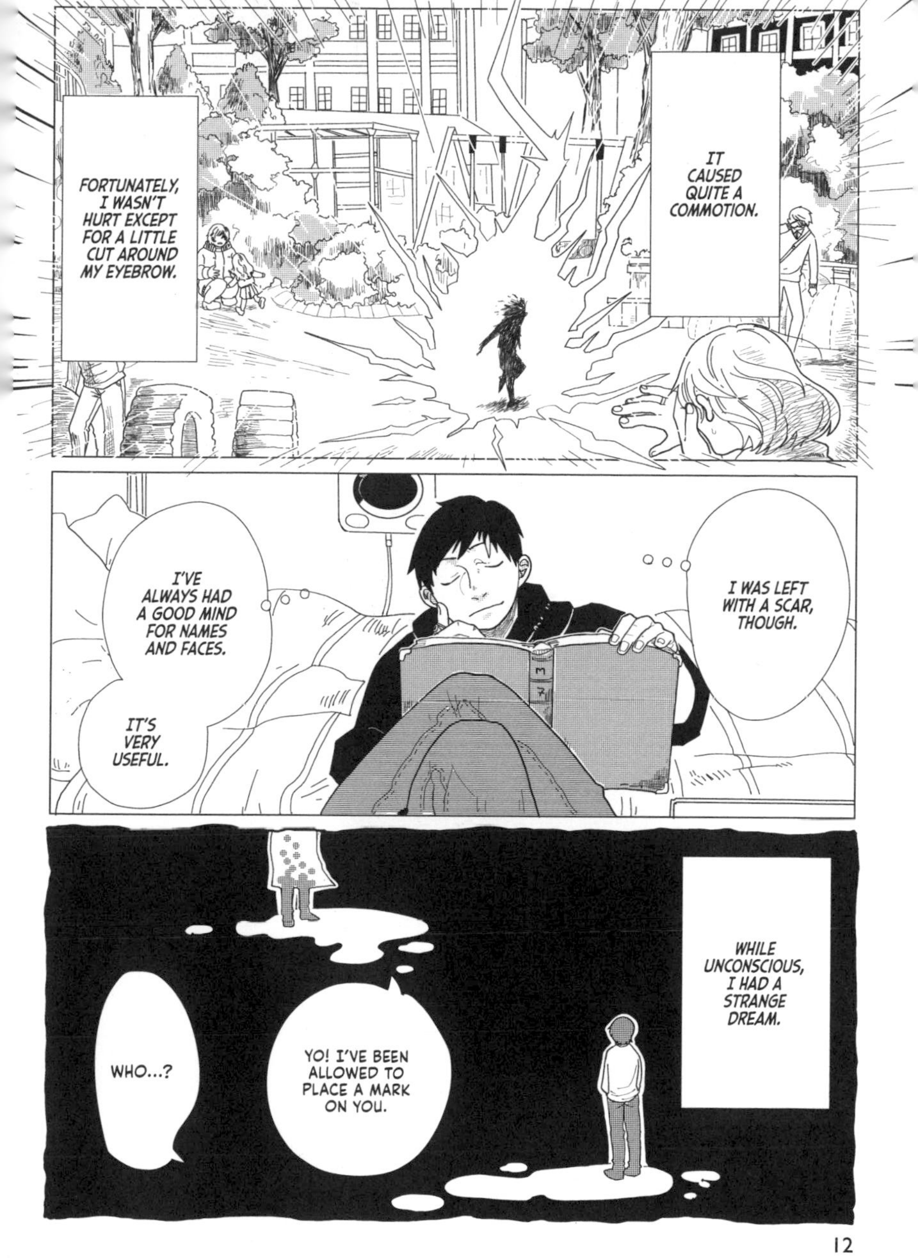
IT CAUSED QUITE A COMMOTION.
FORTUNATELY, I WASN'T HURT EXCEPT FOR A LITTLE CUT AROUND MY EYEBROW.
I WAS LEFT WITH A SCAR, THOUGH.
I'VE ALWAYS HAD A GOOD MIND FOR NAMES AND FACES.
IT'S VERY USEFUL.
WHILE UNCONSCIOUS, I HAD A STRANGE DREAM.
YO! I'VE BEEN ALLOWED TO PLACE A MARK ON YOU.
WHO...?

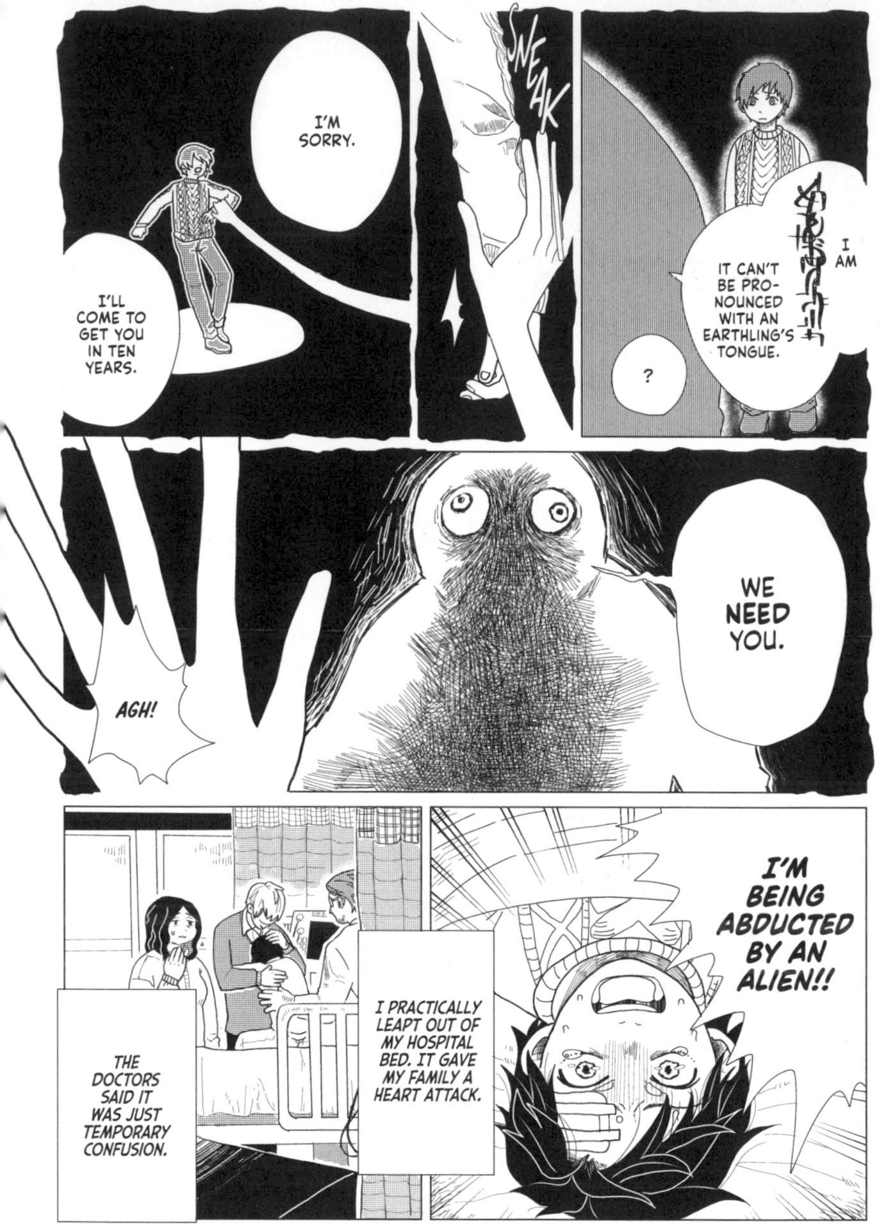
I AM
IT CAN'T BE PRO-NOUNCED WITH AN EARTHLING'S TONGUE.
?
SNEAK
I'M SORRY.
I'LL COME TO GET YOU IN TEN YEARS.
WE NEED YOU.
AGH!
I'M BEING ABDUCTED BY AN ALIEN!!
I PRACTICALLY LEAPT OUT OF MY HOSPITAL BED. IT GAVE MY FAMILY A HEART ATTACK.
THE DOCTORS SAID IT WAS JUST TEMPORARY CONFUSION.

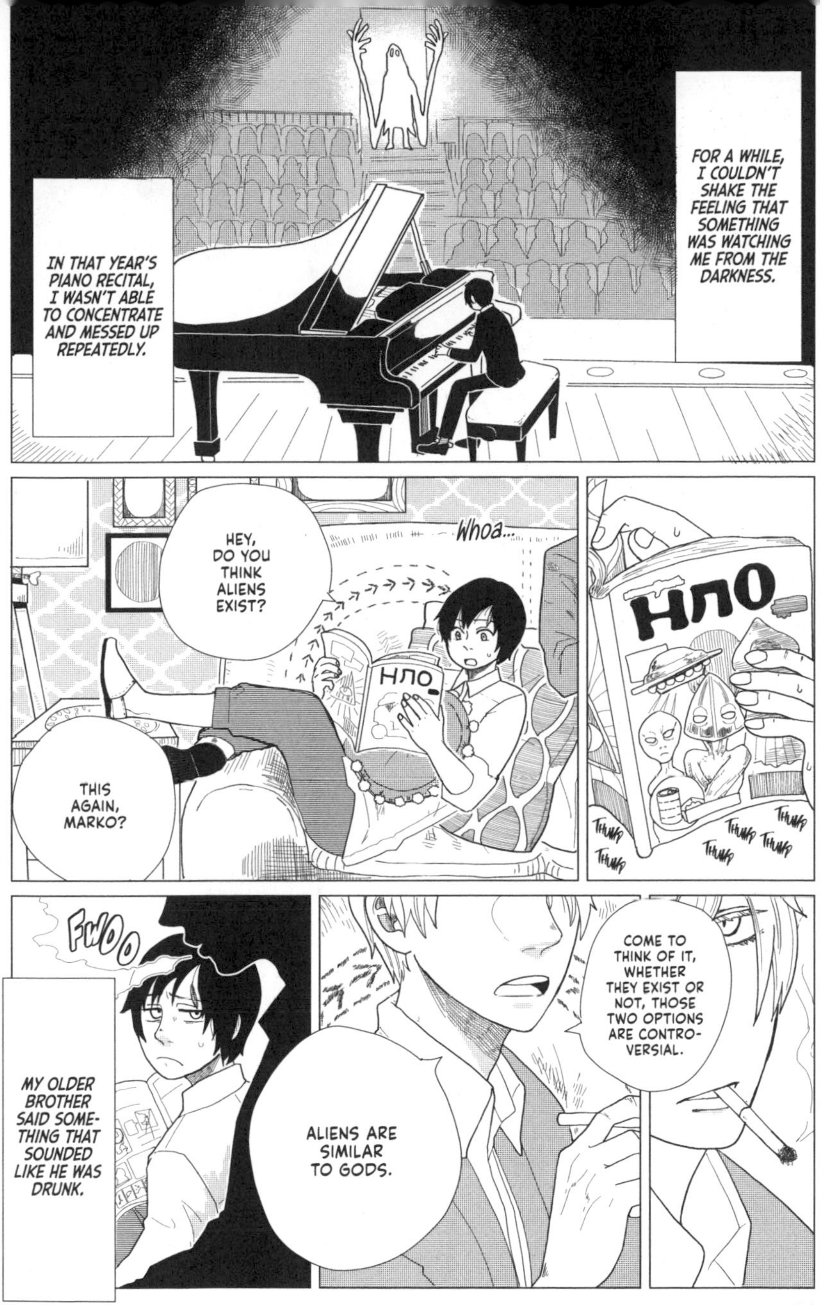
FOR A WHILE, I COULDN'T SHAKE THE FEELING THAT SOMETHING WAS WATCHING ME FROM THE DARKNESS.
IN THAT YEAR'S PIANO RECITAL, I WASN'T ABLE TO CONCENTRATE AND MESSED UP REPEATEDLY.
НЛО
THUMP THUMP THUMP THUMP THUMP
Whoa...
HEY, DO YOU THINK ALIENS EXIST?
НЛО
THIS AGAIN, MARKO?
COME TO THINK OF IT, WHETHER THEY EXIST OR NOT, THOSE TWO OPTIONS ARE CONTRO-VERSIAL.
ALIENS ARE SIMILAR TO GODS.
FWOO
MY OLDER BROTHER SAID SOME-THING THAT SOUNDED LIKE HE WAS DRUNK.

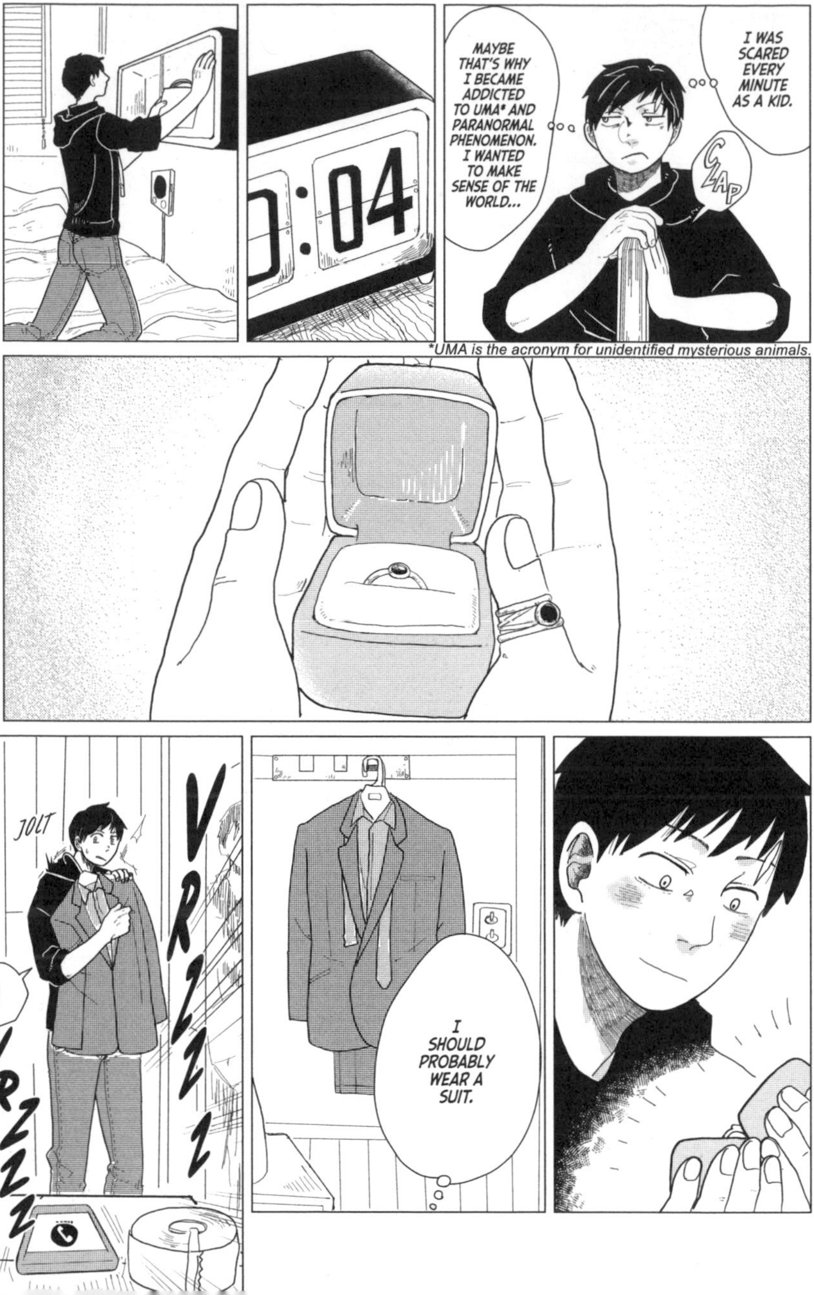
I WAS SCARED EVERY MINUTE AS A KID.
CLAP
MAYBE THAT'S WHY I BECAME ADDICTED TO UMA* AND PARANORMAL PHENOMENON. I WANTED TO MAKE SENSE OF THE WORLD...
I SHOULD PROBABLY WEAR A SUIT.
VRZZZ
JOLT
!
VRZZZZ
*UMA is the acronym for unidentified mysterious animals.

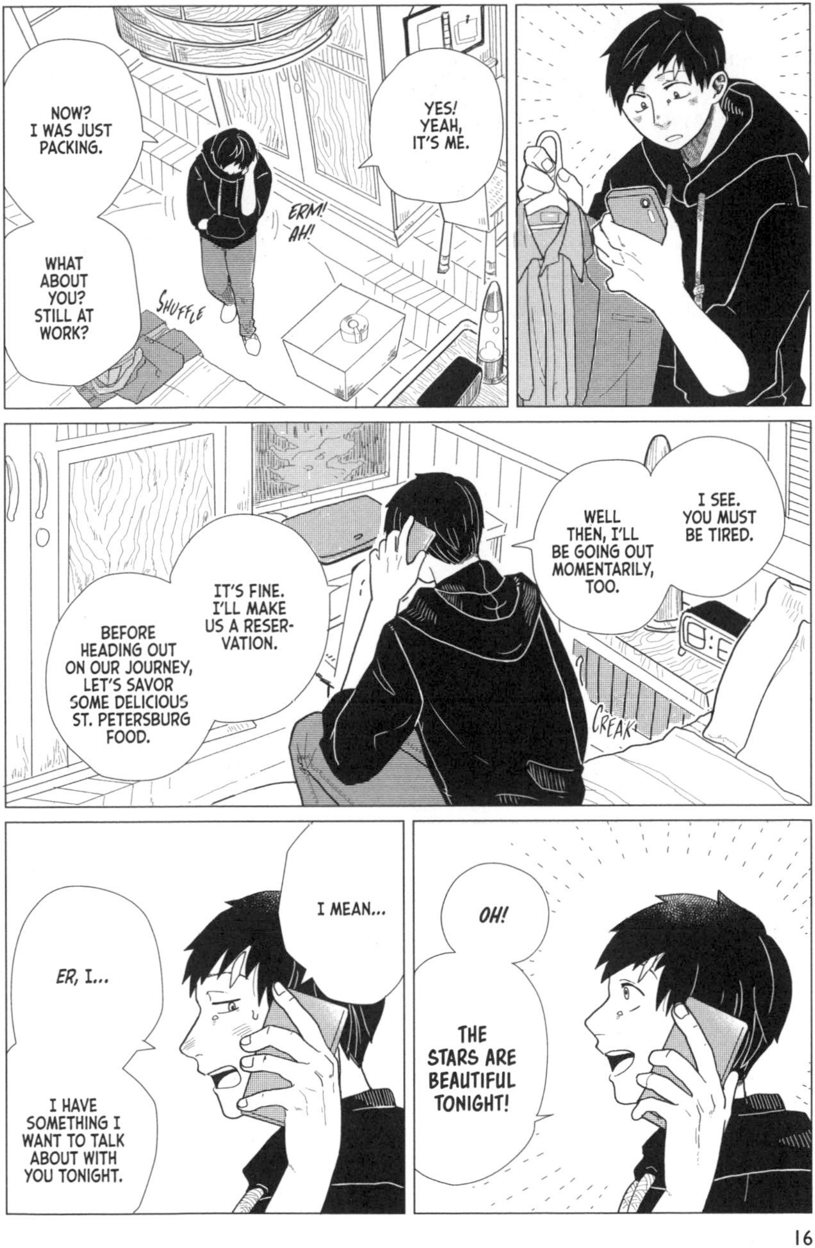
YES! YEAH, IT'S ME.
NOW? I WAS JUST PACKING.
ERM! AH!
WHAT ABOUT YOU? STILL AT WORK?
SHUFFLE
I SEE. YOU MUST BE TIRED.
WELL THEN, I'LL BE GOING OUT MOMENTARILY, TOO.
CREAK
IT'S FINE. I'LL MAKE US A RESERVATION.
BEFORE HEADING OUT ON OUR JOURNEY, LET'S SAVOR SOME DELICIOUS ST. PETERSBURG FOOD.
OH!
THE STARS ARE BEAUTIFUL TONIGHT!
I MEAN...
ER, I...
I HAVE SOMETHING I WANT TO TALK ABOUT WITH YOU TONIGHT.

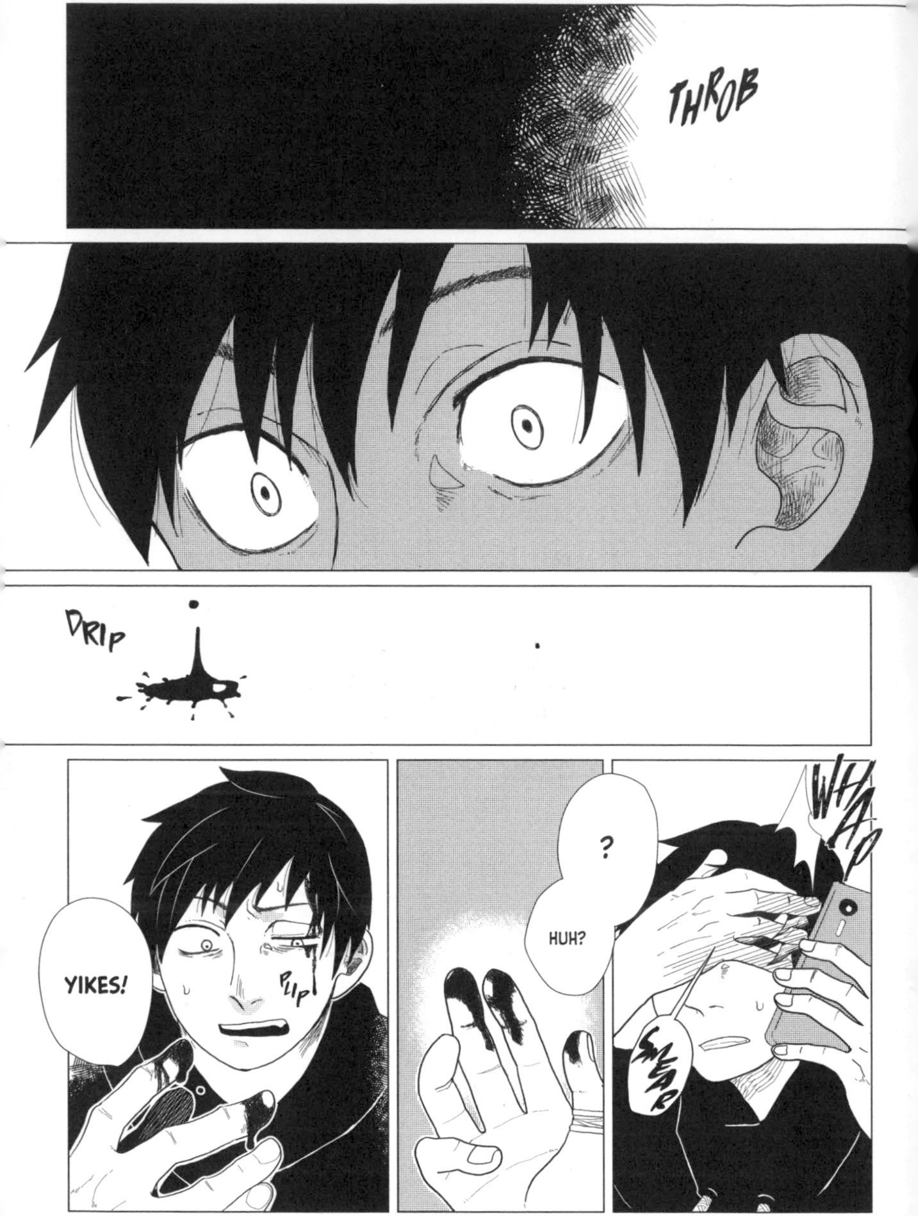
THROB
DRIP
WHAP
SMEAR
?
HUH?
YIKES!
PLIP

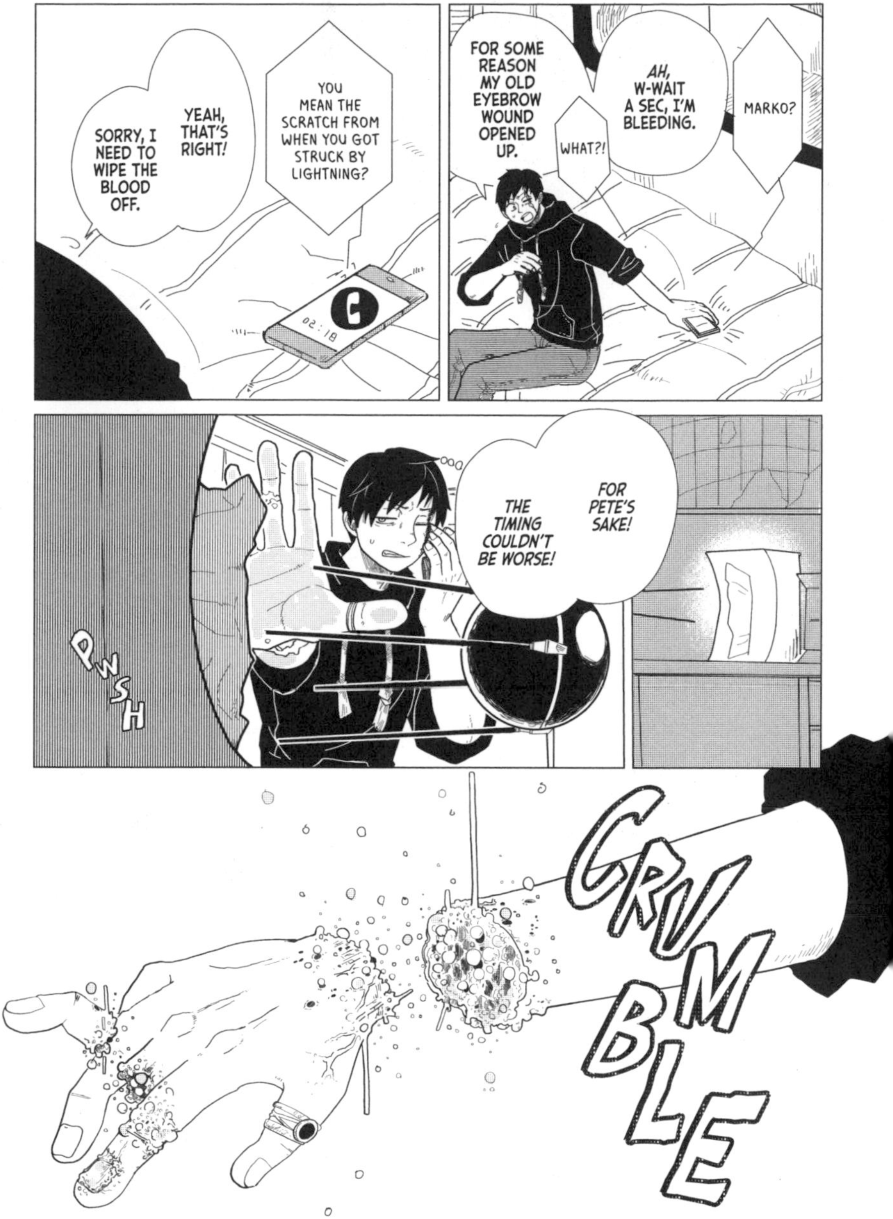
MARKO?
AH, W-WAIT A SEC, I'M BLEEDING.
WHAT?!
FOR SOME REASON MY OLD EYEBROW WOUND OPENED UP.
YOU MEAN THE SCRATCH FROM WHEN YOU GOT STRUCK BY LIGHTNING?
YEAH, THAT'S RIGHT!
SORRY, I NEED TO WIPE THE BLOOD OFF.
FOR PETE'S SAKE!
THE TIMING COULDN'T BE WORSE!
PWSH
CRUMBLE

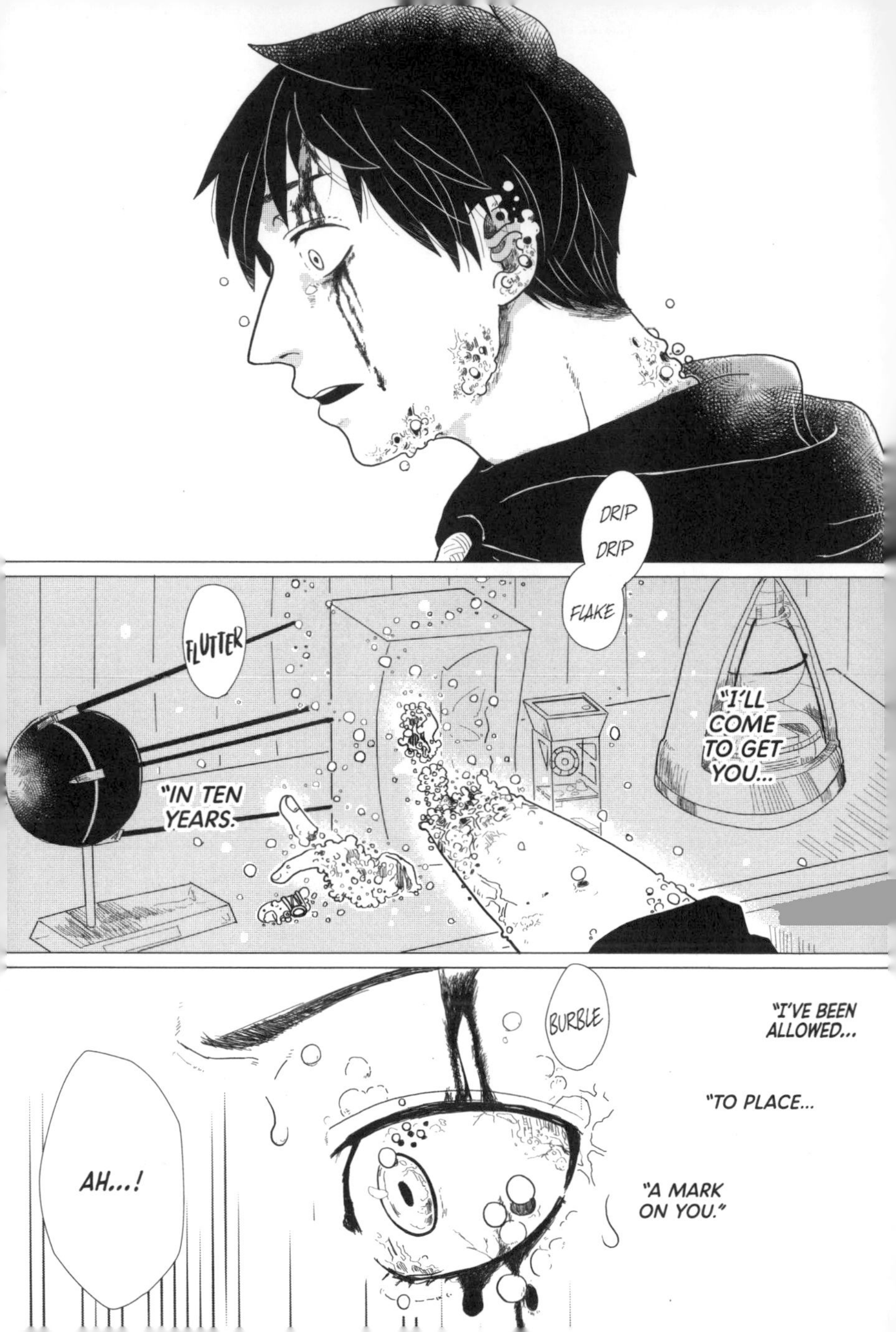
DRIP DRIP
FLAKE
"I'LL COME TO GET YOU...
FLUTTER
"IN TEN YEARS.
"I'VE BEEN ALLOWED...
BURBLE
"TO PLACE...
"A MARK ON YOU."
AH...!

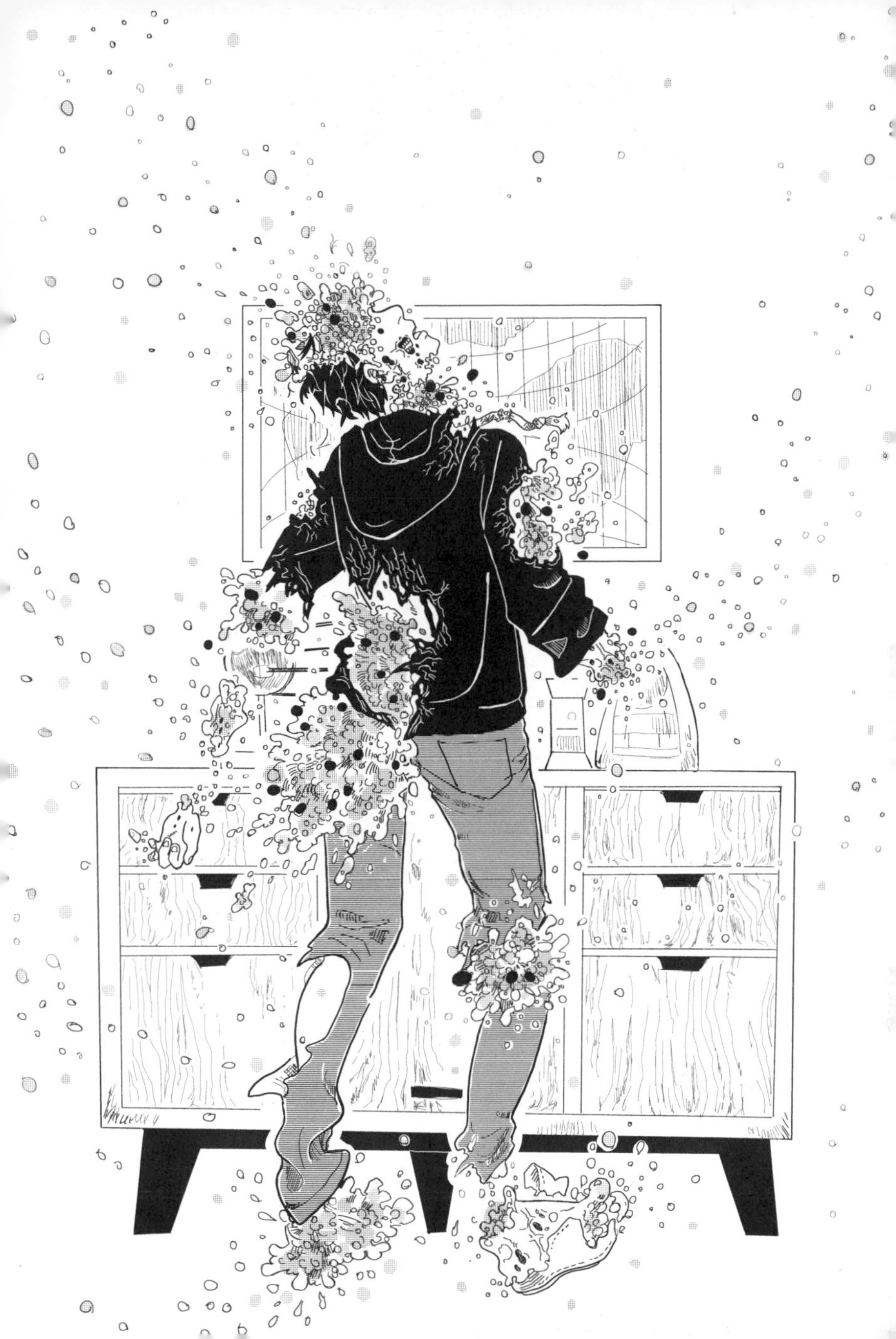

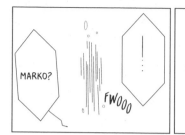

MARKO?

FWOOO

ROLL

ROLL

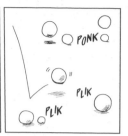

PONK

PLIK

PLIK

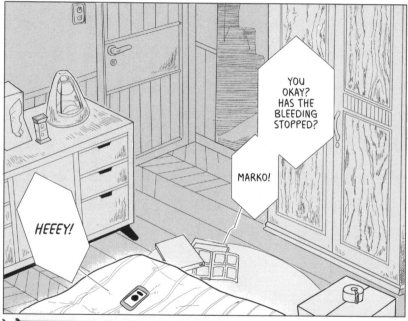

YOU OKAY? HAS THE BLEEDING STOPPED?

MARKO!

HEEEY!

MARKO...?

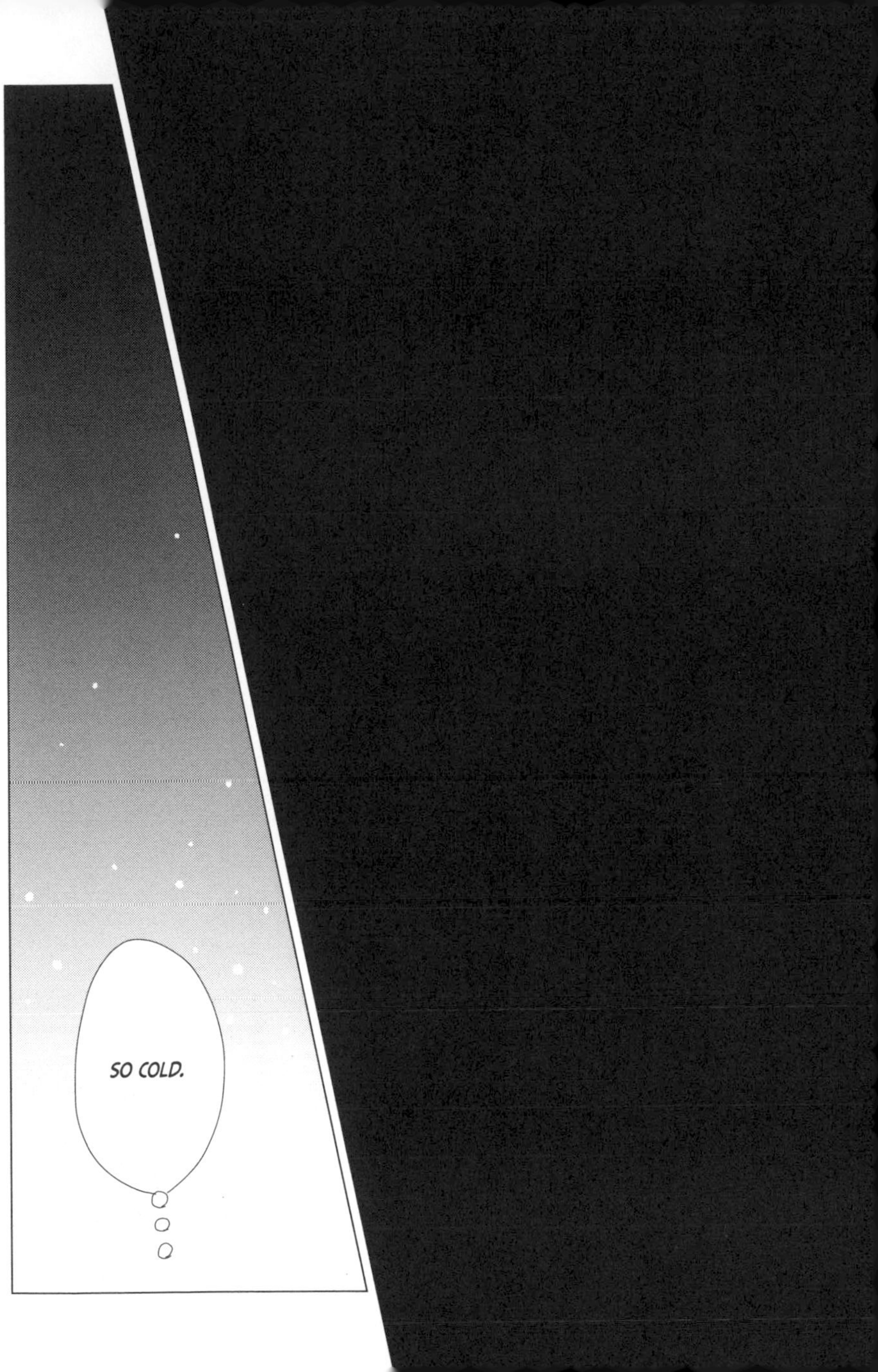
SO COLD.

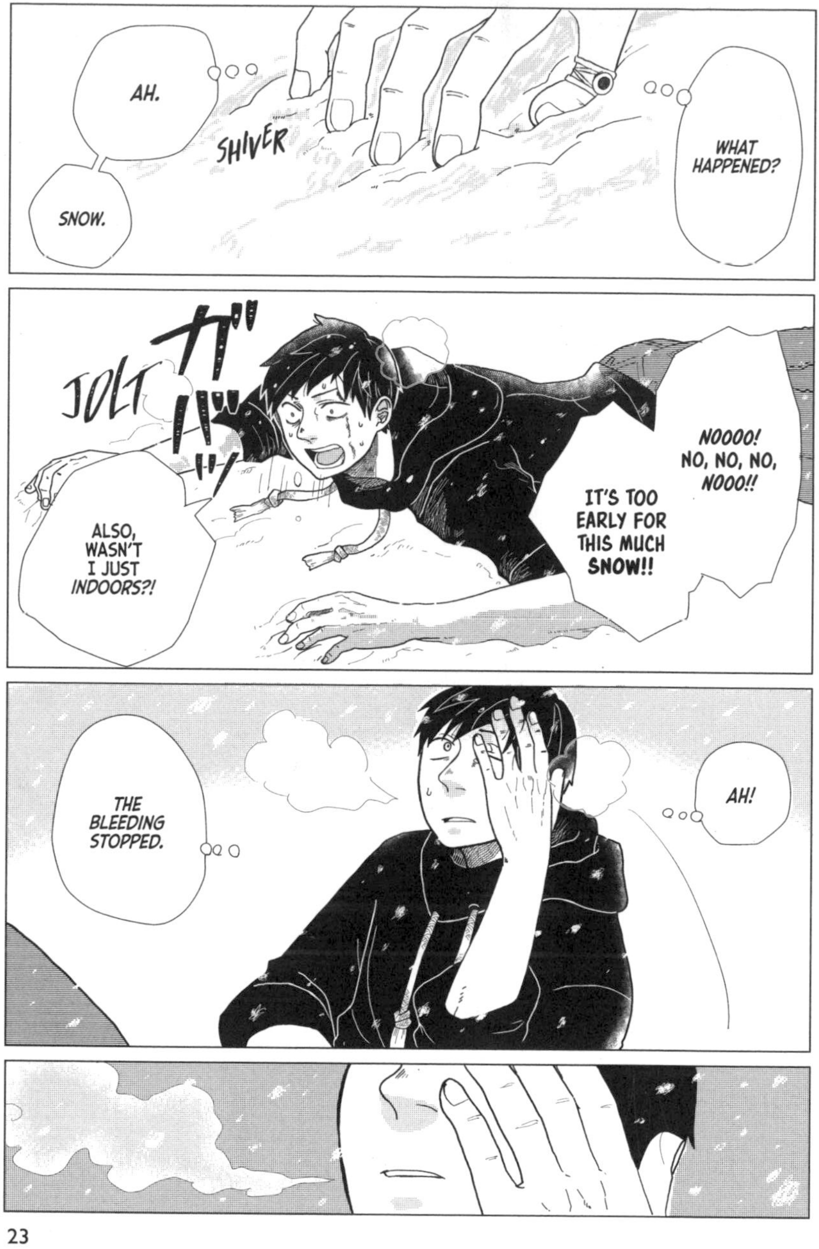
WHAT HAPPENED?
AH.
SHIVER
SNOW.
NOOOO! NO, NO, NO, NOOO!!
IT'S TOO EARLY FOR THIS MUCH SNOW!!
JOLT
ガバッ
ALSO, WASN'T I JUST INDOORS?!
AH!
THE BLEEDING STOPPED.

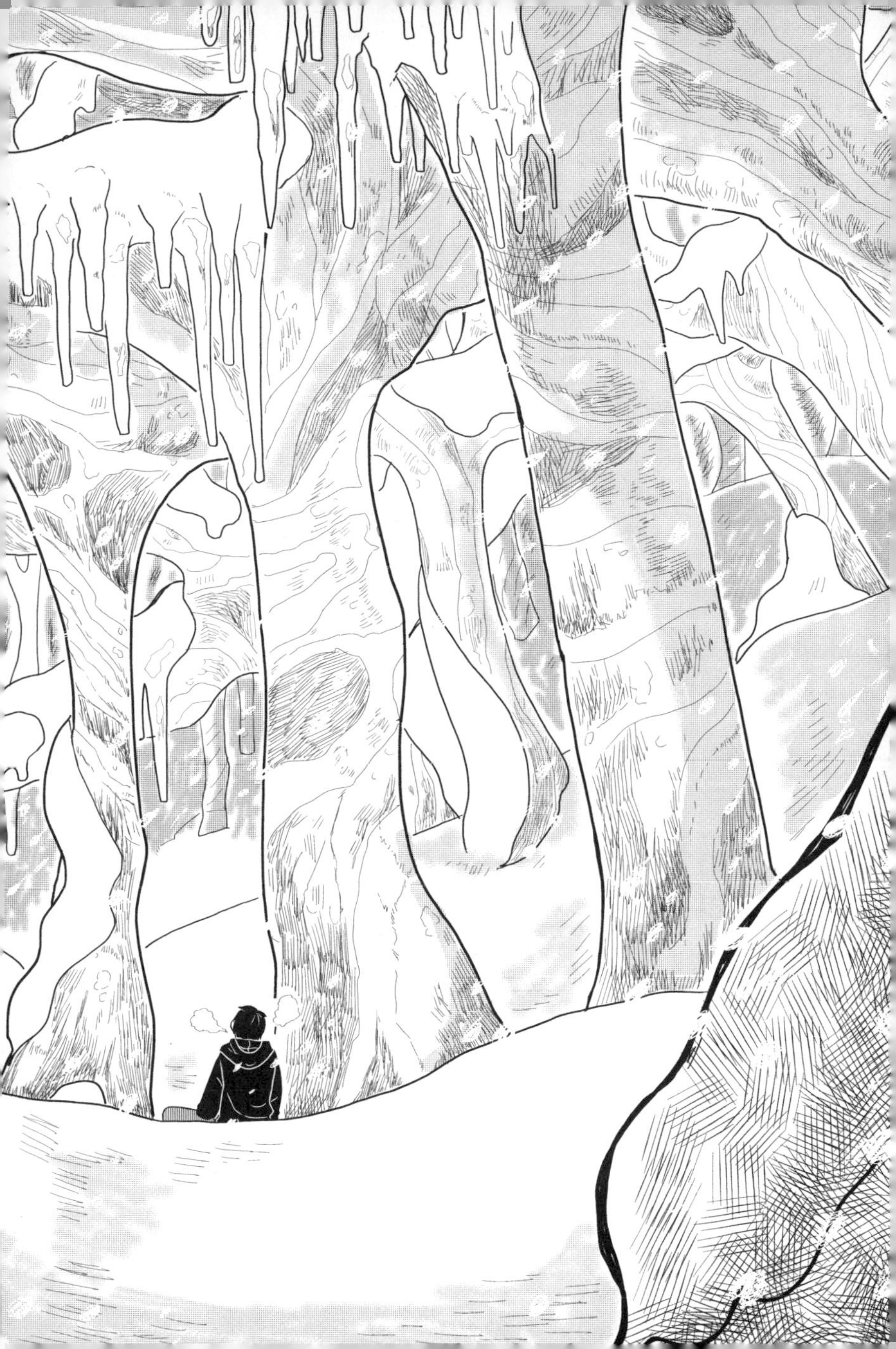

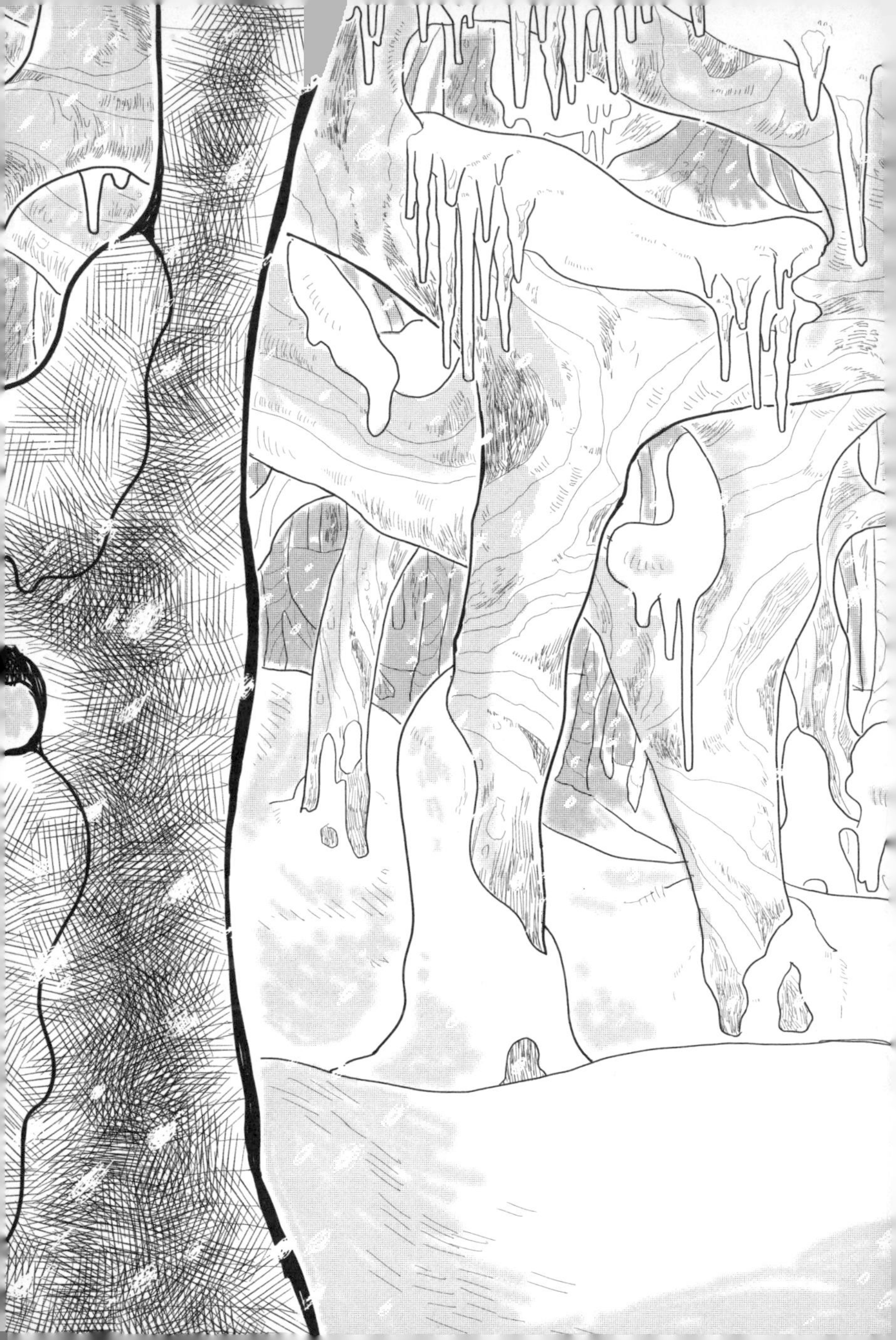

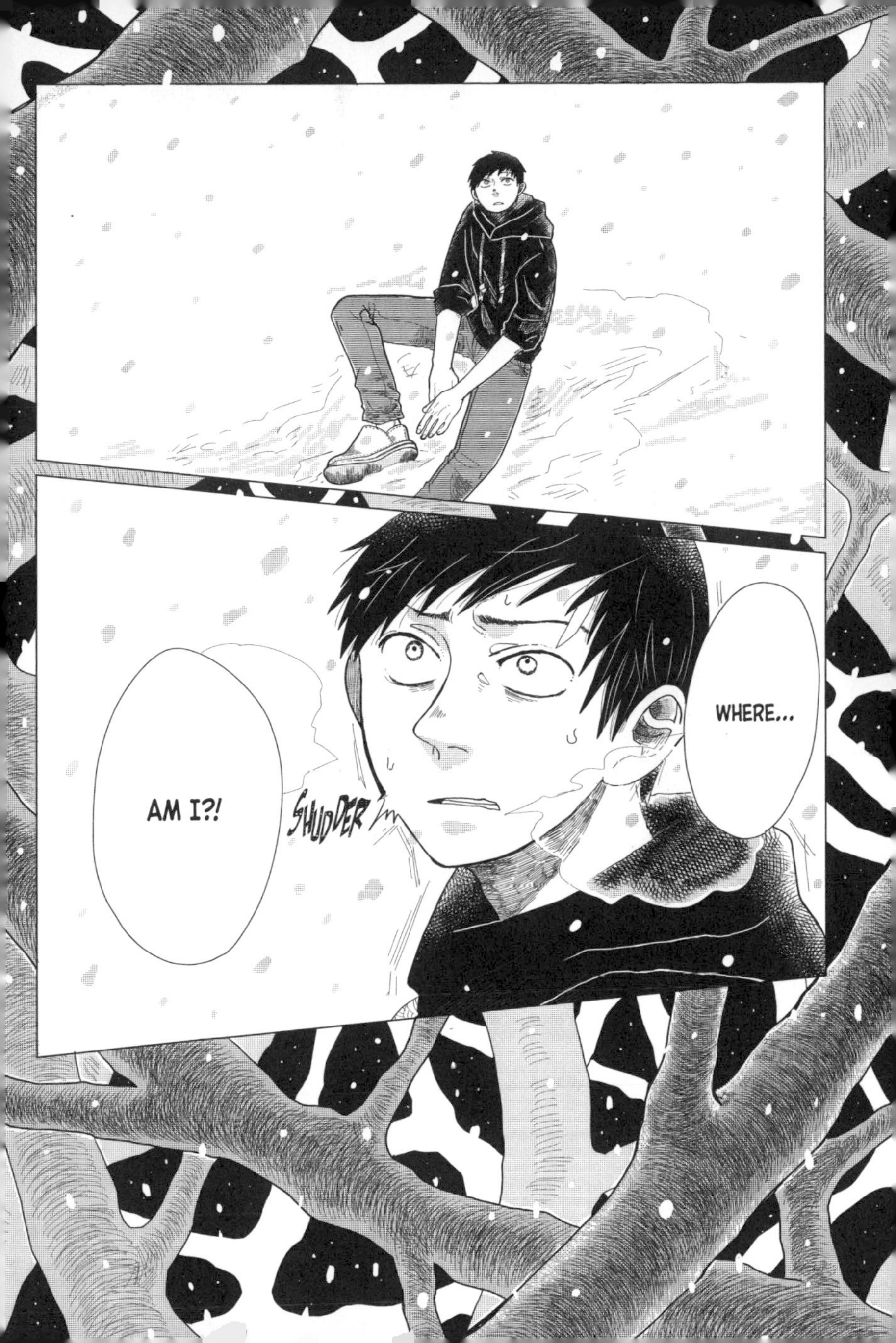
WHERE...
SHUDDER
AM I?!

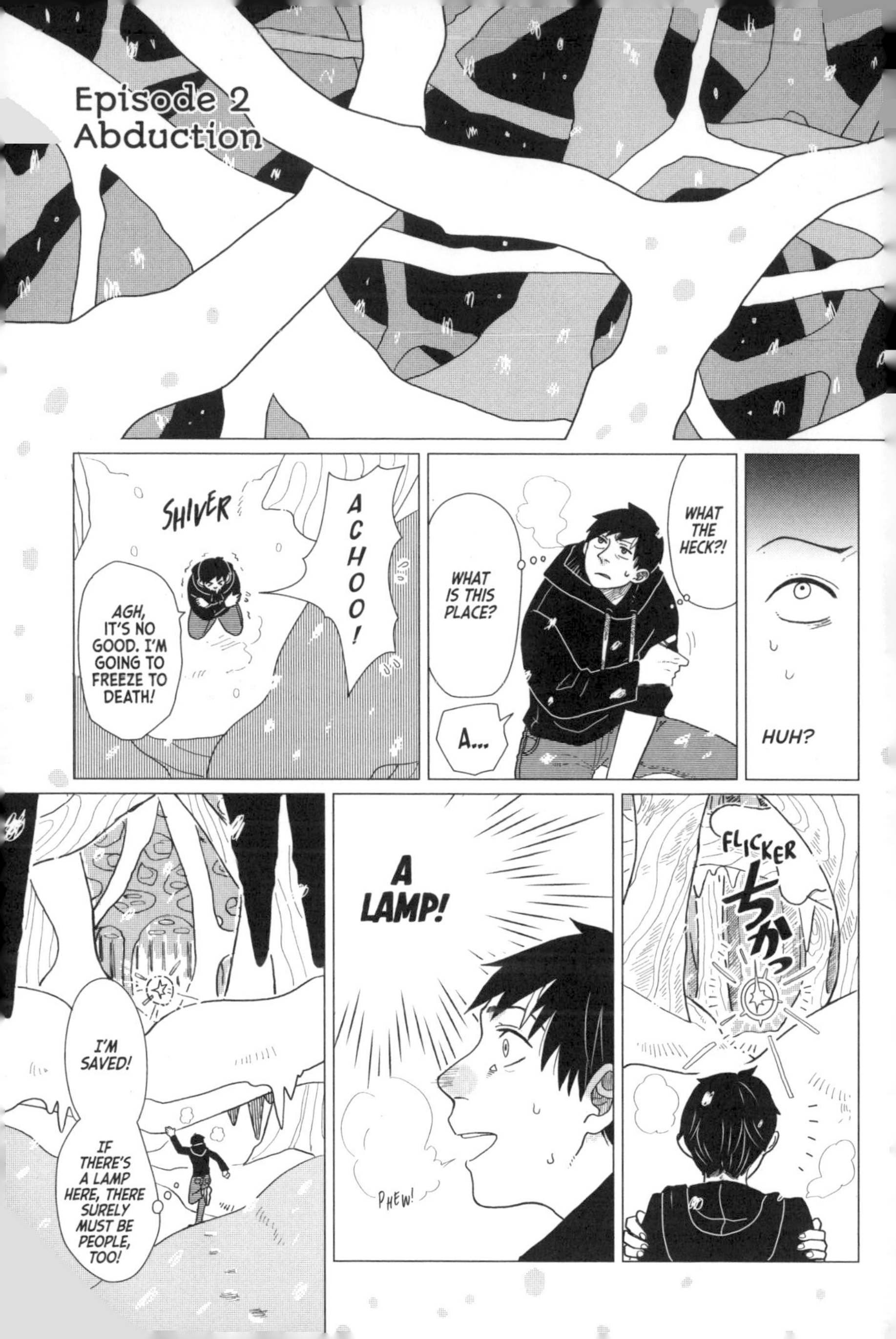
Episode 2
Abduction
HUH?
WHAT THE HECK?!
WHAT IS THIS PLACE?
A...
ACHOO!
SHIVER
AGH, IT'S NO GOOD. I'M GOING TO FREEZE TO DEATH!
FLICKER
ちかっ
A LAMP!
PHEW!
I'M SAVED!
IF THERE'S A LAMP HERE, THERE SURELY MUST BE PEOPLE, TOO!

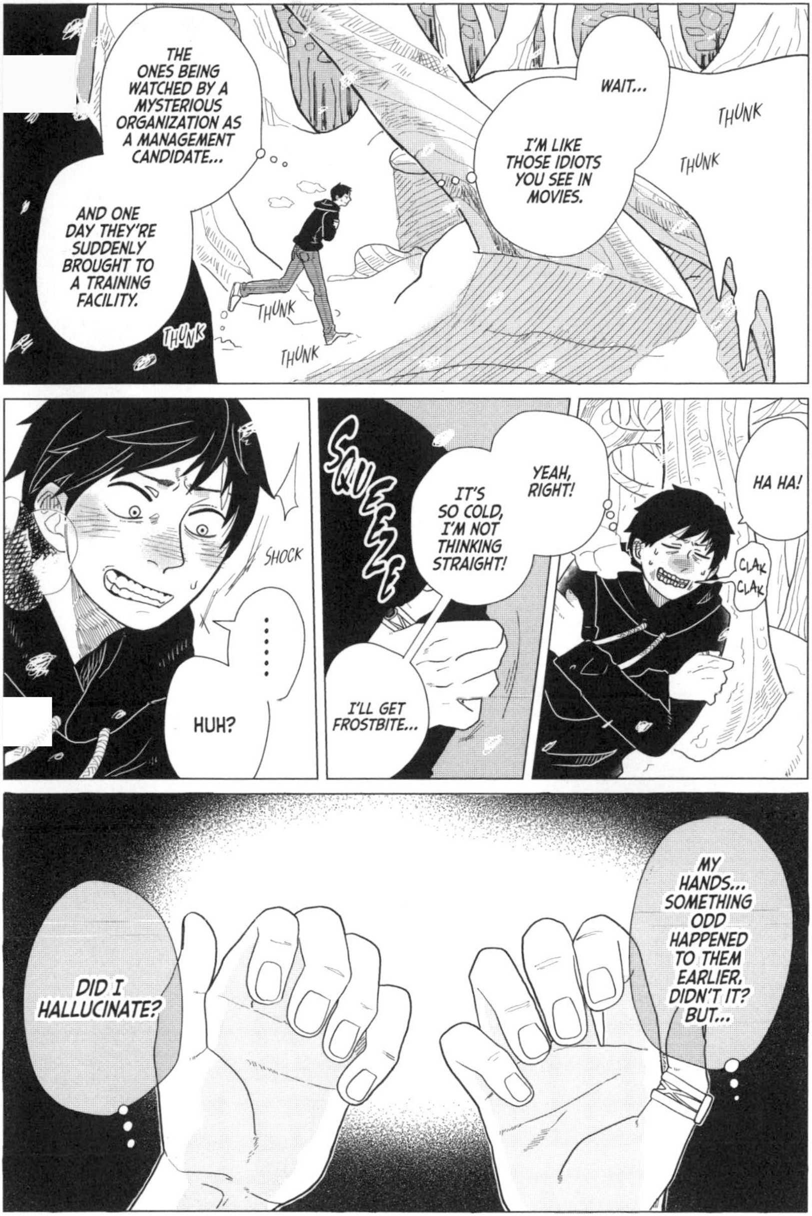
WAIT...
I'M LIKE THOSE IDIOTS YOU SEE IN MOVIES.
THUNK
THUNK
THE ONES BEING WATCHED BY A MYSTERIOUS ORGANIZATION AS A MANAGEMENT CANDIDATE...
AND ONE DAY THEY'RE SUDDENLY BROUGHT TO A TRAINING FACILITY.
THUNK
THUNK
THUNK
HA HA!
YEAH, RIGHT!
CLAK CLAK
SQUEEZE
IT'S SO COLD, I'M NOT THINKING STRAIGHT!
I'LL GET FROSTBITE...
SHOCK
......
HUH?
MY HANDS... SOMETHING ODD HAPPENED TO THEM EARLIER, DIDN'T IT? BUT...
DID I HALLUCINATE?

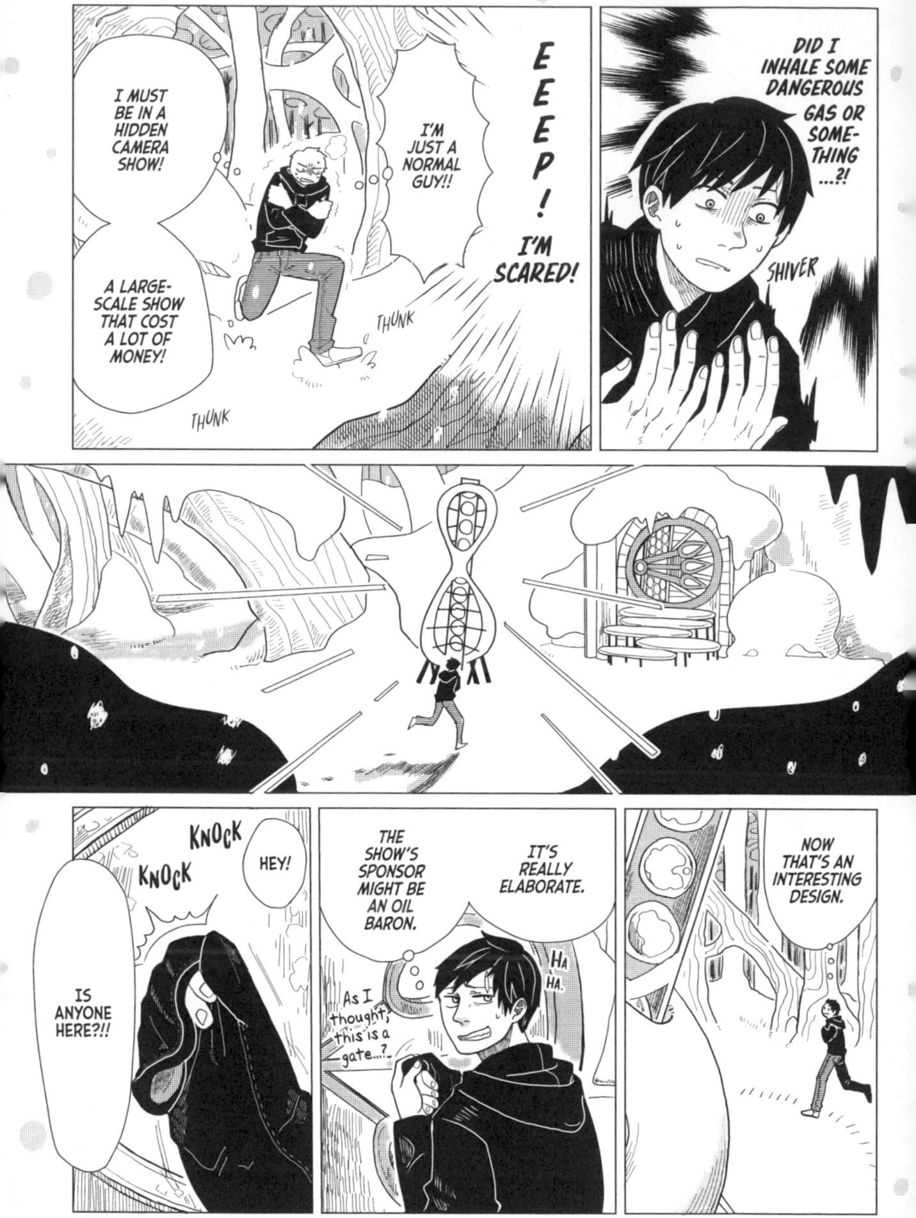
DID I INHALE SOME DANGEROUS GAS OR SOME-THING ...?!
SHIVER
EEEP! I'M SCARED!
I'M JUST A NORMAL GUY!!
I MUST BE IN A HIDDEN CAMERA SHOW!
A LARGE-SCALE SHOW THAT COST A LOT OF MONEY!
THUNK
THUNK
NOW THAT'S AN INTERESTING DESIGN.
IT'S REALLY ELABORATE.
THE SHOW'S SPONSOR MIGHT BE AN OIL BARON.
HA HA.
As I thought, this is a gate...?
HEY!
KNOCK
KNOCK
IS ANYONE HERE?!!

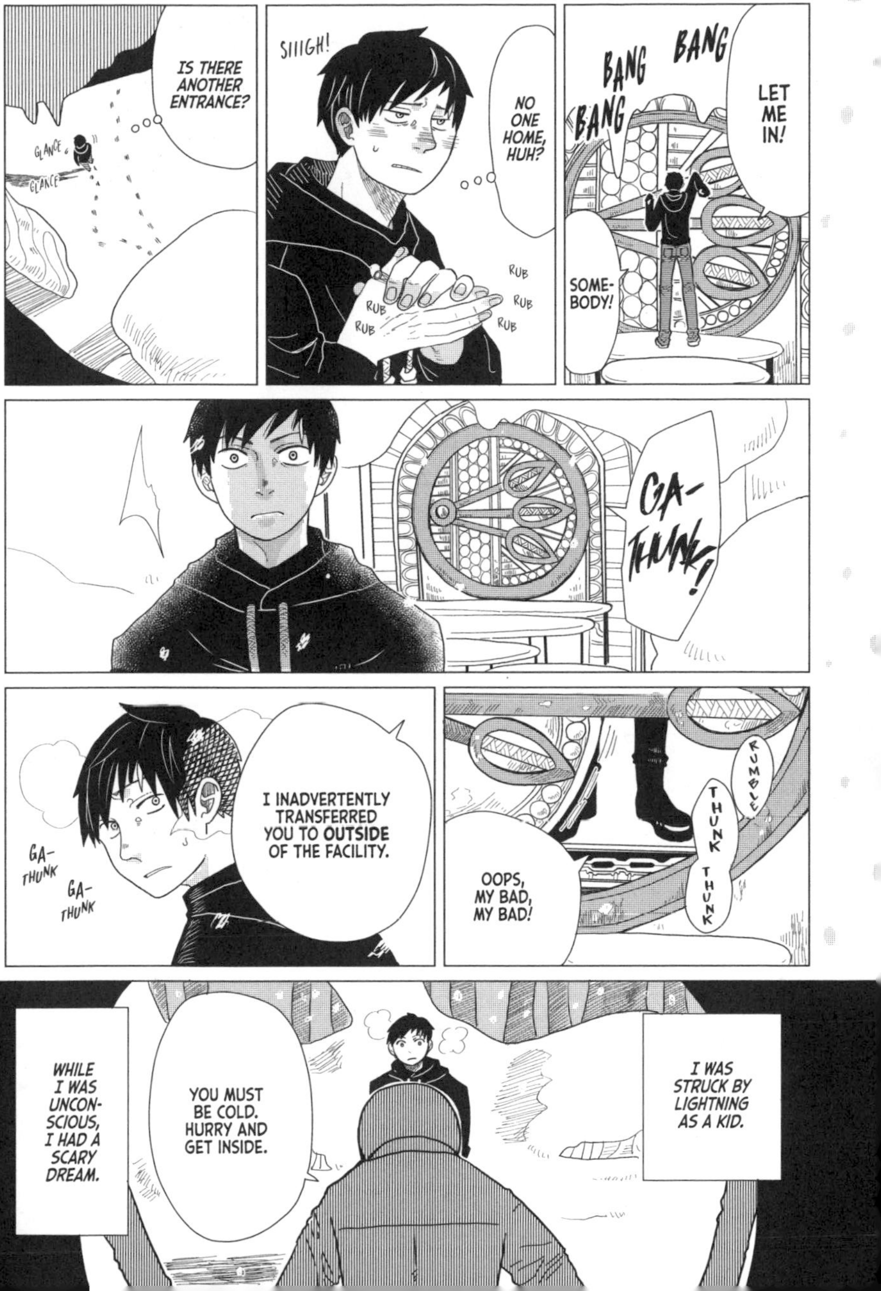
BANG BANG
BANG
BANG
LET ME IN!
SOMEBODY!
SIIIGH!
NO ONE HOME, HUH?
RUB RUB RUB
RUB RUB RUB
IS THERE ANOTHER ENTRANCE?
GLANCE
GLANCE
GA-THUNK!
RUMBLE
THUNK THUNK
OOPS, MY BAD, MY BAD!
I INADVERTENTLY TRANSFERRED YOU TO OUTSIDE OF THE FACILITY.
GA-THUNK
GA-THUNK
I WAS STRUCK BY LIGHTNING AS A KID.
YOU MUST BE COLD. HURRY AND GET INSIDE.
WHILE I WAS UNCONSCIOUS, I HAD A SCARY DREAM.

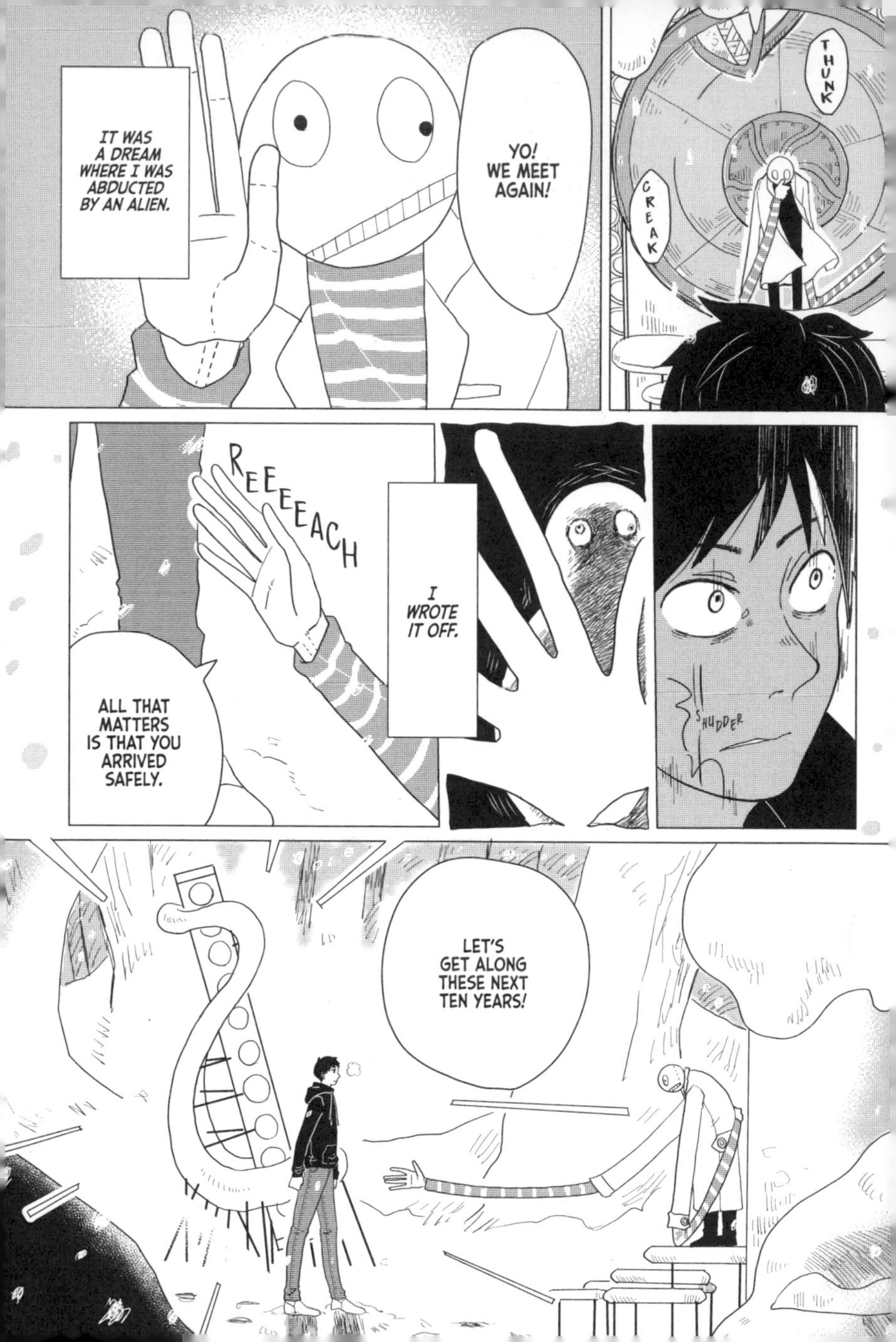
THUNK
CREAK
YO! WE MEET AGAIN!
IT WAS A DREAM WHERE I WAS ABDUCTED BY AN ALIEN.
SHUDDER
I WROTE IT OFF.
REEEEEACH
ALL THAT MATTERS IS THAT YOU ARRIVED SAFELY.
LET'S GET ALONG THESE NEXT TEN YEARS!

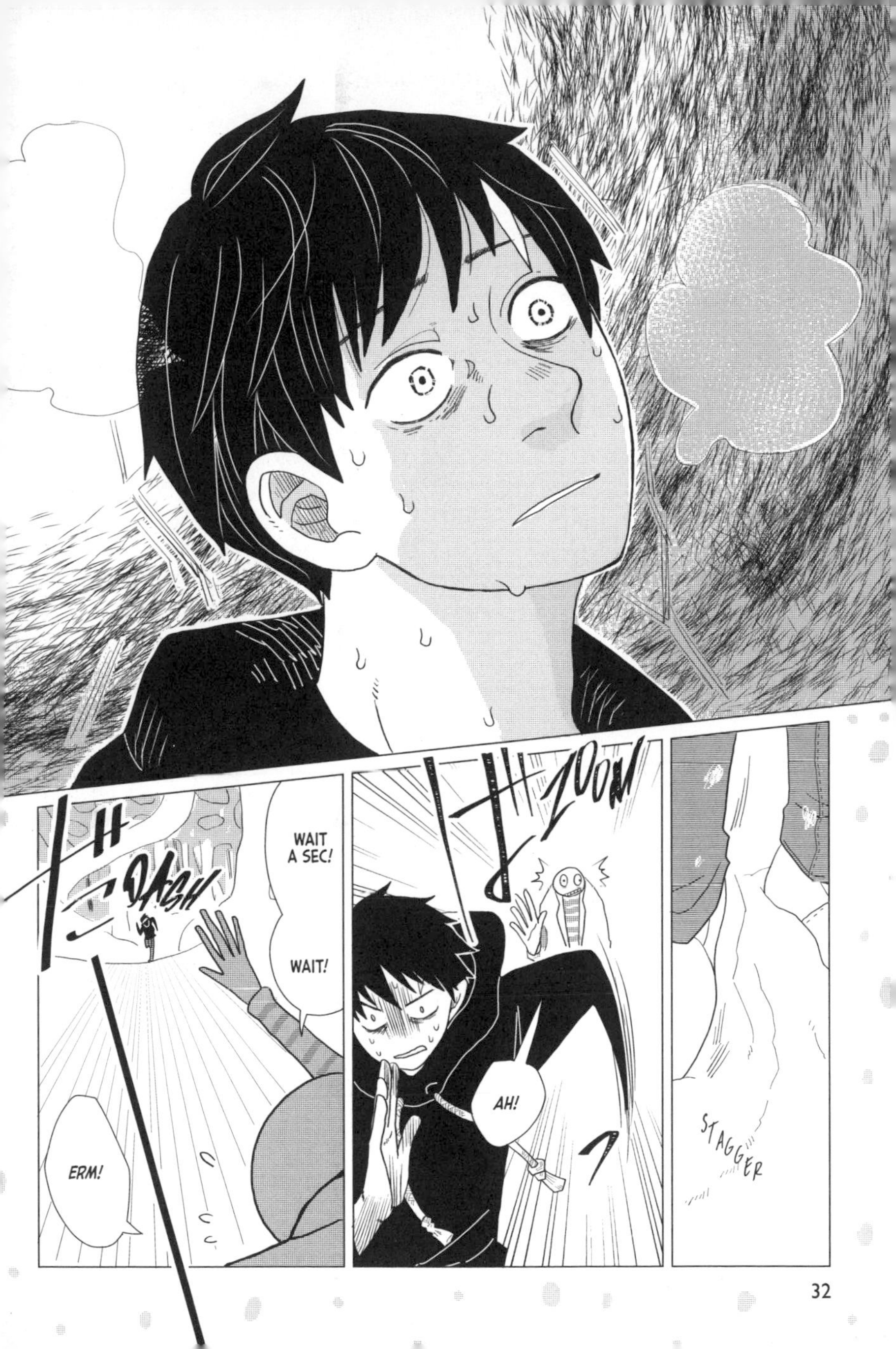
STAGGER
ZOOM
AH!
DASH
WAIT A SEC!
WAIT!
ERM!

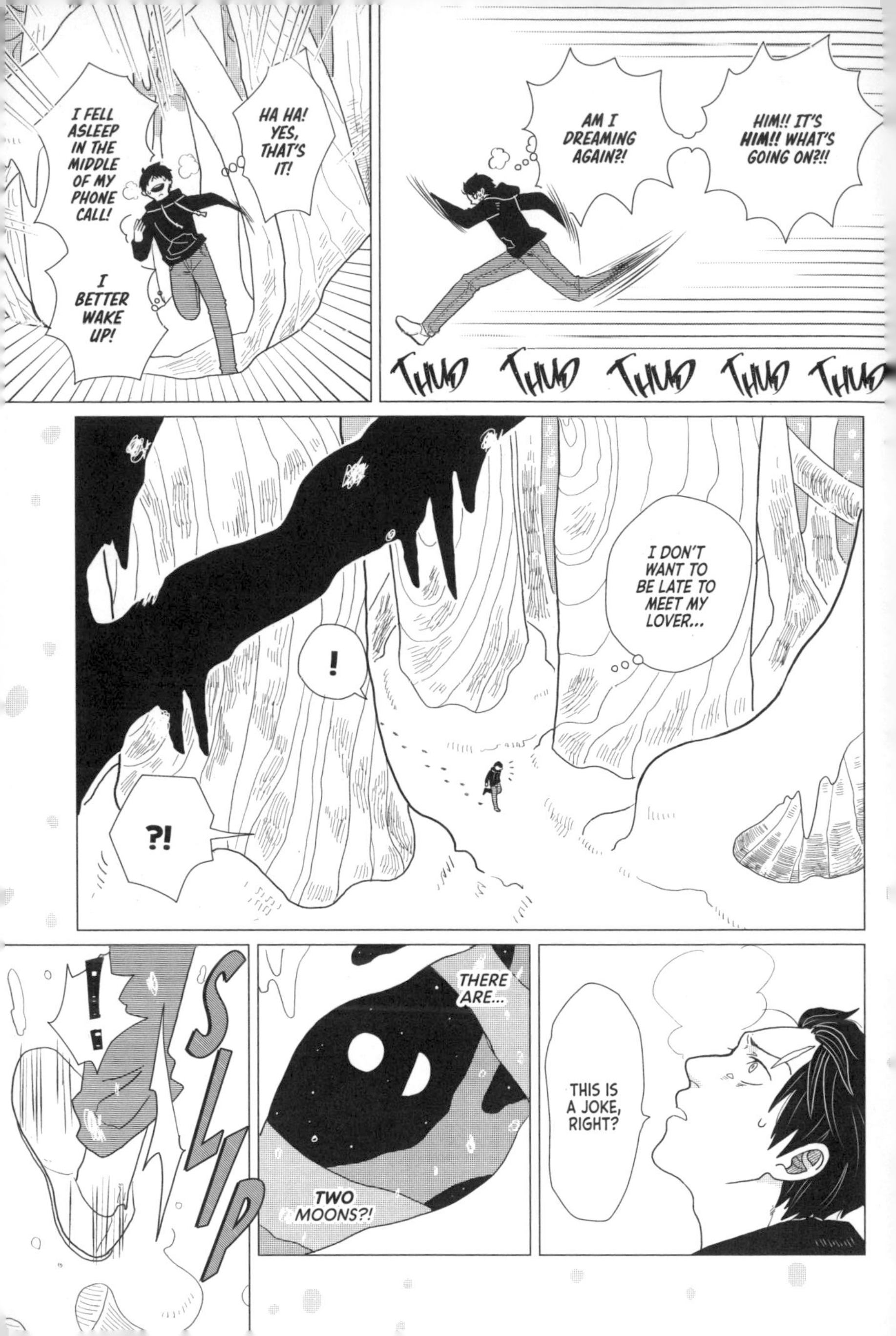
HIM!! IT'S HIM!! WHAT'S GOING ON?!!
AM I DREAMING AGAIN?!
THUD THUD THUD THUD THUD
HA HA! YES, THAT'S IT!
I FELL ASLEEP IN THE MIDDLE OF MY PHONE CALL!
I BETTER WAKE UP!
I DON'T WANT TO BE LATE TO MEET MY LOVER...
!
?!
THIS IS A JOKE, RIGHT?
THERE ARE...
TWO MOONS?!
SLIP
!!

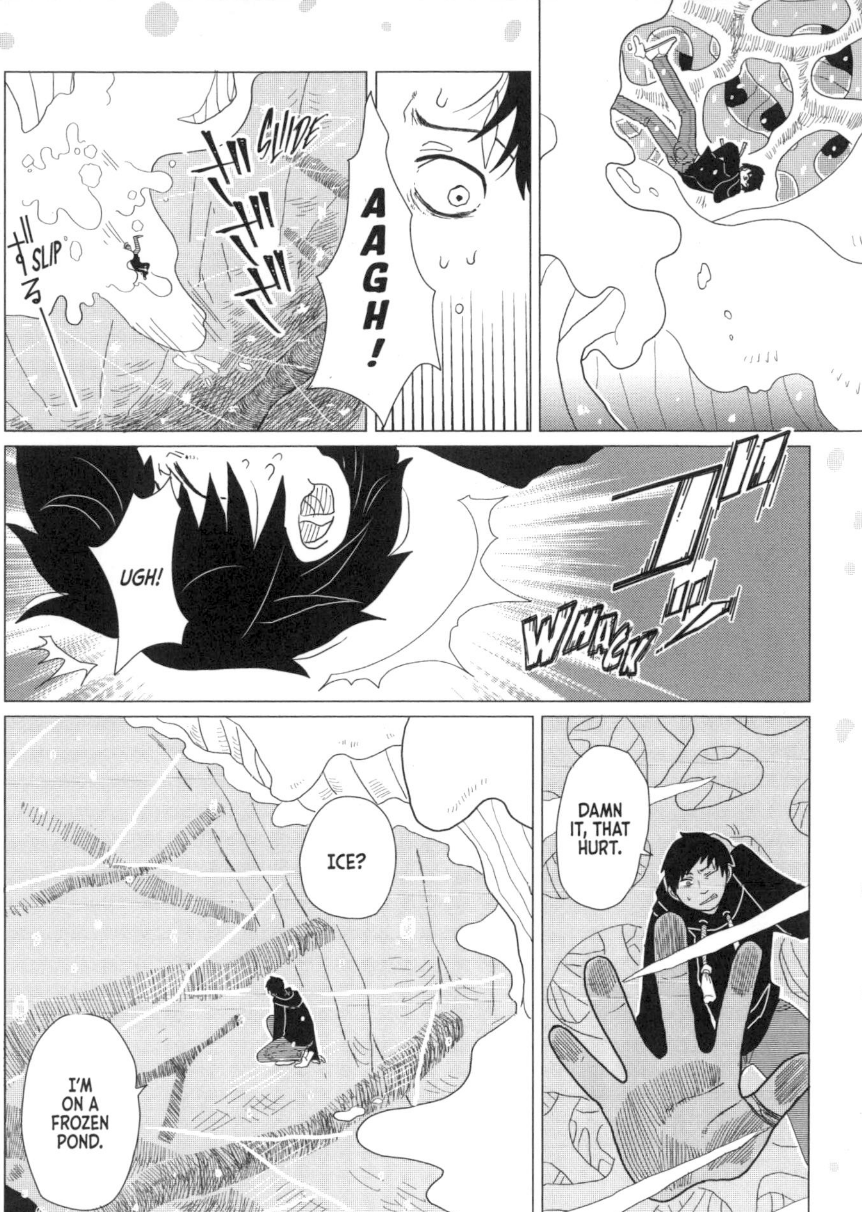
AAGH!
SLIDE
SLIP
WHACK
UGH!
DAMN IT, THAT HURT.
ICE?
I'M ON A FROZEN POND.

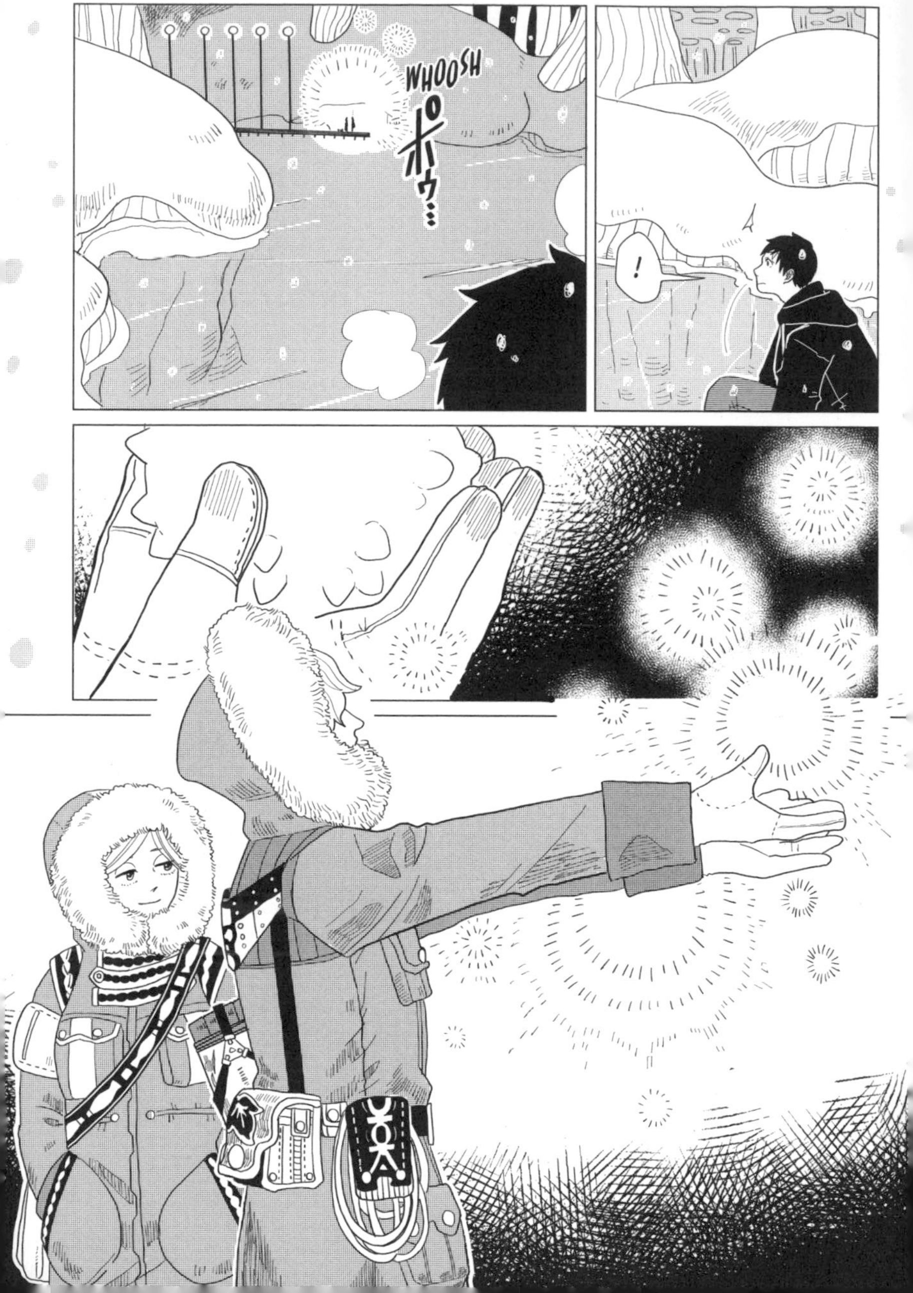
!
WHOOSH
ポホウ…

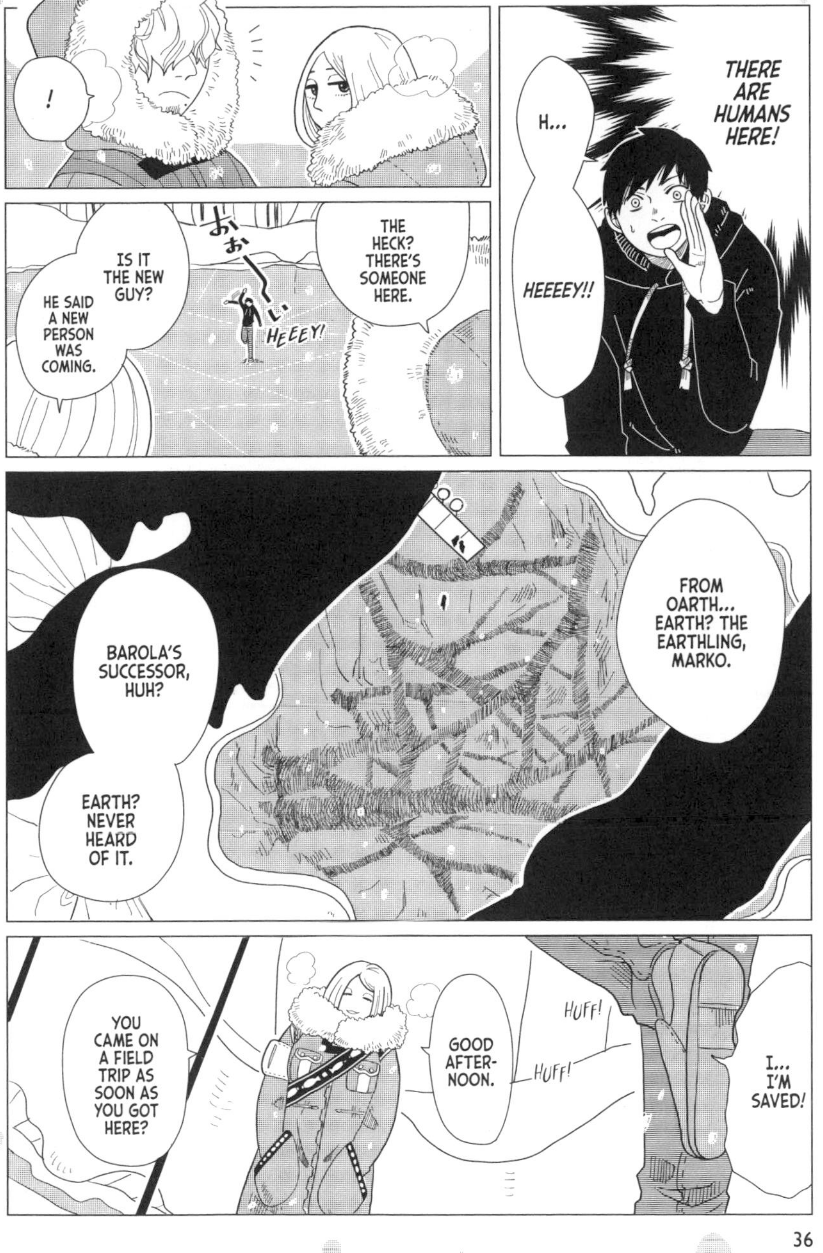
THERE ARE HUMANS HERE!
H...
HEEEEY!!
!
THE HECK? THERE'S SOMEONE HERE.
HEEEY!
IS IT THE NEW GUY?
HE SAID A NEW PERSON WAS COMING.
FROM OARTH... EARTH? THE EARTHLING, MARKO.
BAROLA'S SUCCESSOR, HUH?
EARTH? NEVER HEARD OF IT.
I... I'M SAVED!
HUFF!
HUFF!
GOOD AFTERNOON.
YOU CAME ON A FIELD TRIP AS SOON AS YOU GOT HERE?

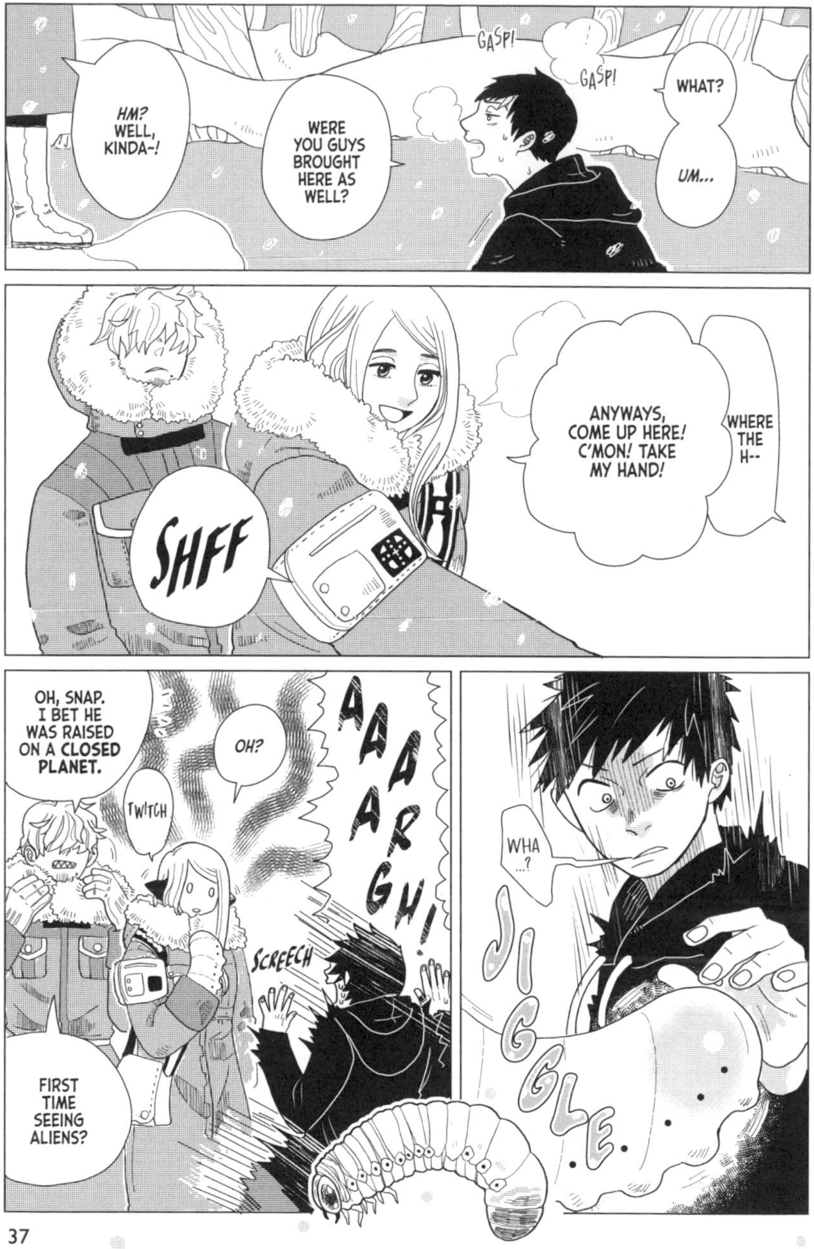
WHAT? UM...
GASP!
GASP!
WERE YOU GUYS BROUGHT HERE AS WELL?
HM? WELL, KINDA~!
WHERE THE H--
ANYWAYS, COME UP HERE! C'MON! TAKE MY HAND!
SHFF
WHA ...?
JIGGLE.
AAAARGH!
OH?
OH, SNAP. I BET HE WAS RAISED ON A **CLOSED PLANET.**
TWITCH
SCREECH
FIRST TIME SEEING ALIENS?

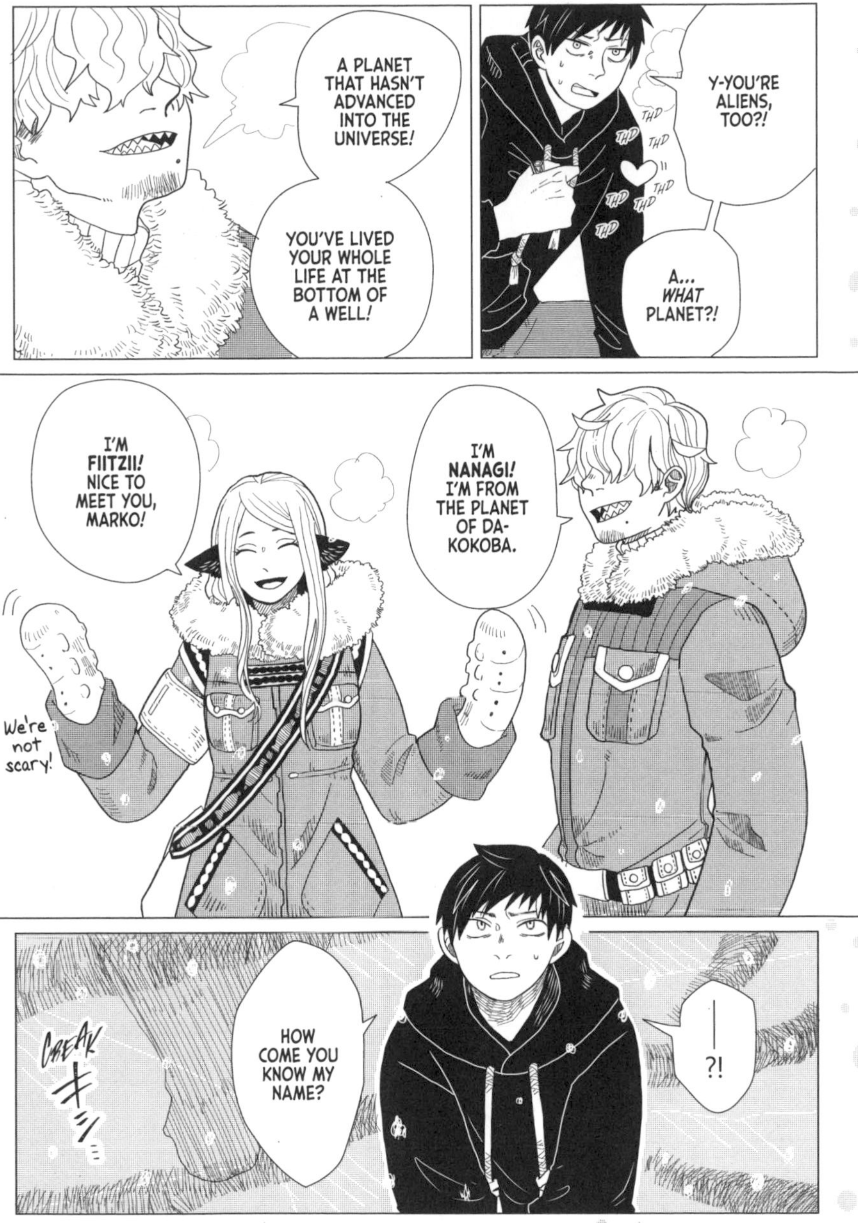
Y-YOU'RE ALIENS, TOO?!
THD THD THD THD THD THD THD
A... WHAT PLANET?!
A PLANET THAT HASN'T ADVANCED INTO THE UNIVERSE!
YOU'VE LIVED YOUR WHOLE LIFE AT THE BOTTOM OF A WELL!
I'M NANAGI! I'M FROM THE PLANET OF DA-KOKOBA.
I'M FIITZII! NICE TO MEET YOU, MARKO!
We're not scary!
―?!
HOW COME YOU KNOW MY NAME?
CREAK

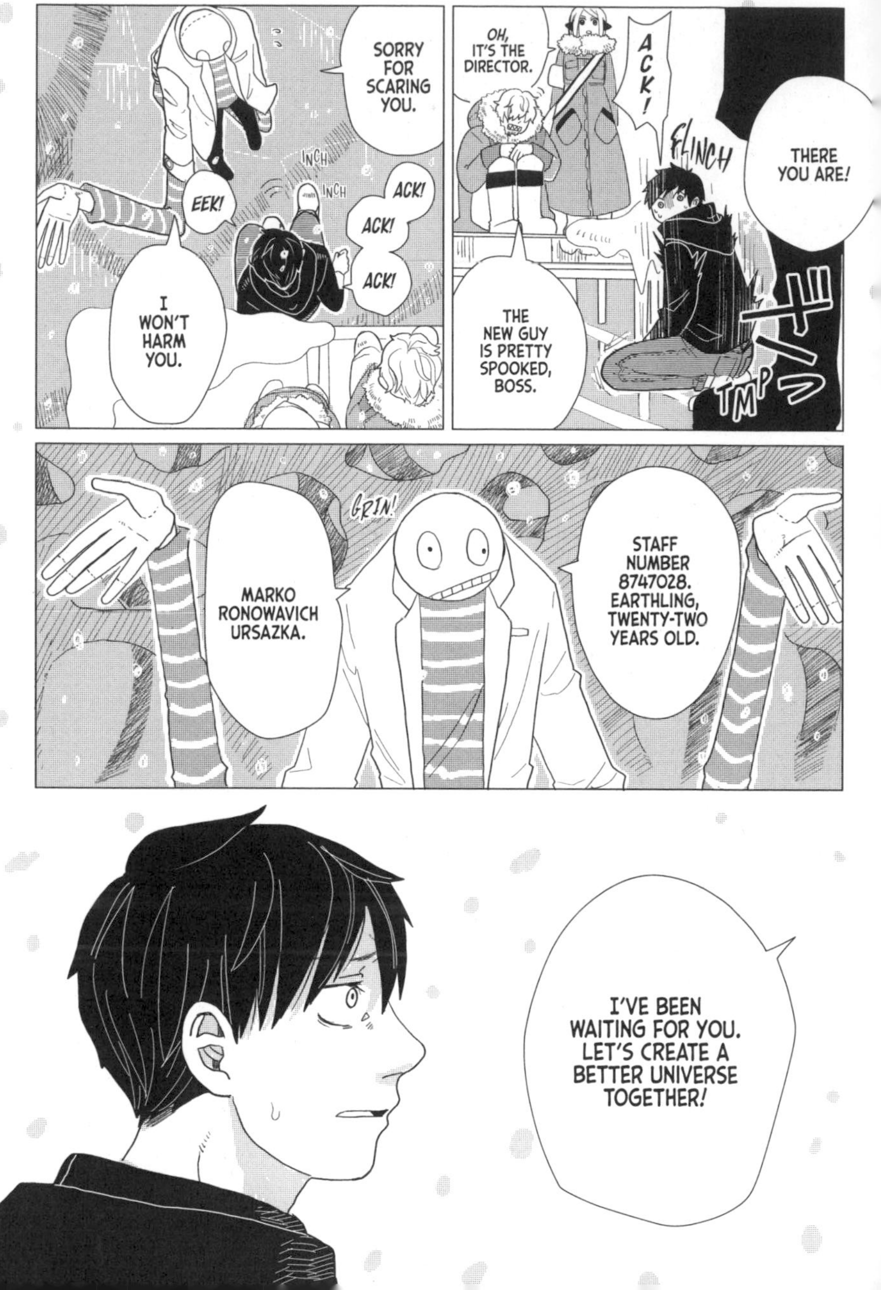
THERE YOU ARE!
FLINCH
ACK!
OH, IT'S THE DIRECTOR.
THE NEW GUY IS PRETTY SPOOKED, BOSS.
TMP
SORRY FOR SCARING YOU.
ACK!
ACK!
ACK!
INCH
INCH
EEK!
I WON'T HARM YOU.
STAFF NUMBER 8747028. EARTHLING, TWENTY-TWO YEARS OLD.
GRIN!
MARKO RONOWAVICH URSAZKA.
I'VE BEEN WAITING FOR YOU. LET'S CREATE A BETTER UNIVERSE TOGETHER!

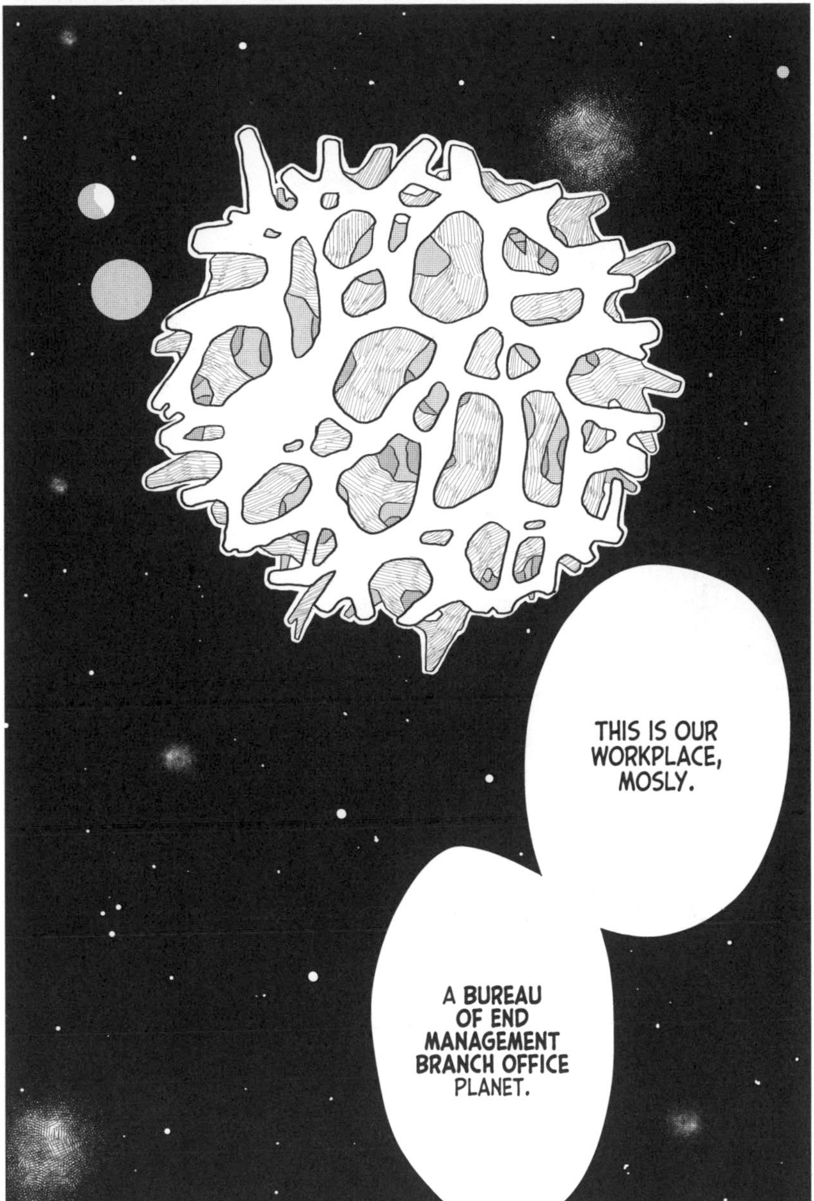
THIS IS OUR WORKPLACE, MOSLY.
A BUREAU OF END MANAGEMENT BRANCH OFFICE PLANET.

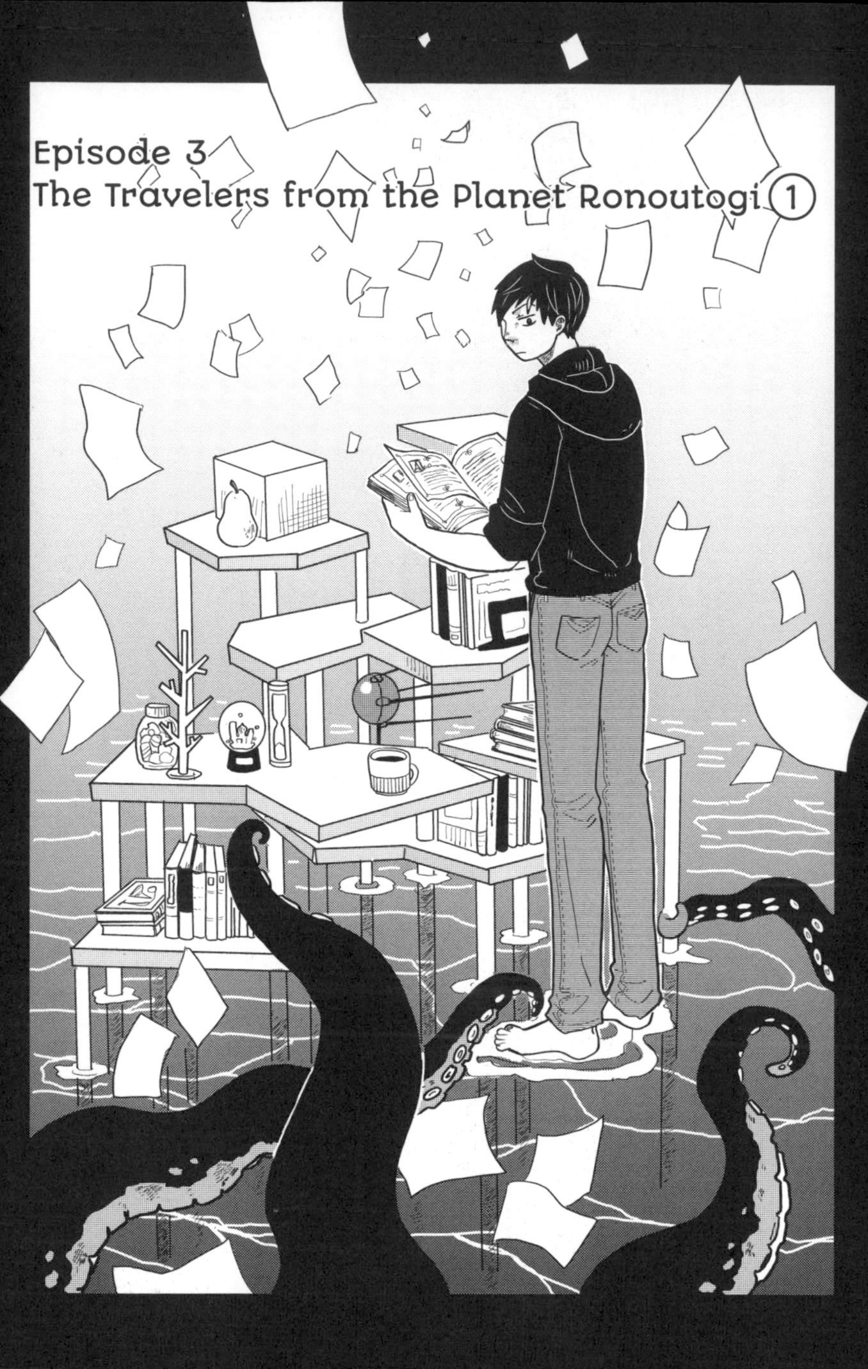
Episode 3
The Travelers from the Planet Ronoutogi 1

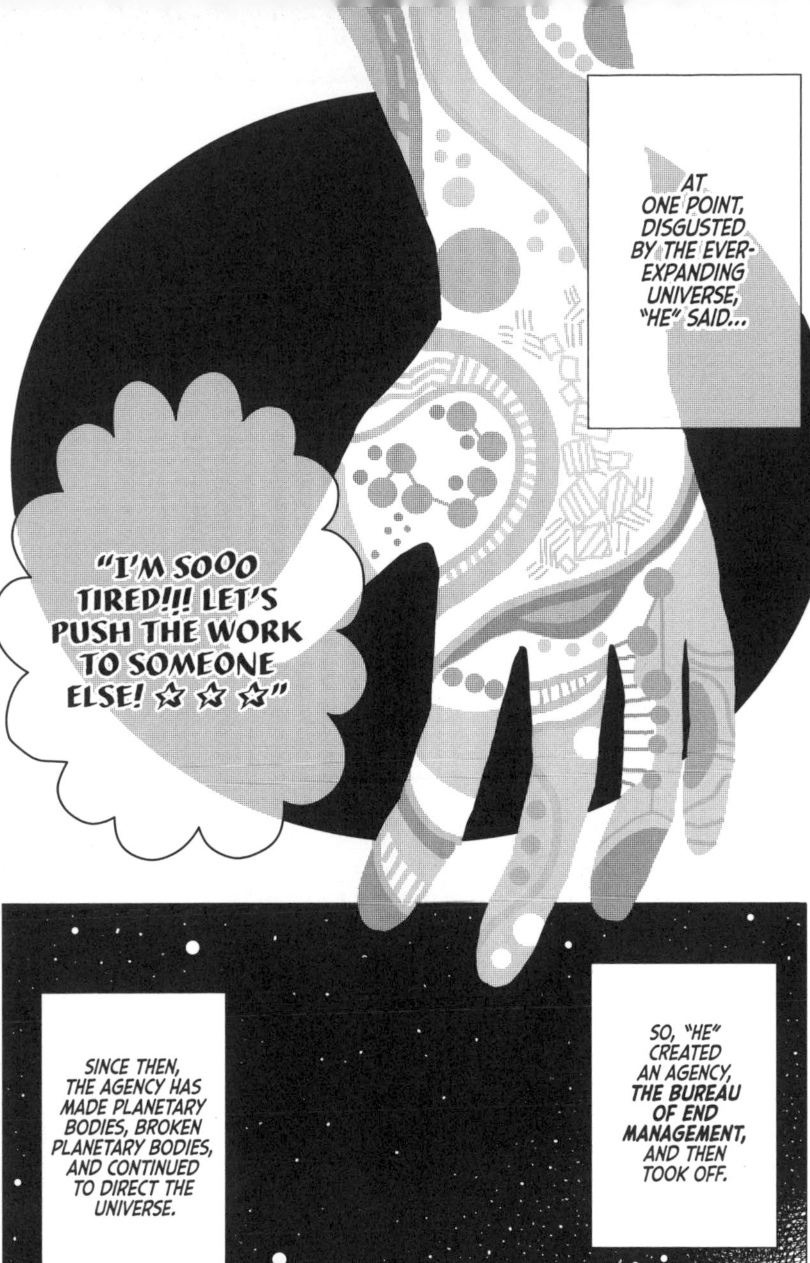
AT ONE POINT, DISGUSTED BY THE EVER-EXPANDING UNIVERSE, "HE" SAID...
"I'M SOOO TIRED!!! LET'S PUSH THE WORK TO SOMEONE ELSE! ☆☆☆"
SO, "HE" CREATED AN AGENCY, **THE BUREAU OF END MANAGEMENT,** AND THEN TOOK OFF.
SINCE THEN, THE AGENCY HAS MADE PLANETARY BODIES, BROKEN PLANETARY BODIES, AND CONTINUED TO DIRECT THE UNIVERSE.

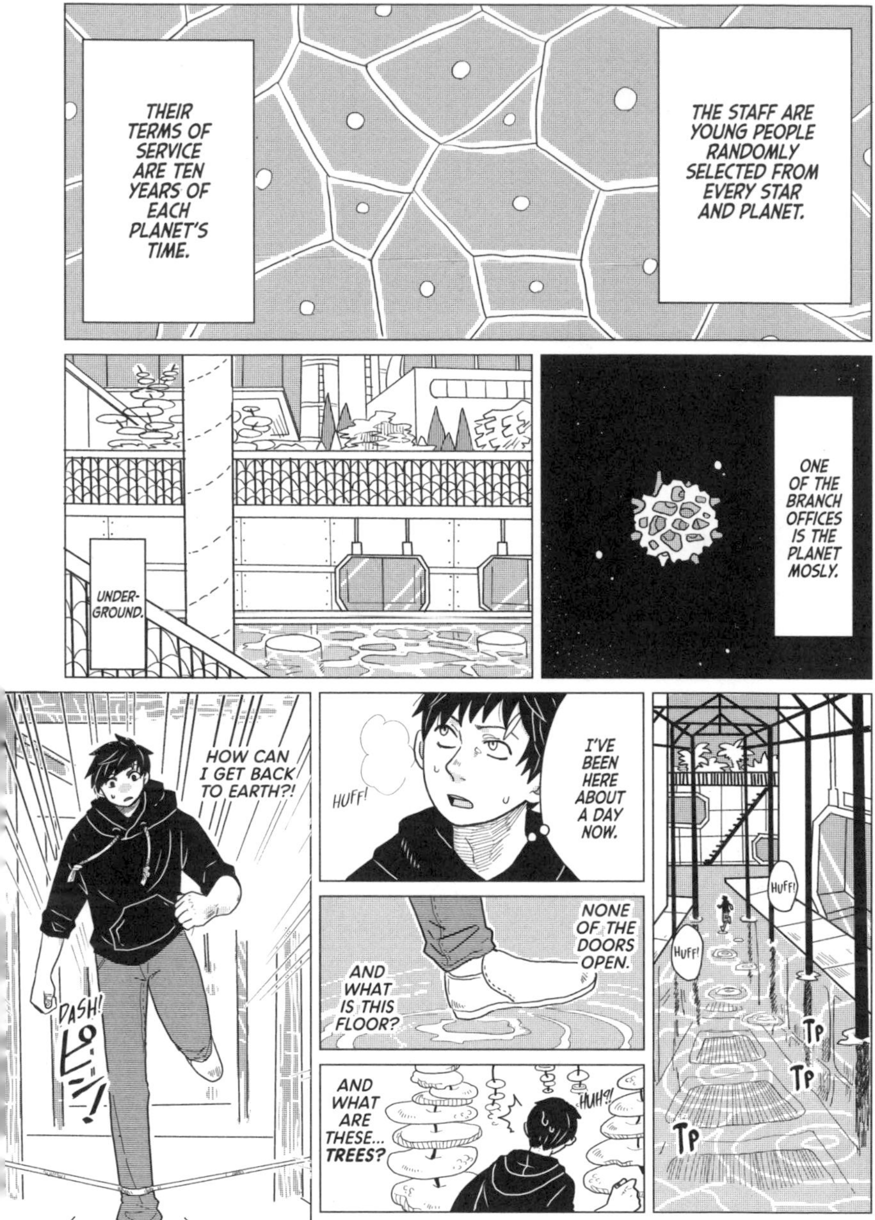
THE STAFF ARE YOUNG PEOPLE RANDOMLY SELECTED FROM EVERY STAR AND PLANET.
THEIR TERMS OF SERVICE ARE TEN YEARS OF EACH PLANET'S TIME.
ONE OF THE BRANCH OFFICES IS THE PLANET MOSLY.
UNDER-GROUND.
HUFF!
HUFF!
TP
TP
TP
I'VE BEEN HERE ABOUT A DAY NOW.
HUFF!
NONE OF THE DOORS OPEN.
AND WHAT IS THIS FLOOR?
HUH?!
AND WHAT ARE THESE... TREES?
HOW CAN I GET BACK TO EARTH?!
DASH!

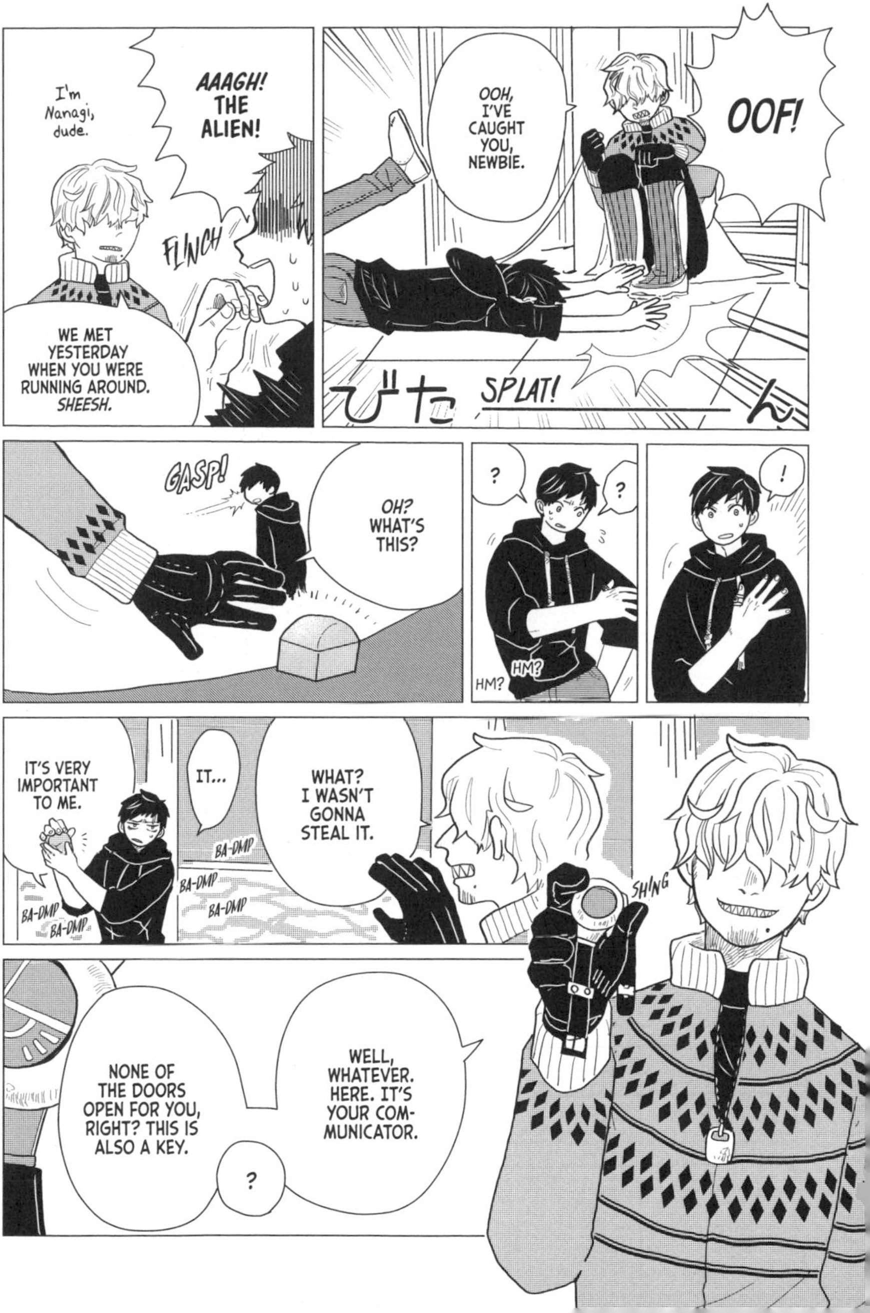
OOF!
OOH, I'VE CAUGHT YOU, NEWBIE.
SPLAT!
AAAGH! THE ALIEN!
I'm Nanagi, dude.
FLINCH
WE MET YESTERDAY WHEN YOU WERE RUNNING AROUND. SHEESH.
!
?
?
HM?
HM?
OH? WHAT'S THIS?
GASP!
SHING
WHAT? I WASN'T GONNA STEAL IT.
IT...
BA-DMP
BA-DMP
BA-DMP
IT'S VERY IMPORTANT TO ME.
BA-DMP
BA-DMP
WELL, WHATEVER. HERE. IT'S YOUR COM-MUNICATOR.
NONE OF THE DOORS OPEN FOR YOU, RIGHT? THIS IS ALSO A KEY.
?

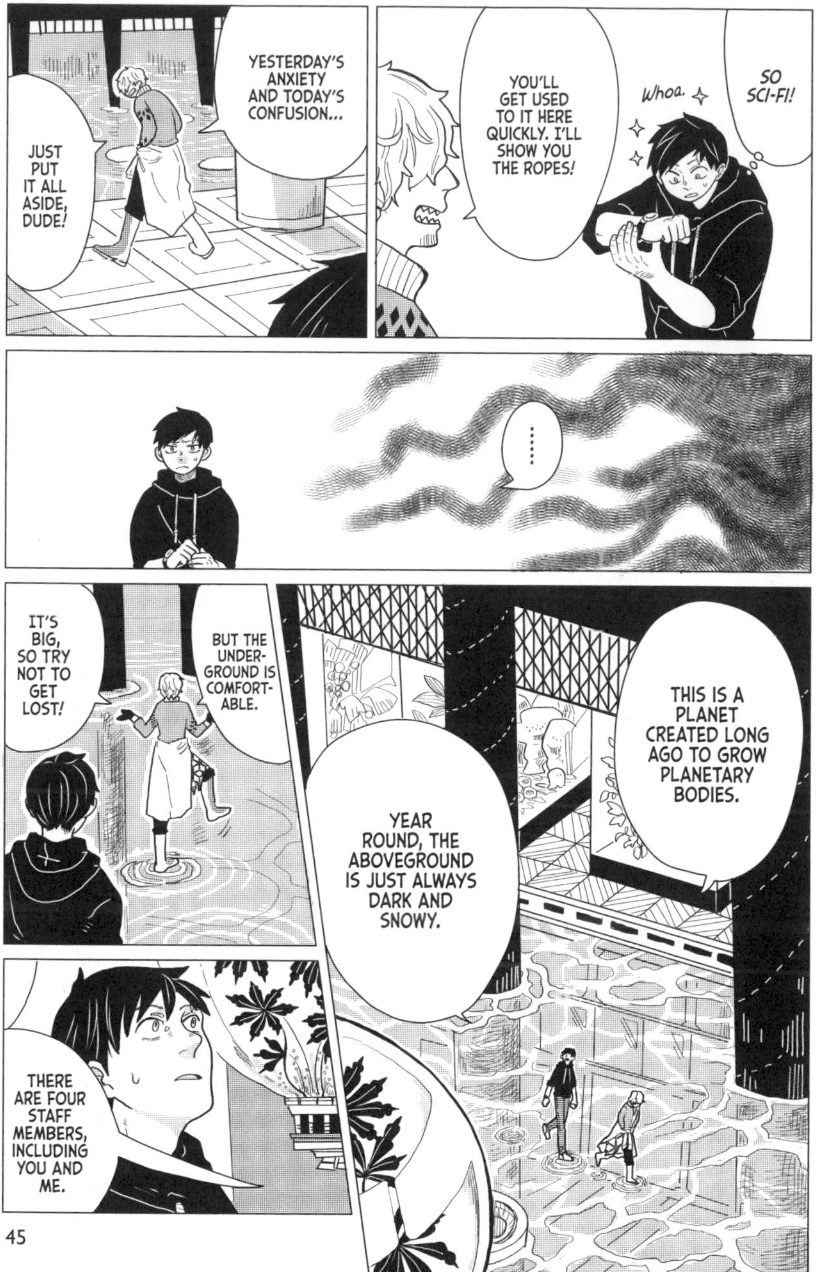
SO SCI-FI!
Whoa.
YOU'LL GET USED TO IT HERE QUICKLY. I'LL SHOW YOU THE ROPES!
YESTERDAY'S ANXIETY AND TODAY'S CONFUSION...
JUST PUT IT ALL ASIDE, DUDE!
......
THIS IS A PLANET CREATED LONG AGO TO GROW PLANETARY BODIES.
YEAR ROUND, THE ABOVEGROUND IS JUST ALWAYS DARK AND SNOWY.
BUT THE UNDER-GROUND IS COMFORT-ABLE.
IT'S BIG, SO TRY NOT TO GET LOST!
THERE ARE FOUR STAFF MEMBERS, INCLUDING YOU AND ME.

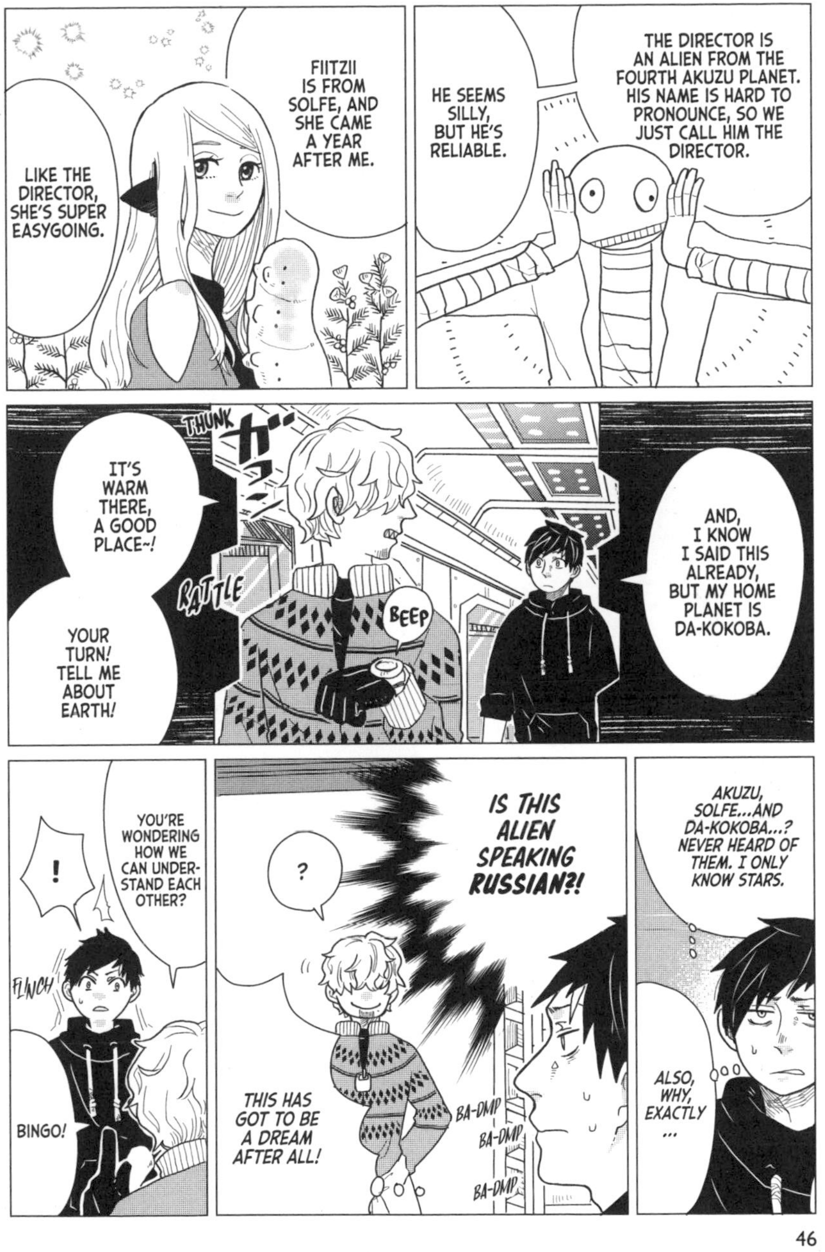
THE DIRECTOR IS AN ALIEN FROM THE FOURTH AKUZU PLANET. HIS NAME IS HARD TO PRONOUNCE, SO WE JUST CALL HIM THE DIRECTOR.
HE SEEMS SILLY, BUT HE'S RELIABLE.
FIITZII IS FROM SOLFE, AND SHE CAME A YEAR AFTER ME.
LIKE THE DIRECTOR, SHE'S SUPER EASYGOING.
AND, I KNOW I SAID THIS ALREADY, BUT MY HOME PLANET IS DA-KOKOBA.
THUNK
BEEP
RATTLE
IT'S WARM THERE, A GOOD PLACE~!
YOUR TURN! TELL ME ABOUT EARTH!
AKUZU, SOLFE...AND DA-KOKOBA...? NEVER HEARD OF THEM. I ONLY KNOW STARS.
ALSO, WHY, EXACTLY ...
IS THIS ALIEN SPEAKING RUSSIAN?!
?
BA-DMP
BA-DMP
BA-DMP
THIS HAS GOT TO BE A DREAM AFTER ALL!
YOU'RE WONDERING HOW WE CAN UNDER-STAND EACH OTHER?
!
FLINCH
BINGO!

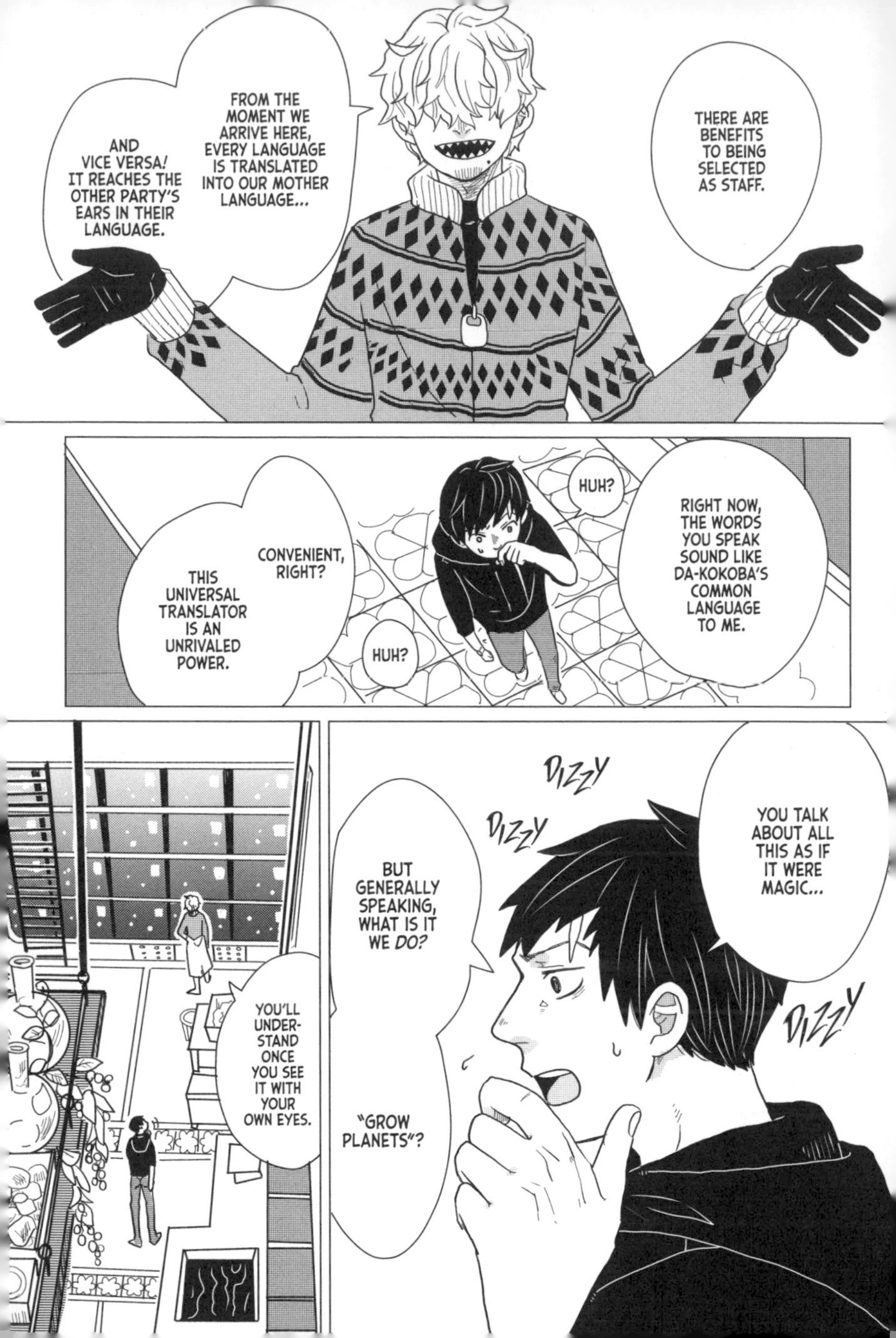
THERE ARE BENEFITS TO BEING SELECTED AS STAFF.
FROM THE MOMENT WE ARRIVE HERE, EVERY LANGUAGE IS TRANSLATED INTO OUR MOTHER LANGUAGE...
AND VICE VERSA! IT REACHES THE OTHER PARTY'S EARS IN THEIR LANGUAGE.
RIGHT NOW, THE WORDS YOU SPEAK SOUND LIKE DA-KOKOBA'S COMMON LANGUAGE TO ME.
HUH?
CONVENIENT, RIGHT?
THIS UNIVERSAL TRANSLATOR IS AN UNRIVALED POWER.
HUH?
DIZZY
YOU TALK ABOUT ALL THIS AS IF IT WERE MAGIC...
DIZZY
BUT GENERALLY SPEAKING, WHAT IS IT WE *DO?*
DIZZY
"GROW PLANETS"?
YOU'LL UNDER-STAND ONCE YOU SEE IT WITH YOUR OWN EYES.

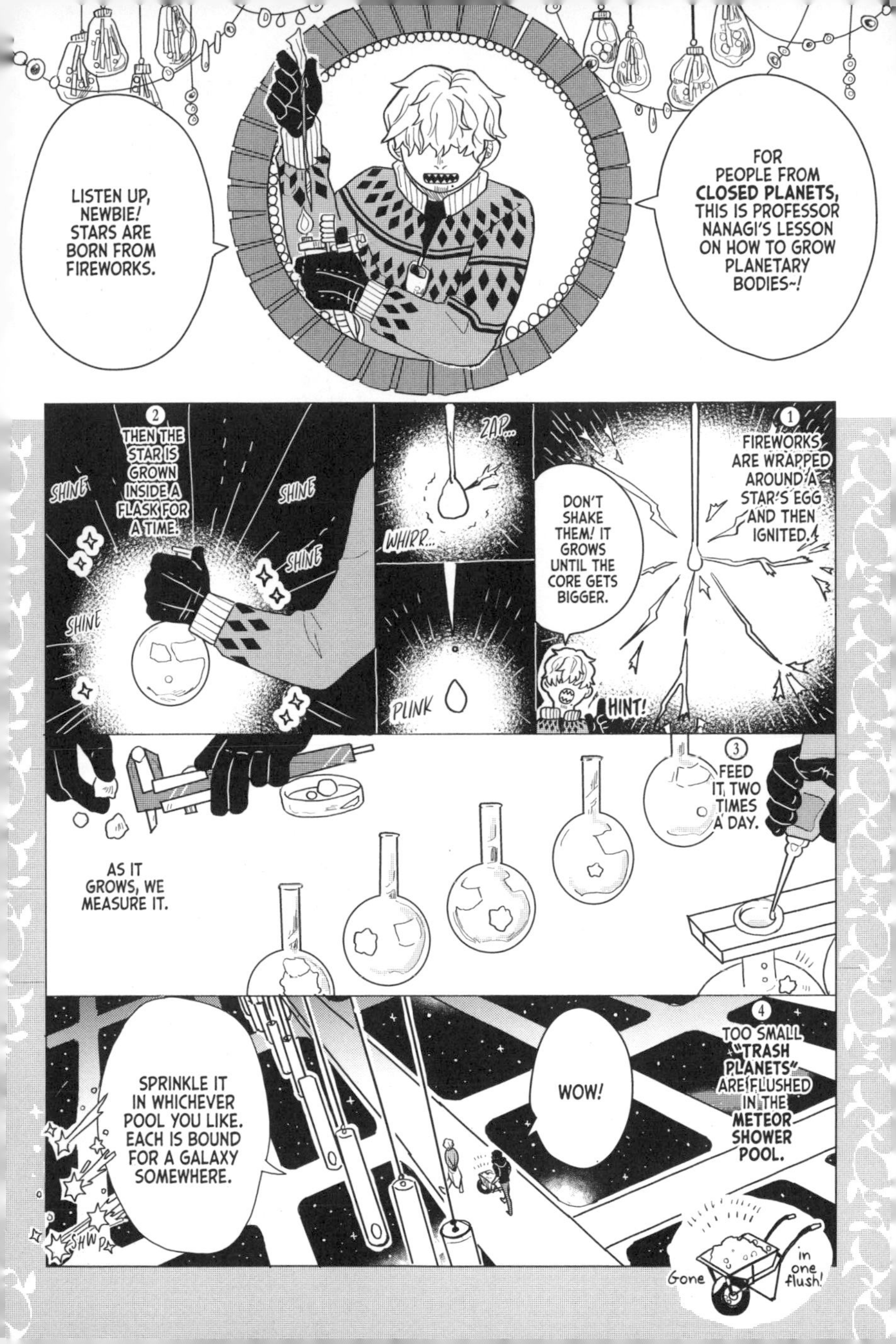
FOR PEOPLE FROM **CLOSED PLANETS,** THIS IS PROFESSOR NANAGI'S LESSON ON HOW TO GROW PLANETARY BODIES~!
LISTEN UP, NEWBIE! STARS ARE BORN FROM FIREWORKS.
1
FIREWORKS ARE WRAPPED AROUND A STAR'S EGG AND THEN IGNITED.
DON'T SHAKE THEM! IT GROWS UNTIL THE CORE GETS BIGGER.
HINT!
ZAP...
WHIRR...
PLINK
2
THEN THE STAR IS GROWN INSIDE A FLASK FOR A TIME.
SHINE
SHINE
SHINE
SHINE
3
FEED IT TWO TIMES A DAY.
AS IT GROWS, WE MEASURE IT.
4
TOO SMALL "TRASH PLANETS" ARE FLUSHED IN THE **METEOR SHOWER POOL.**
WOW!
SPRINKLE IT IN WHICHEVER POOL YOU LIKE. EACH IS BOUND FOR A GALAXY SOMEWHERE.
SHWP
Gone in one flush!

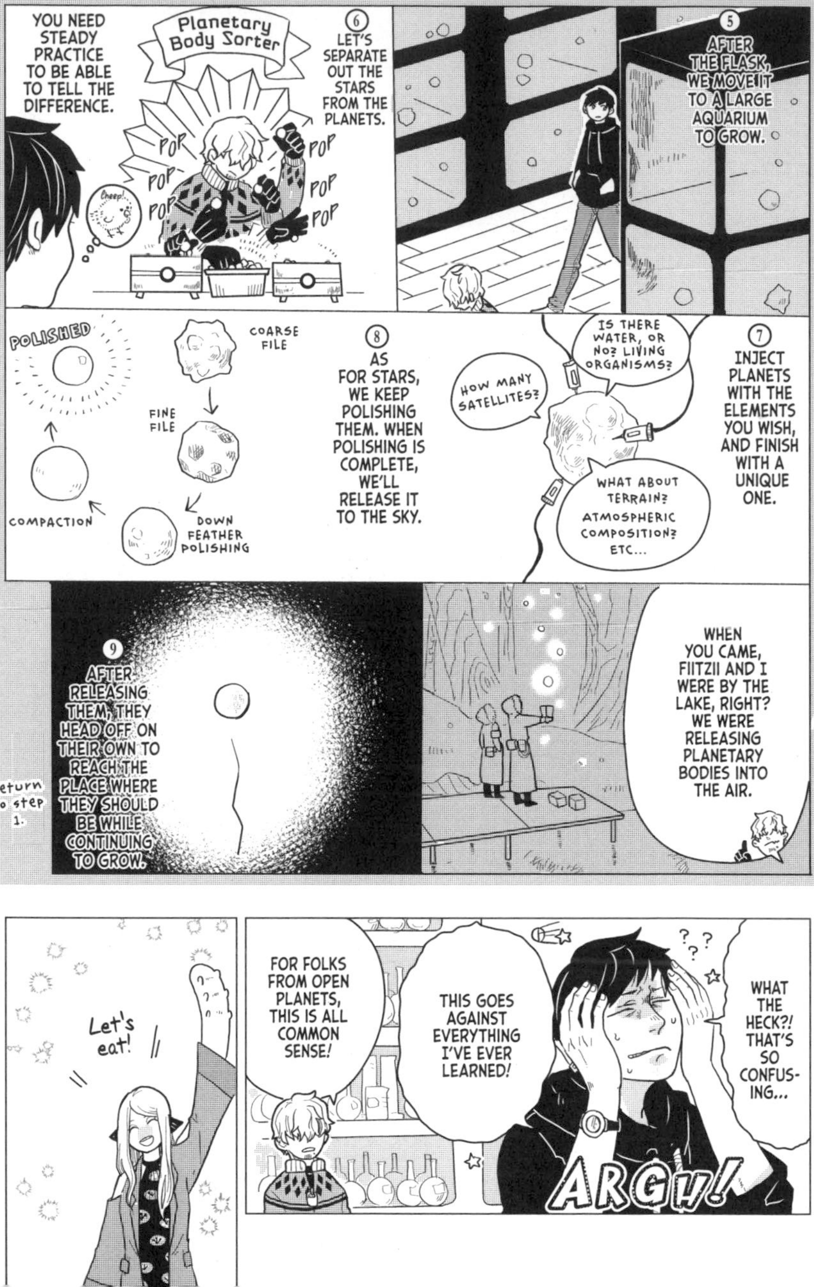
5
AFTER THE FLASK, WE MOVE IT TO A LARGE AQUARIUM TO GROW.
6
LET'S SEPARATE OUT THE STARS FROM THE PLANETS.
Planetary Body Sorter
YOU NEED STEADY PRACTICE TO BE ABLE TO TELL THE DIFFERENCE.
POP
POP
POP
POP
POP
POP
POP
Cheep!
7
INJECT PLANETS WITH THE ELEMENTS YOU WISH, AND FINISH WITH A UNIQUE ONE.
IS THERE WATER, OR NO? LIVING ORGANISMS?
HOW MANY SATELLITES?
WHAT ABOUT TERRAIN? ATMOSPHERIC COMPOSITION? ETC...
8
AS FOR STARS, WE KEEP POLISHING THEM. WHEN POLISHING IS COMPLETE, WE'LL RELEASE IT TO THE SKY.
COARSE FILE
FINE FILE
DOWN FEATHER POLISHING
COMPACTION
POLISHED
WHEN YOU CAME, FIITZII AND I WERE BY THE LAKE, RIGHT? WE WERE RELEASING PLANETARY BODIES INTO THE AIR.
9
AFTER RELEASING THEM, THEY HEAD OFF ON THEIR OWN TO REACH THE PLACE WHERE THEY SHOULD BE WHILE CONTINUING TO GROW.
Return to step 1.
WHAT THE HECK?! THAT'S SO CONFUSING...
THIS GOES AGAINST EVERYTHING I'VE EVER LEARNED!
FOR FOLKS FROM OPEN PLANETS, THIS IS ALL COMMON SENSE!
ARGH!
Let's eat!

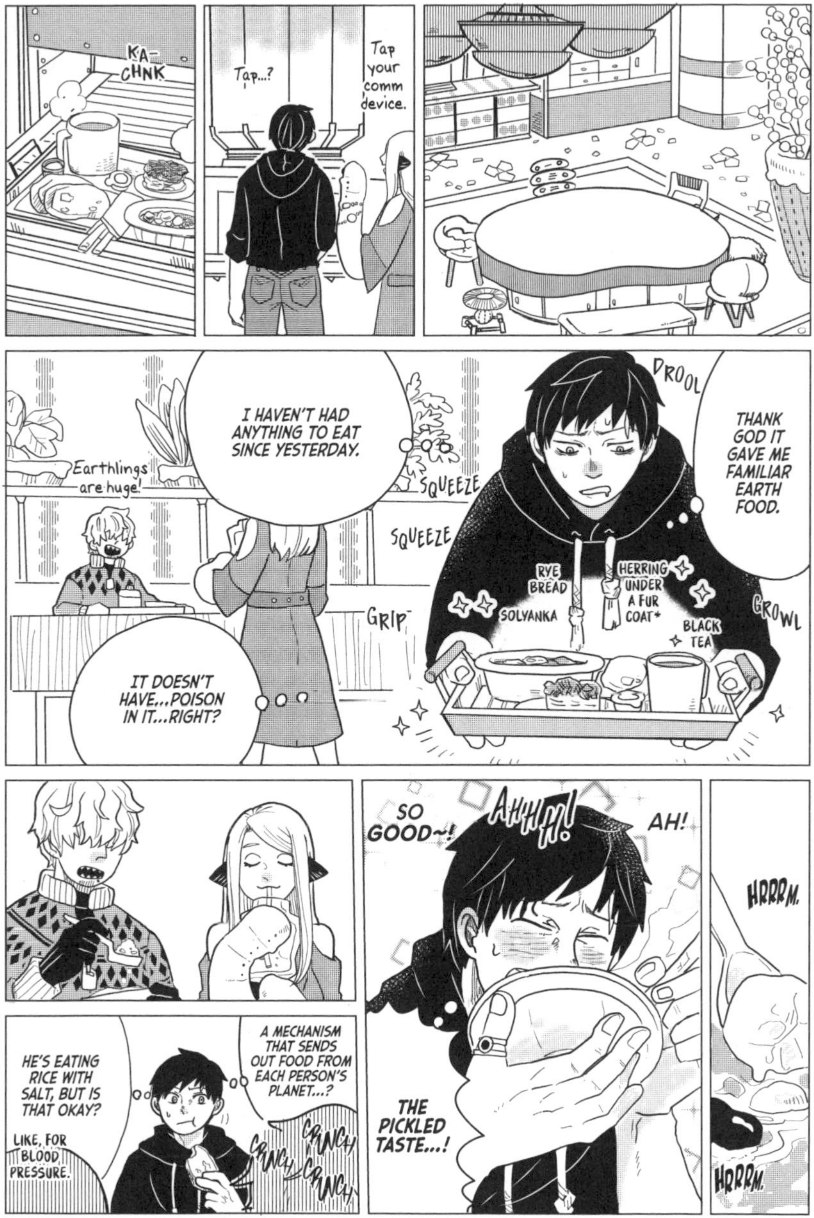
Tap your comm device.
Tap...?
KA-CHNK
DROOL
THANK GOD IT GAVE ME FAMILIAR EARTH FOOD.
GROWL
HERRING UNDER A FUR COAT*
RYE BREAD
SOLYANKA
BLACK TEA
I HAVEN'T HAD ANYTHING TO EAT SINCE YESTERDAY.
SQUEEZE
SQUEEZE
Earthlings are huge!
GRIP
IT DOESN'T HAVE...POISON IN IT...RIGHT?
HRRRM.
HRRRM.
AH!
AHHHH!
SO GOOD~!
THE PICKLED TASTE...!
A MECHANISM THAT SENDS OUT FOOD FROM EACH PERSON'S PLANET...?
HE'S EATING RICE WITH SALT, BUT IS THAT OKAY?
LIKE, FOR BLOOD PRESSURE.
CRUNCH
CRUNCH
CRUNCH
CRUNCH

*Herring under a fur coat is a type of Russian salad that layers fish under vegetables.

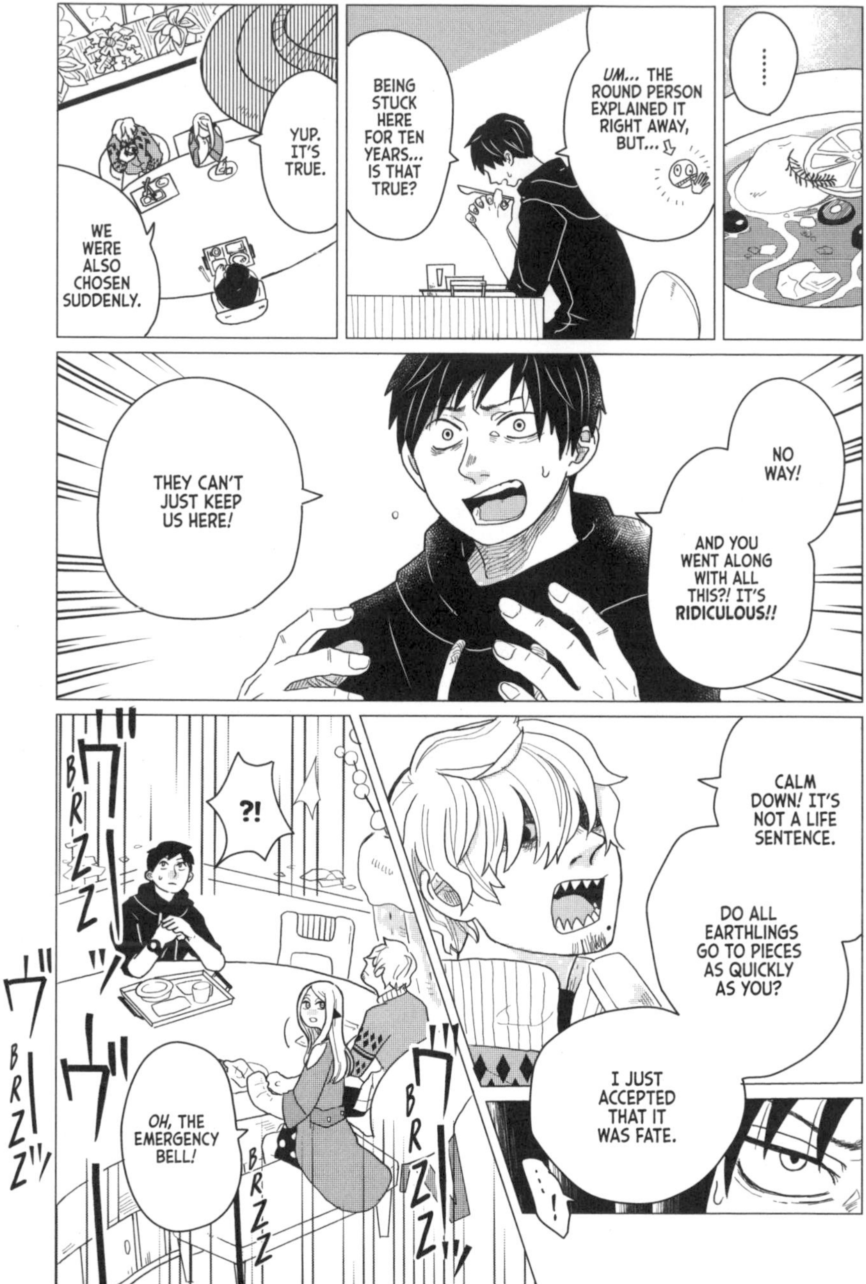
......
UM... THE ROUND PERSON EXPLAINED IT RIGHT AWAY, BUT...
BEING STUCK HERE FOR TEN YEARS... IS THAT TRUE?
YUP. IT'S TRUE.
WE WERE ALSO CHOSEN SUDDENLY.
NO WAY!
AND YOU WENT ALONG WITH ALL THIS?! IT'S **RIDICULOUS!!**
THEY CAN'T JUST KEEP US HERE!
CALM DOWN! IT'S NOT A LIFE SENTENCE.
DO ALL EARTHLINGS GO TO PIECES AS QUICKLY AS YOU?
I JUST ACCEPTED THAT IT WAS FATE.
...!
BRZZ
?!
BRZZ
OH, THE EMERGENCY BELL!
BRZZ
BRZZ

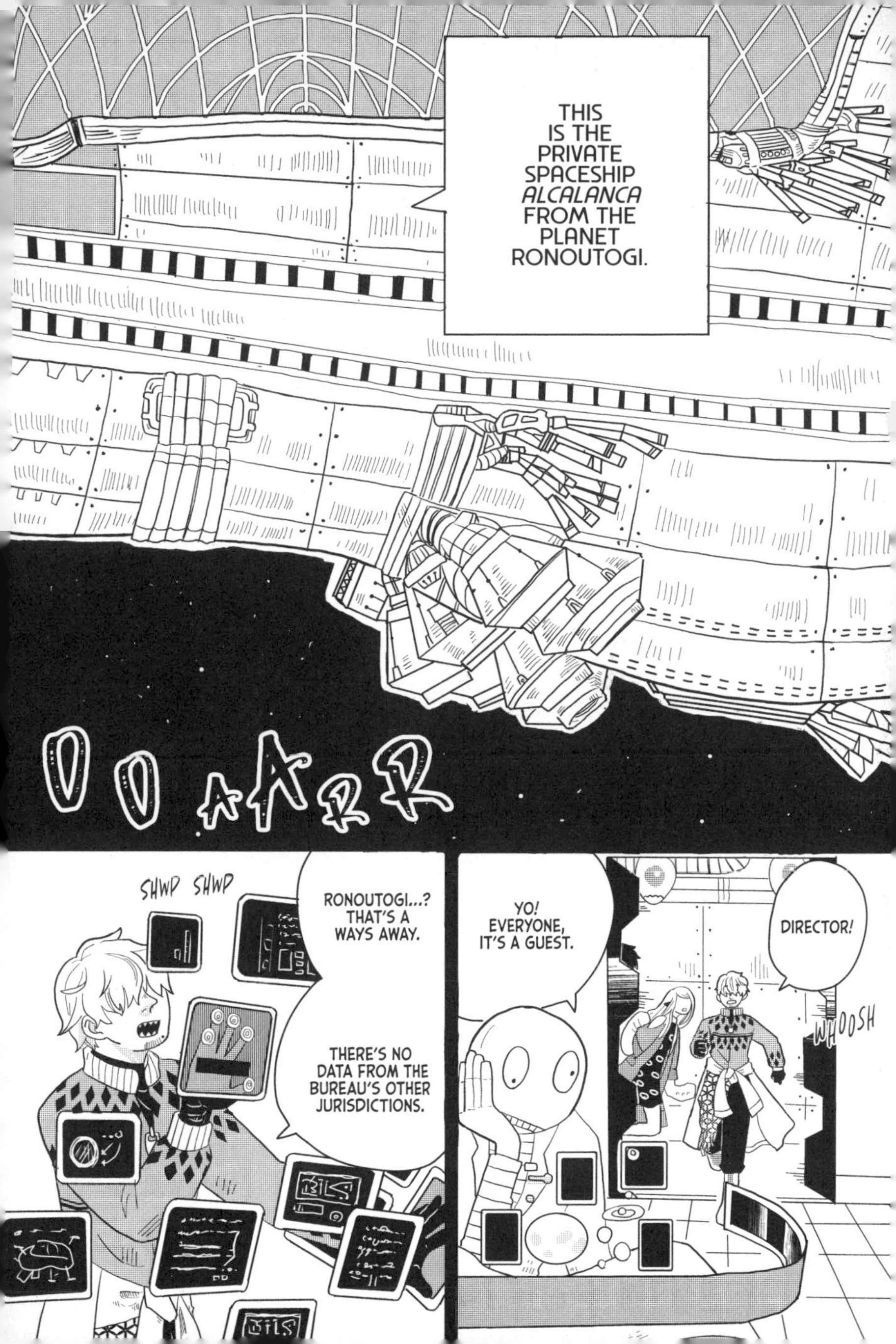
THIS IS THE PRIVATE SPACESHIP *ALCALANCA* FROM THE PLANET RONOUTOGI.
DIRECTOR!
YO! EVERYONE, IT'S A GUEST.
WHOOSH
RONOUTOGI...? THAT'S A WAYS AWAY.
SHWP SHWP
THERE'S NO DATA FROM THE BUREAU'S OTHER JURISDICTIONS.

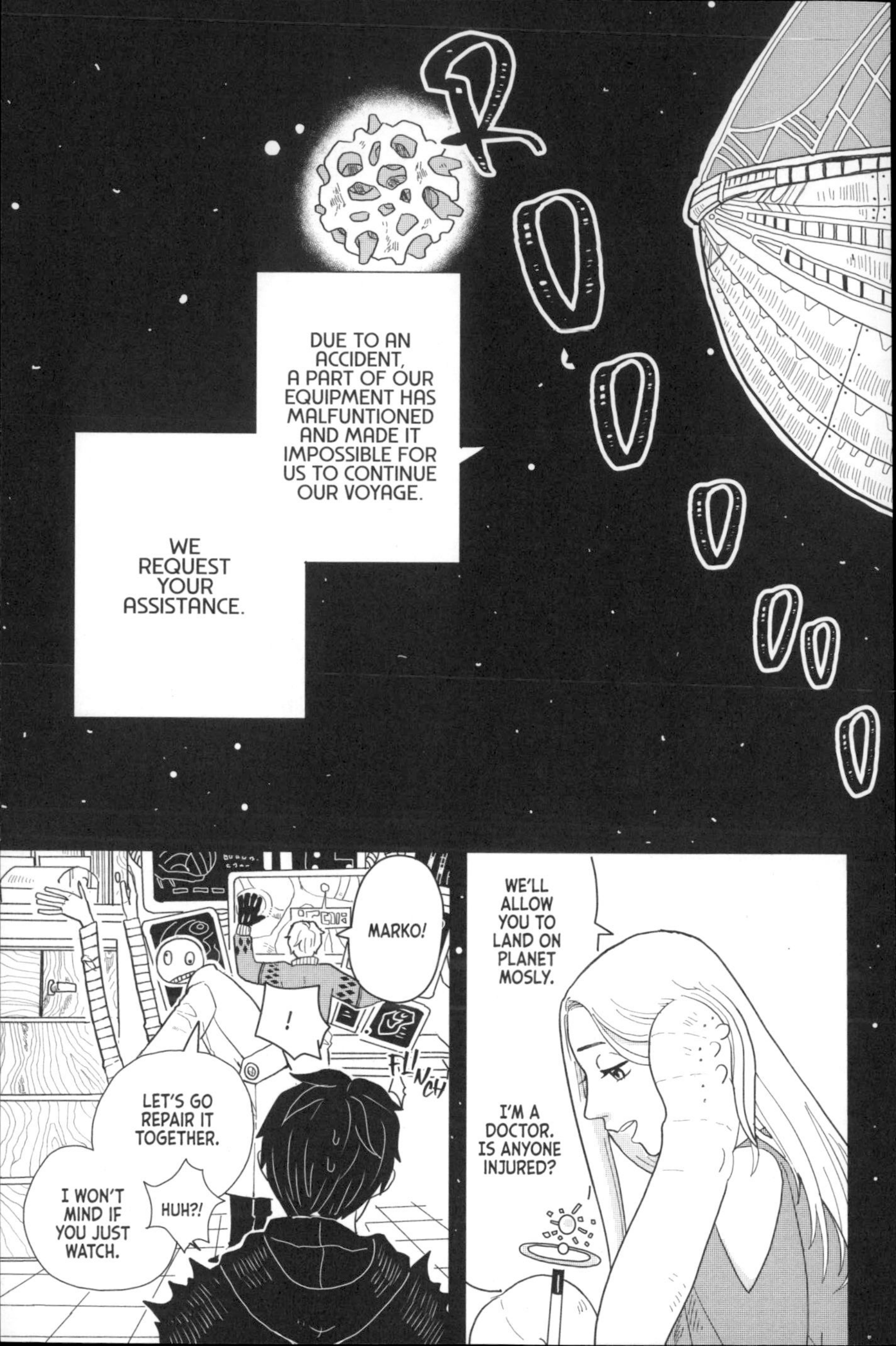
DUE TO AN ACCIDENT, A PART OF OUR EQUIPMENT HAS MALFUNTIONED AND MADE IT IMPOSSIBLE FOR US TO CONTINUE OUR VOYAGE.
WE REQUEST YOUR ASSISTANCE.
WE'LL ALLOW YOU TO LAND ON PLANET MOSLY.
I'M A DOCTOR. IS ANYONE INJURED?
MARKO!
!
FLINCH
LET'S GO REPAIR IT TOGETHER.
HUH?!
I WON'T MIND IF YOU JUST WATCH.

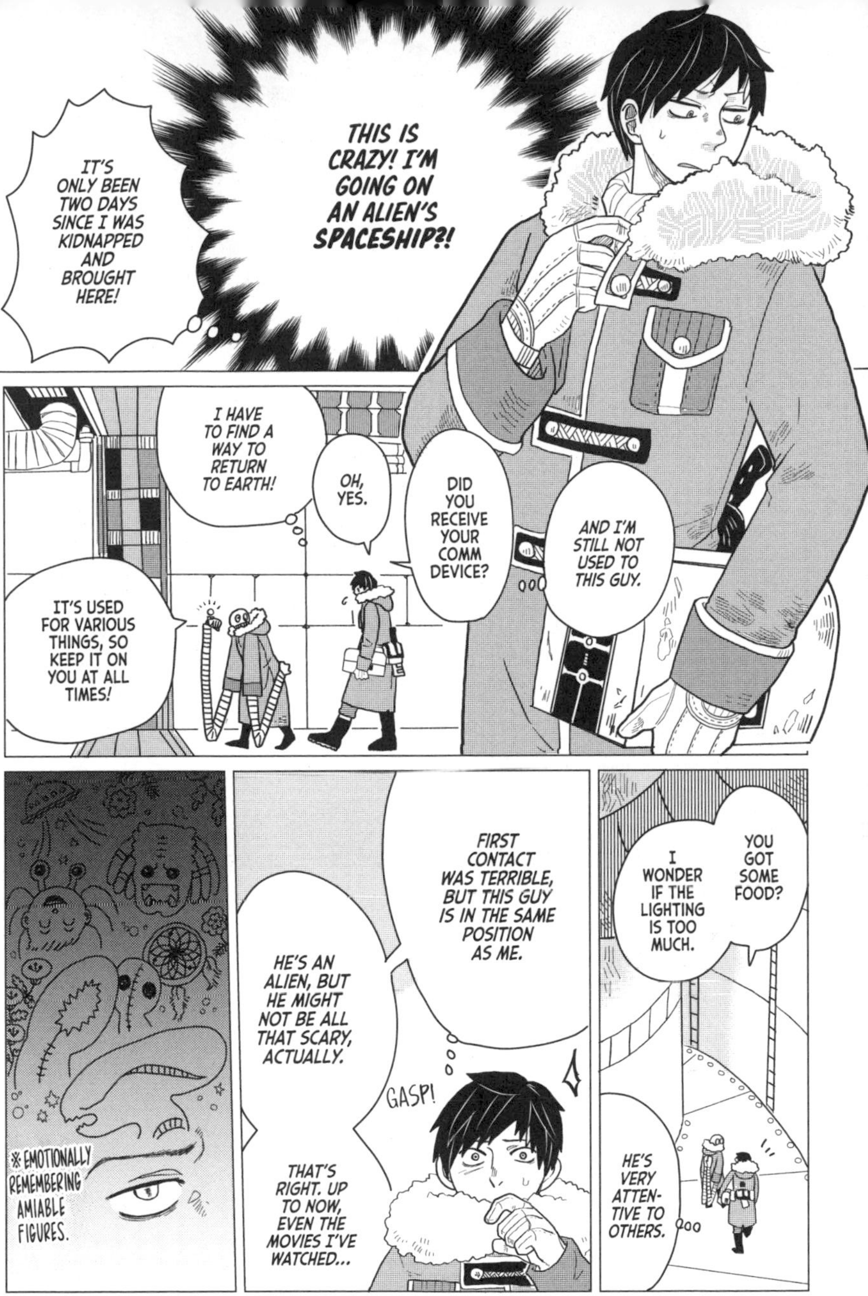
THIS IS CRAZY! I'M GOING ON AN ALIEN'S SPACESHIP?!
IT'S ONLY BEEN TWO DAYS SINCE I WAS KIDNAPPED AND BROUGHT HERE!
AND I'M STILL NOT USED TO THIS GUY.
DID YOU RECEIVE YOUR COMM DEVICE?
OH, YES.
I HAVE TO FIND A WAY TO RETURN TO EARTH!
IT'S USED FOR VARIOUS THINGS, SO KEEP IT ON YOU AT ALL TIMES!
YOU GOT SOME FOOD?
I WONDER IF THE LIGHTING IS TOO MUCH.
HE'S VERY ATTEN-TIVE TO OTHERS.
FIRST CONTACT WAS TERRIBLE, BUT THIS GUY IS IN THE SAME POSITION AS ME.
HE'S AN ALIEN, BUT HE MIGHT NOT BE ALL THAT SCARY, ACTUALLY.
GASP!
THAT'S RIGHT. UP TO NOW, EVEN THE MOVIES I'VE WATCHED...
※EMOTIONALLY REMEMBERING AMIABLE FIGURES.

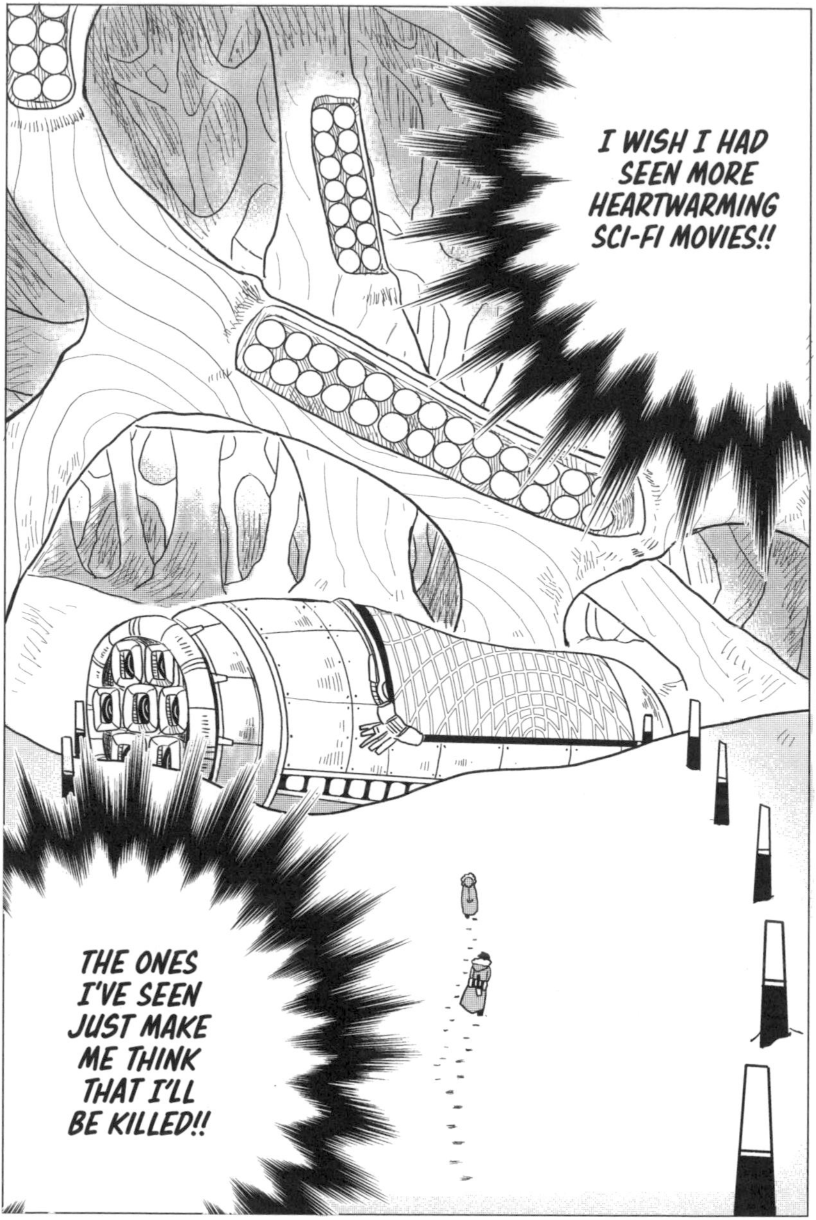
I WISH I HAD SEEN MORE HEARTWARMING SCI-FI MOVIES!!
THE ONES I'VE SEEN JUST MAKE ME THINK THAT I'LL BE KILLED!!

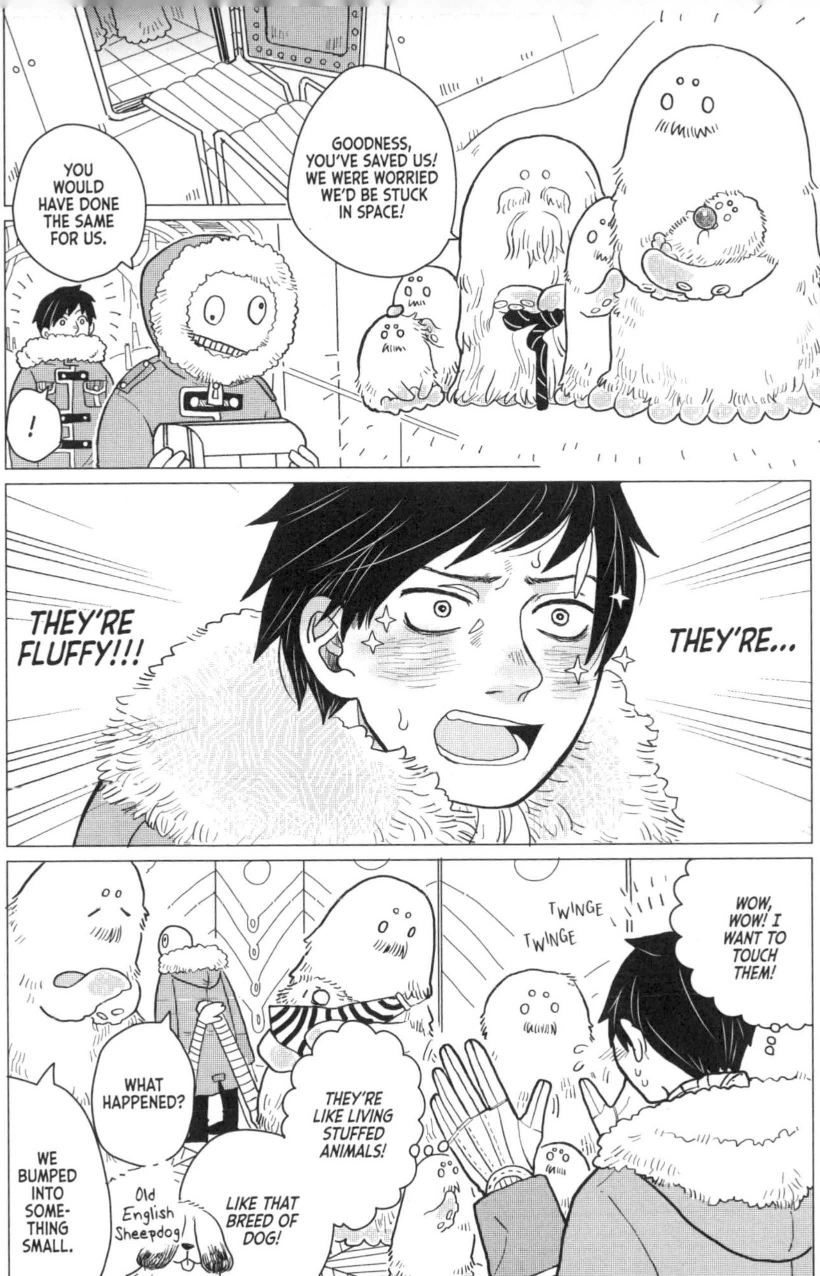
GOODNESS, YOU'VE SAVED US! WE WERE WORRIED WE'D BE STUCK IN SPACE!
YOU WOULD HAVE DONE THE SAME FOR US.
!
THEY'RE...
THEY'RE FLUFFY!!!
WOW, WOW! I WANT TO TOUCH THEM!
TWINGE
TWINGE
THEY'RE LIKE LIVING STUFFED ANIMALS!
WHAT HAPPENED?
LIKE THAT BREED OF DOG!
Old English Sheepdog
WE BUMPED INTO SOME-THING SMALL.

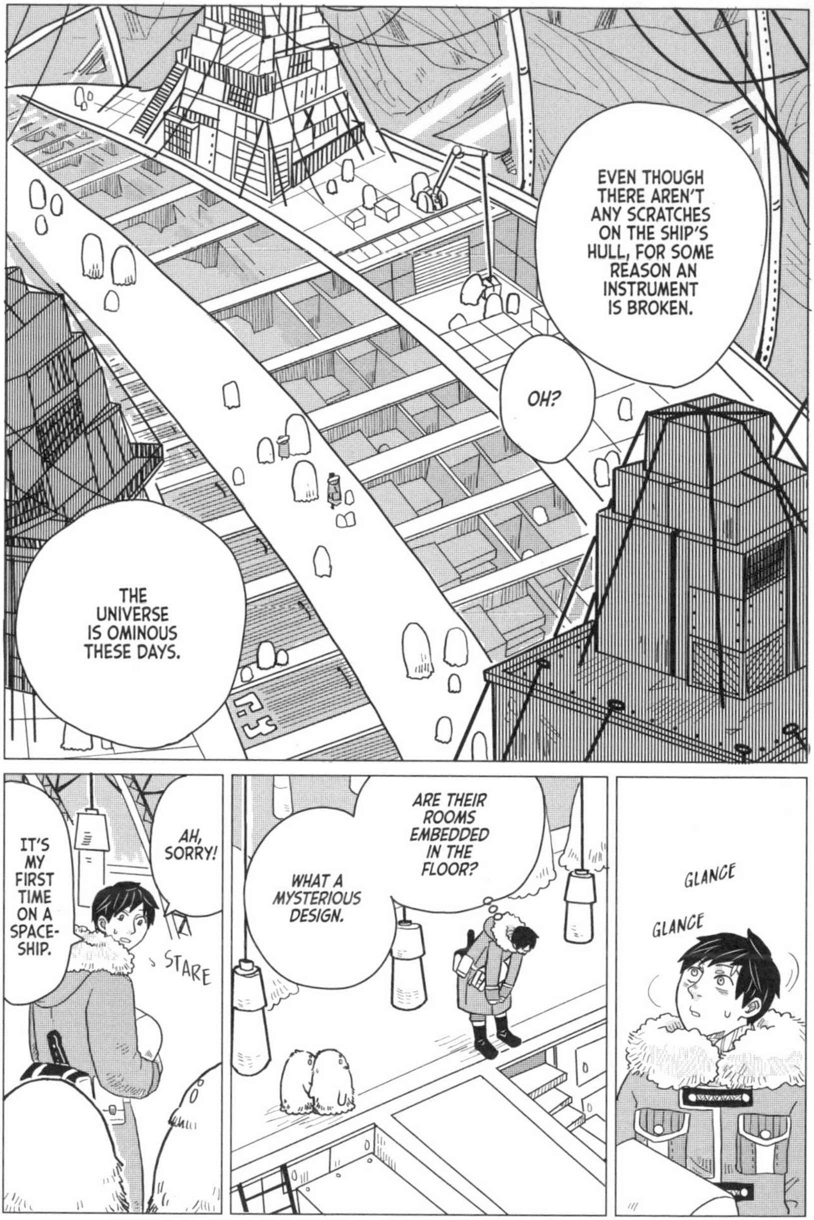
EVEN THOUGH THERE AREN'T ANY SCRATCHES ON THE SHIP'S HULL, FOR SOME REASON AN INSTRUMENT IS BROKEN.
OH?
THE UNIVERSE IS OMINOUS THESE DAYS.
GLANCE
GLANCE
ARE THEIR ROOMS EMBEDDED IN THE FLOOR?
WHAT A MYSTERIOUS DESIGN.
AH, SORRY!
IT'S MY FIRST TIME ON A SPACE-SHIP.
STARE

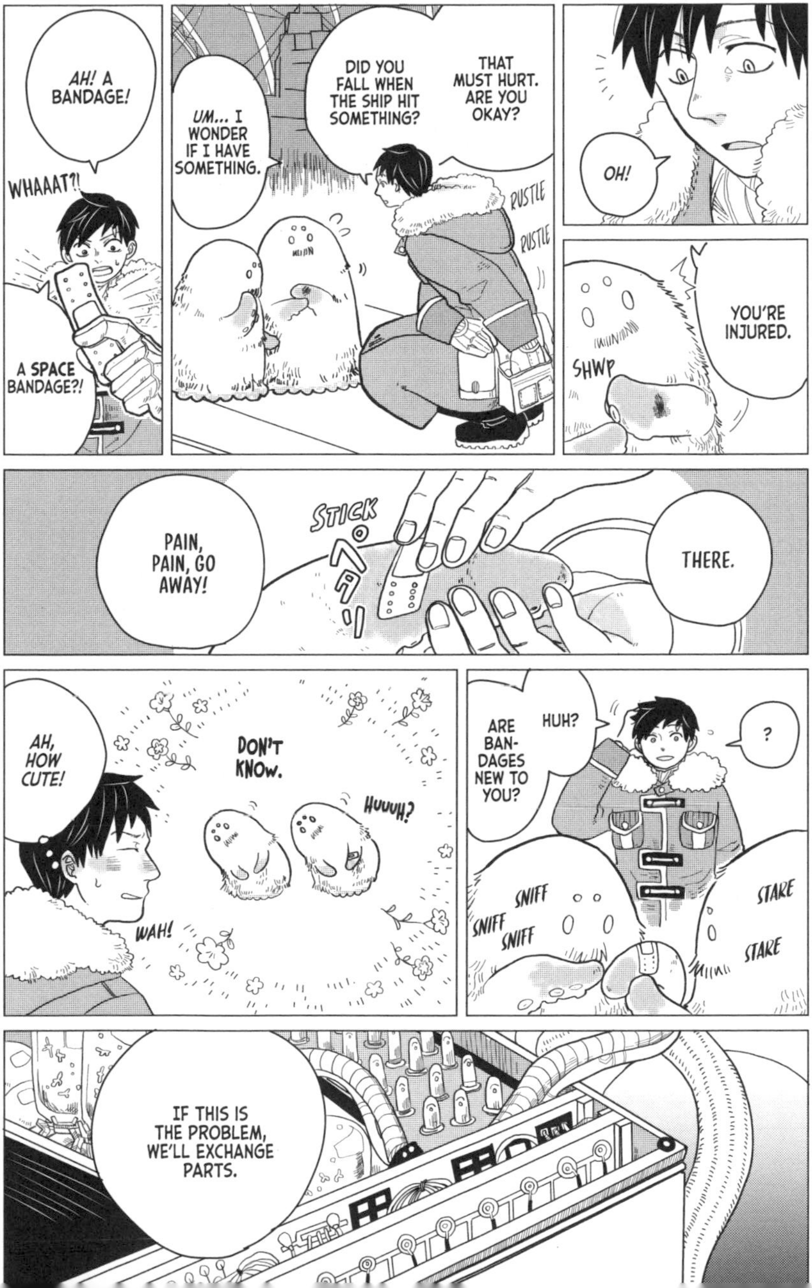
OH!
YOU'RE INJURED.
SHWP
THAT MUST HURT. ARE YOU OKAY?
DID YOU FALL WHEN THE SHIP HIT SOMETHING?
UM... I WONDER IF I HAVE SOMETHING.
RUSTLE
RUSTLE
AH! A BANDAGE!
WHAAAT?!
A SPACE BANDAGE?!
THERE.
STICK
PAIN, PAIN, GO AWAY!
?
HUH?
ARE BAN-DAGES NEW TO YOU?
SNIFF
SNIFF
SNIFF
STARE
STARE
DON'T KNOW.
HUUUH?
AH, HOW CUTE!
WAH!
IF THIS IS THE PROBLEM, WE'LL EXCHANGE PARTS.

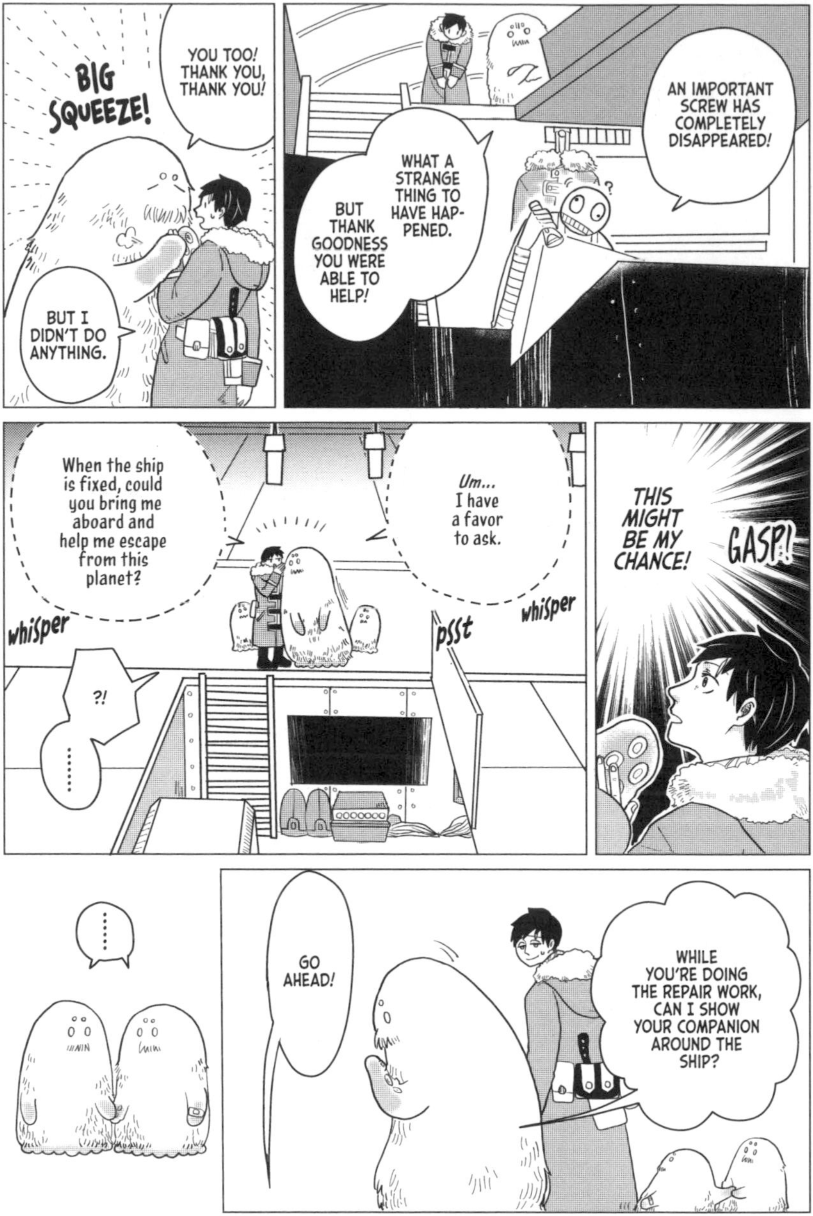
AN IMPORTANT SCREW HAS COMPLETELY DISAPPEARED!
WHAT A STRANGE THING TO HAVE HAP-PENED.
BUT THANK GOODNESS YOU WERE ABLE TO HELP!
YOU TOO! THANK YOU, THANK YOU!
BIG SQUEEZE!
BUT I DIDN'T DO ANYTHING.
GASP!
THIS MIGHT BE MY CHANCE!
Um... I have a favor to ask.
whisper
psst
When the ship is fixed, could you bring me aboard and help me escape from this planet?
whisper
?!
......
WHILE YOU'RE DOING THE REPAIR WORK, CAN I SHOW YOUR COMPANION AROUND THE SHIP?
GO AHEAD!
......

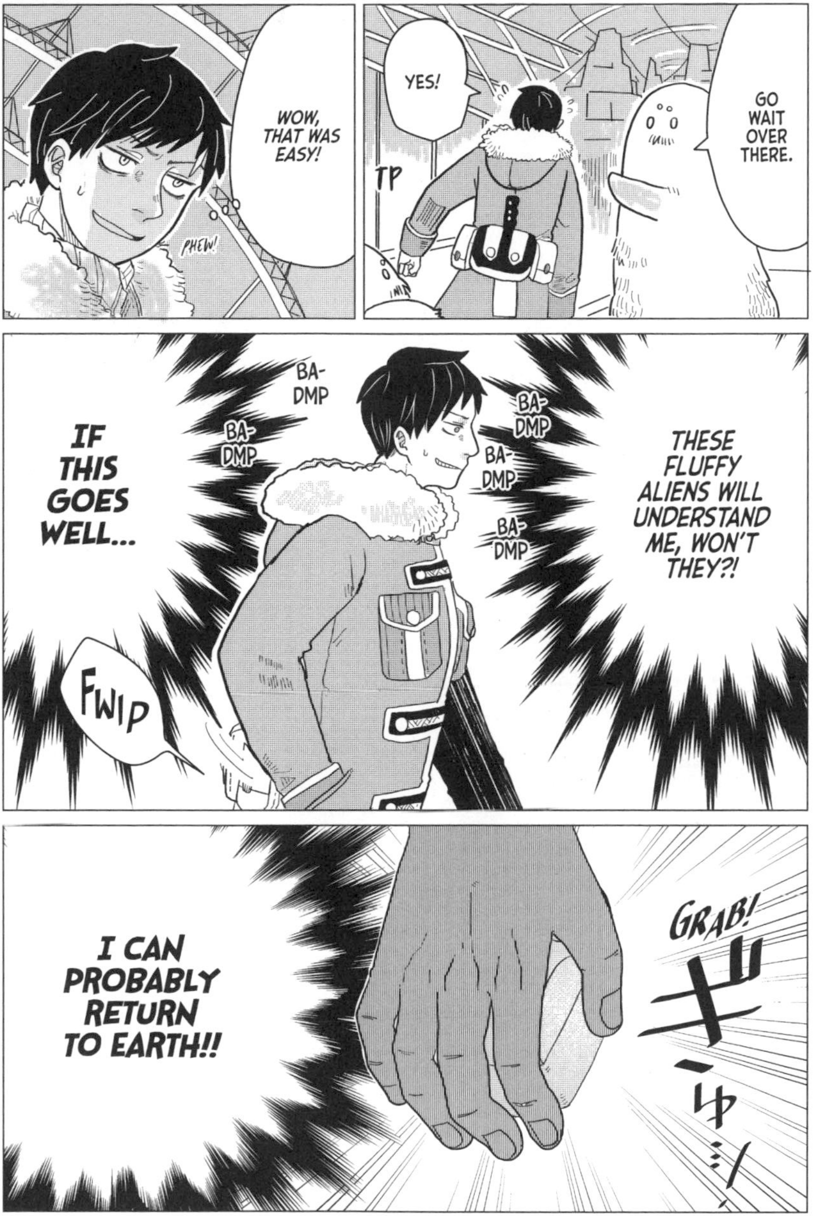
GO WAIT OVER THERE.
YES!
TP
WOW, THAT WAS EASY!
PHEW!
THESE FLUFFY ALIENS WILL UNDERSTAND ME, WON'T THEY?!
BA-DMP
BA-DMP
BA-DMP
BA-DMP
BA-DMP
IF THIS GOES WELL...
FWIP
GRAB!
I CAN PROBABLY RETURN TO EARTH!!

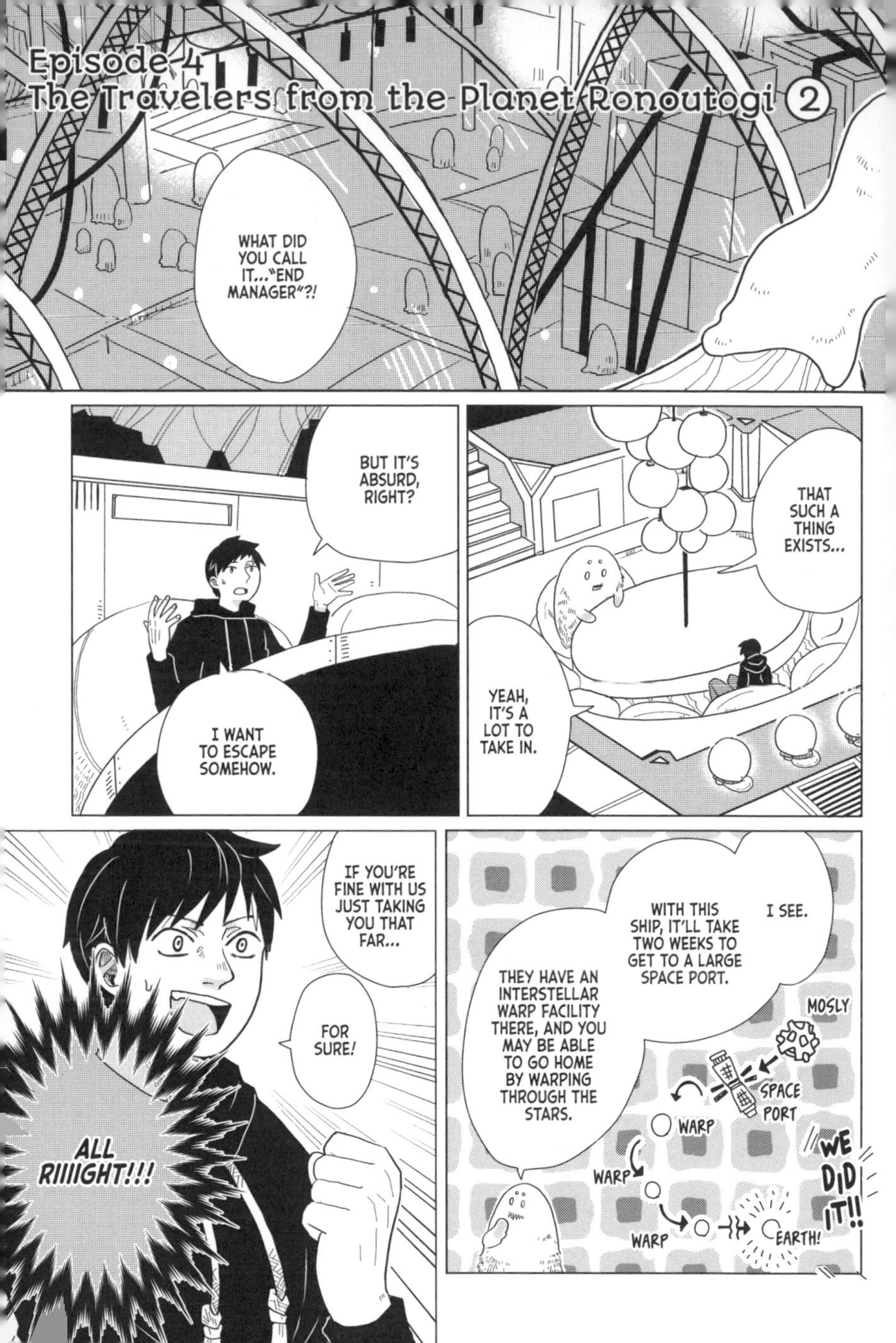
Episode 4
The Travelers from the Planet Ronoutogi ②
WHAT DID YOU CALL IT..."END MANAGER"?!
THAT SUCH A THING EXISTS...
YEAH, IT'S A LOT TO TAKE IN.
BUT IT'S ABSURD, RIGHT?
I WANT TO ESCAPE SOMEHOW.
I SEE.
WITH THIS SHIP, IT'LL TAKE TWO WEEKS TO GET TO A LARGE SPACE PORT.
THEY HAVE AN INTERSTELLAR WARP FACILITY THERE, AND YOU MAY BE ABLE TO GO HOME BY WARPING THROUGH THE STARS.
MOSLY
SPACE PORT
WARP
WARP
WARP
EARTH!
WE DID IT!!
IF YOU'RE FINE WITH US JUST TAKING YOU THAT FAR...
FOR SURE!
ALL RIIIIGHT!!!

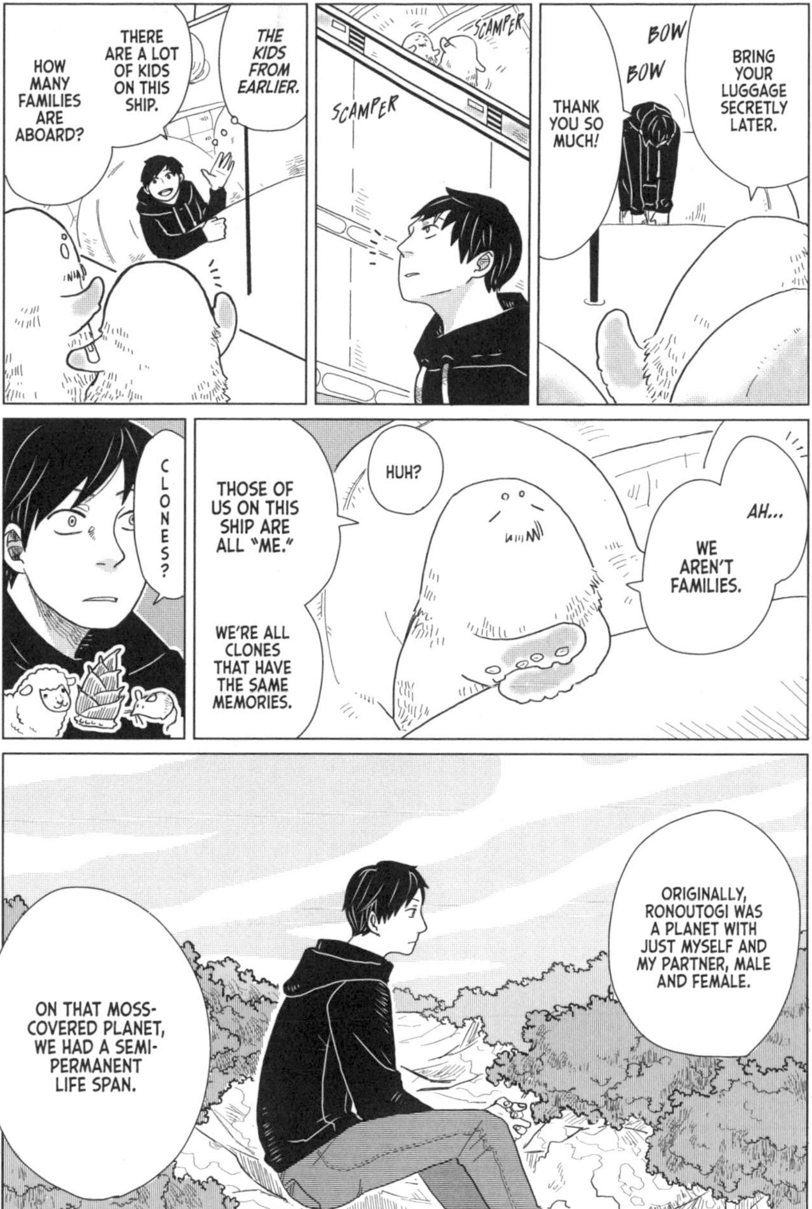
BRING YOUR LUGGAGE SECRETLY LATER.
BOW
BOW
THANK YOU SO MUCH!
SCAMPER
SCAMPER
THE KIDS FROM EARLIER.
THERE ARE A LOT OF KIDS ON THIS SHIP.
HOW MANY FAMILIES ARE ABOARD?
AH...
WE AREN'T FAMILIES.
HUH?
THOSE OF US ON THIS SHIP ARE ALL "ME."
WE'RE ALL CLONES THAT HAVE THE SAME MEMORIES.
CLONES?
ORIGINALLY, RONOUTOGI WAS A PLANET WITH JUST MYSELF AND MY PARTNER, MALE AND FEMALE.
ON THAT MOSS-COVERED PLANET, WE HAD A SEMI-PERMANENT LIFE SPAN.

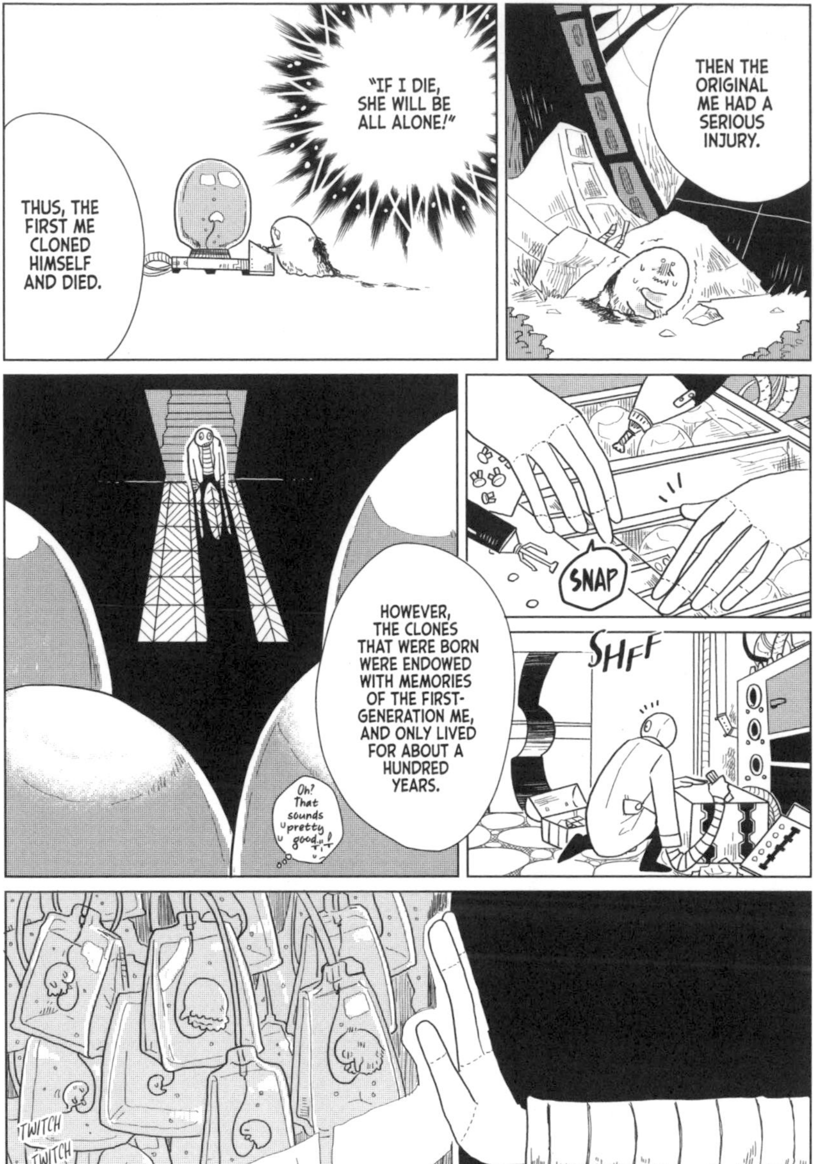
THEN THE ORIGINAL ME HAD A SERIOUS INJURY.
"IF I DIE, SHE WILL BE ALL ALONE!"
THUS, THE FIRST ME CLONED HIMSELF AND DIED.
SNAP
SHFF
HOWEVER, THE CLONES THAT WERE BORN WERE ENDOWED WITH MEMORIES OF THE FIRST-GENERATION ME, AND ONLY LIVED FOR ABOUT A HUNDRED YEARS.
Oh? That sounds pretty good...!
TWITCH
TWITCH

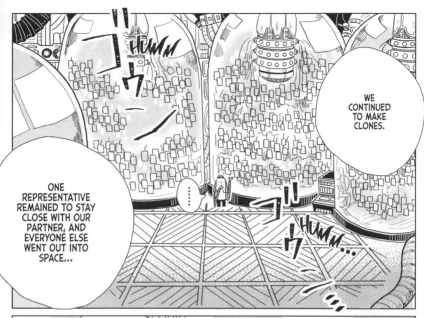

WE CONTINUED TO MAKE CLONES.

ONE REPRESENTATIVE REMAINED TO STAY CLOSE WITH OUR PARTNER, AND EVERYONE ELSE WENT OUT INTO SPACE...

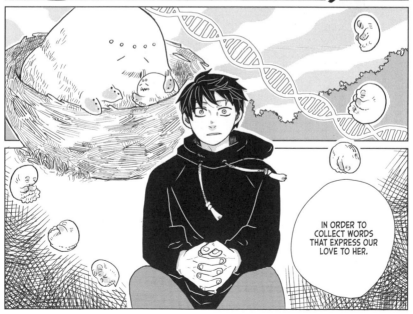

IN ORDER TO COLLECT WORDS THAT EXPRESS OUR LOVE TO HER.

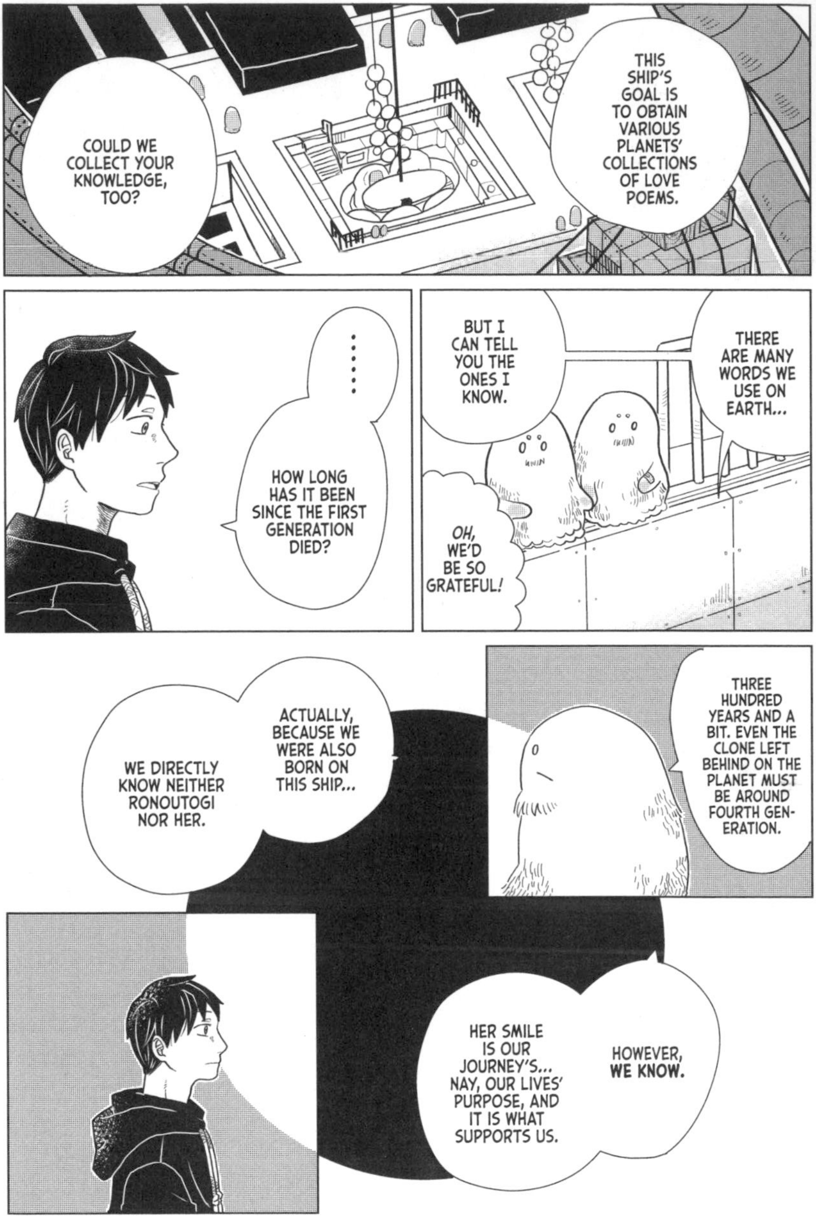
THIS SHIP'S GOAL IS TO OBTAIN VARIOUS PLANETS' COLLECTIONS OF LOVE POEMS.
COULD WE COLLECT YOUR KNOWLEDGE, TOO?
THERE ARE MANY WORDS WE USE ON EARTH...
BUT I CAN TELL YOU THE ONES I KNOW.
OH, WE'D BE SO GRATEFUL!
......
HOW LONG HAS IT BEEN SINCE THE FIRST GENERATION DIED?
THREE HUNDRED YEARS AND A BIT. EVEN THE CLONE LEFT BEHIND ON THE PLANET MUST BE AROUND FOURTH GENERATION.
ACTUALLY, BECAUSE WE WERE ALSO BORN ON THIS SHIP...
WE DIRECTLY KNOW NEITHER RONOUTOGI NOR HER.
HOWEVER, **WE KNOW.**
HER SMILE IS OUR JOURNEY'S... NAY, OUR LIVES' PURPOSE, AND IT IS WHAT SUPPORTS US.

*Venus' Flower Basket: A sea sponge in which a male and female pair of sponge shrimp spend their lifetimes as companions.

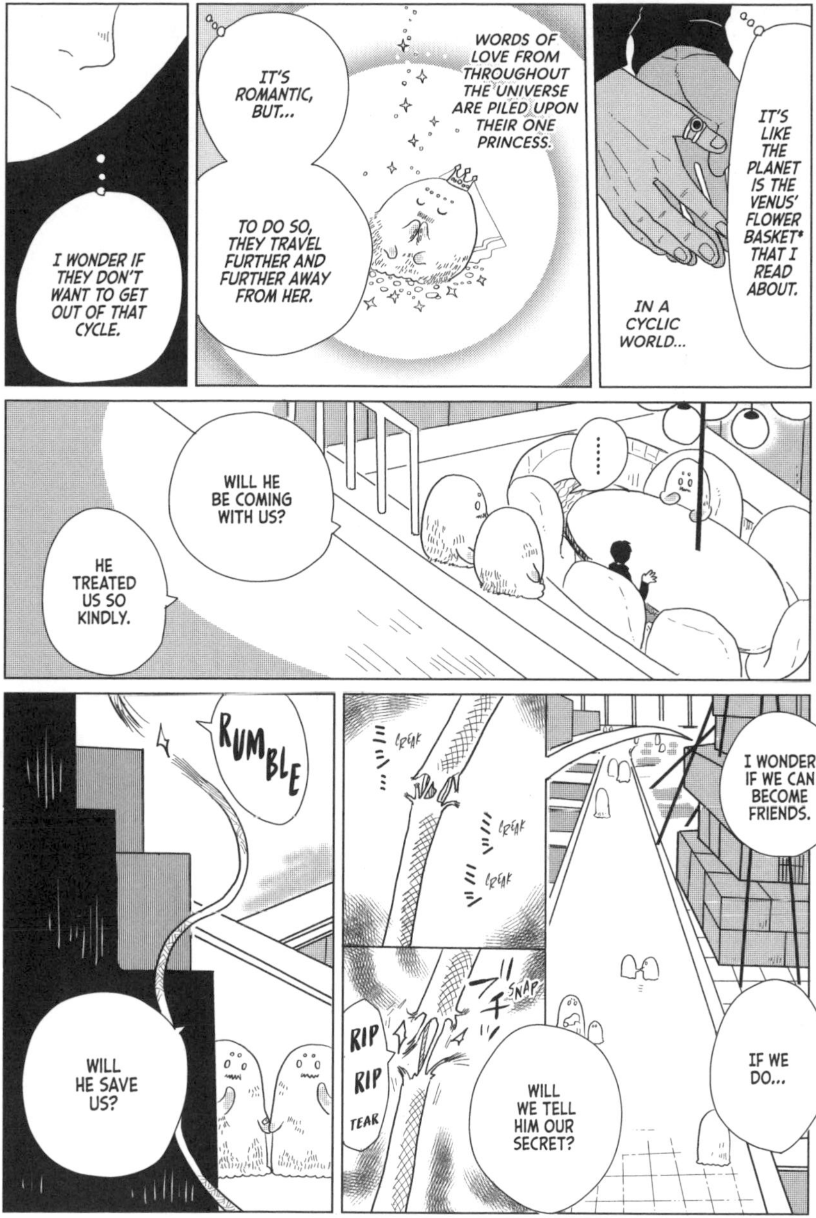
IT'S LIKE THE PLANET IS THE VENUS' FLOWER BASKET* THAT I READ ABOUT.
IN A CYCLIC WORLD...
WORDS OF LOVE FROM THROUGHOUT THE UNIVERSE ARE PILED UPON THEIR ONE PRINCESS.
IT'S ROMANTIC, BUT...
TO DO SO, THEY TRAVEL FURTHER AND FURTHER AWAY FROM HER.
I WONDER IF THEY DON'T WANT TO GET OUT OF THAT CYCLE.
......
WILL HE BE COMING WITH US?
HE TREATED US SO KINDLY.
I WONDER IF WE CAN BECOME FRIENDS.
IF WE DO...
WILL WE TELL HIM OUR SECRET?
CREAK
CREAK
CREAK
SNAP
RIP
RIP
TEAR
RUMBLE
WILL HE SAVE US?

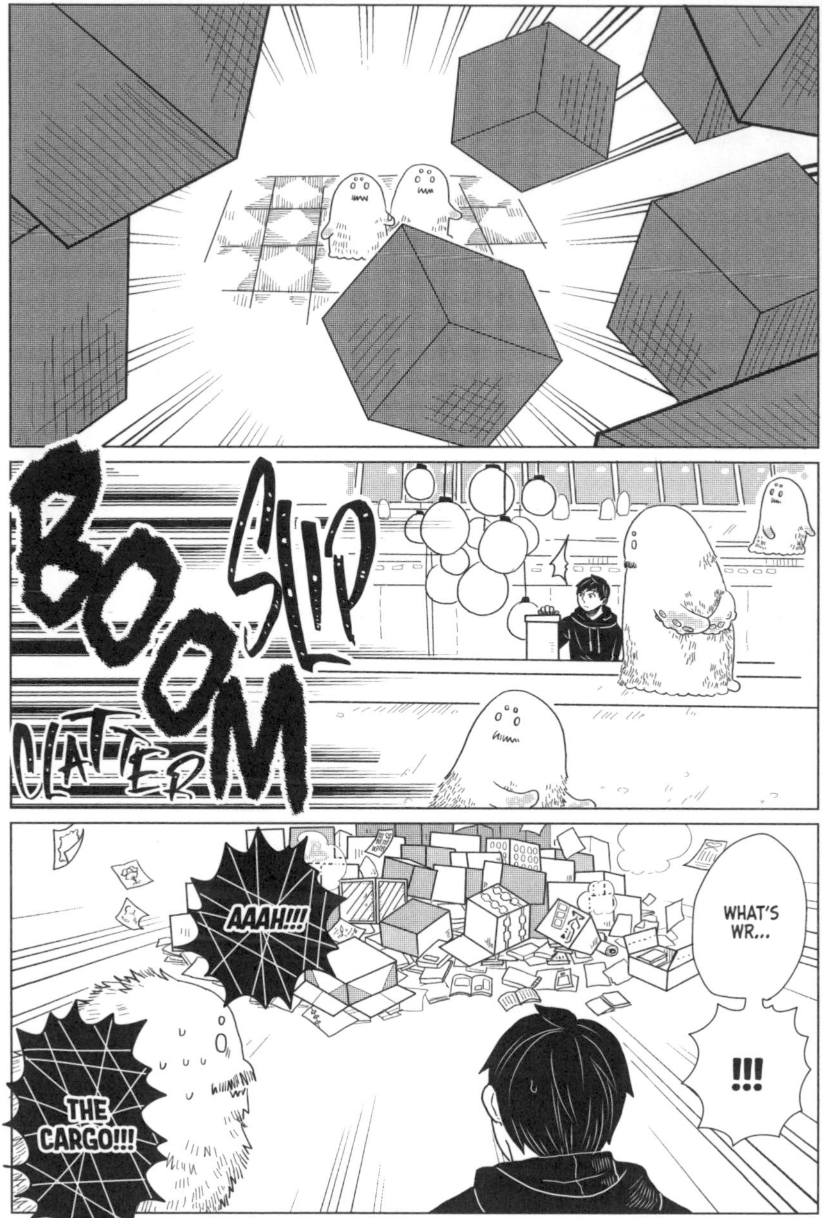
SLIP
BOOM
CLATTER
WHAT'S WR...
!!!
AAAH!!!
THE CARGO!!!

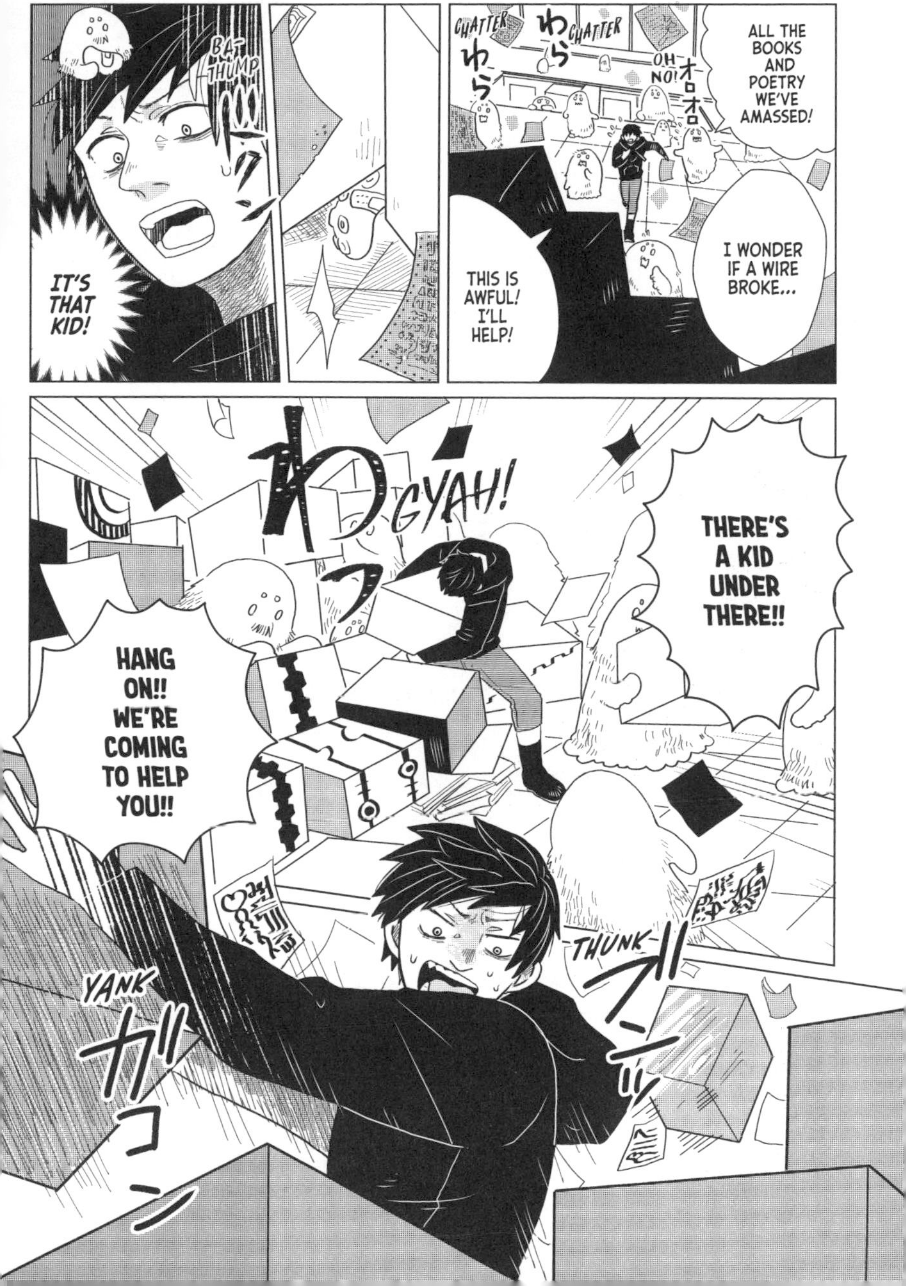
ALL THE BOOKS AND POETRY WE'VE AMASSED!
OH NO!
CHATTER
CHATTER
I WONDER IF A WIRE BROKE...
THIS IS AWFUL! I'LL HELP!
BA-THUMP
IT'S THAT KID!
THERE'S A KID UNDER THERE!!
GYAH!
HANG ON!! WE'RE COMING TO HELP YOU!!
THUNK
YANK

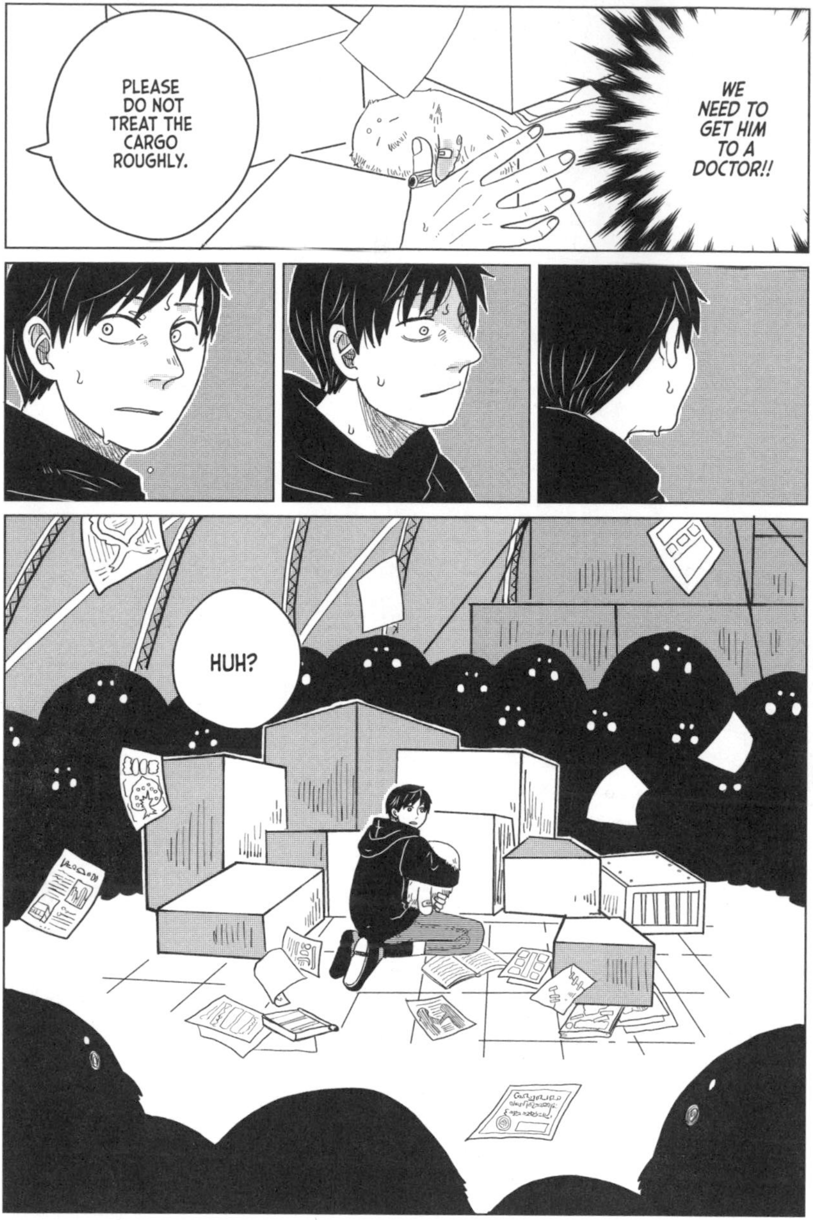
WE NEED TO GET HIM TO A DOCTOR!!
PLEASE DO NOT TREAT THE CARGO ROUGHLY.
HUH?

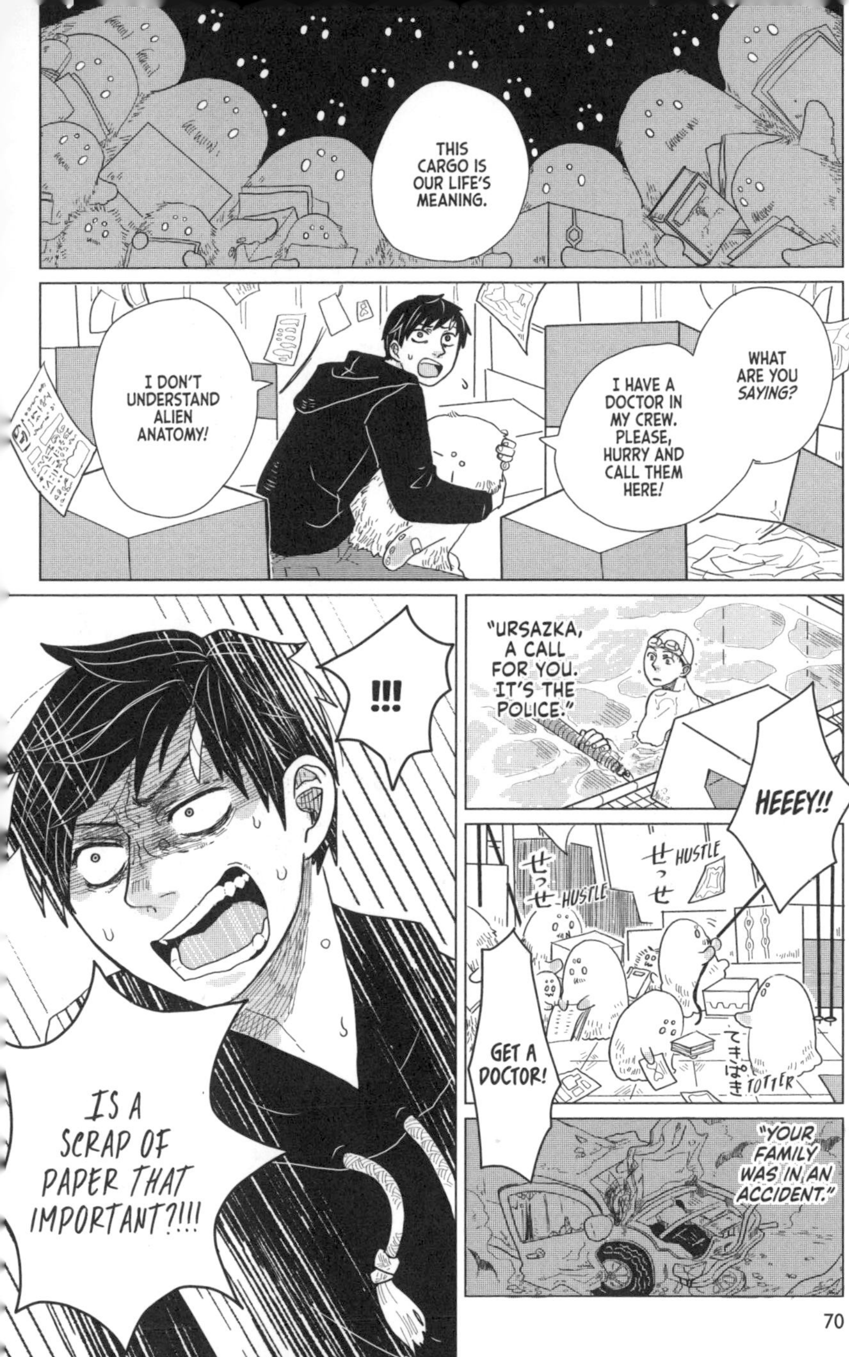
THIS CARGO IS OUR LIFE'S MEANING.
WHAT ARE YOU SAYING?
I HAVE A DOCTOR IN MY CREW. PLEASE, HURRY AND CALL THEM HERE!
I DON'T UNDERSTAND ALIEN ANATOMY!
"URSAZKA, A CALL FOR YOU. IT'S THE POLICE."
HEEEY!!
せっせ HUSTLE
せっせ HUSTLE
てきぱき TOTTER
GET A DOCTOR!
"YOUR FAMILY WAS IN AN ACCIDENT."
!!!
IS A SCRAP OF PAPER THAT IMPORTANT?!!!

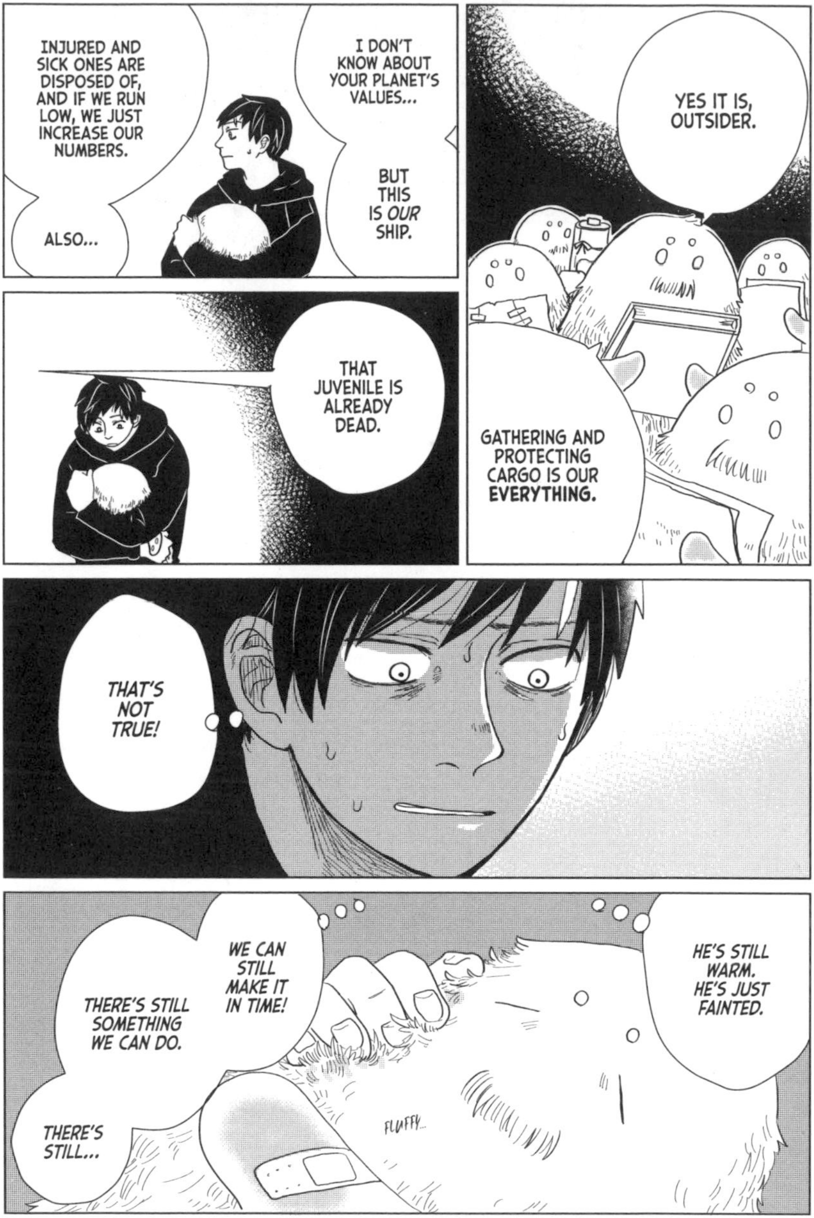
YES IT IS, OUTSIDER.
GATHERING AND PROTECTING CARGO IS OUR EVERYTHING.
I DON'T KNOW ABOUT YOUR PLANET'S VALUES...
BUT THIS IS OUR SHIP.
INJURED AND SICK ONES ARE DISPOSED OF, AND IF WE RUN LOW, WE JUST INCREASE OUR NUMBERS.
ALSO...
THAT JUVENILE IS ALREADY DEAD.
THAT'S NOT TRUE!
HE'S STILL WARM. HE'S JUST FAINTED.
WE CAN STILL MAKE IT IN TIME!
THERE'S STILL SOMETHING WE CAN DO.
FLUFFY...
THERE'S STILL...

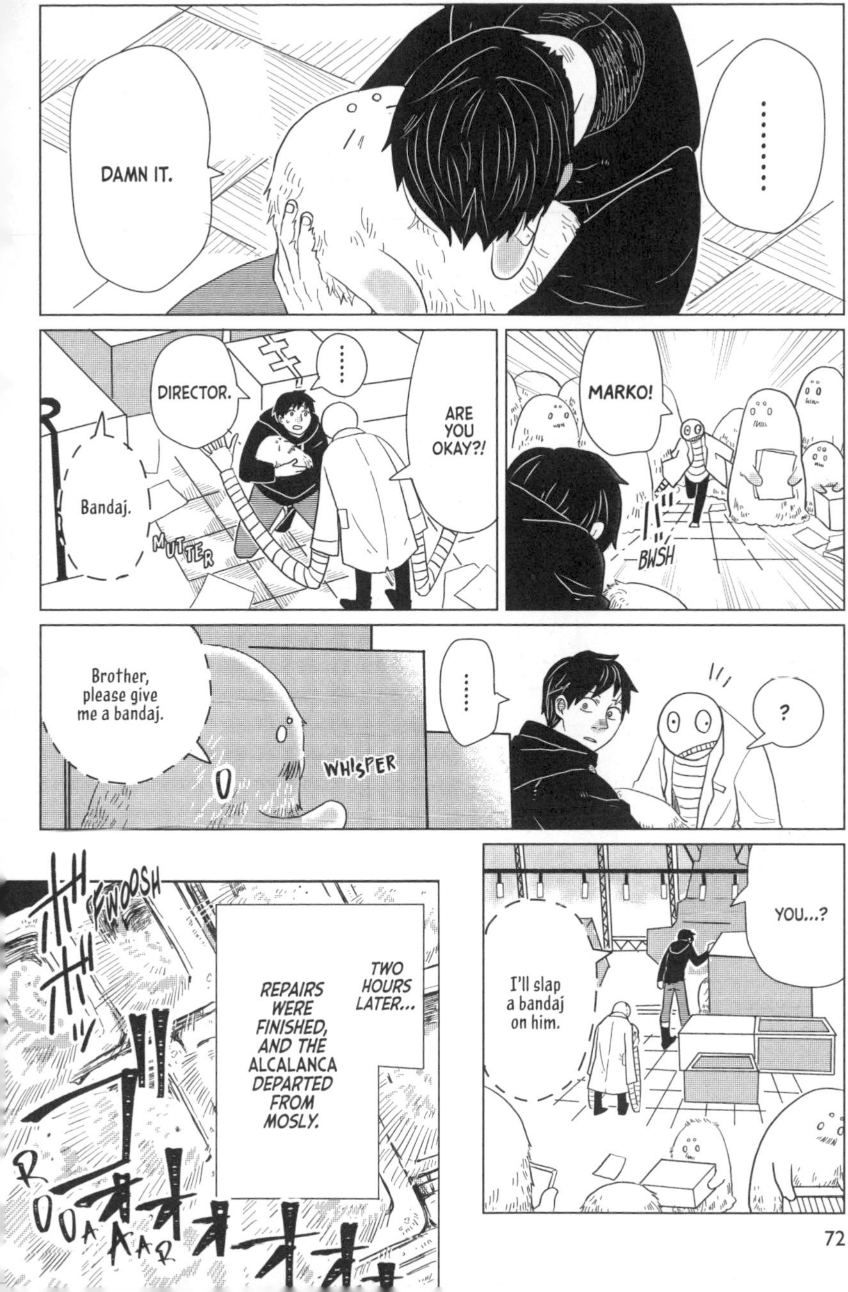

……
DAMN IT.
MARKO!
BWSH
ARE YOU OKAY?!
……
DIRECTOR.
Bandaj.
MUTTER
?
……
WHISPER
Brother, please give me a bandaj.
YOU...?
I'll slap a bandaj on him.
TWO HOURS LATER...
REPAIRS WERE FINISHED, AND THE ALCALANCA DEPARTED FROM MOSLY.
FWOOSH
ROOAAAR

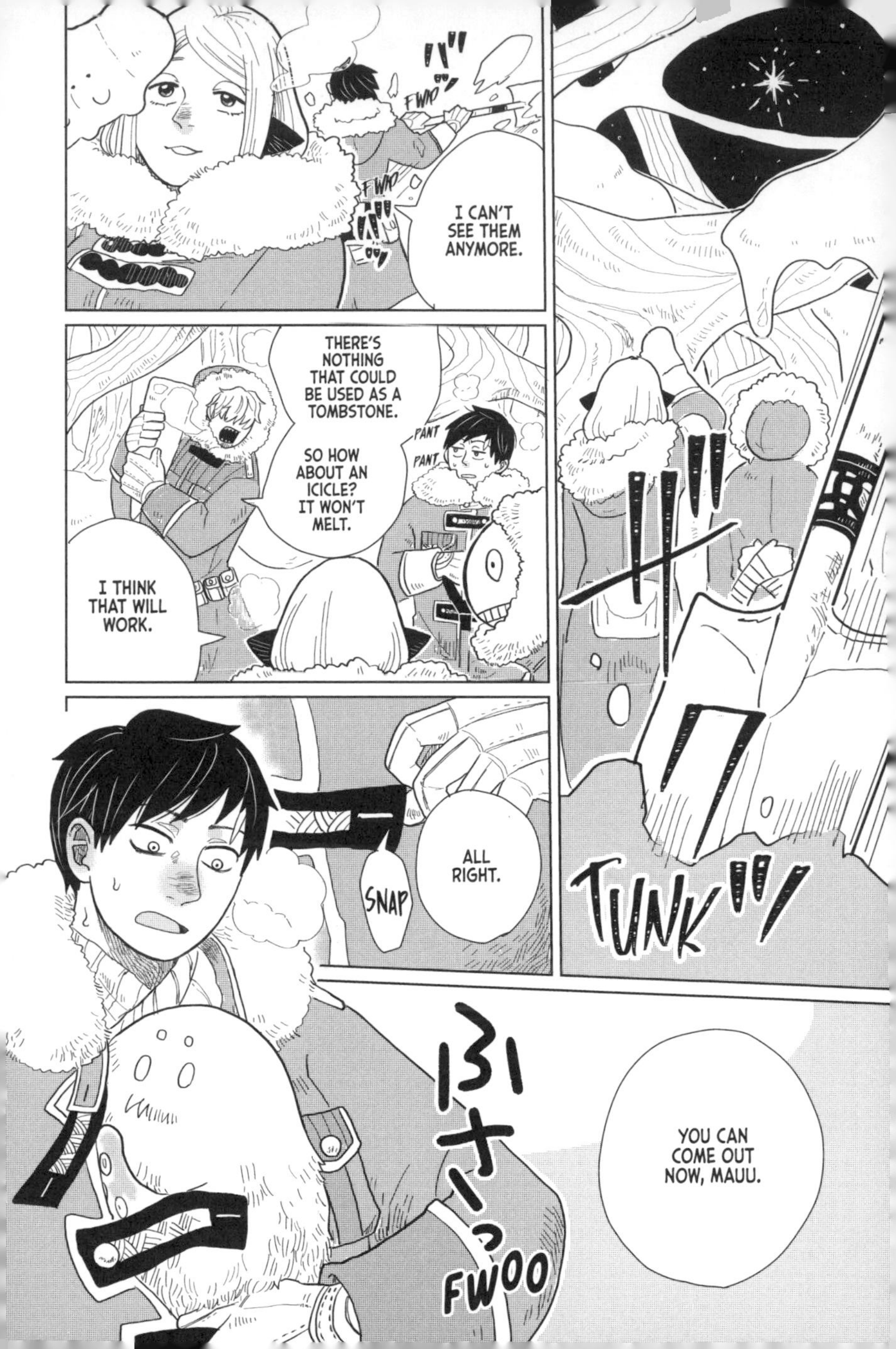
TUNK
FWIP
FWIP
I CAN'T SEE THEM ANYMORE.
THERE'S NOTHING THAT COULD BE USED AS A TOMBSTONE.
SO HOW ABOUT AN ICICLE? IT WON'T MELT.
PANT
PANT
I THINK THAT WILL WORK.
ALL RIGHT.
SNAP
YOU CAN COME OUT NOW, MAUU.
ふさっ
FWOO

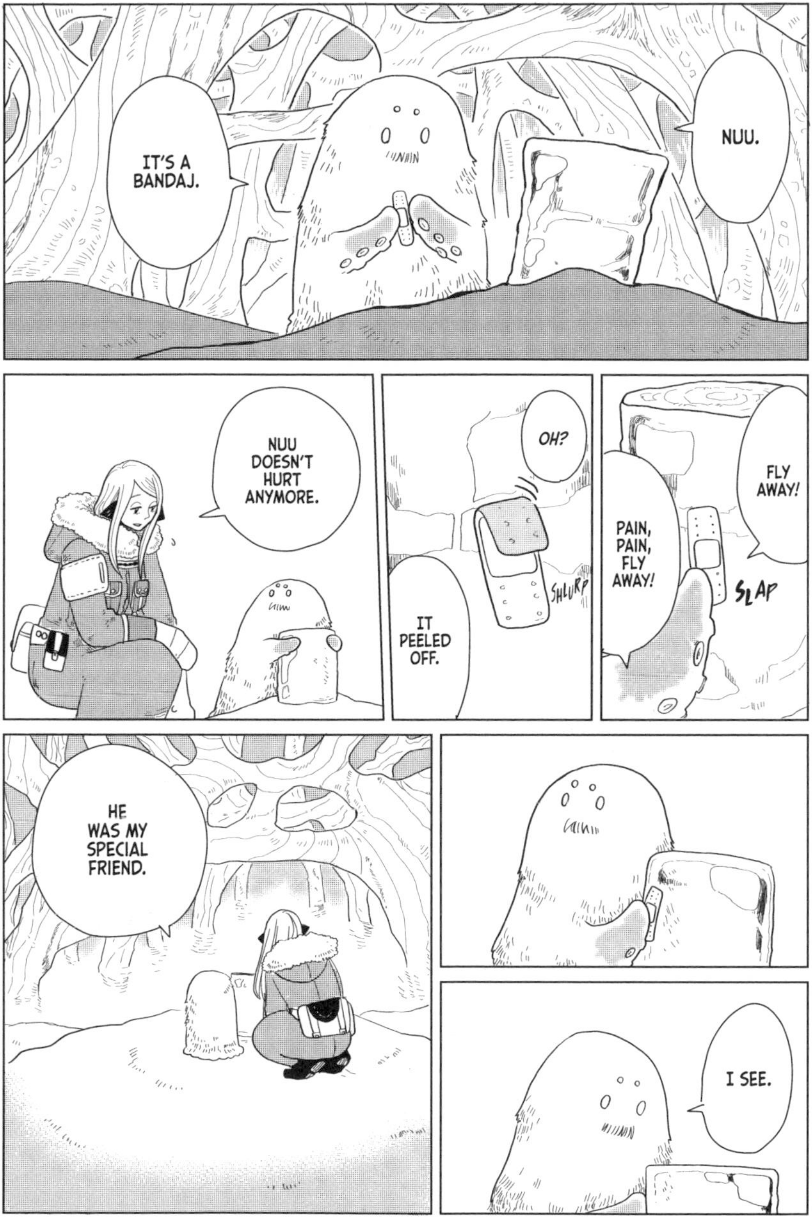
NUU.
IT'S A BANDAJ.
FLY AWAY!
PAIN, PAIN, FLY AWAY!
SLAP
OH?
SHLURP
IT PEELED OFF.
NUU DOESN'T HURT ANYMORE.
I SEE.
HE WAS MY SPECIAL FRIEND.

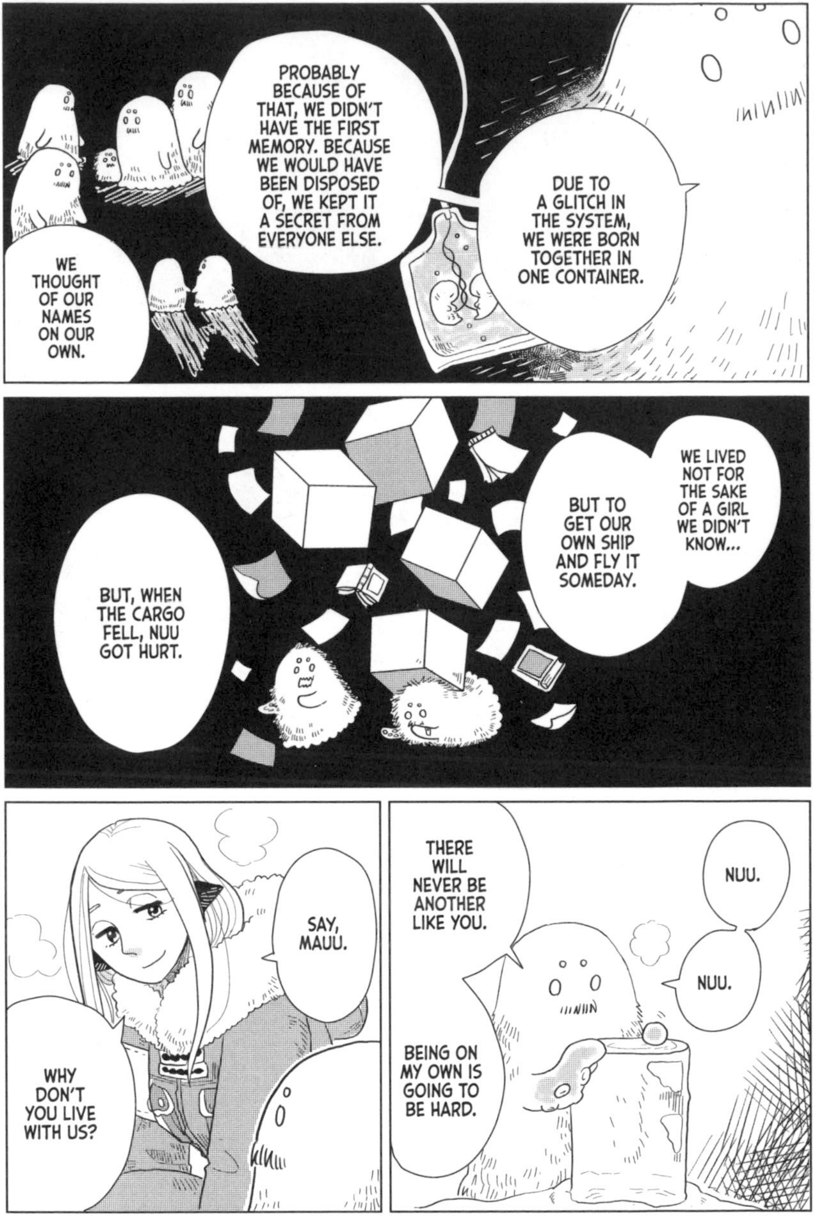
DUE TO A GLITCH IN THE SYSTEM, WE WERE BORN TOGETHER IN ONE CONTAINER.
PROBABLY BECAUSE OF THAT, WE DIDN'T HAVE THE FIRST MEMORY. BECAUSE WE WOULD HAVE BEEN DISPOSED OF, WE KEPT IT A SECRET FROM EVERYONE ELSE.
WE THOUGHT OF OUR NAMES ON OUR OWN.
WE LIVED NOT FOR THE SAKE OF A GIRL WE DIDN'T KNOW...
BUT TO GET OUR OWN SHIP AND FLY IT SOMEDAY.
BUT, WHEN THE CARGO FELL, NUU GOT HURT.
NUU.
NUU.
THERE WILL NEVER BE ANOTHER LIKE YOU.
BEING ON MY OWN IS GOING TO BE HARD.
SAY, MAUU.
WHY DON'T YOU LIVE WITH US?

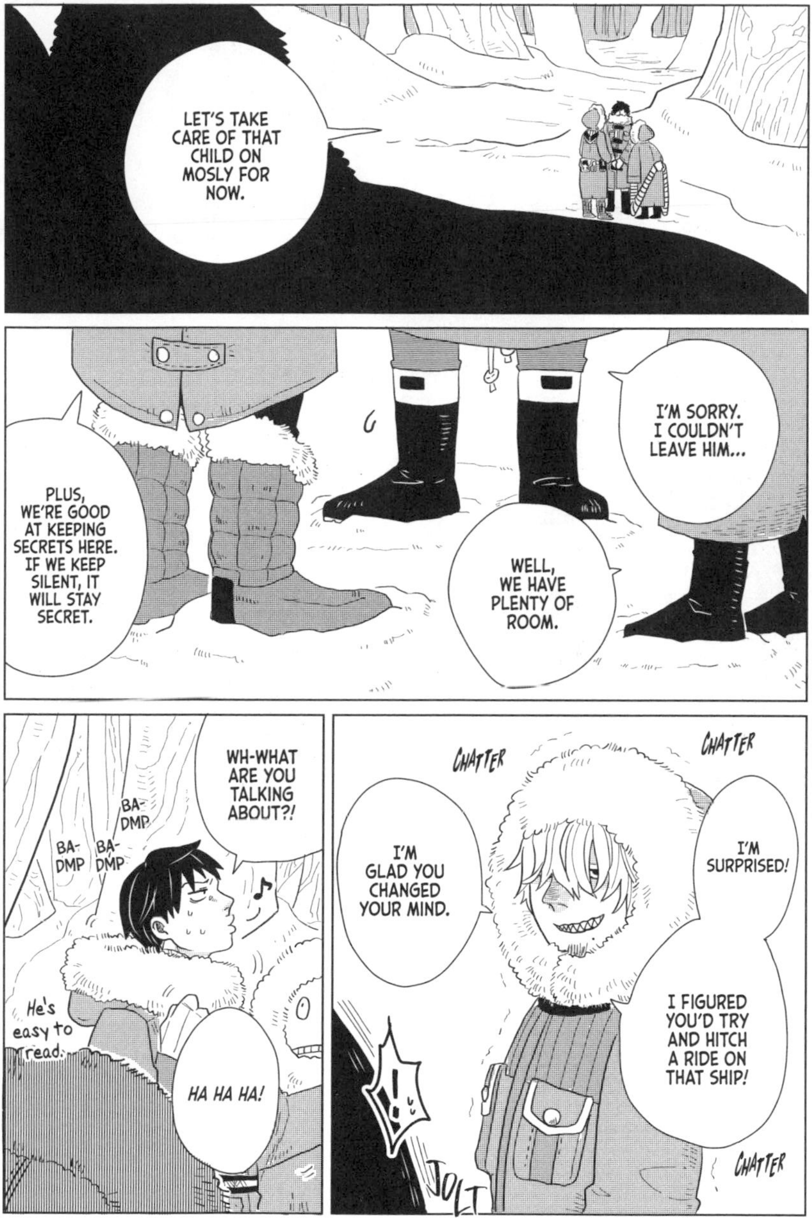
LET'S TAKE CARE OF THAT CHILD ON MOSLY FOR NOW.
I'M SORRY. I COULDN'T LEAVE HIM...
WELL, WE HAVE PLENTY OF ROOM.
PLUS, WE'RE GOOD AT KEEPING SECRETS HERE. IF WE KEEP SILENT, IT WILL STAY SECRET.
CHATTER
CHATTER
I'M SURPRISED!
I'M GLAD YOU CHANGED YOUR MIND.
I FIGURED YOU'D TRY AND HITCH A RIDE ON THAT SHIP!
CHATTER
JOLT
WH-WHAT ARE YOU TALKING ABOUT?!
BA-DMP
BA-DMP
BA-DMP
He's easy to read.
HA HA HA!

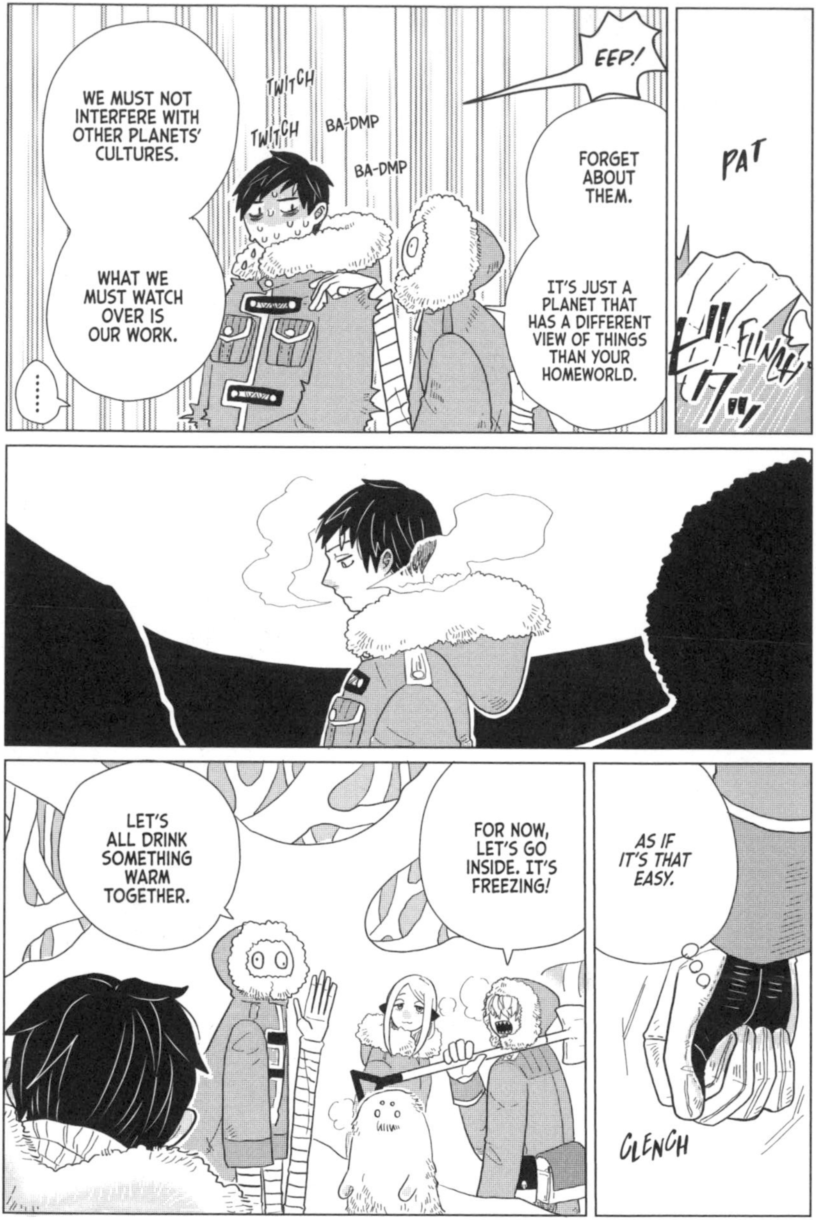
PAT
FLINCH
EEP!
FORGET ABOUT THEM.
IT'S JUST A PLANET THAT HAS A DIFFERENT VIEW OF THINGS THAN YOUR HOMEWORLD.
BA-DMP
BA-DMP
TWITCH
TWITCH
WE MUST NOT INTERFERE WITH OTHER PLANETS' CULTURES.
WHAT WE MUST WATCH OVER IS OUR WORK.
……
AS IF IT'S THAT EASY.
CLENCH
FOR NOW, LET'S GO INSIDE. IT'S FREEZING!
LET'S ALL DRINK SOMETHING WARM TOGETHER.

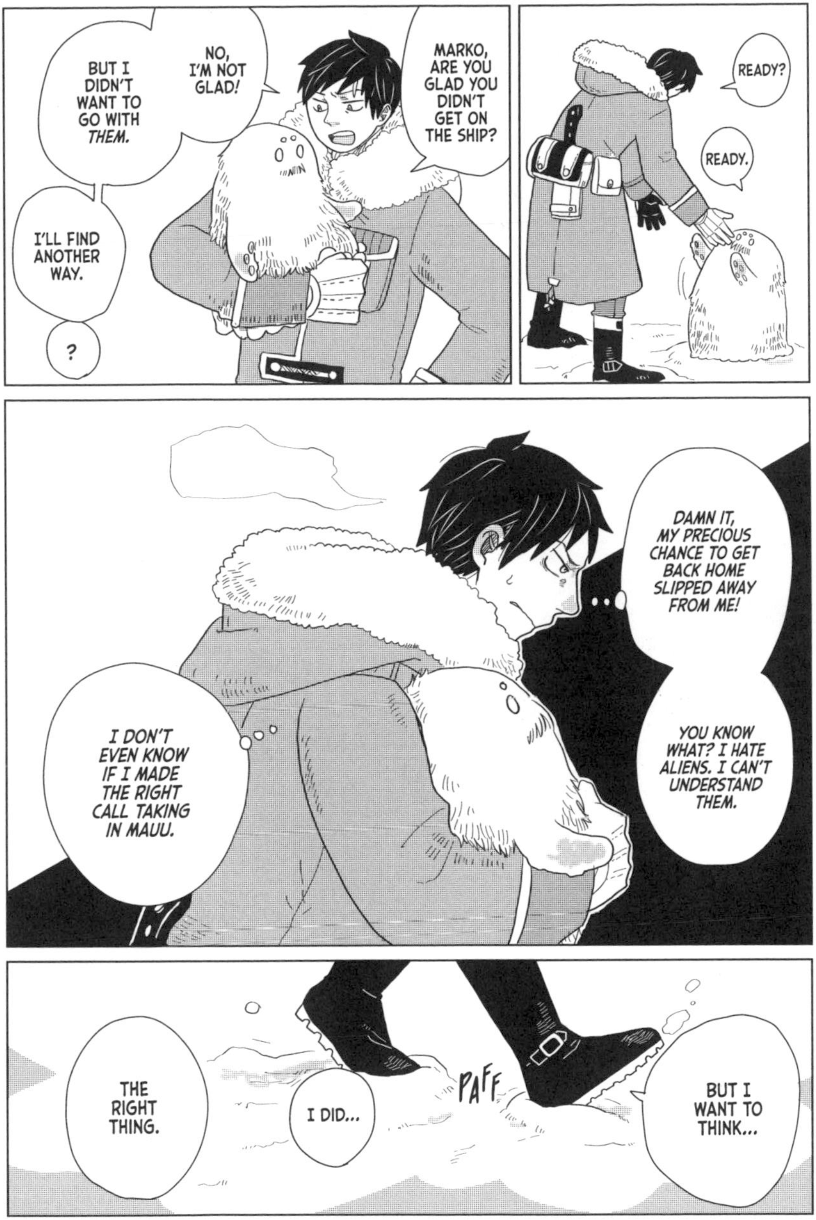
READY?
READY.
MARKO, ARE YOU GLAD YOU DIDN'T GET ON THE SHIP?
NO, I'M NOT GLAD!
BUT I DIDN'T WANT TO GO WITH *THEM.*
I'LL FIND ANOTHER WAY.
?
DAMN IT, MY PRECIOUS CHANCE TO GET BACK HOME SLIPPED AWAY FROM ME!
YOU KNOW WHAT? I HATE ALIENS. I CAN'T UNDERSTAND THEM.
I DON'T EVEN KNOW IF I MADE THE RIGHT CALL TAKING IN MAUU.
BUT I WANT TO THINK...
PAFF
I DID...
THE RIGHT THING.

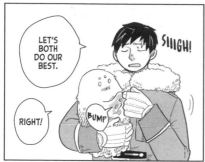

LET'S BOTH DO OUR BEST.

RIGHT!

SIIIGH!

BUMP

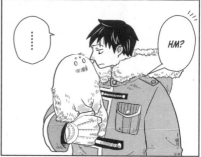

. . . .

HM?

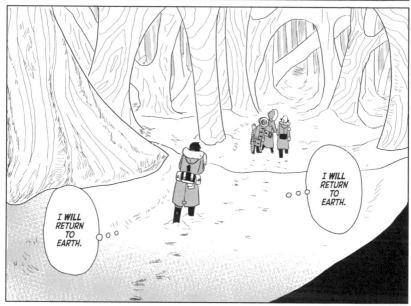

I WILL RETURN TO EARTH.

I WILL RETURN TO EARTH.

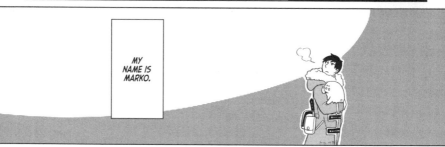

MY NAME IS MARKO.

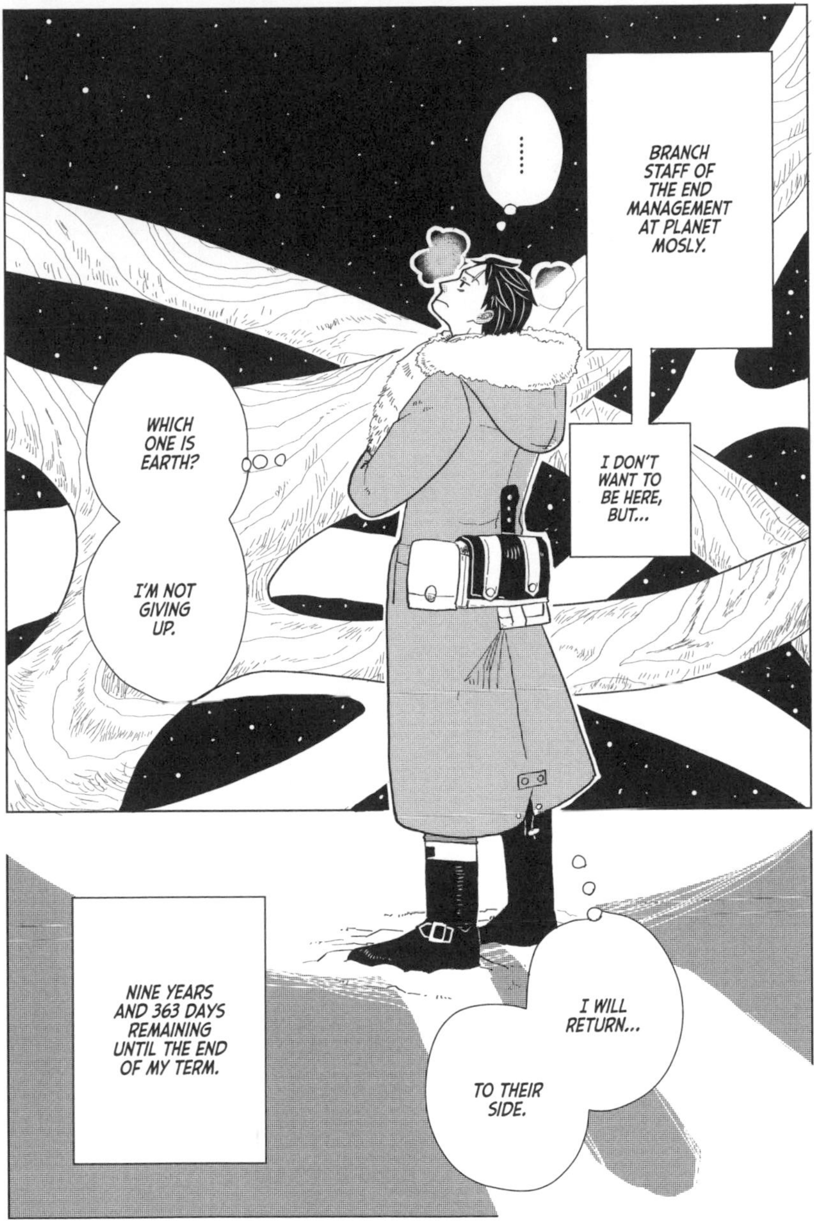
BRANCH STAFF OF THE END MANAGEMENT AT PLANET MOSLY.
......
I DON'T WANT TO BE HERE, BUT...
WHICH ONE IS EARTH?
I'M NOT GIVING UP.
I WILL RETURN...
TO THEIR SIDE.
NINE YEARS AND 363 DAYS REMAINING UNTIL THE END OF MY TERM.

Episode 5: Horshe 8's Space Fireworks

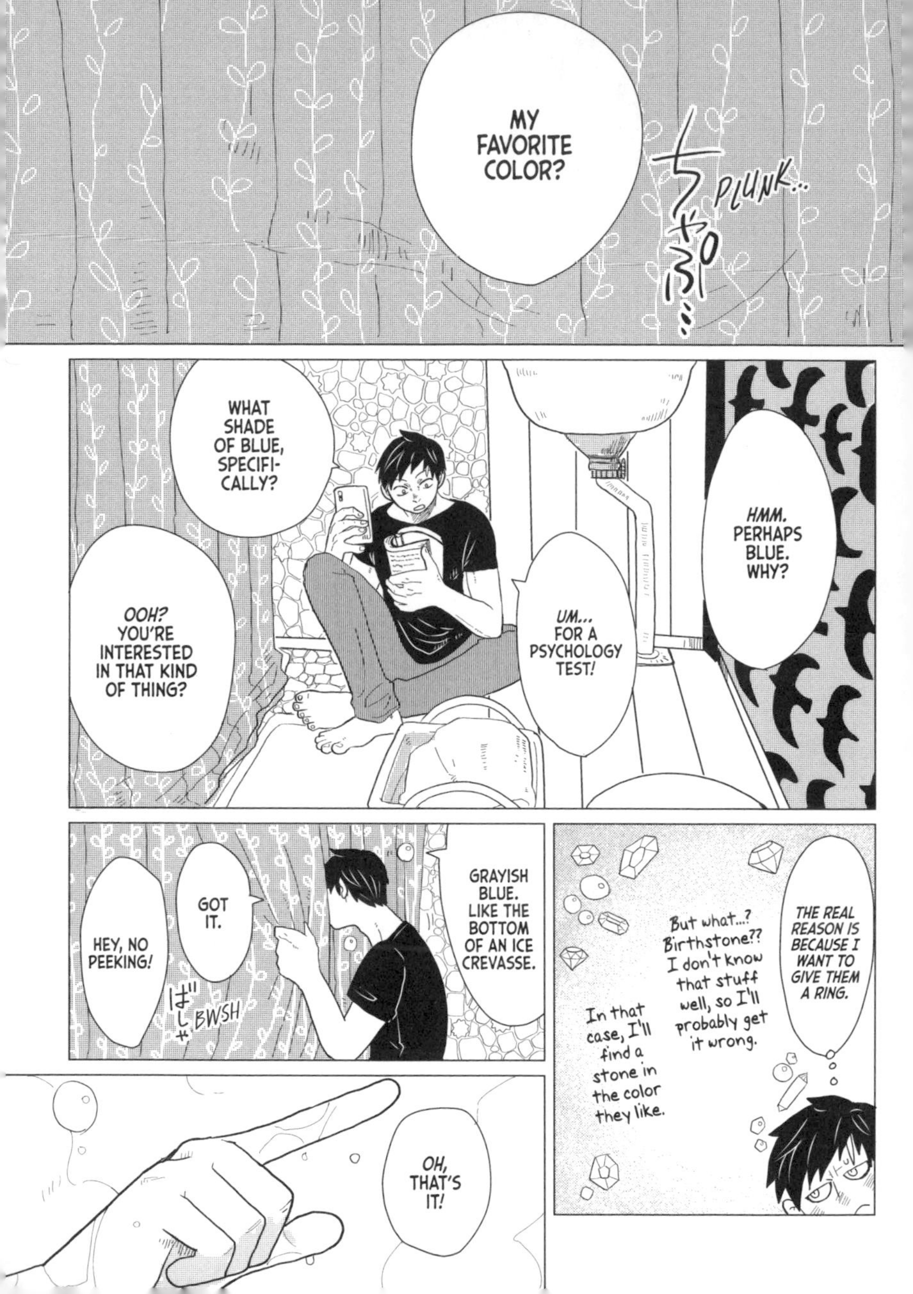
MY FAVORITE COLOR?
ちゃぷ… PLUNK...
HMM. PERHAPS BLUE. WHY?
UM... FOR A PSYCHOLOGY TEST!
WHAT SHADE OF BLUE, SPECIFICALLY?
OOH? YOU'RE INTERESTED IN THAT KIND OF THING?
THE REAL REASON IS BECAUSE I WANT TO GIVE THEM A RING.
But what...? Birthstone?? I don't know that stuff well, so I'll probably get it wrong.
In that case, I'll find a stone in the color they like.
GRAYISH BLUE. LIKE THE BOTTOM OF AN ICE CREVASSE.
GOT IT.
HEY, NO PEEKING!
ばしゃ BWSH
OH, THAT'S IT!

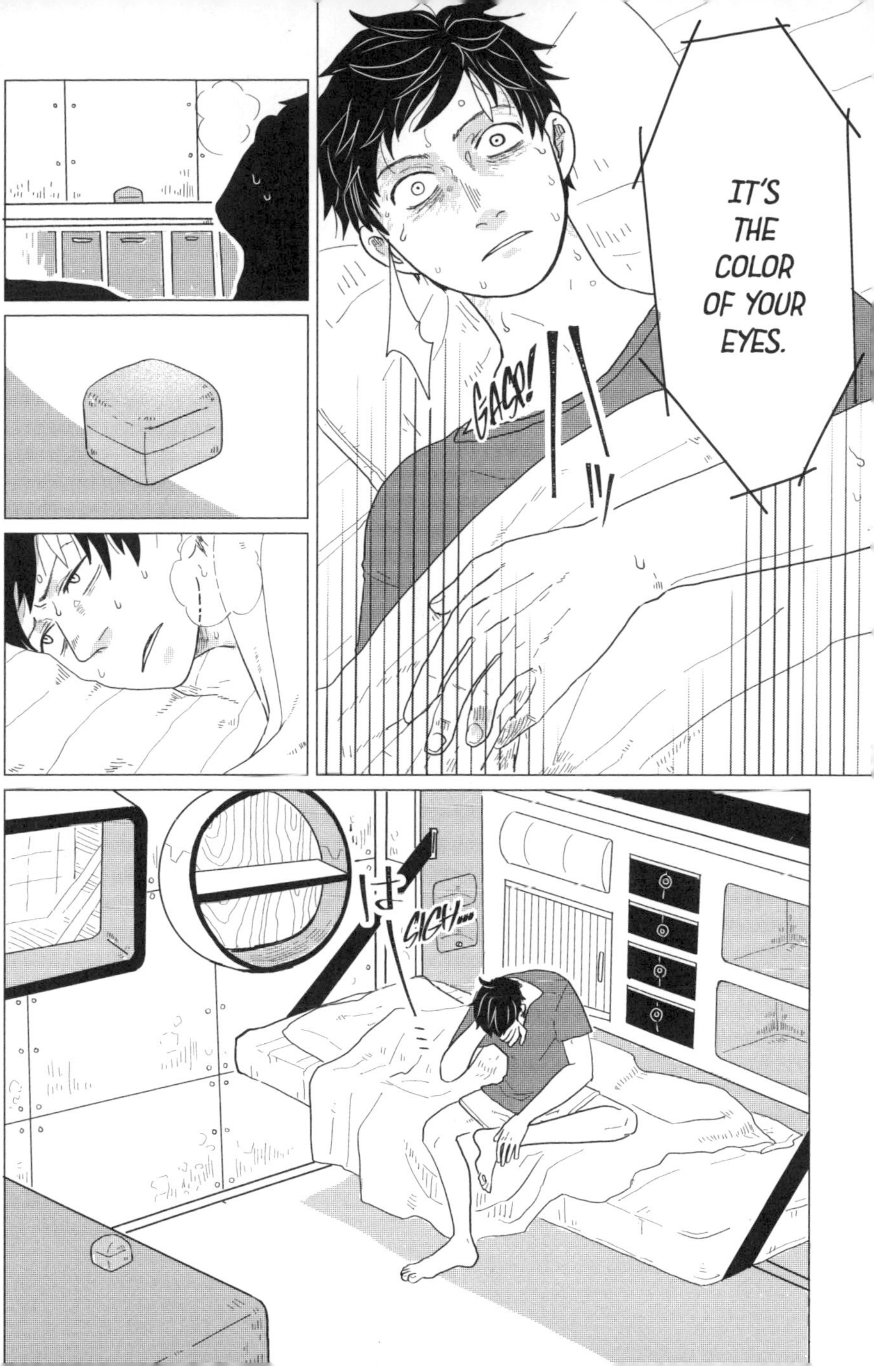
IT'S THE COLOR OF YOUR EYES.
GASP!
は
SIGH...

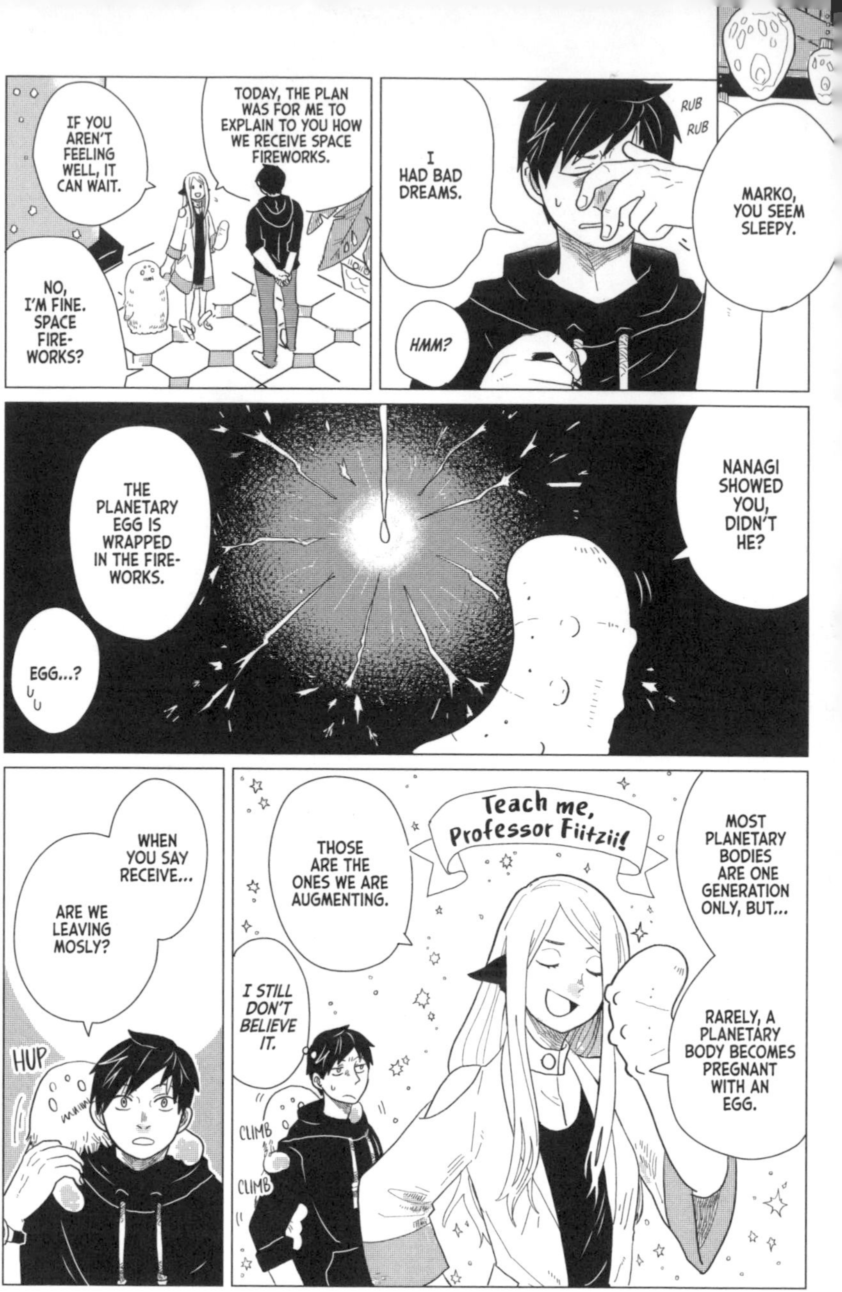
MARKO, YOU SEEM SLEEPY.
HMM?
RUB
RUB
I HAD BAD DREAMS.
TODAY, THE PLAN WAS FOR ME TO EXPLAIN TO YOU HOW WE RECEIVE SPACE FIREWORKS.
IF YOU AREN'T FEELING WELL, IT CAN WAIT.
NO, I'M FINE. SPACE FIRE-WORKS?
NANAGI SHOWED YOU, DIDN'T HE?
THE PLANETARY EGG IS WRAPPED IN THE FIRE-WORKS.
EGG...?
MOST PLANETARY BODIES ARE ONE GENERATION ONLY, BUT...
Teach me, Professor Fiitzii!
RARELY, A PLANETARY BODY BECOMES PREGNANT WITH AN EGG.
THOSE ARE THE ONES WE ARE AUGMENTING.
I STILL DON'T BELIEVE IT.
CLIMB
CLIMB
WHEN YOU SAY RECEIVE...
ARE WE LEAVING MOSLY?
HUP

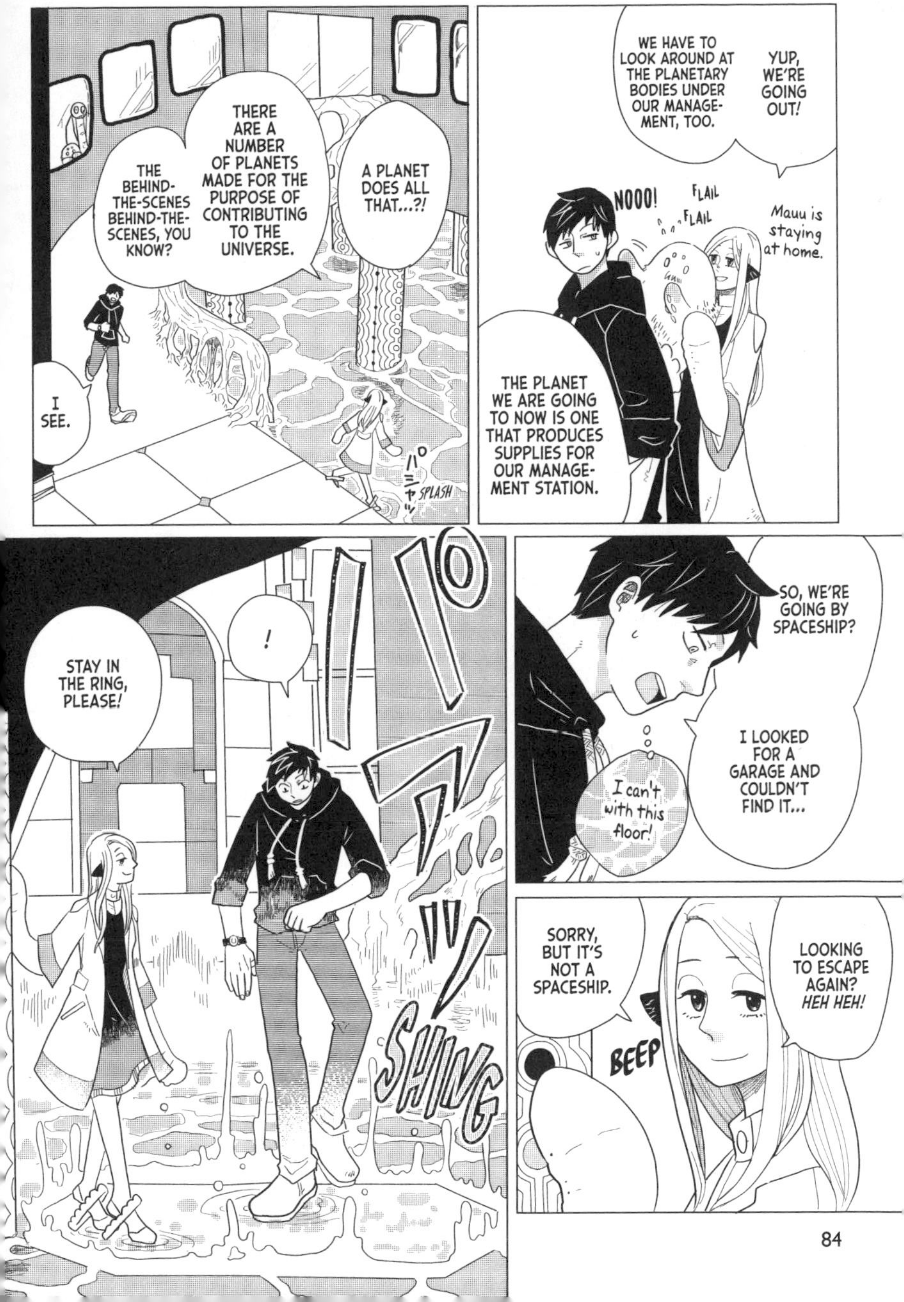
YUP, WE'RE GOING OUT!
WE HAVE TO LOOK AROUND AT THE PLANETARY BODIES UNDER OUR MANAGE-MENT, TOO.
FLAIL
FLAIL
Mauu is staying at home.
NOOO!
THE PLANET WE ARE GOING TO NOW IS ONE THAT PRODUCES SUPPLIES FOR OUR MANAGE-MENT STATION.
A PLANET DOES ALL THAT...?!
THERE ARE A NUMBER OF PLANETS MADE FOR THE PURPOSE OF CONTRIBUTING TO THE UNIVERSE.
THE BEHIND-THE-SCENES BEHIND-THE-SCENES, YOU KNOW?
I SEE.
SPLASH
SO, WE'RE GOING BY SPACESHIP?
I LOOKED FOR A GARAGE AND COULDN'T FIND IT...
I can't with this floor!
LOOKING TO ESCAPE AGAIN? *HEH HEH!*
SORRY, BUT IT'S NOT A SPACESHIP.
BEEP
!
SHING
STAY IN THE RING, PLEASE!

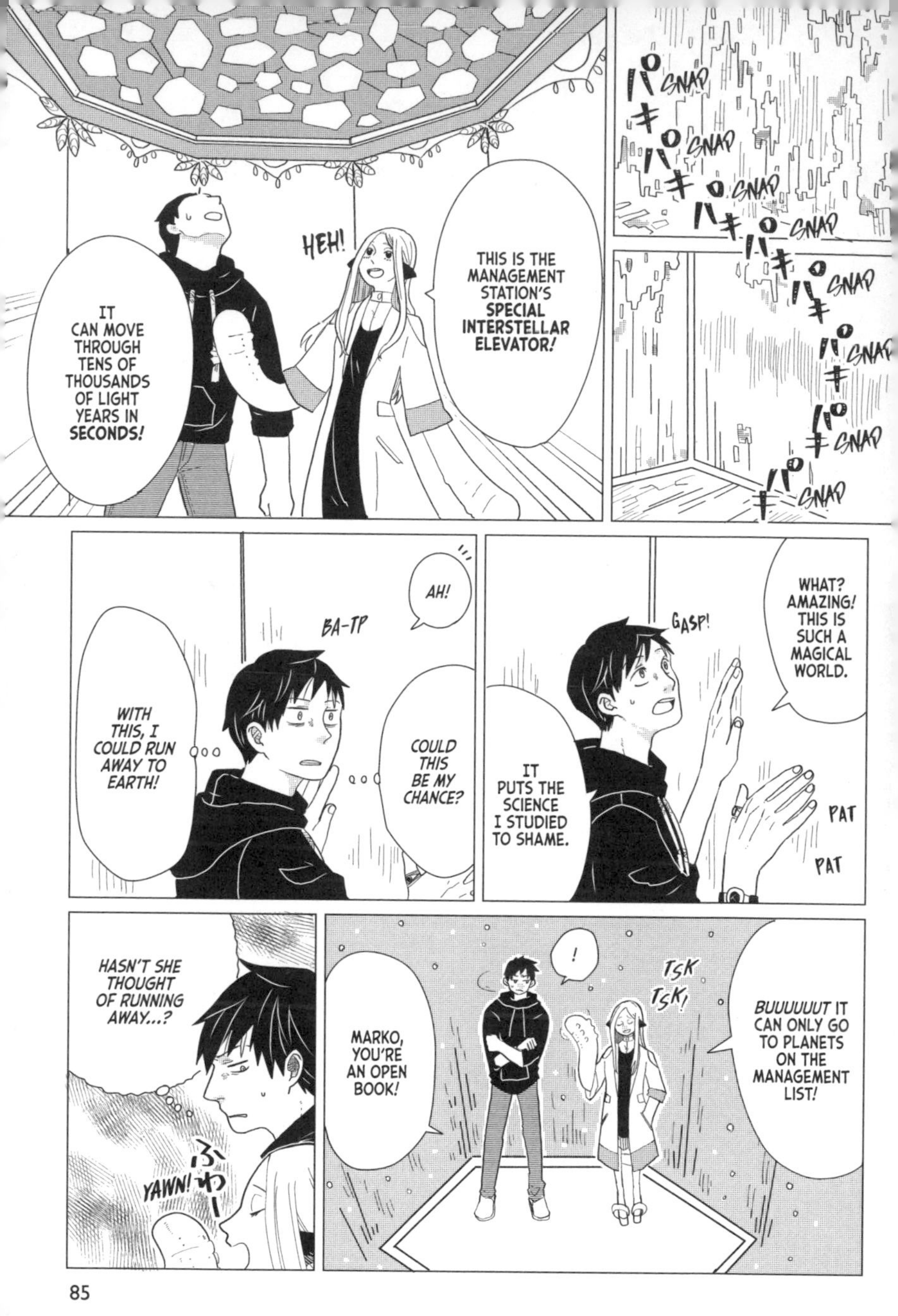
パキ SNAP
パキ SNAP
パキ SNAP
パキ SNAP
パキ SNAP
パキ SNAP
パキ SNAP
SNAP
パキ SNAP
HEH!
THIS IS THE MANAGEMENT STATION'S SPECIAL INTERSTELLAR ELEVATOR!
IT CAN MOVE THROUGH TENS OF THOUSANDS OF LIGHT YEARS IN SECONDS!
GASP!
WHAT? AMAZING! THIS IS SUCH A MAGICAL WORLD.
IT PUTS THE SCIENCE I STUDIED TO SHAME.
PAT
PAT
AH!
BA-TP
COULD THIS BE MY CHANCE?
WITH THIS, I COULD RUN AWAY TO EARTH!
BUUUUUUT IT CAN ONLY GO TO PLANETS ON THE MANAGEMENT LIST!
TSK TSK!
!
MARKO, YOU'RE AN OPEN BOOK!
HASN'T SHE THOUGHT OF RUNNING AWAY...?
ふわー
YAWN!

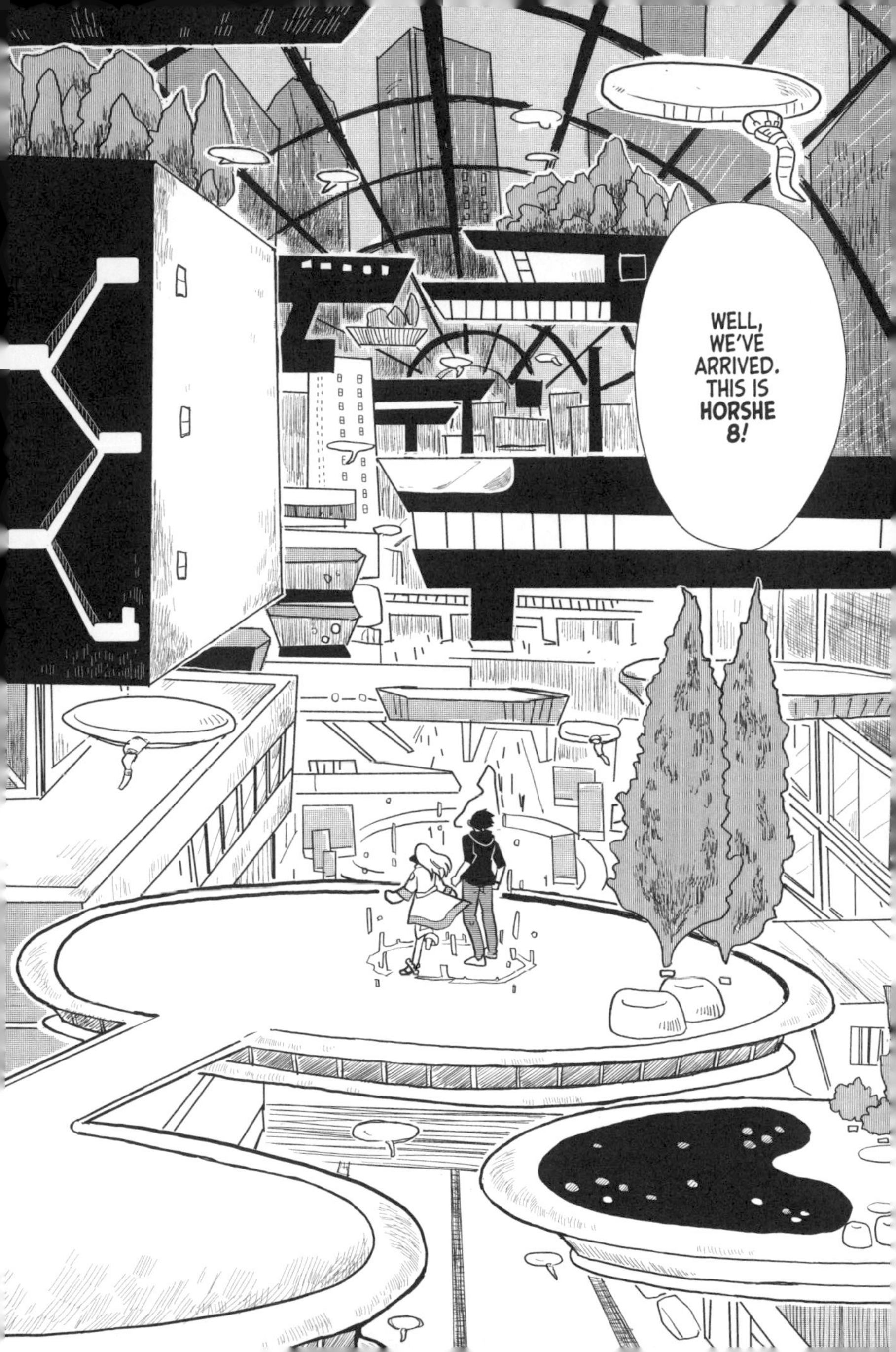
WELL, WE'VE ARRIVED. THIS IS HORSHE 8!

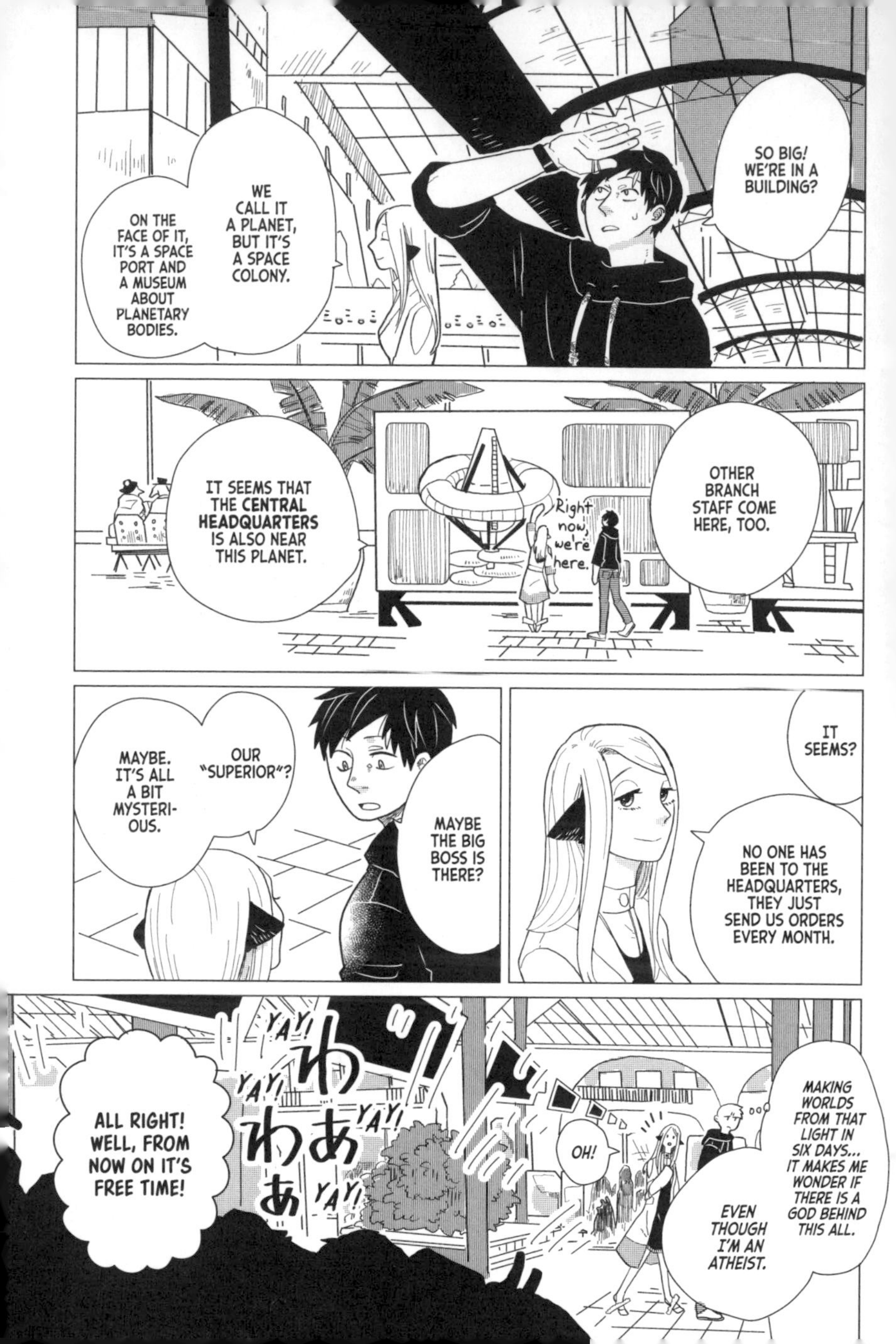
SO BIG! WE'RE IN A BUILDING?
WE CALL IT A PLANET, BUT IT'S A SPACE COLONY.
ON THE FACE OF IT, IT'S A SPACE PORT AND A MUSEUM ABOUT PLANETARY BODIES.
OTHER BRANCH STAFF COME HERE, TOO.
Right now, we're here.
IT SEEMS THAT THE **CENTRAL HEADQUARTERS** IS ALSO NEAR THIS PLANET.
IT SEEMS?
NO ONE HAS BEEN TO THE HEADQUARTERS, THEY JUST SEND US ORDERS EVERY MONTH.
MAYBE THE BIG BOSS IS THERE?
OUR "SUPERIOR"?
MAYBE. IT'S ALL A BIT MYSTERIOUS.
MAKING WORLDS FROM THAT LIGHT IN SIX DAYS... IT MAKES ME WONDER IF THERE IS A GOD BEHIND THIS ALL.
EVEN THOUGH I'M AN ATHEIST.
OH!
わ YAY!
わあ YAY! YAY!
あ YAY!
ALL RIGHT! WELL, FROM NOW ON IT'S FREE TIME!

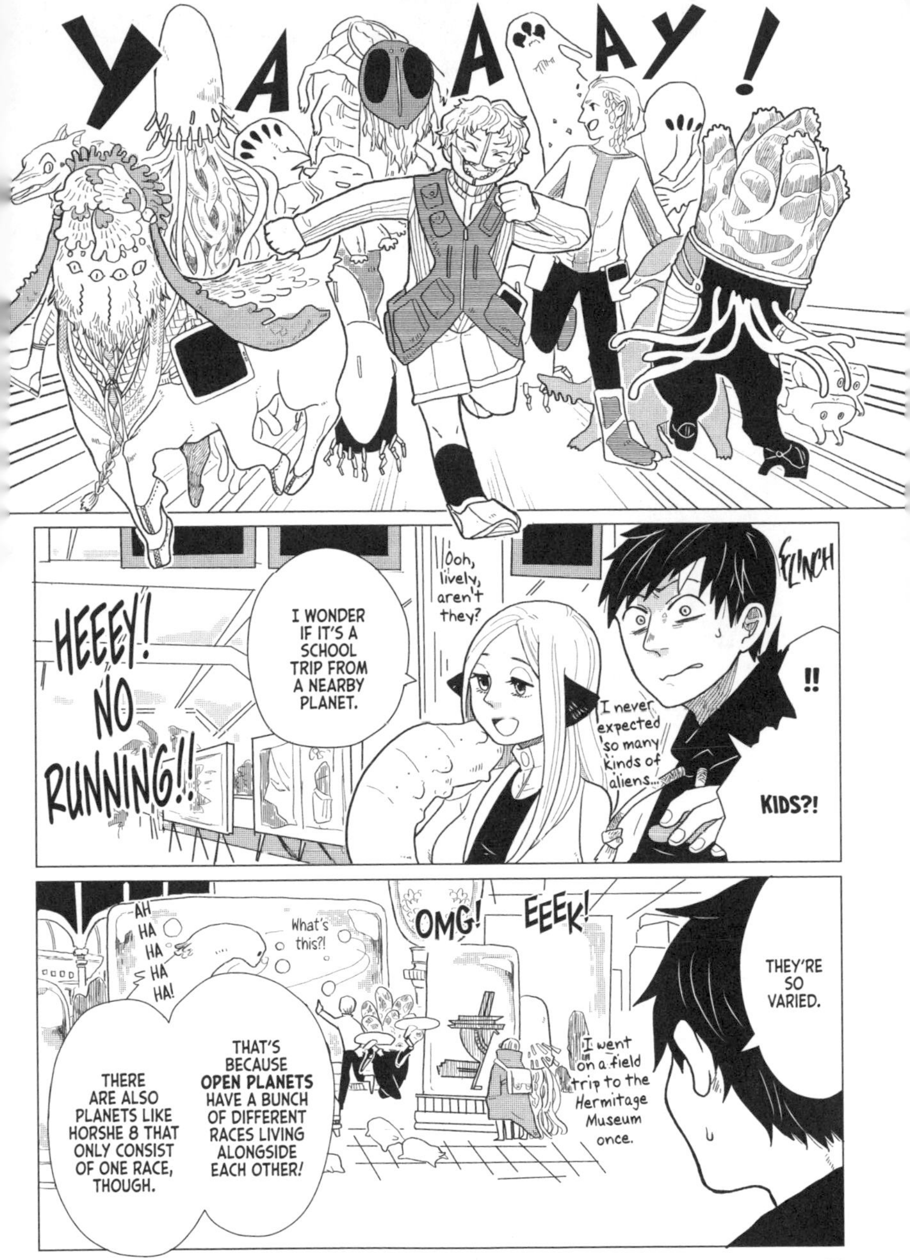
YAAAY!
FLINCH
!!
Ooh, lively, aren't they?
I never expected so many kinds of aliens...
KIDS?!
I WONDER IF IT'S A SCHOOL TRIP FROM A NEARBY PLANET.
HEEEY! NO RUNNING!!
THEY'RE SO VARIED.
I went on a field trip to the Hermitage Museum once.
EEEK!
OMG!
What's this?!
AH HA HA HA HA!
THAT'S BECAUSE **OPEN PLANETS** HAVE A BUNCH OF DIFFERENT RACES LIVING ALONGSIDE EACH OTHER!
THERE ARE ALSO PLANETS LIKE HORSHE 8 THAT ONLY CONSIST OF ONE RACE, THOUGH.

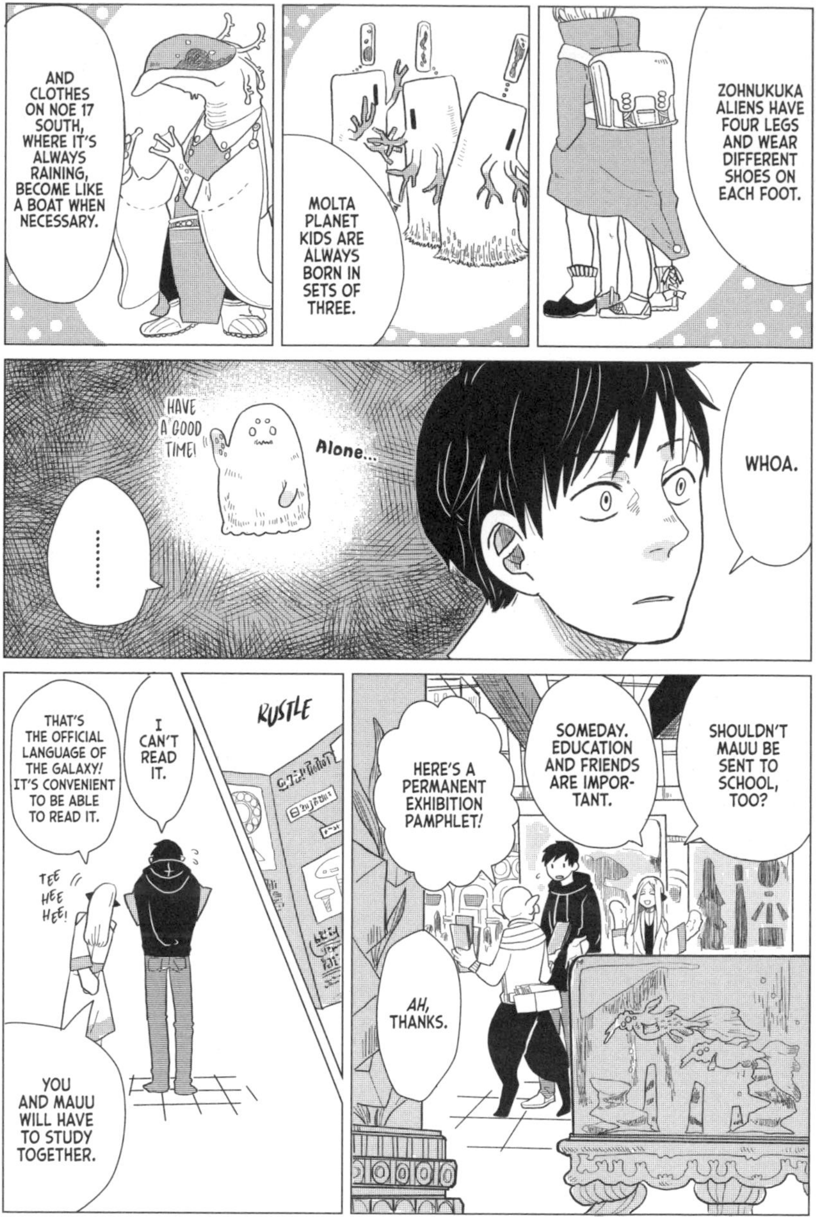
ZOHNUKUKA ALIENS HAVE FOUR LEGS AND WEAR DIFFERENT SHOES ON EACH FOOT.
MOLTA PLANET KIDS ARE ALWAYS BORN IN SETS OF THREE.
AND CLOTHES ON NOE 17 SOUTH, WHERE IT'S ALWAYS RAINING, BECOME LIKE A BOAT WHEN NECESSARY.
WHOA.
Alone...
HAVE A GOOD TIME!
......
SHOULDN'T MAUU BE SENT TO SCHOOL, TOO?
SOMEDAY. EDUCATION AND FRIENDS ARE IMPORTANT.
HERE'S A PERMANENT EXHIBITION PAMPHLET!
AH, THANKS.
RUSTLE
I CAN'T READ IT.
THAT'S THE OFFICIAL LANGUAGE OF THE GALAXY! IT'S CONVENIENT TO BE ABLE TO READ IT.
TEE HEE HEE!
YOU AND MAUU WILL HAVE TO STUDY TOGETHER.

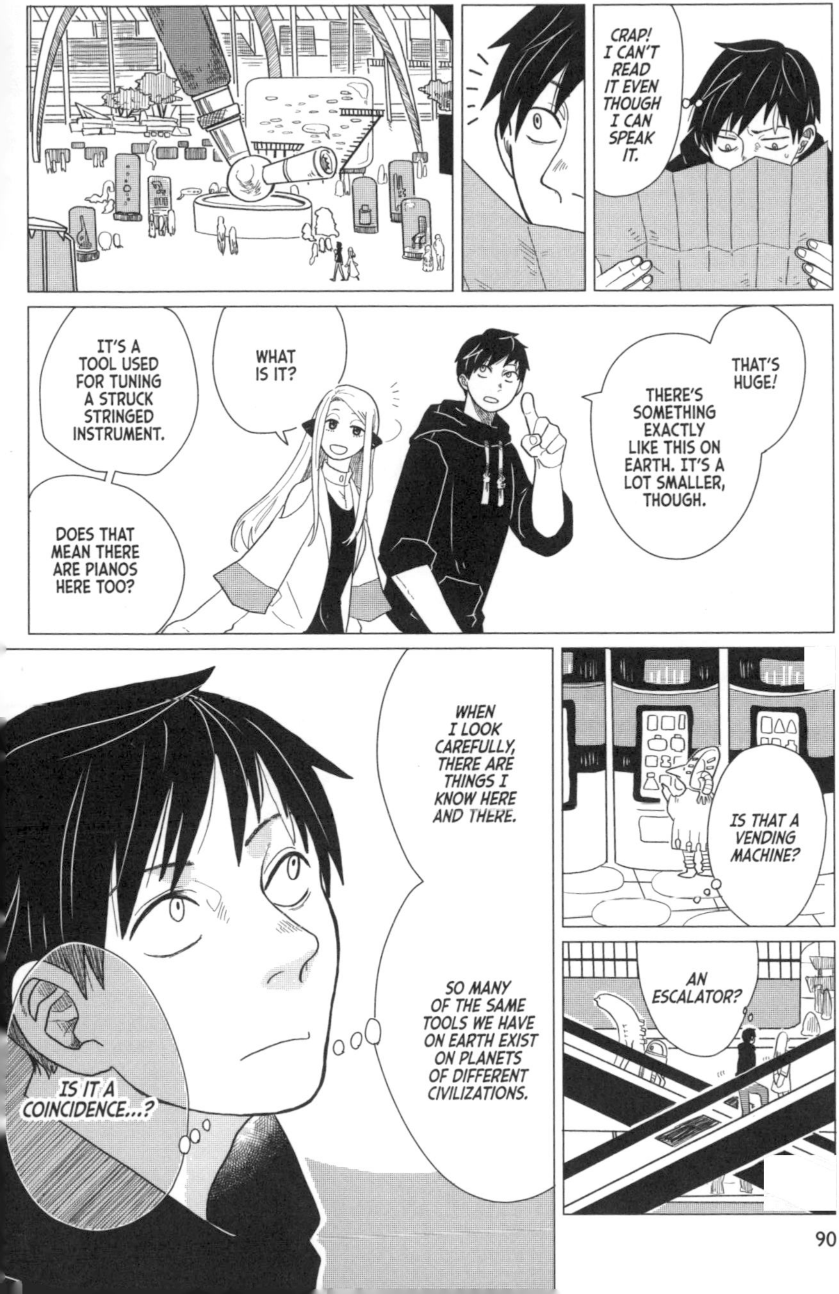
CRAP! I CAN'T READ IT EVEN THOUGH I CAN SPEAK IT.
THAT'S HUGE!
THERE'S SOMETHING EXACTLY LIKE THIS ON EARTH. IT'S A LOT SMALLER, THOUGH.
WHAT IS IT?
IT'S A TOOL USED FOR TUNING A STRUCK STRINGED INSTRUMENT.
DOES THAT MEAN THERE ARE PIANOS HERE TOO?
IS THAT A VENDING MACHINE?
AN ESCALATOR?
WHEN I LOOK CAREFULLY, THERE ARE THINGS I KNOW HERE AND THERE.
SO MANY OF THE SAME TOOLS WE HAVE ON EARTH EXIST ON PLANETS OF DIFFERENT CIVILIZATIONS.
IS IT A COINCIDENCE...?

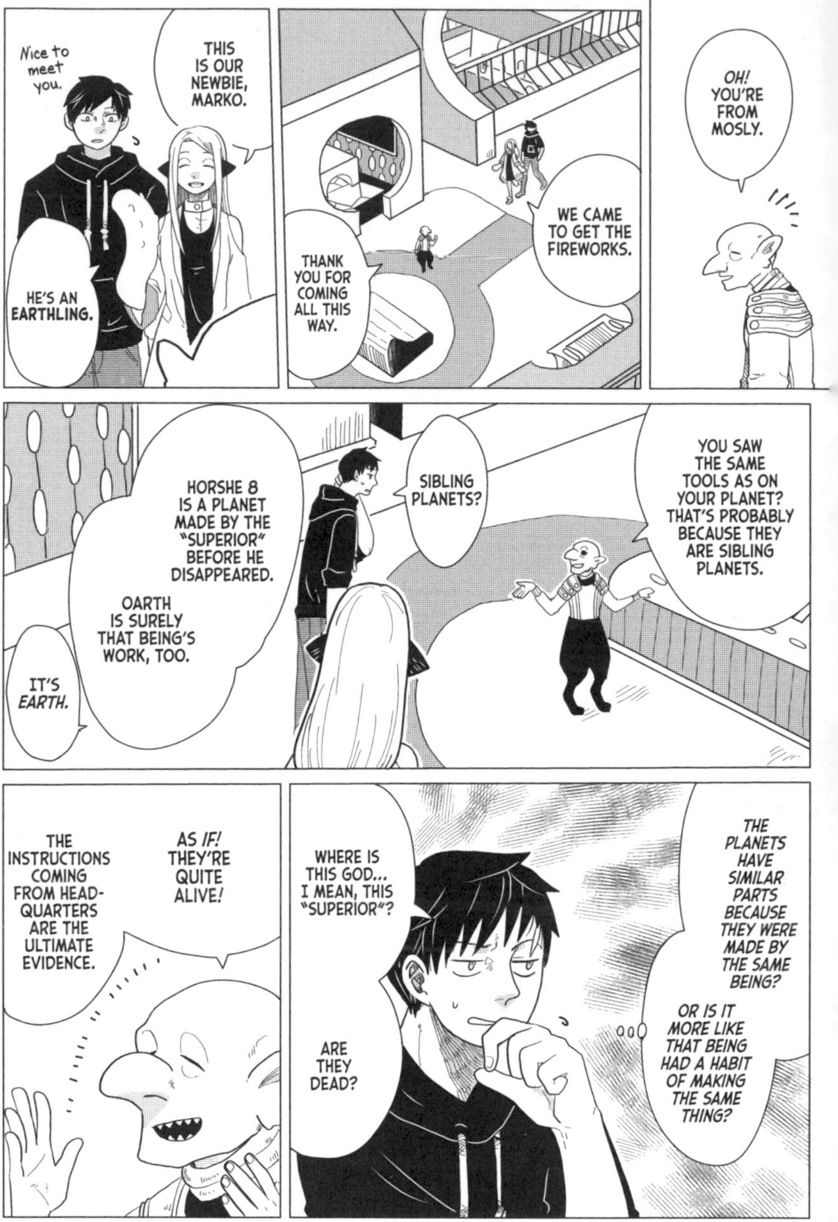
OH! YOU'RE FROM MOSLY.
WE CAME TO GET THE FIREWORKS.
THANK YOU FOR COMING ALL THIS WAY.
THIS IS OUR NEWBIE, MARKO.
HE'S AN EARTHLING.
Nice to meet you.
YOU SAW THE SAME TOOLS AS ON YOUR PLANET? THAT'S PROBABLY BECAUSE THEY ARE SIBLING PLANETS.
SIBLING PLANETS?
HORSHE 8 IS A PLANET MADE BY THE "SUPERIOR" BEFORE HE DISAPPEARED.
OARTH IS SURELY THAT BEING'S WORK, TOO.
IT'S *EARTH.*
THE PLANETS HAVE SIMILAR PARTS BECAUSE THEY WERE MADE BY THE SAME BEING?
OR IS IT MORE LIKE THAT BEING HAD A HABIT OF MAKING THE SAME THING?
WHERE IS THIS GOD... I MEAN, THIS "SUPERIOR"?
ARE THEY DEAD?
AS *IF!* THEY'RE QUITE ALIVE*!*
THE INSTRUCTIONS COMING FROM HEAD-QUARTERS ARE THE ULTIMATE EVIDENCE.

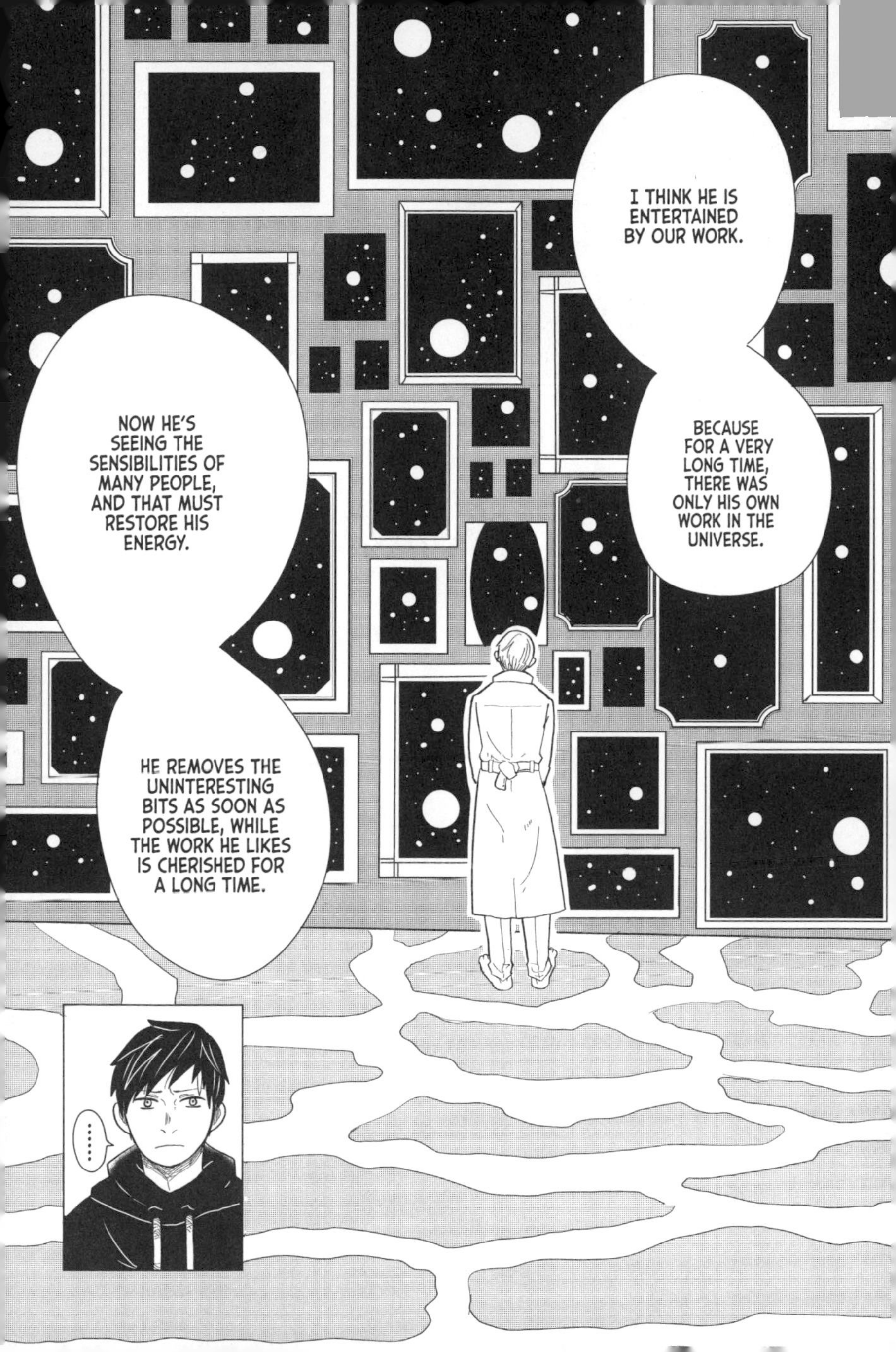
I THINK HE IS ENTERTAINED BY OUR WORK.
BECAUSE FOR A VERY LONG TIME, THERE WAS ONLY HIS OWN WORK IN THE UNIVERSE.
NOW HE'S SEEING THE SENSIBILITIES OF MANY PEOPLE, AND THAT MUST RESTORE HIS ENERGY.
HE REMOVES THE UNINTERESTING BITS AS SOON AS POSSIBLE, WHILE THE WORK HE LIKES IS CHERISHED FOR A LONG TIME.
......

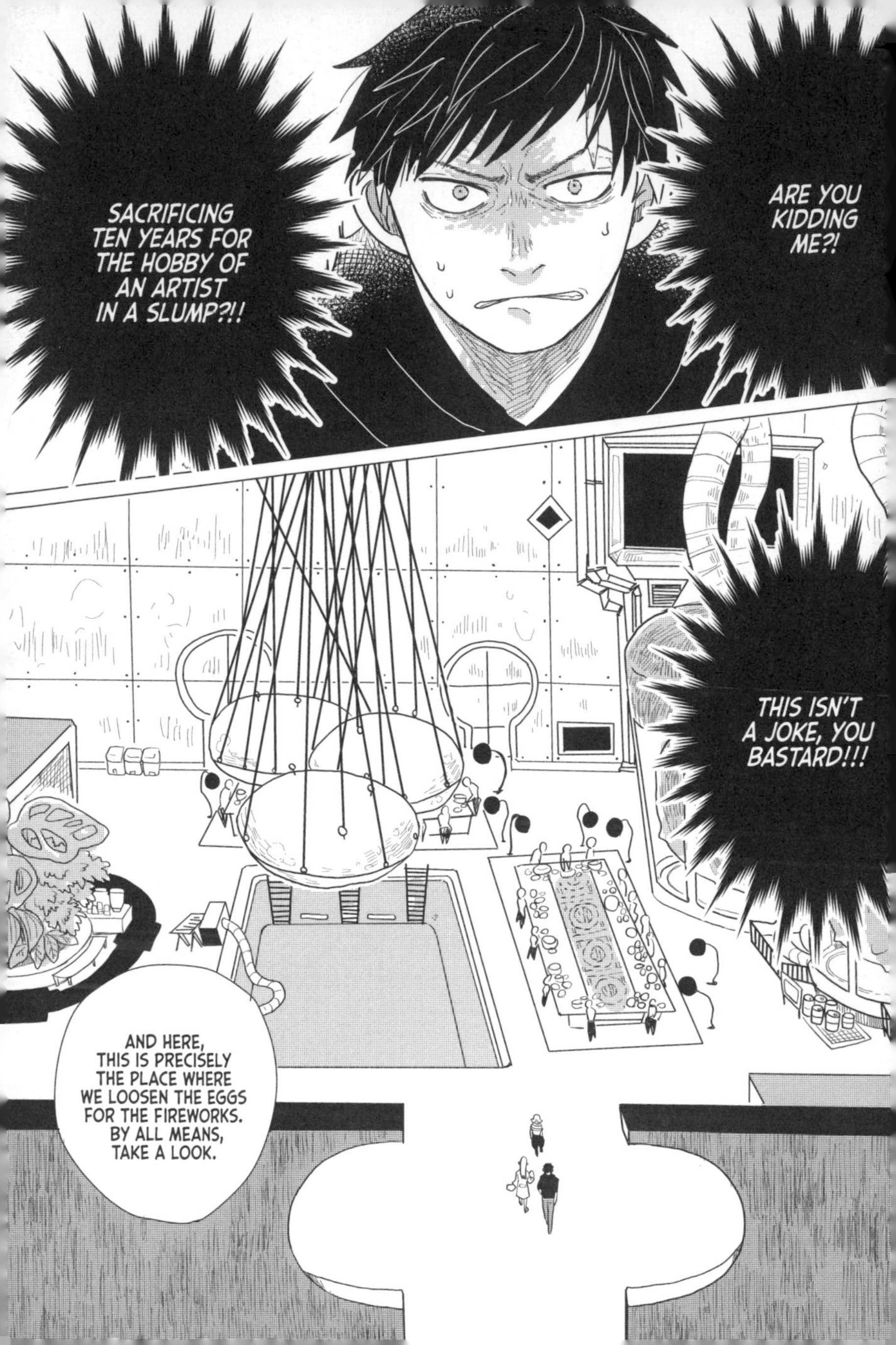
ARE YOU KIDDING ME?!
SACRIFICING TEN YEARS FOR THE HOBBY OF AN ARTIST IN A SLUMP?!!
THIS ISN'T A JOKE, YOU BASTARD!!!
AND HERE, THIS IS PRECISELY THE PLACE WHERE WE LOOSEN THE EGGS FOR THE FIREWORKS. BY ALL MEANS, TAKE A LOOK.

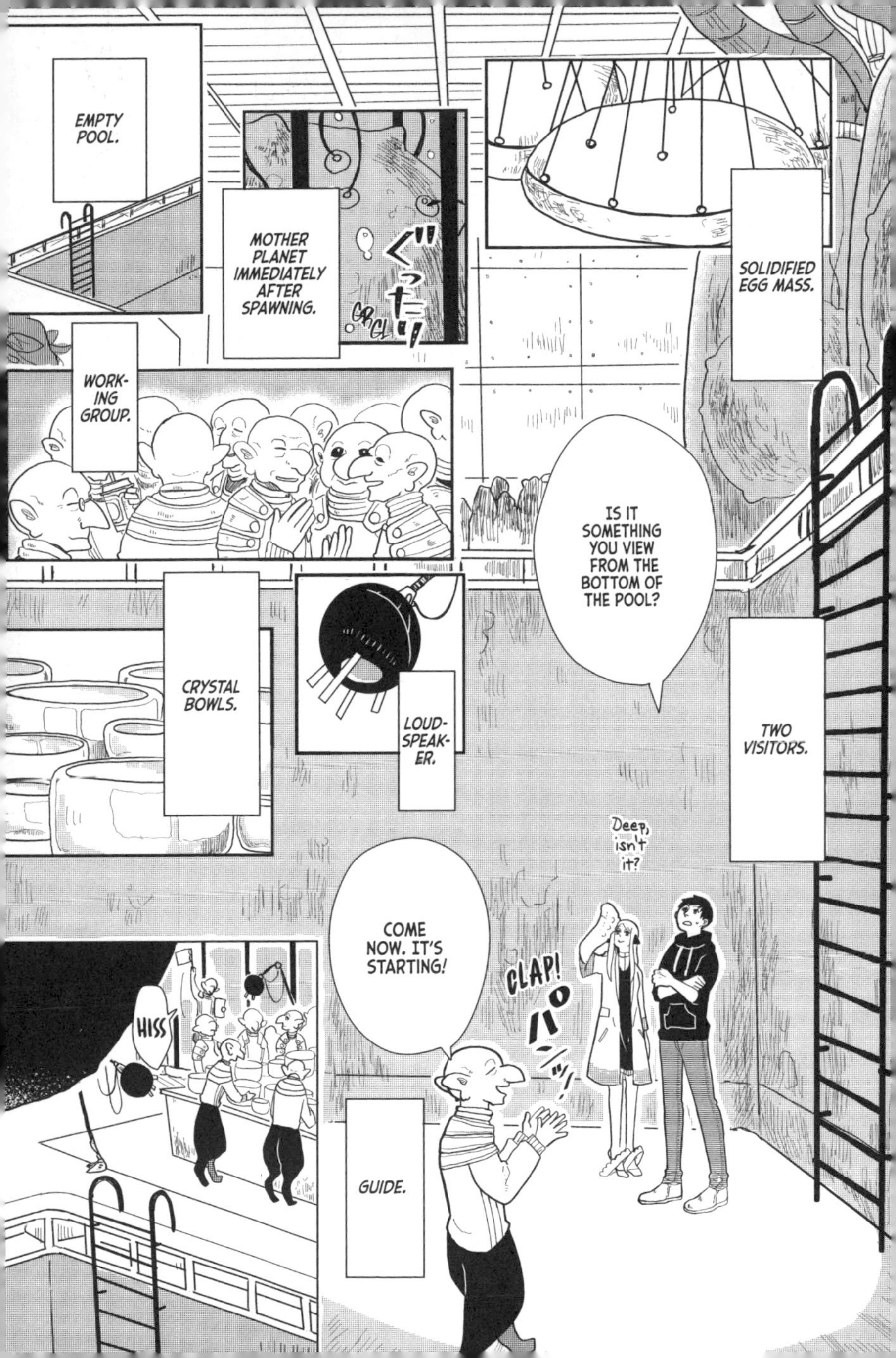
SOLIDIFIED EGG MASS.
MOTHER PLANET IMMEDIATELY AFTER SPAWNING.
GRGL
EMPTY POOL.
WORKING GROUP.
IS IT SOMETHING YOU VIEW FROM THE BOTTOM OF THE POOL?
TWO VISITORS.
LOUD-SPEAK-ER.
CRYSTAL BOWLS.
Deep, isn't it?
CLAP!
COME NOW. IT'S STARTING!
GUIDE.
HISS

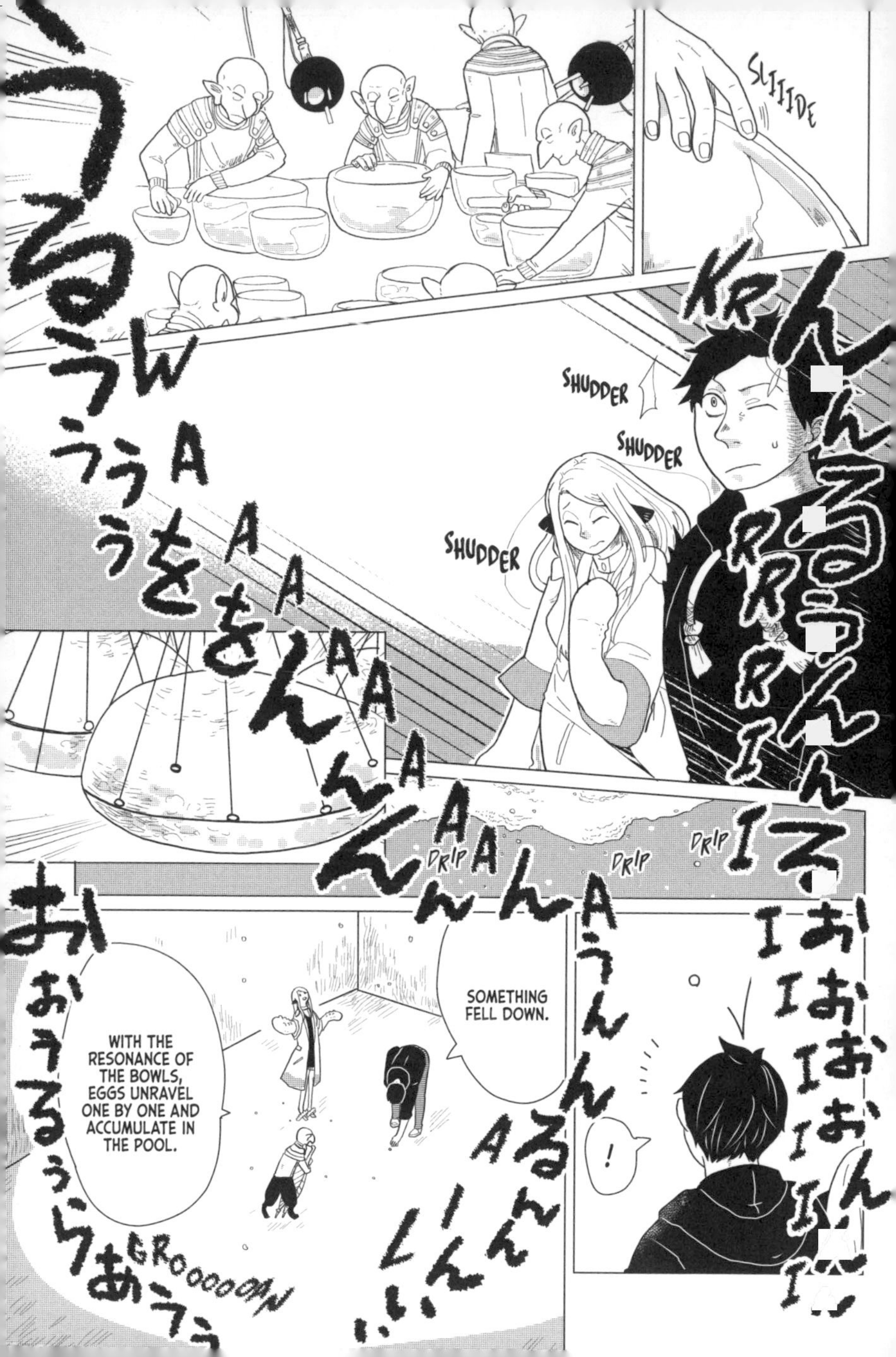

SLIIIDE
KRRRRIIIII
SHUDDER
SHUDDER
SHUDDER
WAAAAAAAAAA
DRIP
DRIP
DRIP
!
SOMETHING FELL DOWN.
WITH THE RESONANCE OF THE BOWLS, EGGS UNRAVEL ONE BY ONE AND ACCUMULATE IN THE POOL.
GROOOOOAN

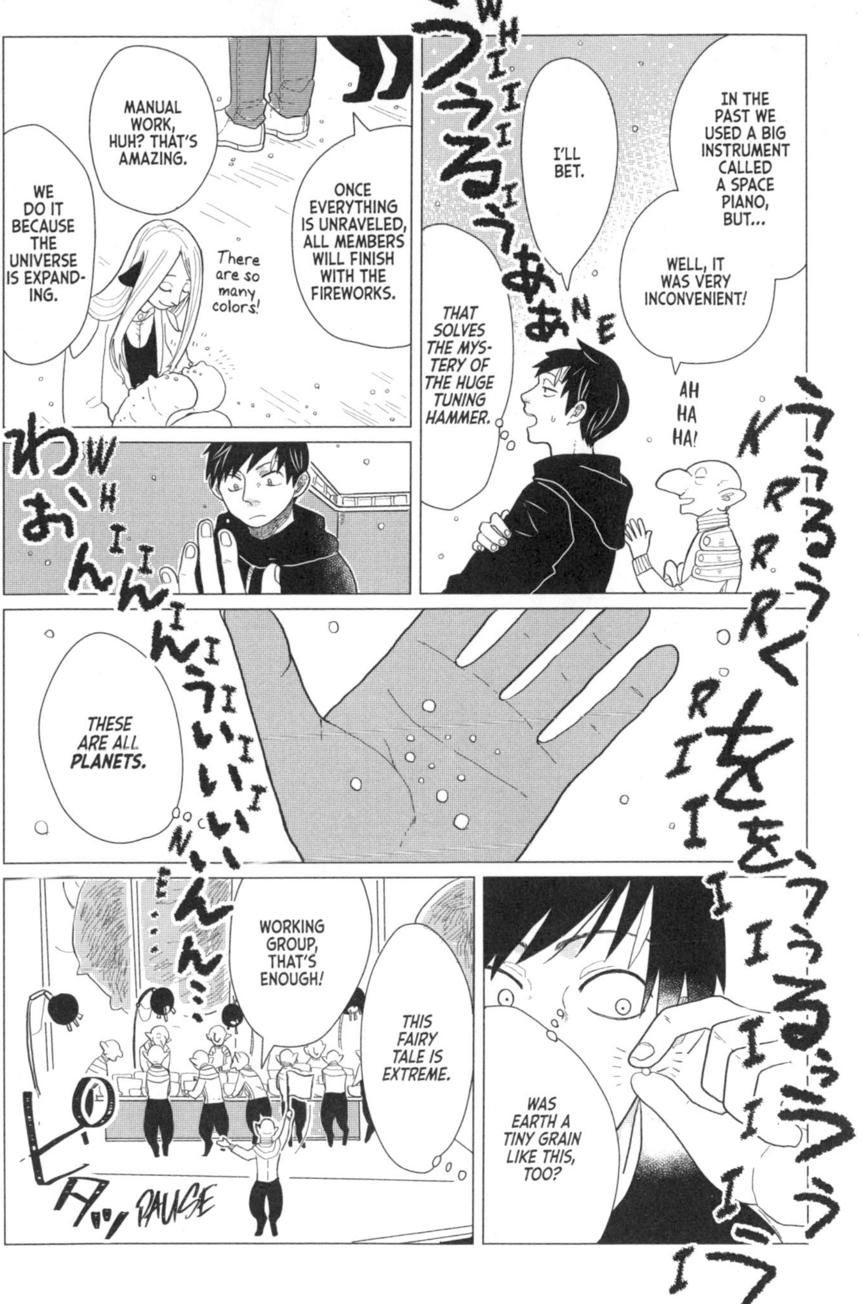
IN THE PAST WE USED A BIG INSTRUMENT CALLED A SPACE PIANO, BUT...
WELL, IT WAS VERY INCONVENIENT!
I'LL BET.
WHIIIIINE
THAT SOLVES THE MYSTERY OF THE HUGE TUNING HAMMER.
AH HA HA!
MANUAL WORK, HUH? THAT'S AMAZING.
ONCE EVERYTHING IS UNRAVELED, ALL MEMBERS WILL FINISH WITH THE FIREWORKS.
There are so many colors!
WE DO IT BECAUSE THE UNIVERSE IS EXPAND-ING.
WHIIIIIIINE
KRRRRIIIIIIII
THESE ARE ALL PLANETS.
WAS EARTH A TINY GRAIN LIKE THIS, TOO?
WORKING GROUP, THAT'S ENOUGH!
THIS FAIRY TALE IS EXTREME.
PAUSE

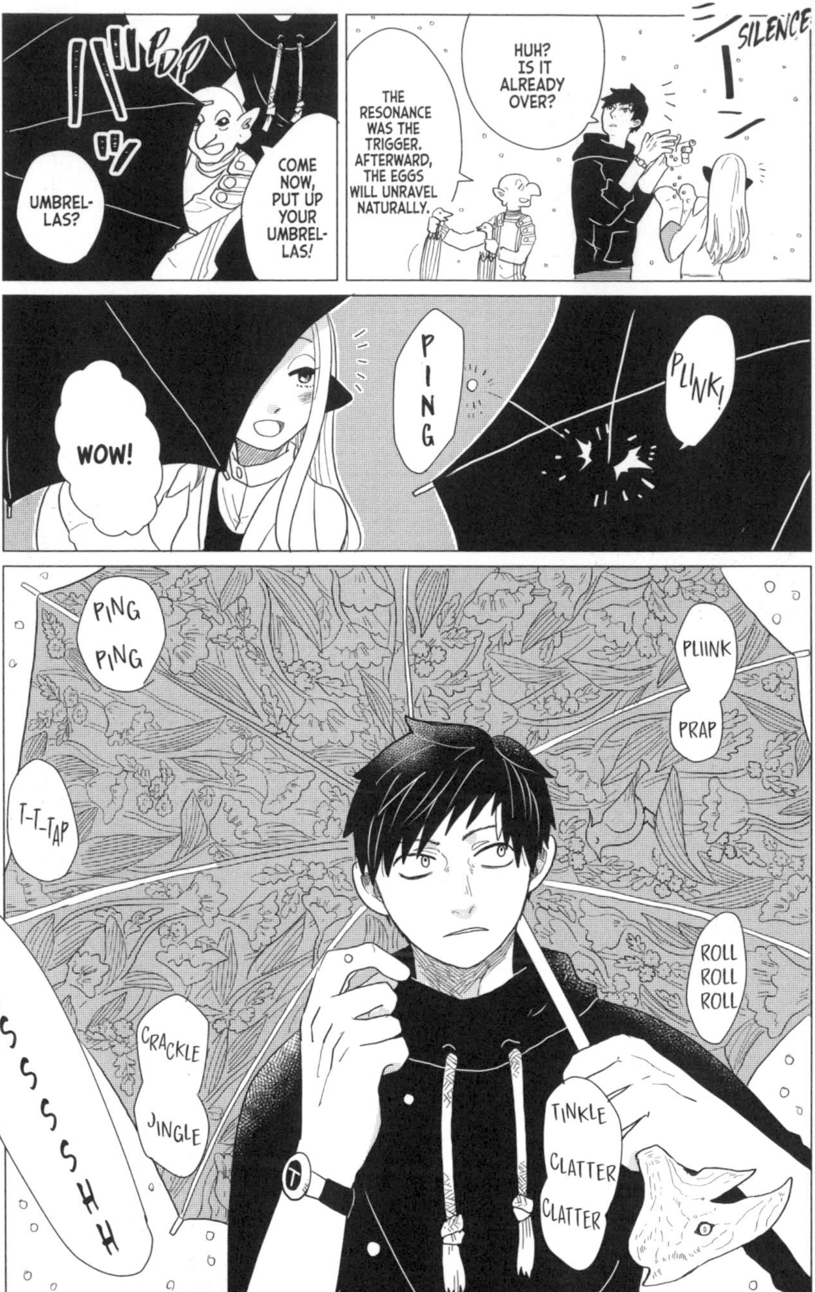
SILENCE
HUH? IS IT ALREADY OVER?
THE RESONANCE WAS THE TRIGGER. AFTERWARD, THE EGGS WILL UNRAVEL NATURALLY.
COME NOW, PUT UP YOUR UMBREL-LAS!
UMBREL-LAS?
PLINK!
PING
WOW!
PLIINK
PRAP
PING PING
ROLL ROLL ROLL
T-T-TAP
TINKLE
CLATTER
CLATTER
CRACKLE
JINGLE
FWSSSSSHH

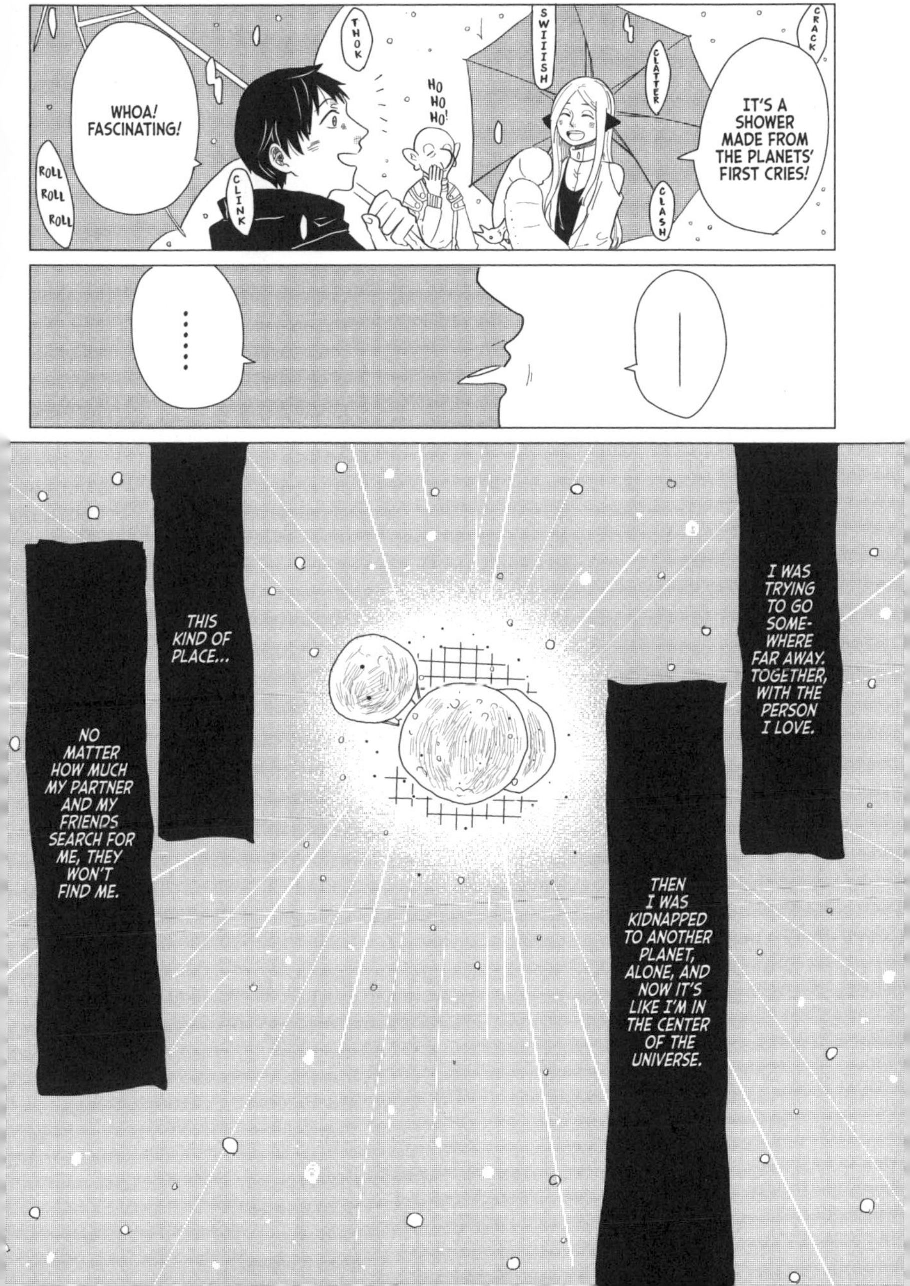
CRACK
IT'S A SHOWER MADE FROM THE PLANETS' FIRST CRIES!
CLATTER
CLASH
SWIIISH
HO HO HO!
THOK
WHOA! FASCINATING!
CLINK
ROLL ROLL ROLL
—
......
I WAS TRYING TO GO SOME-WHERE FAR AWAY. TOGETHER, WITH THE PERSON I LOVE.
THEN I WAS KIDNAPPED TO ANOTHER PLANET, ALONE, AND NOW IT'S LIKE I'M IN THE CENTER OF THE UNIVERSE.
THIS KIND OF PLACE...
NO MATTER HOW MUCH MY PARTNER AND MY FRIENDS SEARCH FOR ME, THEY WON'T FIND ME.

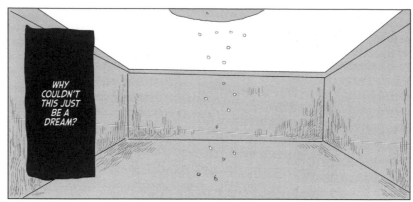

WHY COULDN'T THIS JUST BE A DREAM?
ぺたり SLAP
HERE YOU GO! SPACE FIREWORKS.
PLEASE GROW GOOD PLANETARY BODIES!

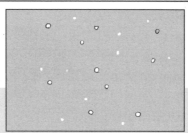

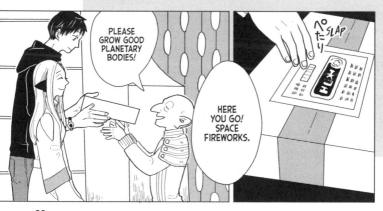

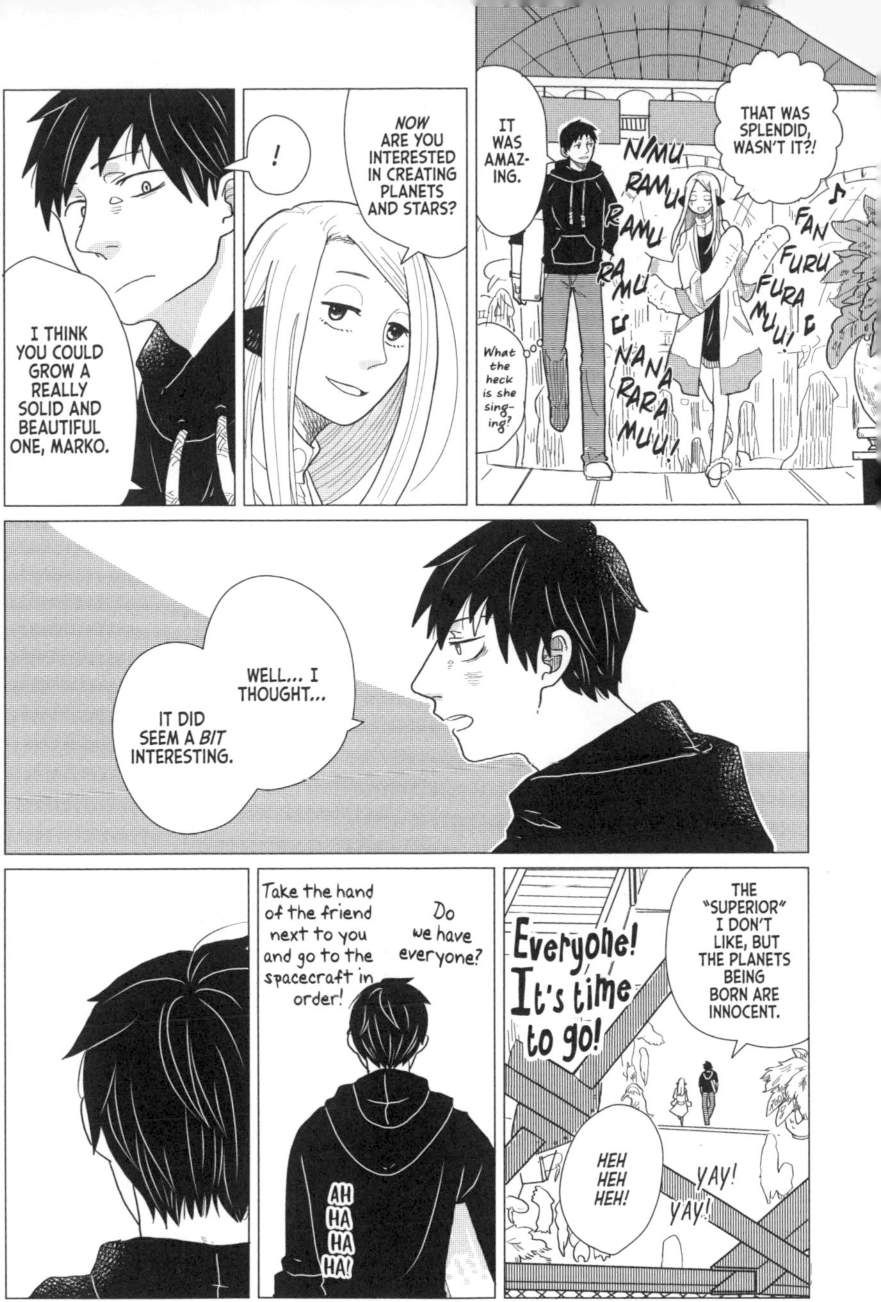
THAT WAS SPLENDID, WASN'T IT?!
FAN FURU FURA MUUU! ♪
IT WAS AMAZ-ING.
NIMU RAMU RAMU RAMU RAMU ♪ NANA RARA MUUU!
What the heck is she sing-ing?
NOW ARE YOU INTERESTED IN CREATING PLANETS AND STARS?
!
I THINK YOU COULD GROW A REALLY SOLID AND BEAUTIFUL ONE, MARKO.
WELL... I THOUGHT...
IT DID SEEM A BIT INTERESTING.
THE "SUPERIOR" I DON'T LIKE, BUT THE PLANETS BEING BORN ARE INNOCENT.
Everyone! It's time to go!
YAY!
YAY!
HEH HEH HEH!
Do we have everyone?
Take the hand of the friend next to you and go to the spacecraft in order!
AH HA HA HA!

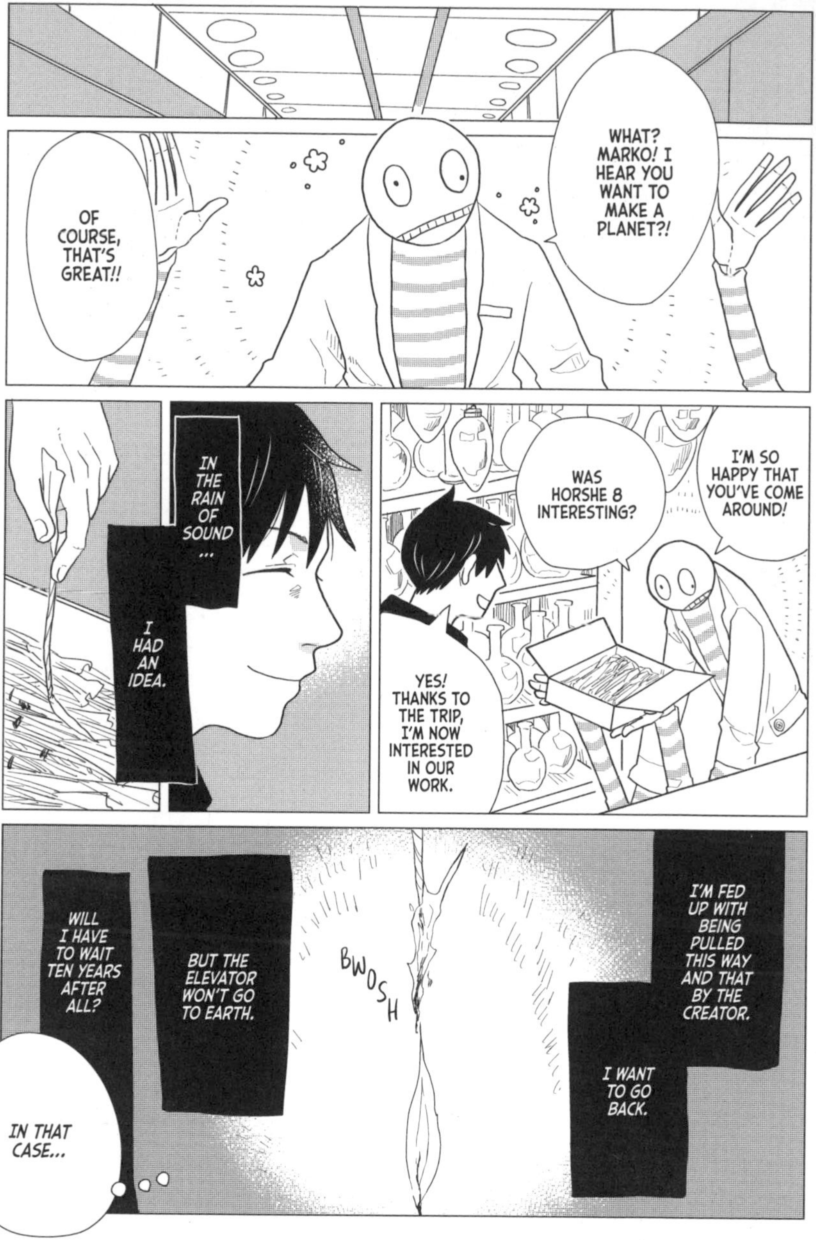
WHAT? MARKO! I HEAR YOU WANT TO MAKE A PLANET?!
OF COURSE, THAT'S GREAT!!
I'M SO HAPPY THAT YOU'VE COME AROUND!
WAS HORSHE 8 INTERESTING?
YES! THANKS TO THE TRIP, I'M NOW INTERESTED IN OUR WORK.
IN THE RAIN OF SOUND...
I HAD AN IDEA.
I'M FED UP WITH BEING PULLED THIS WAY AND THAT BY THE CREATOR.
I WANT TO GO BACK.
BWOSH
BUT THE ELEVATOR WON'T GO TO EARTH.
WILL I HAVE TO WAIT TEN YEARS AFTER ALL?
IN THAT CASE...

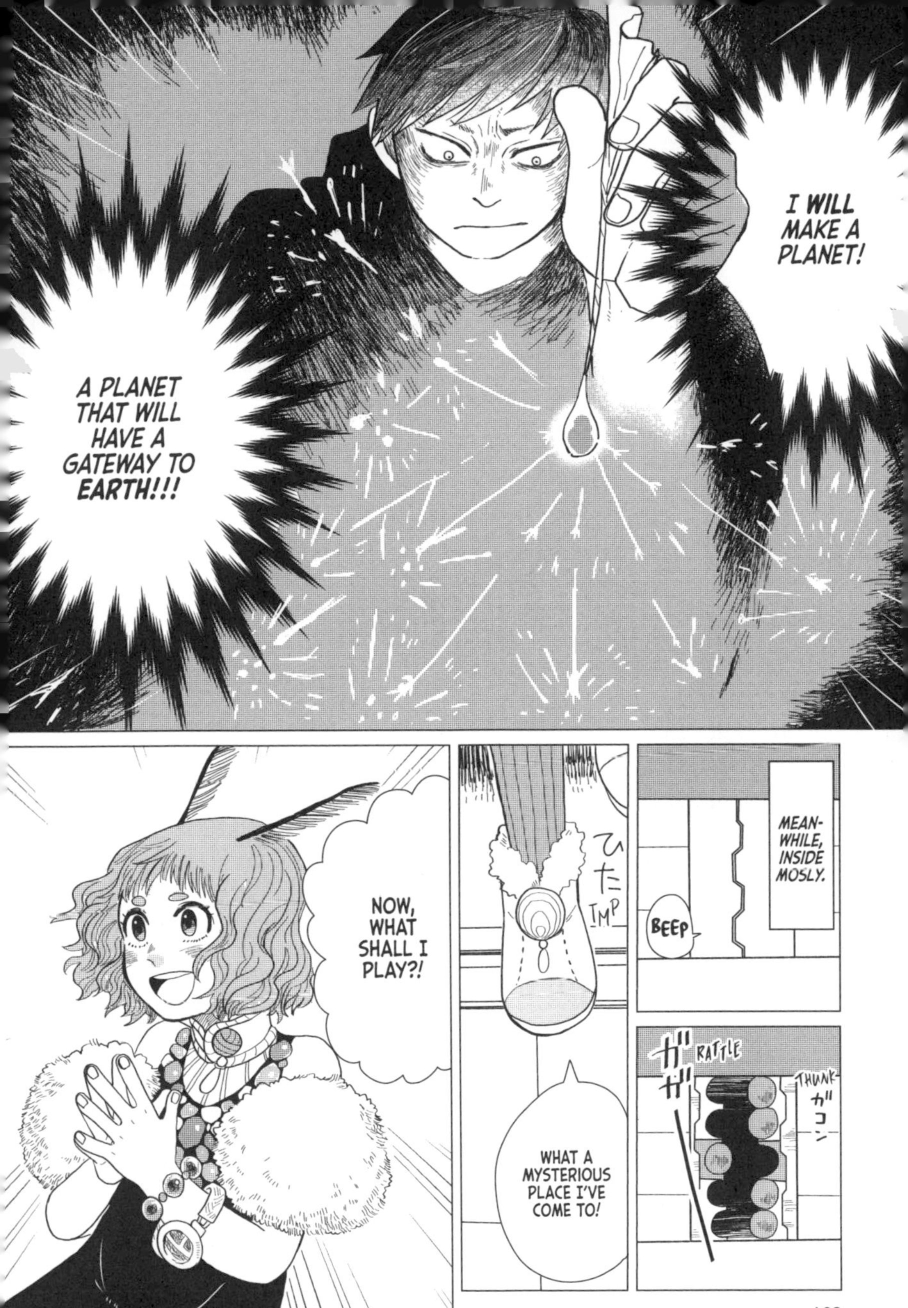
I WILL MAKE A PLANET!
A PLANET THAT WILL HAVE A GATEWAY TO EARTH!!!
MEAN-WHILE, INSIDE MOSLY.
BEEP
ガガ RATTLE
THUNK ガコン
ひた TMP
WHAT A MYSTERIOUS PLACE I'VE COME TO!
NOW, WHAT SHALL I PLAY?!

Episode 6: The Stone-Eating Creatures of the Planet Kiara

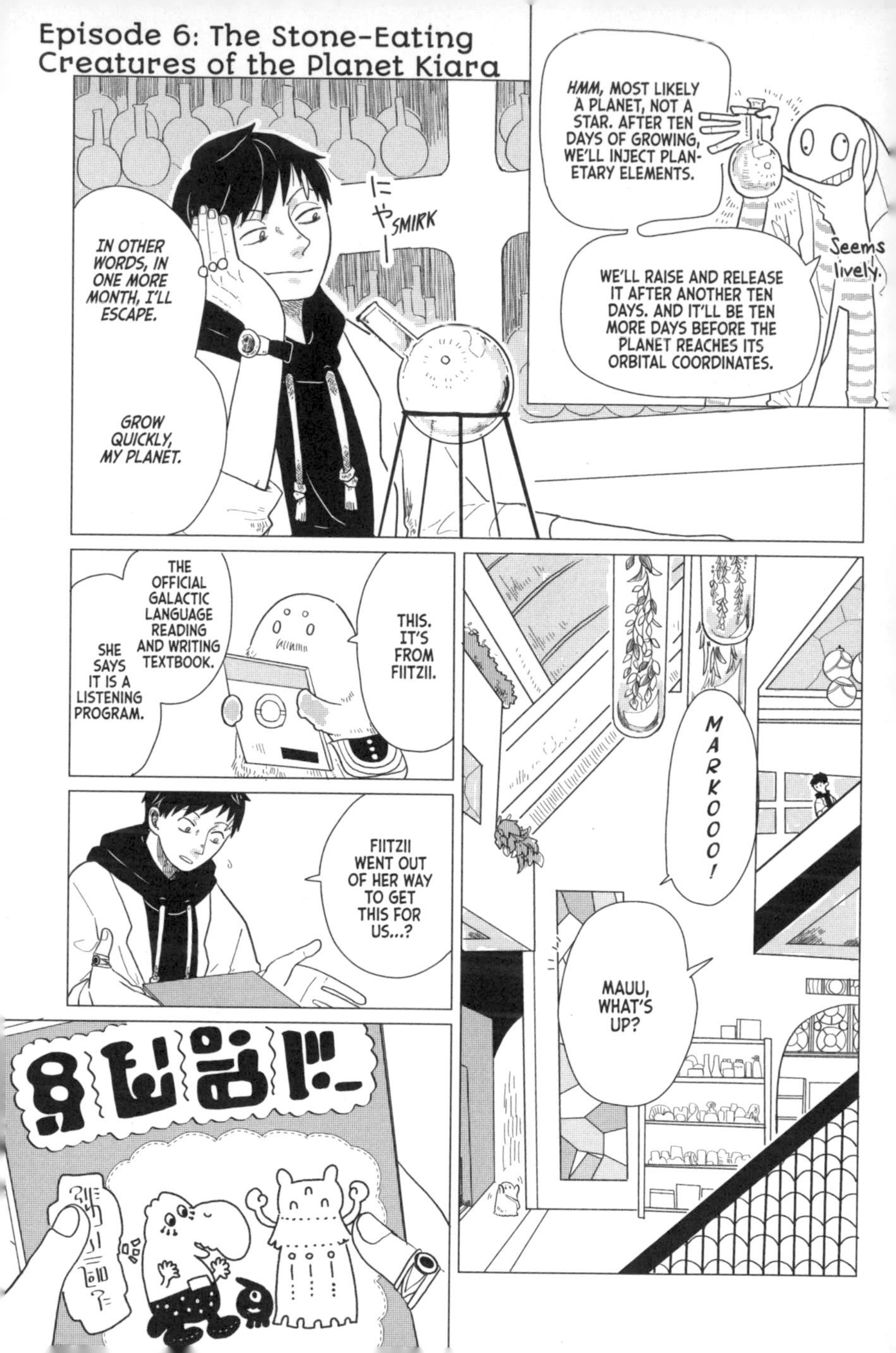
HMM, MOST LIKELY A PLANET, NOT A STAR. AFTER TEN DAYS OF GROWING, WE'LL INJECT PLANETARY ELEMENTS.
WE'LL RAISE AND RELEASE IT AFTER ANOTHER TEN DAYS. AND IT'LL BE TEN MORE DAYS BEFORE THE PLANET REACHES ITS ORBITAL COORDINATES.
Seems lively.
にやー SMIRK
IN OTHER WORDS, IN ONE MORE MONTH, I'LL ESCAPE.
GROW QUICKLY, MY PLANET.
MARKOOO!
MAUU, WHAT'S UP?
THIS. IT'S FROM FIITZII.
THE OFFICIAL GALACTIC LANGUAGE READING AND WRITING TEXTBOOK.
SHE SAYS IT IS A LISTENING PROGRAM.
FIITZII WENT OUT OF HER WAY TO GET THIS FOR US...?

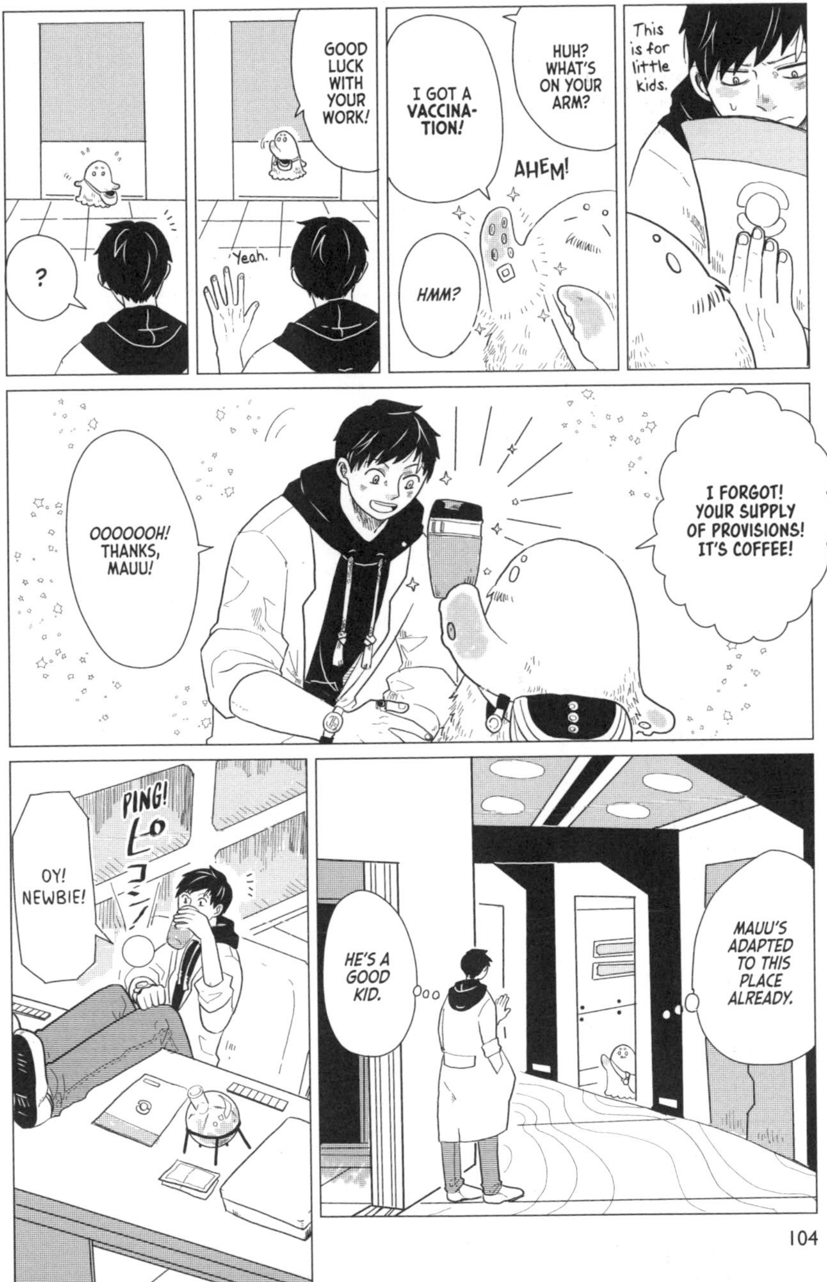
This is for little kids.
HUH? WHAT'S ON YOUR ARM?
I GOT A VACCINATION!
AHEM!
HMM?
GOOD LUCK WITH YOUR WORK!
Yeah.
?
I FORGOT! YOUR SUPPLY OF PROVISIONS! IT'S COFFEE!
OOOOOOH! THANKS, MAUU!
MAUU'S ADAPTED TO THIS PLACE ALREADY.
HE'S A GOOD KID.
PING!
OY! NEWBIE!

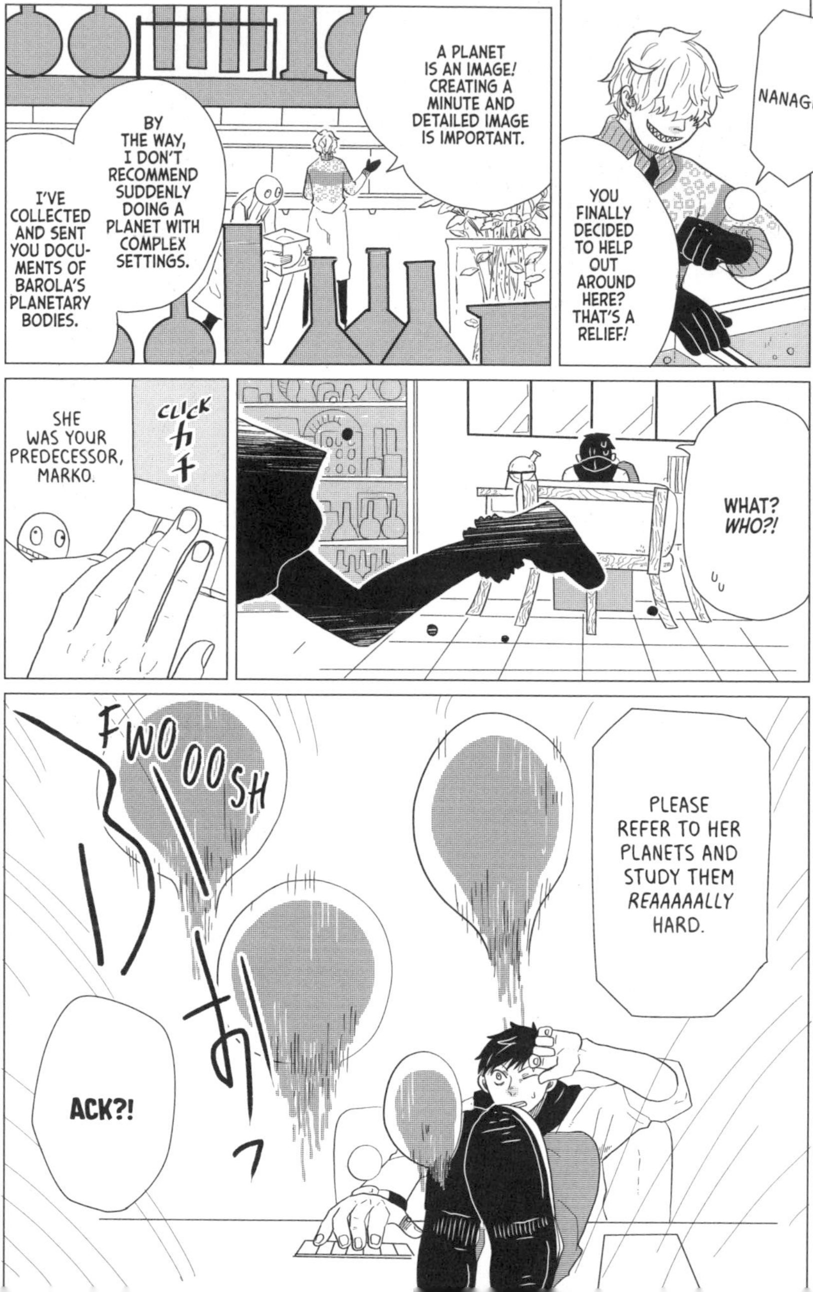
NANAGI?
YOU FINALLY DECIDED TO HELP OUT AROUND HERE? THAT'S A RELIEF!
A PLANET IS AN IMAGE! CREATING A MINUTE AND DETAILED IMAGE IS IMPORTANT.
BY THE WAY, I DON'T RECOMMEND SUDDENLY DOING A PLANET WITH COMPLEX SETTINGS.
I'VE COLLECTED AND SENT YOU DOCUMENTS OF BAROLA'S PLANETARY BODIES.
WHAT? WHO?!
CLICK カチ
SHE WAS YOUR PREDECESSOR, MARKO.
PLEASE REFER TO HER PLANETS AND STUDY THEM REAAAAALLY HARD.
FWOOOSH
ACK?!

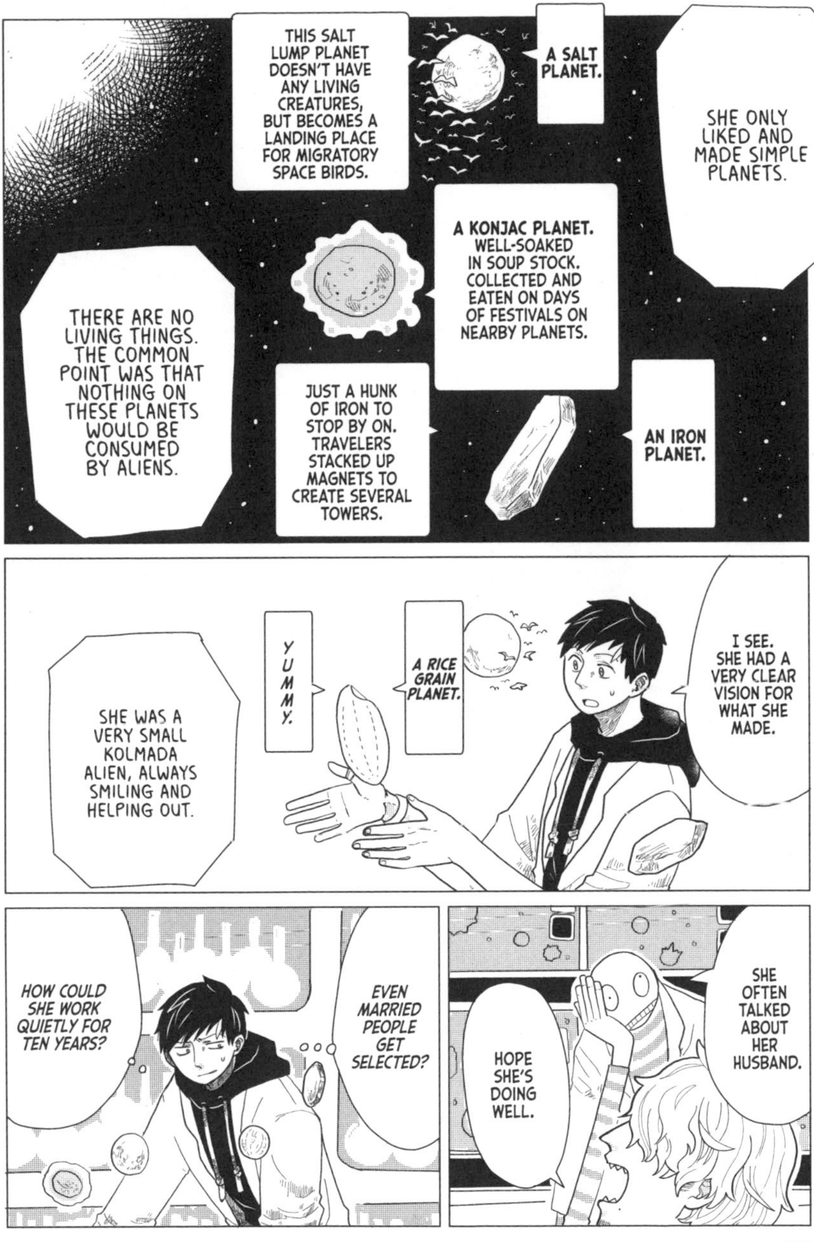
SHE ONLY LIKED AND MADE SIMPLE PLANETS.
A SALT PLANET.
THIS SALT LUMP PLANET DOESN'T HAVE ANY LIVING CREATURES, BUT BECOMES A LANDING PLACE FOR MIGRATORY SPACE BIRDS.
A KONJAC PLANET. WELL-SOAKED IN SOUP STOCK. COLLECTED AND EATEN ON DAYS OF FESTIVALS ON NEARBY PLANETS.
AN IRON PLANET.
JUST A HUNK OF IRON TO STOP BY ON. TRAVELERS STACKED UP MAGNETS TO CREATE SEVERAL TOWERS.
THERE ARE NO LIVING THINGS. THE COMMON POINT WAS THAT NOTHING ON THESE PLANETS WOULD BE CONSUMED BY ALIENS.
I SEE. SHE HAD A VERY CLEAR VISION FOR WHAT SHE MADE.
A RICE GRAIN PLANET.
YUMMY.
SHE WAS A VERY SMALL KOLMADA ALIEN, ALWAYS SMILING AND HELPING OUT.
SHE OFTEN TALKED ABOUT HER HUSBAND.
HOPE SHE'S DOING WELL.
EVEN MARRIED PEOPLE GET SELECTED?
HOW COULD SHE WORK QUIETLY FOR TEN YEARS?

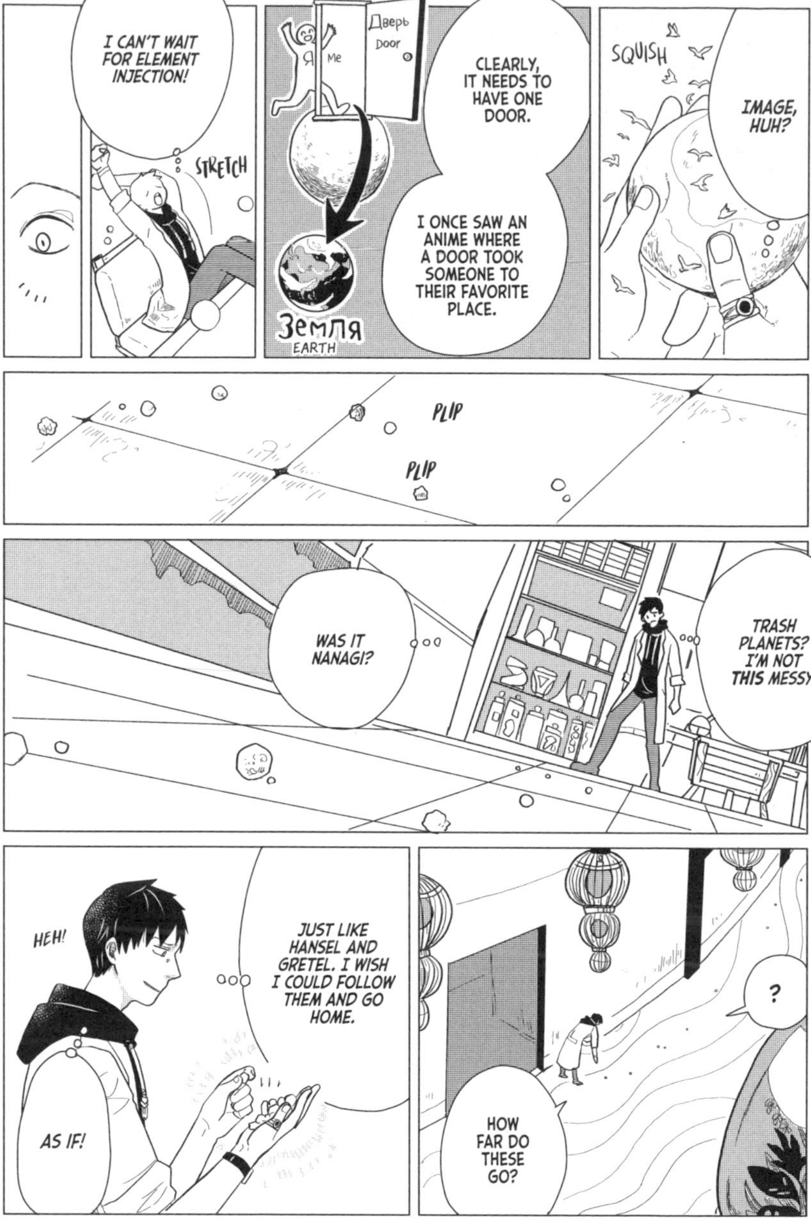
SQUISH
IMAGE, HUH?
Дверь
Door
Я
Me
CLEARLY, IT NEEDS TO HAVE ONE DOOR.
I ONCE SAW AN ANIME WHERE A DOOR TOOK SOMEONE TO THEIR FAVORITE PLACE.
Земля
EARTH
I CAN'T WAIT FOR ELEMENT INJECTION!
STRETCH
PLIP
PLIP
TRASH PLANETS? I'M NOT THIS MESSY.
WAS IT NANAGI?
?
HOW FAR DO THESE GO?
JUST LIKE HANSEL AND GRETEL. I WISH I COULD FOLLOW THEM AND GO HOME.
HEH!
AS IF!

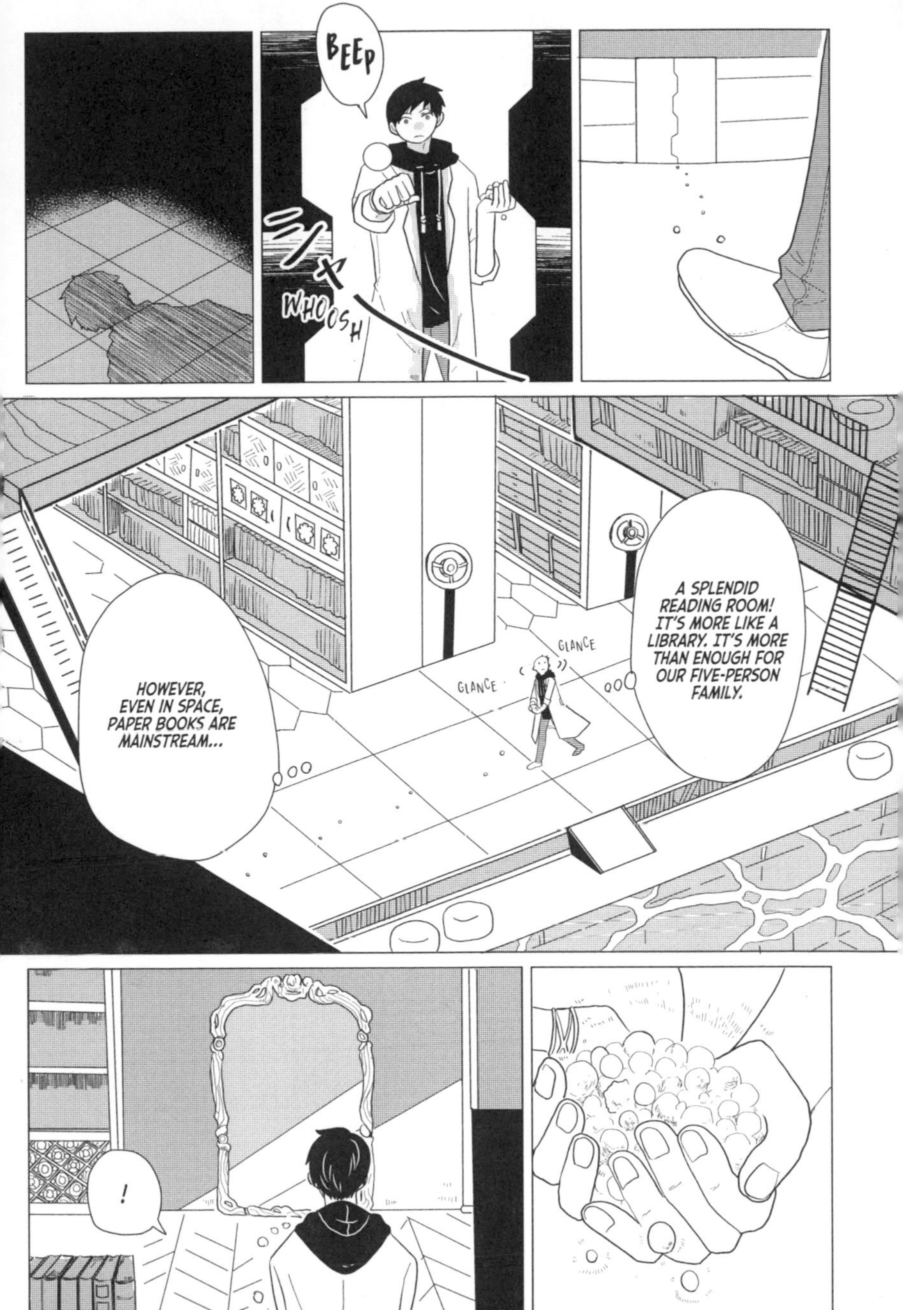
BEEP
WHOOSH
A SPLENDID READING ROOM! IT'S MORE LIKE A LIBRARY. IT'S MORE THAN ENOUGH FOR OUR FIVE-PERSON FAMILY.
GLANCE
GLANCE
HOWEVER, EVEN IN SPACE, PAPER BOOKS ARE MAINSTREAM...
!

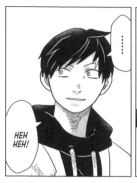

HEH HEH!

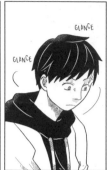

GLANCE

GLANCE

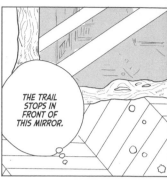

THE TRAIL STOPS IN FRONT OF THIS MIRROR.

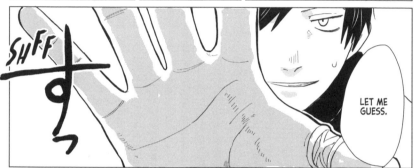

SHFF

LET ME GUESS.

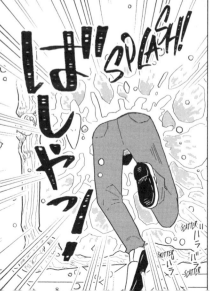

SPLASH!

SCATTER

SKITTER

SCATTER

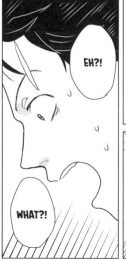

EH?!

WHAT?!

PAT

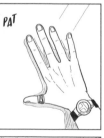

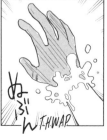

THWAP

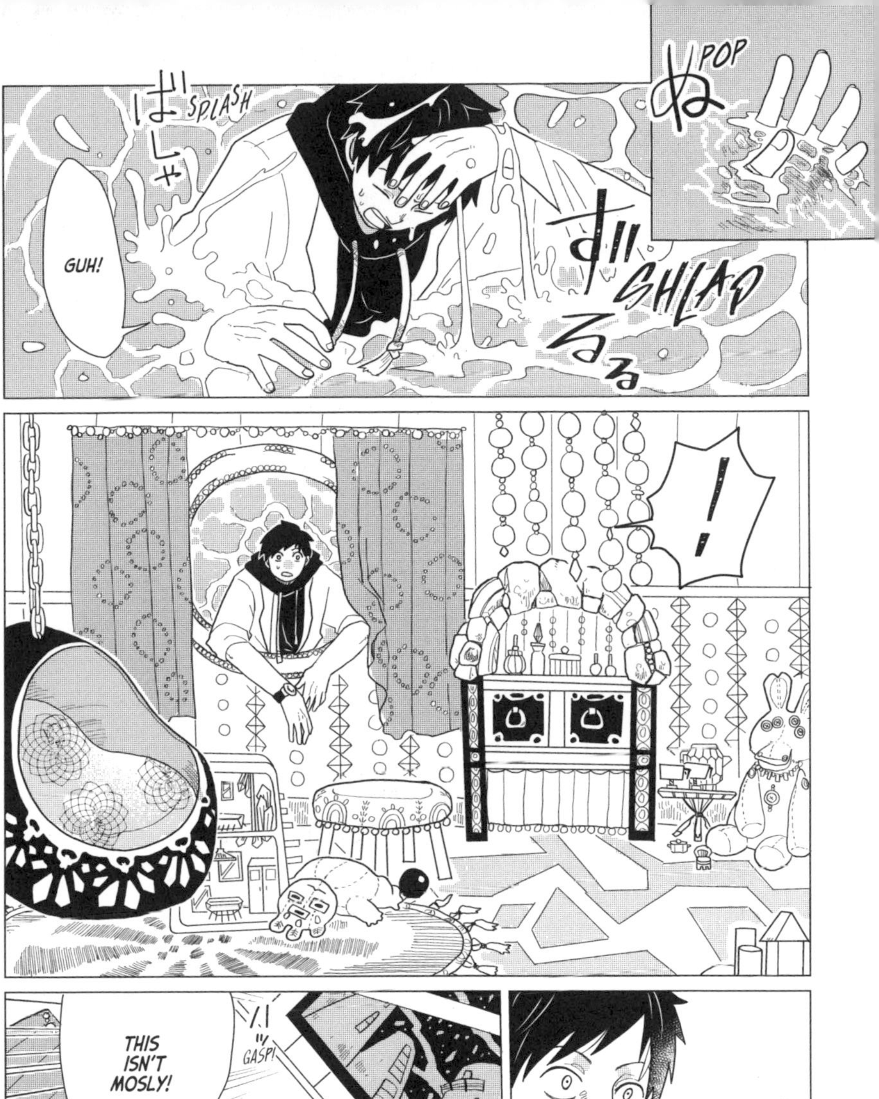
ぬ
POP
ぱしゃ
SPLASH
ずるる
SHLAP
GUH!
!
A KID'S ROOM?!
GASP!
THIS ISN'T MOSLY!

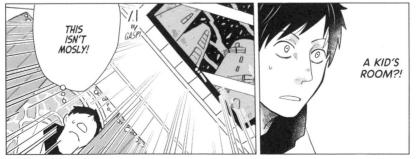

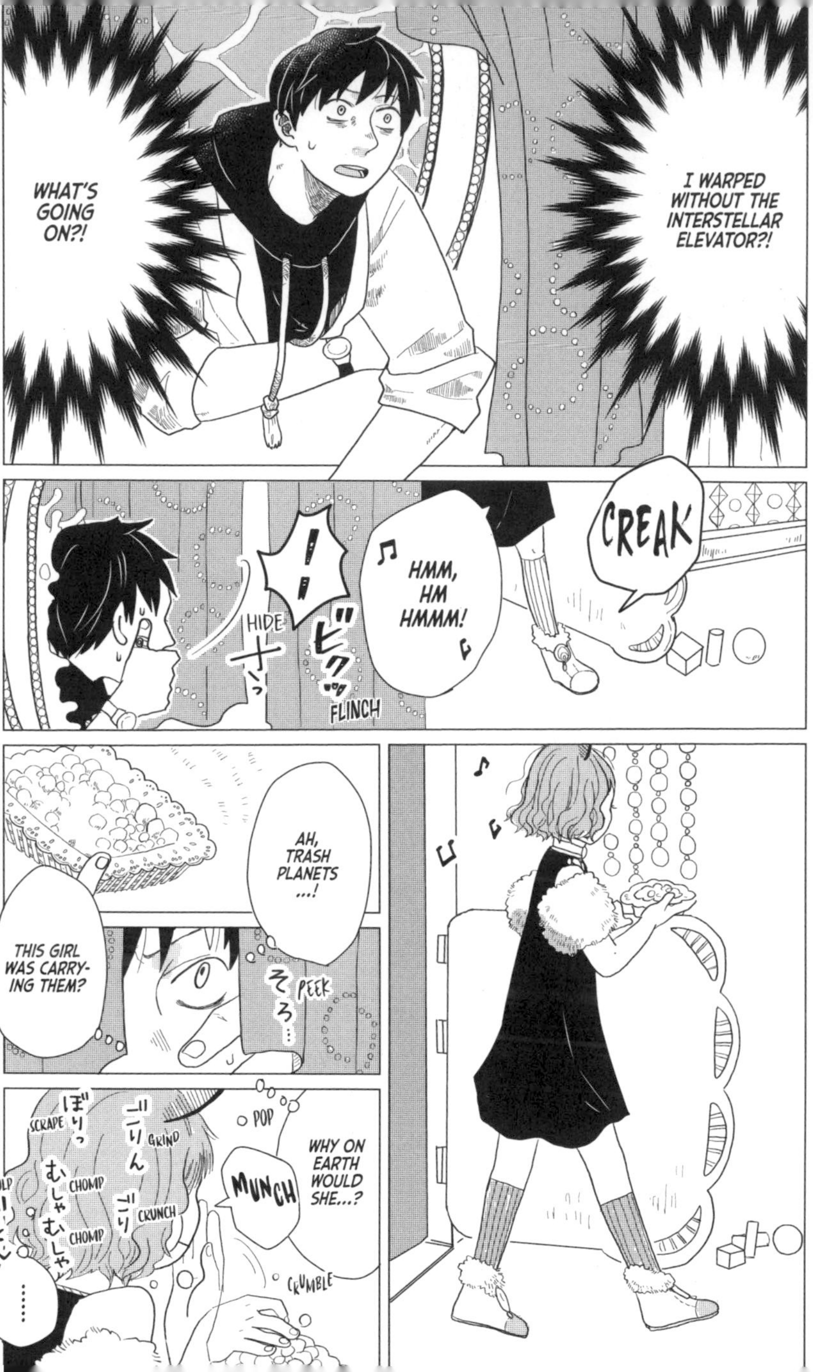
I WARPED WITHOUT THE INTERSTELLAR ELEVATOR?!
WHAT'S GOING ON?!
CREAK
HMM, HM HMMM!
!!
ビクッ
FLINCH
HIDE
サッ
AH, TRASH PLANETS...!
THIS GIRL WAS CARRYING THEM?
そろ…
PEEK
POP
WHY ON EARTH WOULD SHE...?
MUNCH
ごりん
GRIND
ぼりっ
SCRAPE
ごり
CRUNCH
むしゃむしゃ
CHOMP
CHOMP
ごくん
GULP
CRUMBLE
……

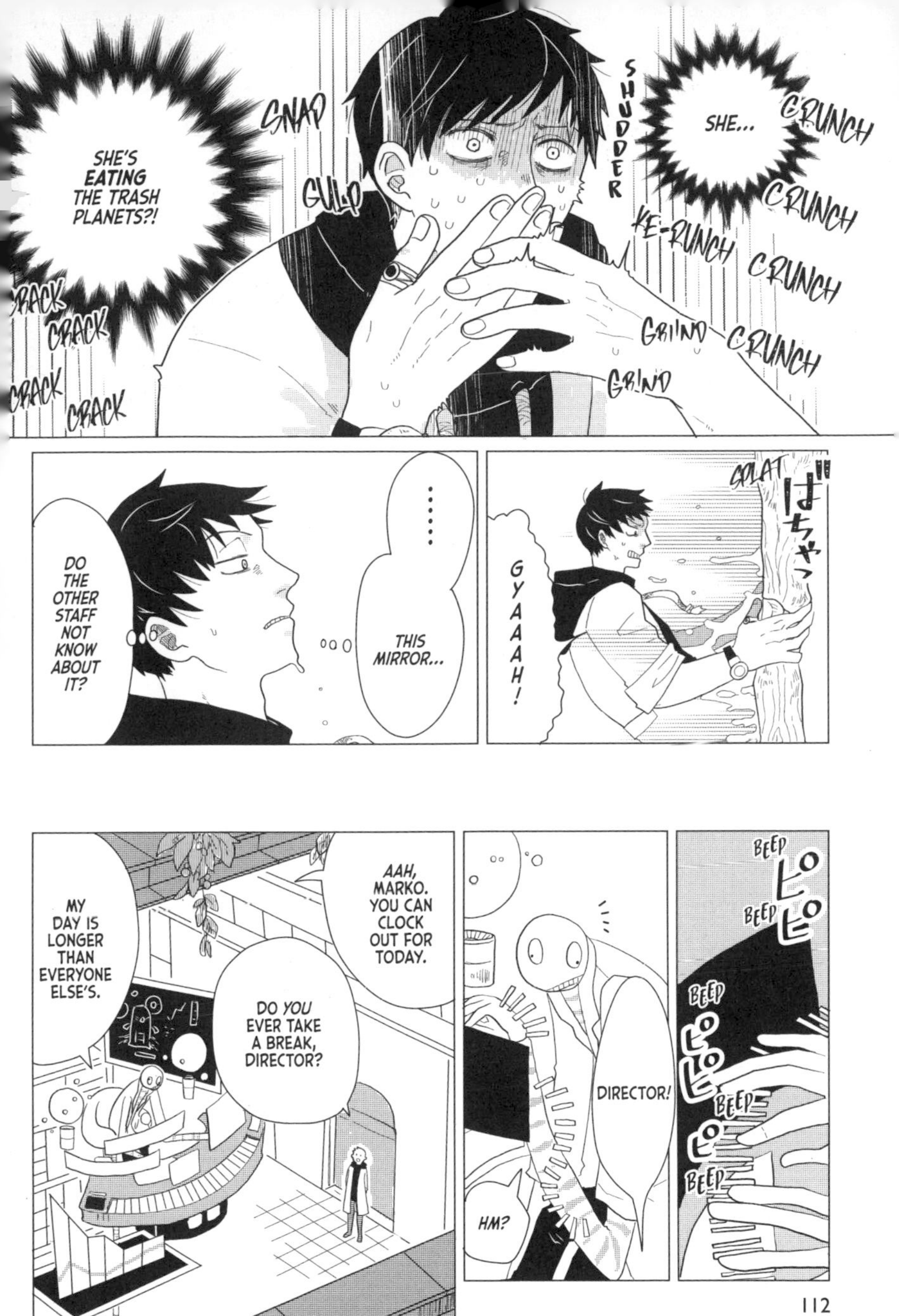
SHUDDER
SHE...
CRUNCH
CRUNCH
KE-RUNCH
CRUNCH
GRIND
CRUNCH
GRIND
SNAP
GULP
SHE'S EATING THE TRASH PLANETS?!
CRACK
CRACK
CRACK
CRACK
SPLAT
ばちゃっ
GYAAAAH!
......
THIS MIRROR...
DO THE OTHER STAFF NOT KNOW ABOUT IT?
BEEP
ピロ
BEEP
ピロ
BEEP
ピロピロ
BEEP
ピロ
BEEP
DIRECTOR!
HM?
AAH, MARKO. YOU CAN CLOCK OUT FOR TODAY.
DO *YOU* EVER TAKE A BREAK, DIRECTOR?
MY DAY IS LONGER THAN EVERYONE ELSE'S.

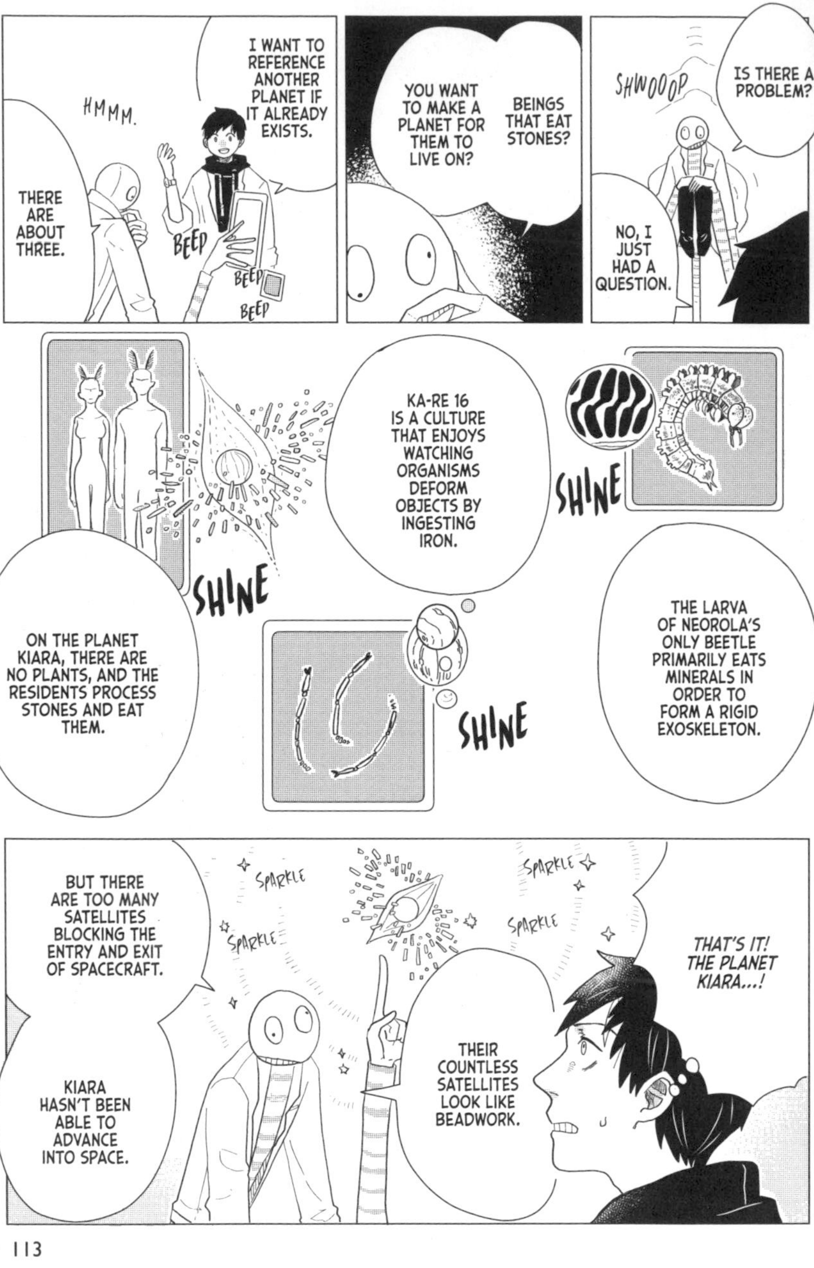

IS THERE A PROBLEM?
SHWOOOP
NO, I JUST HAD A QUESTION.
BEINGS THAT EAT STONES?
YOU WANT TO MAKE A PLANET FOR THEM TO LIVE ON?
I WANT TO REFERENCE ANOTHER PLANET IF IT ALREADY EXISTS.
HMMM.
BEEP
BEEP
BEEP
THERE ARE ABOUT THREE.
SHINE
THE LARVA OF NEOROLA'S ONLY BEETLE PRIMARILY EATS MINERALS IN ORDER TO FORM A RIGID EXOSKELETON.
KA-RE 16 IS A CULTURE THAT ENJOYS WATCHING ORGANISMS DEFORM OBJECTS BY INGESTING IRON.
SHINE
SHINE
ON THE PLANET KIARA, THERE ARE NO PLANTS, AND THE RESIDENTS PROCESS STONES AND EAT THEM.
THAT'S IT! THE PLANET KIARA...!
SPARKLE
SPARKLE
SPARKLE
SPARKLE
THEIR COUNTLESS SATELLITES LOOK LIKE BEADWORK.
BUT THERE ARE TOO MANY SATELLITES BLOCKING THE ENTRY AND EXIT OF SPACECRAFT.
KIARA HASN'T BEEN ABLE TO ADVANCE INTO SPACE.

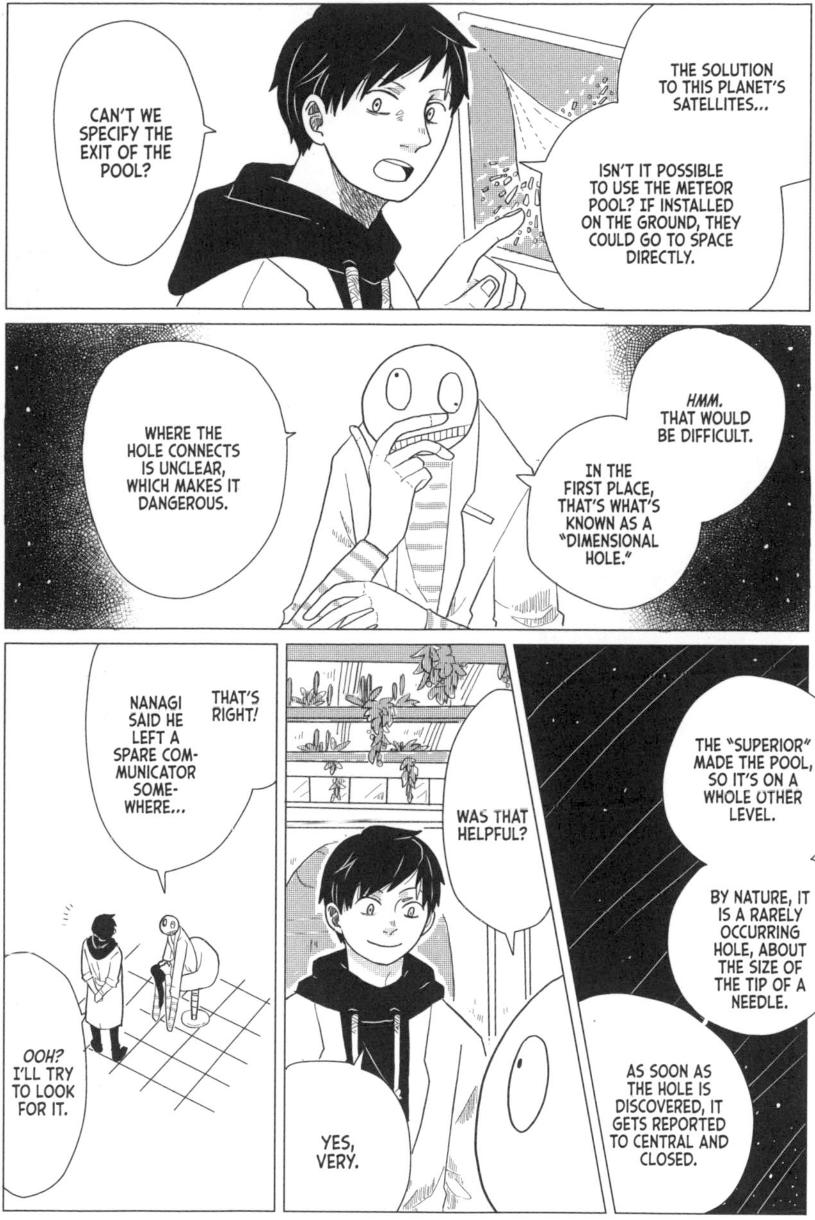
THE SOLUTION TO THIS PLANET'S SATELLITES...
ISN'T IT POSSIBLE TO USE THE METEOR POOL? IF INSTALLED ON THE GROUND, THEY COULD GO TO SPACE DIRECTLY.
CAN'T WE SPECIFY THE EXIT OF THE POOL?
HMM. THAT WOULD BE DIFFICULT.
IN THE FIRST PLACE, THAT'S WHAT'S KNOWN AS A "DIMENSIONAL HOLE."
WHERE THE HOLE CONNECTS IS UNCLEAR, WHICH MAKES IT DANGEROUS.
THE "SUPERIOR" MADE THE POOL, SO IT'S ON A WHOLE OTHER LEVEL.
BY NATURE, IT IS A RARELY OCCURRING HOLE, ABOUT THE SIZE OF THE TIP OF A NEEDLE.
AS SOON AS THE HOLE IS DISCOVERED, IT GETS REPORTED TO CENTRAL AND CLOSED.
WAS THAT HELPFUL?
YES, VERY.
THAT'S RIGHT!
NANAGI SAID HE LEFT A SPARE COM-MUNICATOR SOME-WHERE...
OOH? I'LL TRY TO LOOK FOR IT.

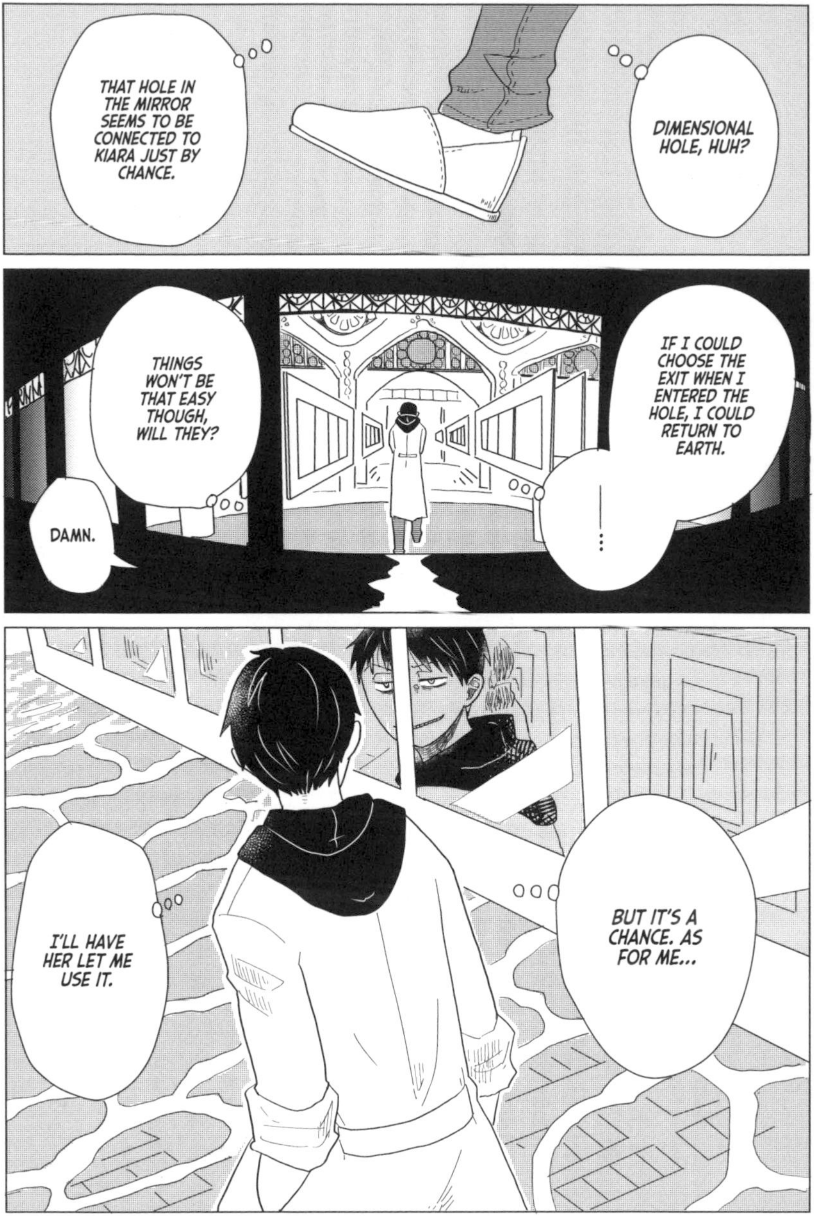
DIMENSIONAL HOLE, HUH?
THAT HOLE IN THE MIRROR SEEMS TO BE CONNECTED TO KIARA JUST BY CHANCE.
IF I COULD CHOOSE THE EXIT WHEN I ENTERED THE HOLE, I COULD RETURN TO EARTH.
...
THINGS WON'T BE THAT EASY THOUGH, WILL THEY?
DAMN.
BUT IT'S A CHANCE. AS FOR ME...
I'LL HAVE HER LET ME USE IT.

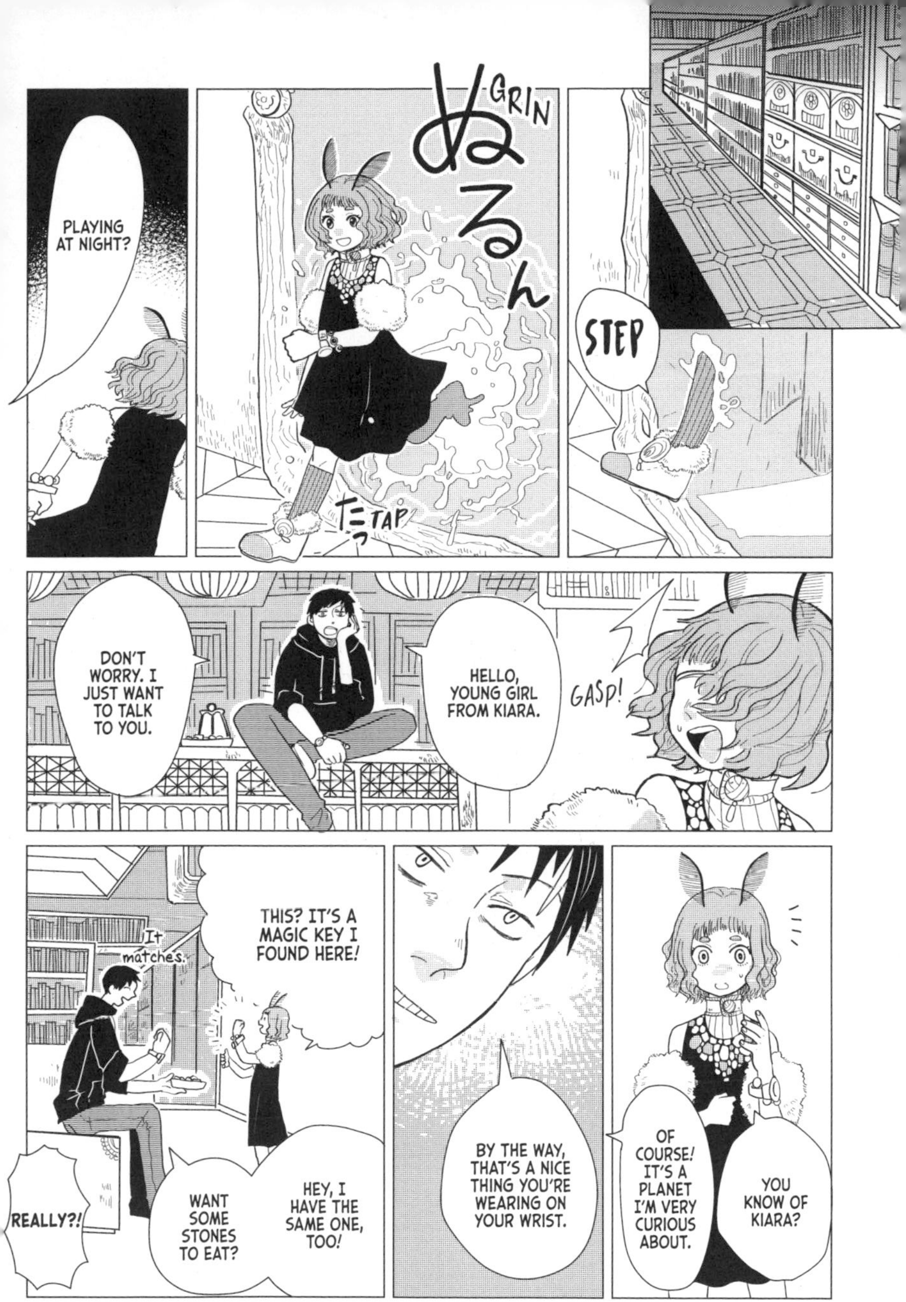
STEP
ぬるん
GRIN
たっ TAP
PLAYING AT NIGHT?
GASP!
HELLO, YOUNG GIRL FROM KIARA.
DON'T WORRY. I JUST WANT TO TALK TO YOU.
YOU KNOW OF KIARA?
OF COURSE! IT'S A PLANET I'M VERY CURIOUS ABOUT.
BY THE WAY, THAT'S A NICE THING YOU'RE WEARING ON YOUR WRIST.
THIS? IT'S A MAGIC KEY I FOUND HERE!
It matches.
HEY, I HAVE THE SAME ONE, TOO!
WANT SOME STONES TO EAT?
REALLY?!

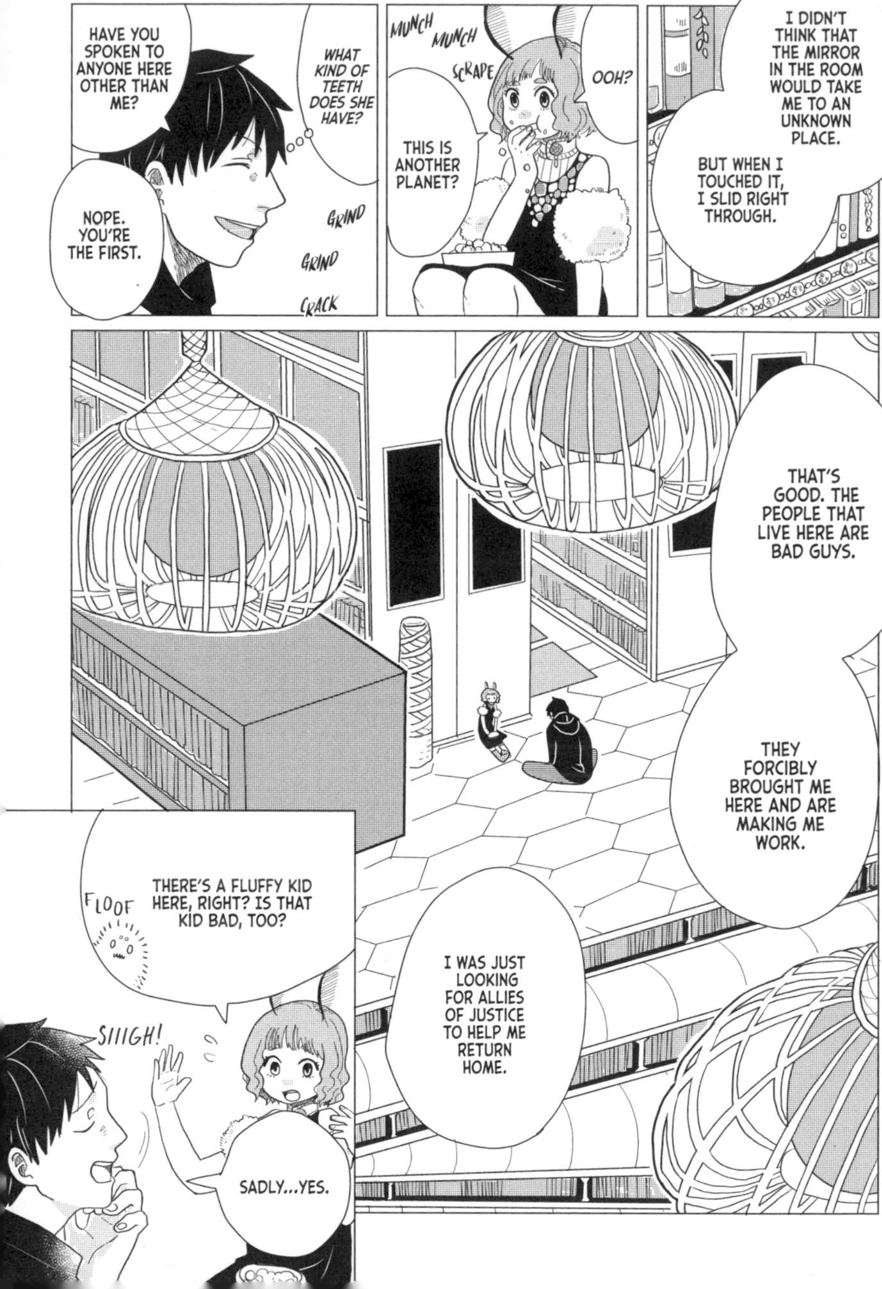
I DIDN'T THINK THAT THE MIRROR IN THE ROOM WOULD TAKE ME TO AN UNKNOWN PLACE.
BUT WHEN I TOUCHED IT, I SLID RIGHT THROUGH.
MUNCH MUNCH
SCRAPE
OOH?
THIS IS ANOTHER PLANET?
WHAT KIND OF TEETH DOES SHE HAVE?
HAVE YOU SPOKEN TO ANYONE HERE OTHER THAN ME?
NOPE. YOU'RE THE FIRST.
GRIND
GRIND
CRACK
THAT'S GOOD. THE PEOPLE THAT LIVE HERE ARE BAD GUYS.
THEY FORCIBLY BROUGHT ME HERE AND ARE MAKING ME WORK.
I WAS JUST LOOKING FOR ALLIES OF JUSTICE TO HELP ME RETURN HOME.
THERE'S A FLUFFY KID HERE, RIGHT? IS THAT KID BAD, TOO?
FLOOF
SIIIGH!
SADLY...YES.

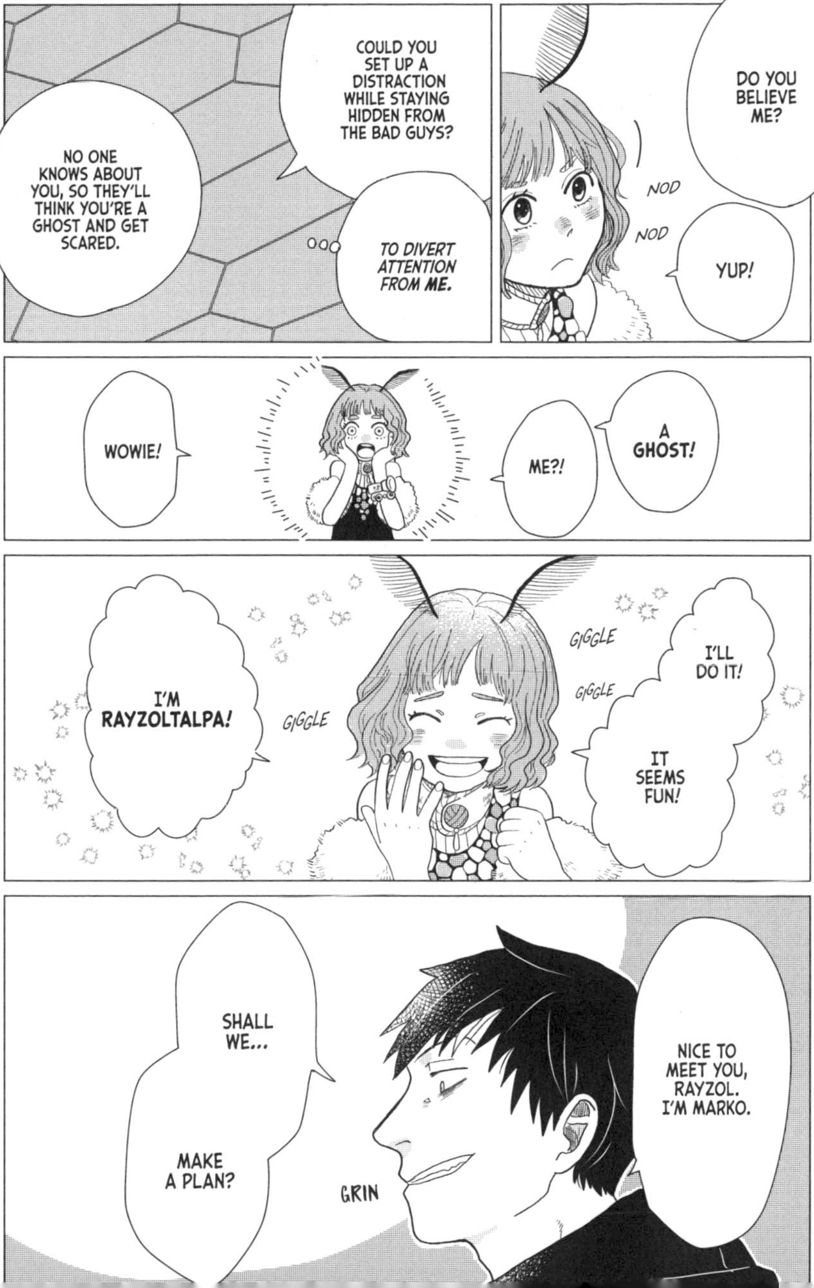
DO YOU BELIEVE ME?
NOD
NOD
YUP!
COULD YOU SET UP A DISTRACTION WHILE STAYING HIDDEN FROM THE BAD GUYS?
TO DIVERT ATTENTION FROM ME.
NO ONE KNOWS ABOUT YOU, SO THEY'LL THINK YOU'RE A GHOST AND GET SCARED.
A GHOST!
ME?!
WOWIE!
I'LL DO IT!
IT SEEMS FUN!
GIGGLE
GIGGLE
GIGGLE
I'M RAYZOLTALPA!
NICE TO MEET YOU, RAYZOL. I'M MARKO.
GRIN
SHALL WE...
MAKE A PLAN?

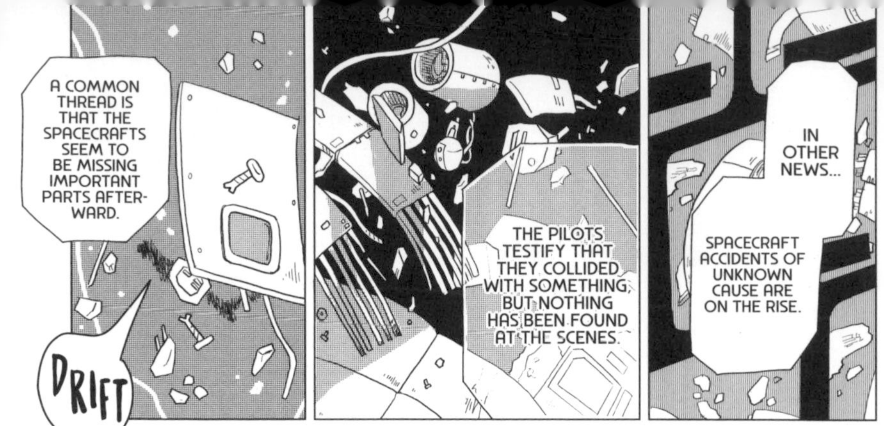
IN OTHER NEWS...
SPACECRAFT ACCIDENTS OF UNKNOWN CAUSE ARE ON THE RISE.
THE PILOTS TESTIFY THAT THEY COLLIDED WITH SOMETHING, BUT NOTHING HAS BEEN FOUND AT THE SCENES.
A COMMON THREAD IS THAT THE SPACECRAFTS SEEM TO BE MISSING IMPORTANT PARTS AFTERWARD.
DRIFT

Episode 7: Escape ①

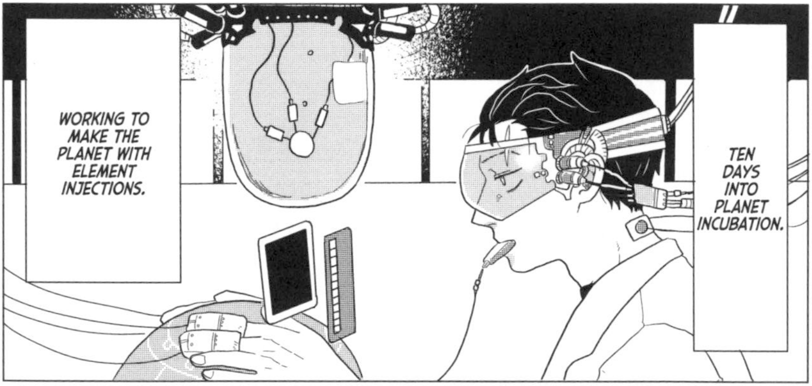
TEN DAYS INTO PLANET INCUBATION.
WORKING TO MAKE THE PLANET WITH ELEMENT INJECTIONS.

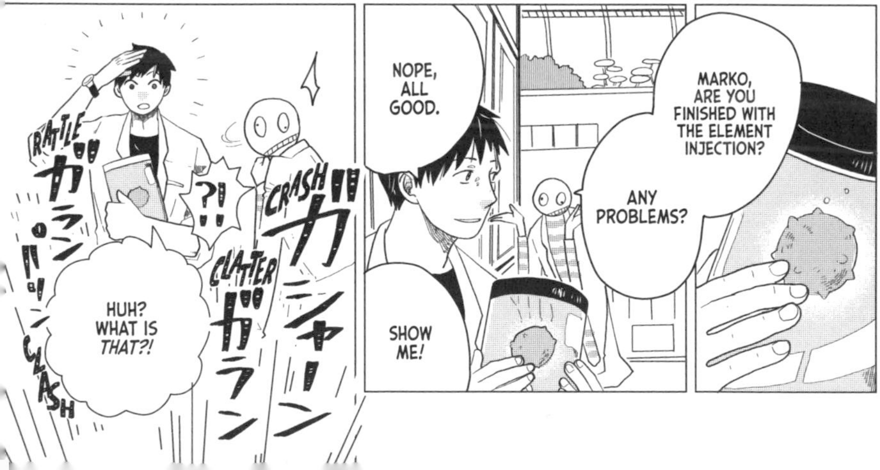
MARKO, ARE YOU FINISHED WITH THE ELEMENT INJECTION?
ANY PROBLEMS?
NOPE, ALL GOOD.
SHOW ME!
CRASH カシャーン
CLATTER ガラン
?!
RATTLE カラン
HUH? WHAT IS THAT?!
パリーン
CLASH

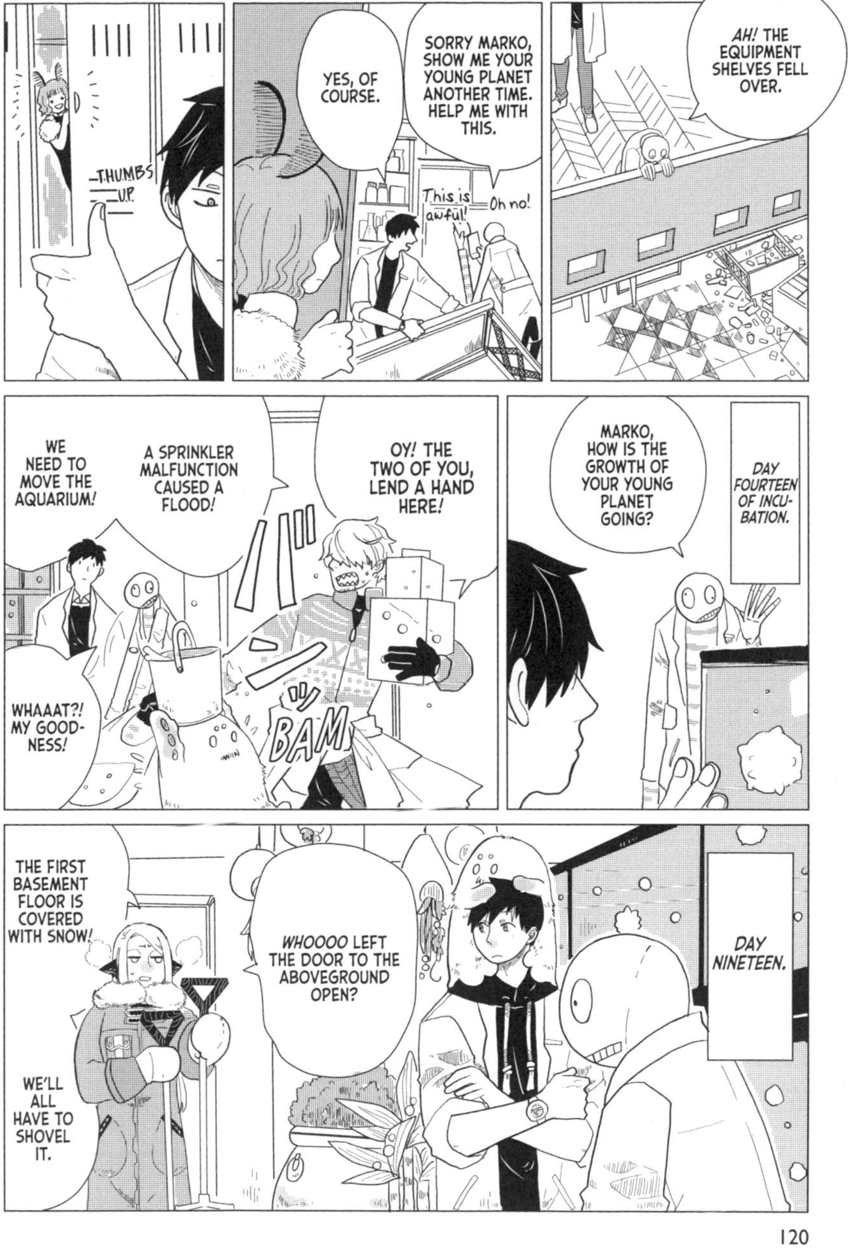
AH! THE EQUIPMENT SHELVES FELL OVER.
SORRY MARKO, SHOW ME YOUR YOUNG PLANET ANOTHER TIME. HELP ME WITH THIS.
YES, OF COURSE.
Oh no!
This is awful!
THUMBS UP
DAY FOURTEEN OF INCU-BATION.
MARKO, HOW IS THE GROWTH OF YOUR YOUNG PLANET GOING?
OY! THE TWO OF YOU, LEND A HAND HERE!
A SPRINKLER MALFUNCTION CAUSED A FLOOD!
WE NEED TO MOVE THE AQUARIUM!
BAM
WHAAAT?! MY GOOD-NESS!
DAY NINETEEN.
WHOOOO LEFT THE DOOR TO THE ABOVEGROUND OPEN?
THE FIRST BASEMENT FLOOR IS COVERED WITH SNOW!
WE'LL ALL HAVE TO SHOVEL IT.

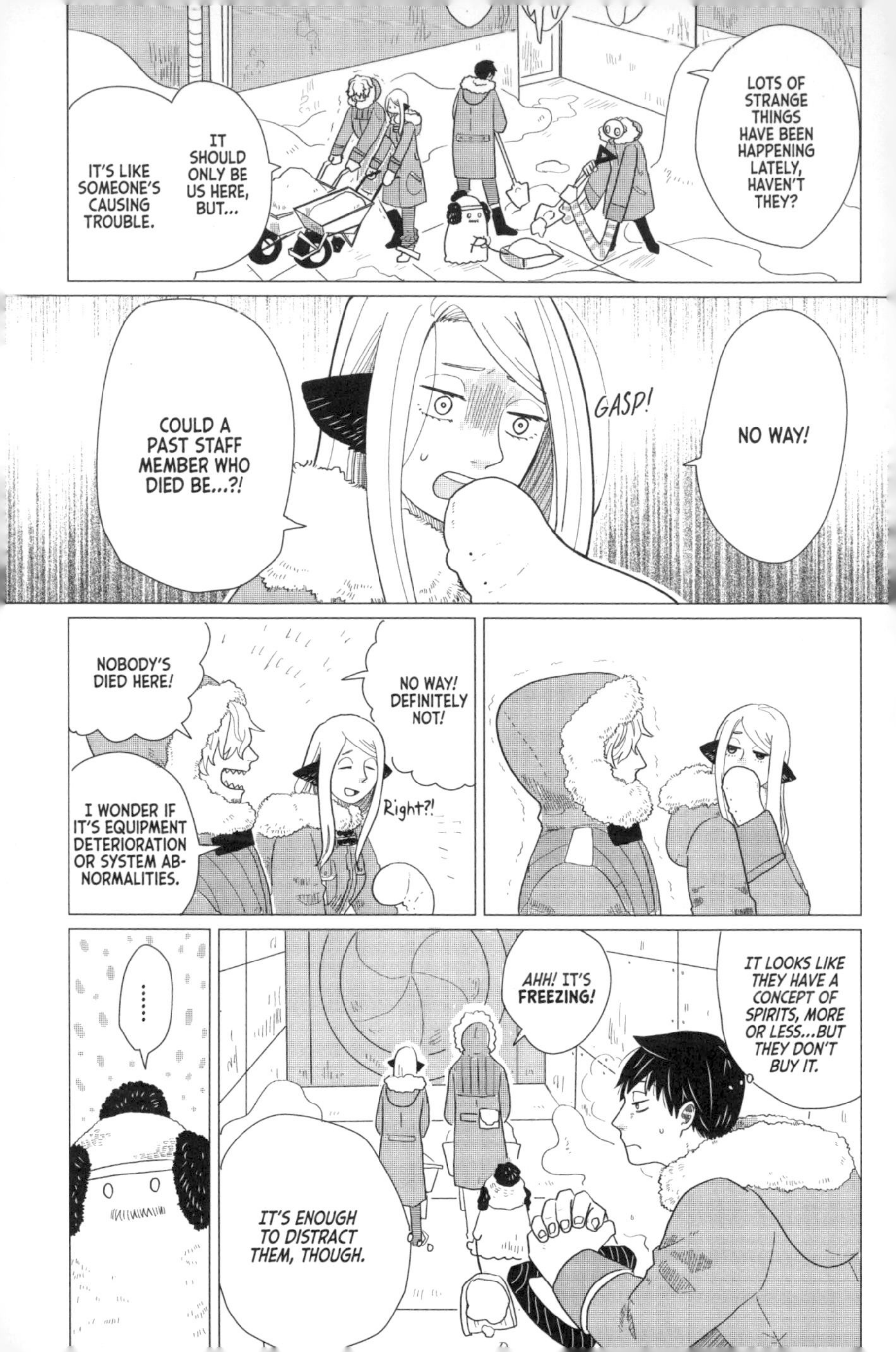
LOTS OF STRANGE THINGS HAVE BEEN HAPPENING LATELY, HAVEN'T THEY?
IT SHOULD ONLY BE US HERE, BUT...
IT'S LIKE SOMEONE'S CAUSING TROUBLE.
NO WAY!
GASP!
COULD A PAST STAFF MEMBER WHO DIED BE...?!
NO WAY! DEFINITELY NOT!
NOBODY'S DIED HERE!
Right?!
I WONDER IF IT'S EQUIPMENT DETERIORATION OR SYSTEM AB-NORMALITIES.
IT LOOKS LIKE THEY HAVE A CONCEPT OF SPIRITS, MORE OR LESS...BUT THEY DON'T BUY IT.
AHH! IT'S FREEZING!
IT'S ENOUGH TO DISTRACT THEM, THOUGH.
......

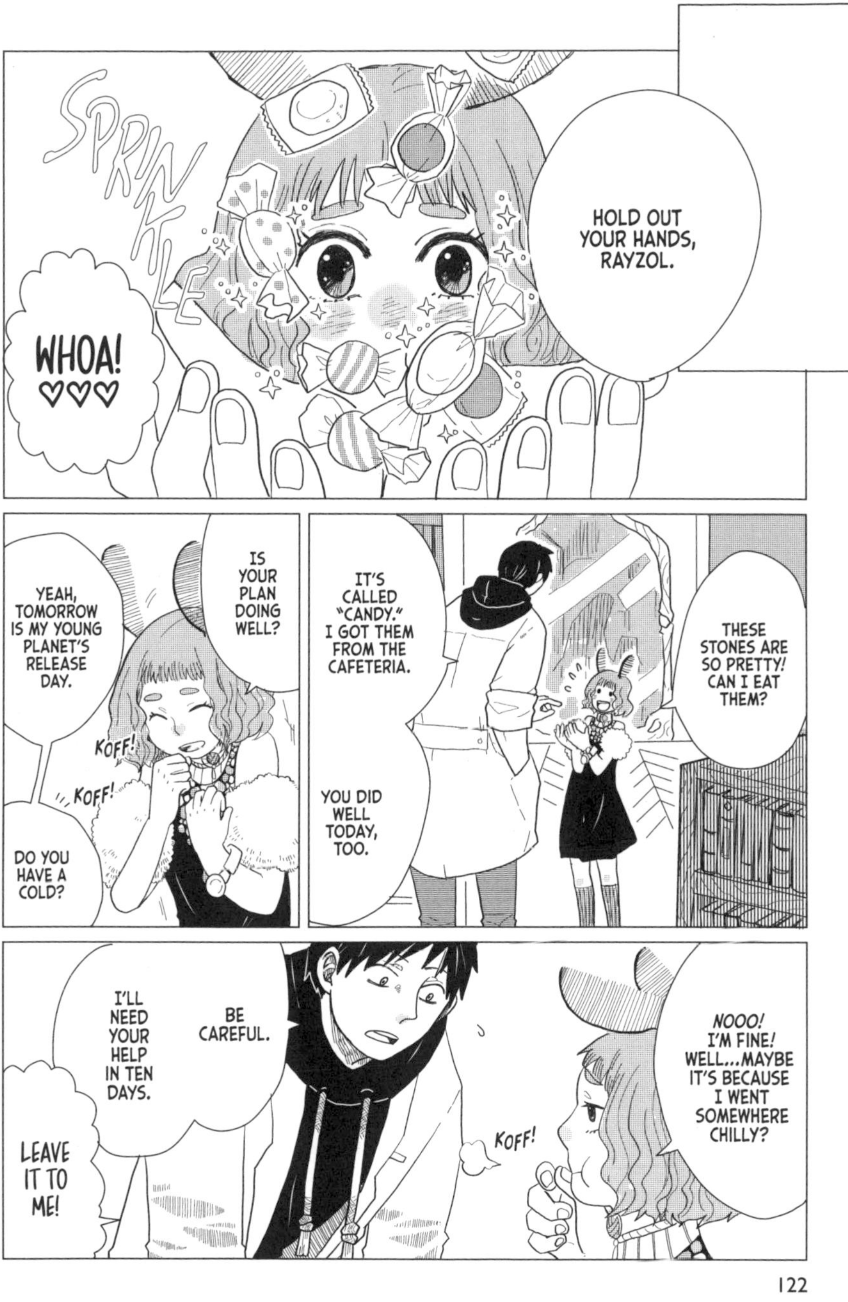
HOLD OUT YOUR HANDS, RAYZOL.
SPRINKLE
WHOA! ♡♡♡
THESE STONES ARE SO PRETTY! CAN I EAT THEM?
IT'S CALLED "CANDY." I GOT THEM FROM THE CAFETERIA.
YOU DID WELL TODAY, TOO.
IS YOUR PLAN DOING WELL?
YEAH, TOMORROW IS MY YOUNG PLANET'S RELEASE DAY.
KOFF!
KOFF!
DO YOU HAVE A COLD?
NOOO! I'M FINE! WELL...MAYBE IT'S BECAUSE I WENT SOMEWHERE CHILLY?
KOFF!
BE CAREFUL.
I'LL NEED YOUR HELP IN TEN DAYS.
LEAVE IT TO ME!

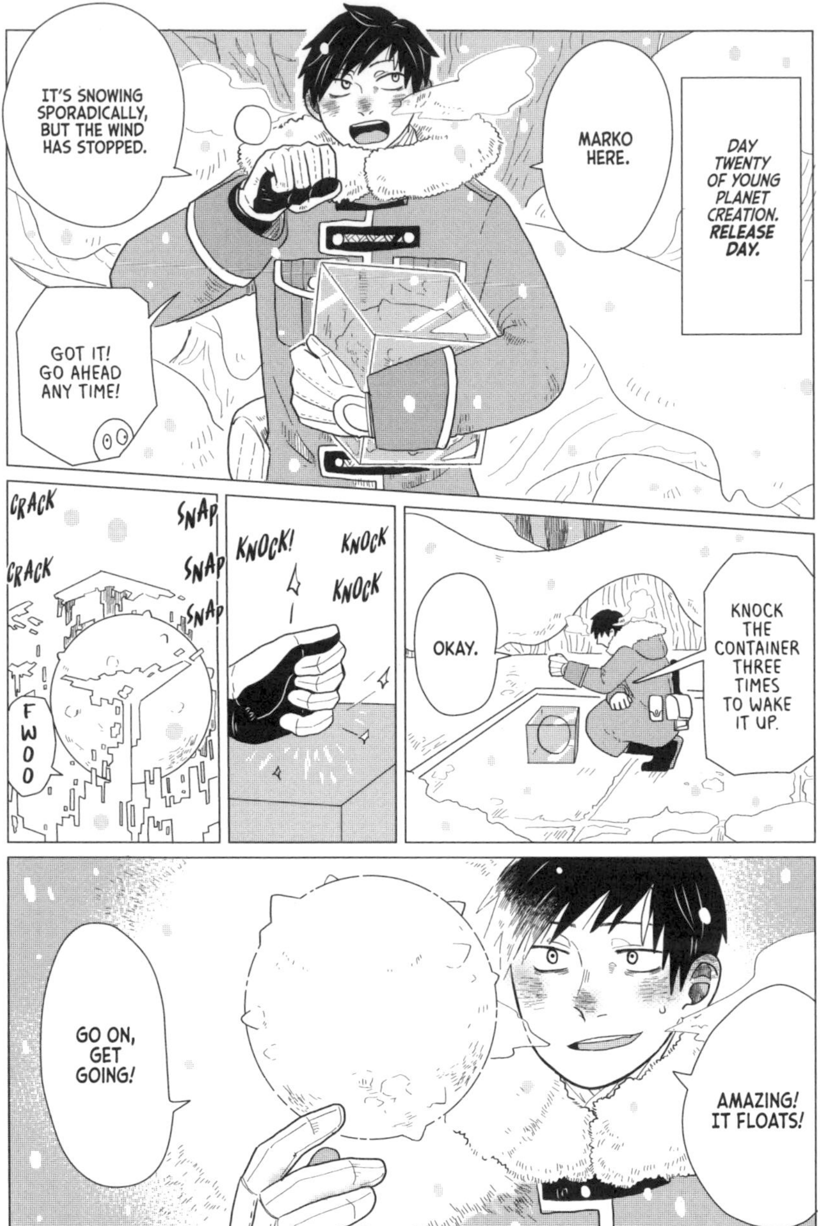
DAY TWENTY OF YOUNG PLANET CREATION. RELEASE DAY.
MARKO HERE.
IT'S SNOWING SPORADICALLY, BUT THE WIND HAS STOPPED.
GOT IT! GO AHEAD ANY TIME!
KNOCK THE CONTAINER THREE TIMES TO WAKE IT UP.
OKAY.
KNOCK!
KNOCK
KNOCK
SNAP
SNAP
SNAP
CRACK
CRACK
FWOO
AMAZING! IT FLOATS!
GO ON, GET GOING!

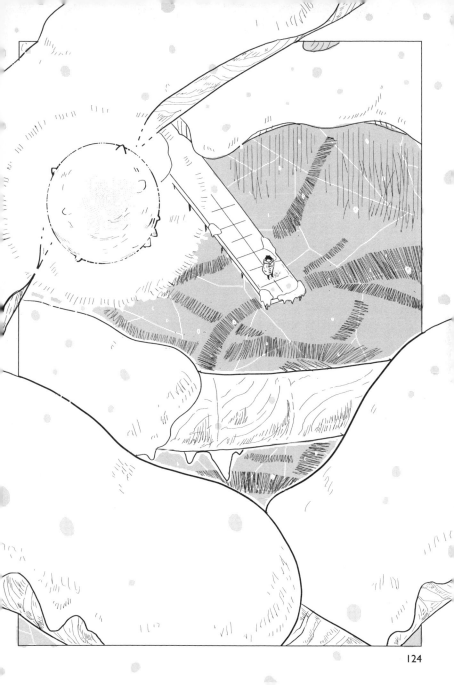

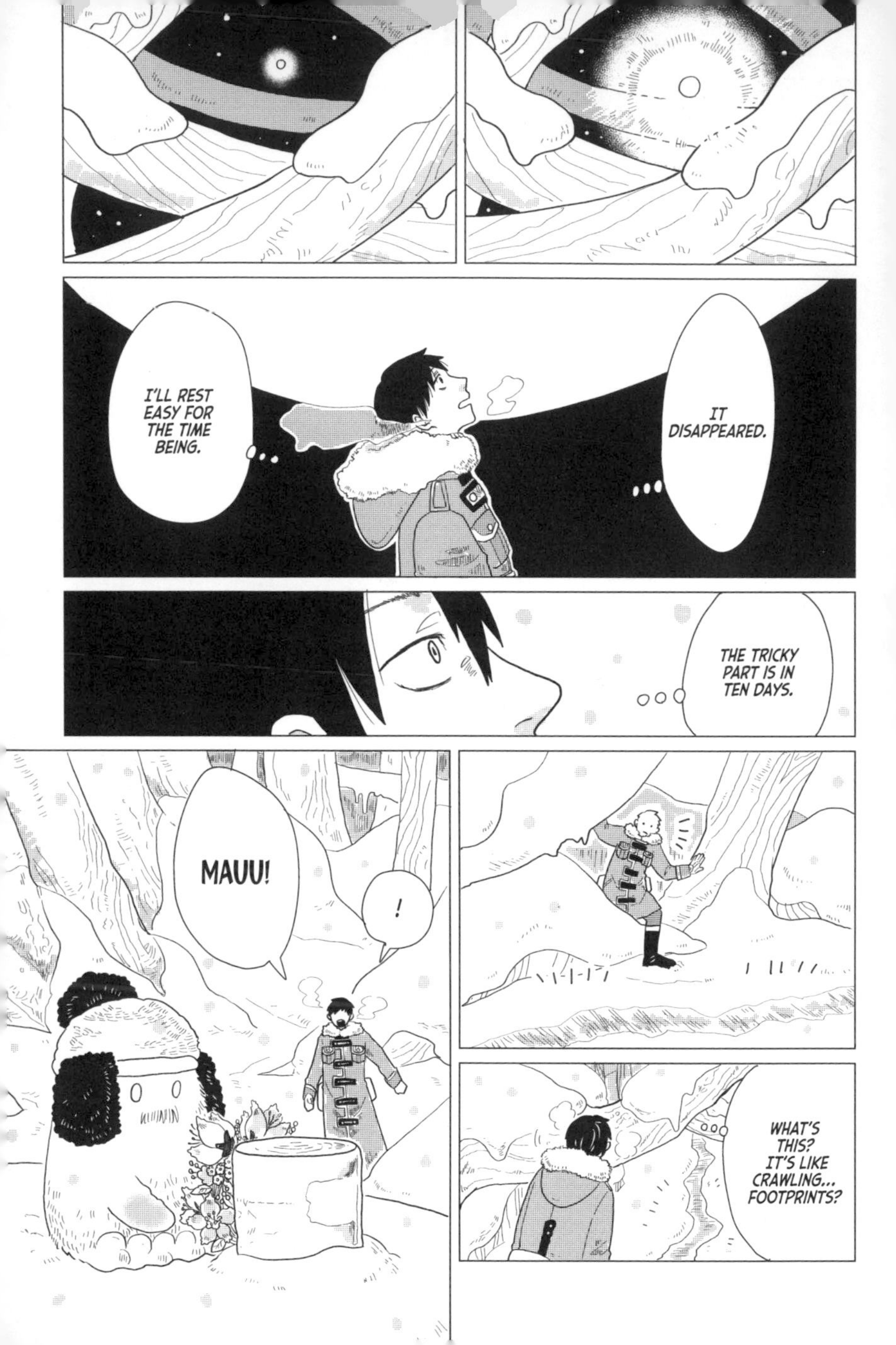

IT DISAPPEARED.
I'LL REST EASY FOR THE TIME BEING.
THE TRICKY PART IS IN TEN DAYS.
WHAT'S THIS? IT'S LIKE CRAWLING... FOOTPRINTS?
MAUU!
!

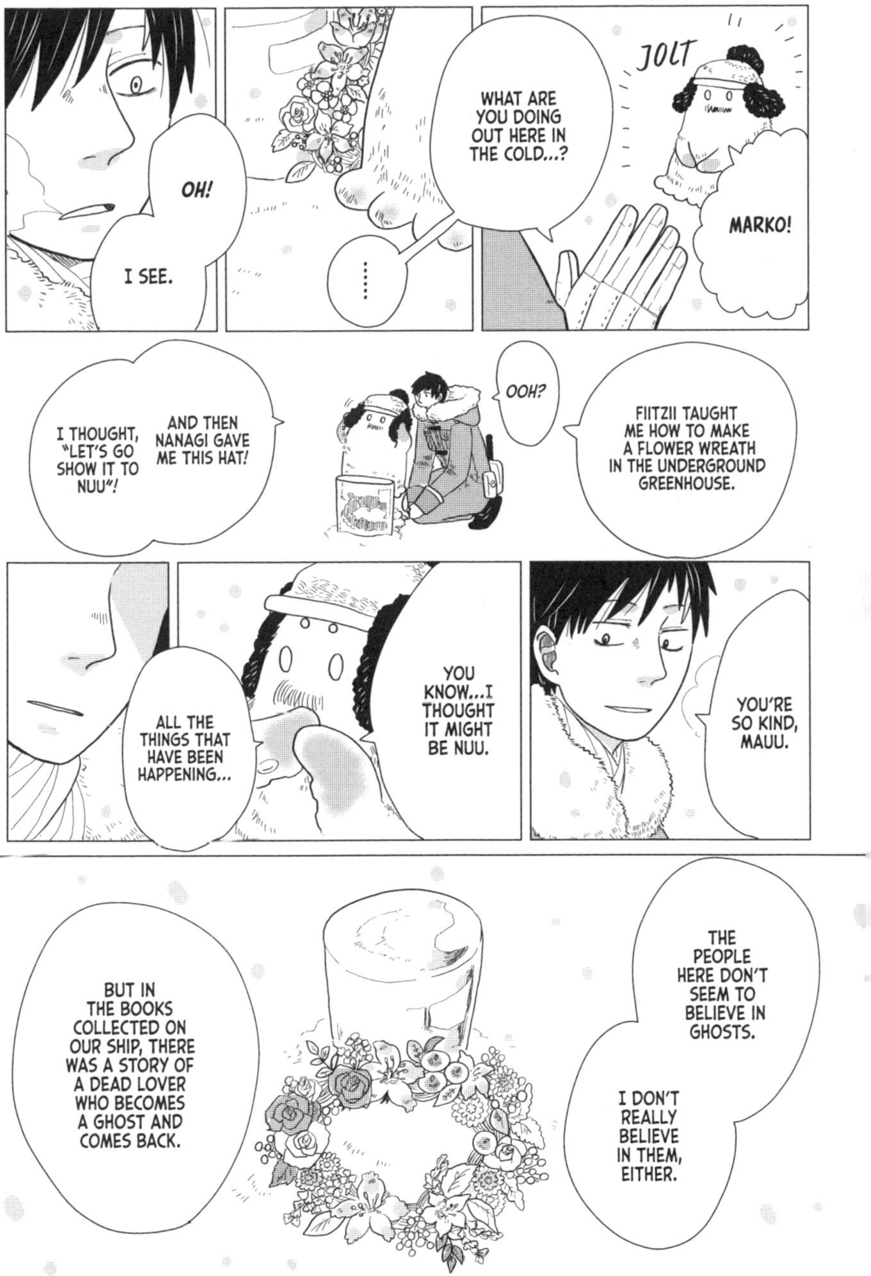
JOLT
MARKO!
WHAT ARE YOU DOING OUT HERE IN THE COLD...?
......
OH!
I SEE.
FIITZII TAUGHT ME HOW TO MAKE A FLOWER WREATH IN THE UNDERGROUND GREENHOUSE.
OOH?
AND THEN NANAGI GAVE ME THIS HAT!
I THOUGHT, "LET'S GO SHOW IT TO NUU"!
YOU'RE SO KIND, MAUU.
YOU KNOW...I THOUGHT IT MIGHT BE NUU.
ALL THE THINGS THAT HAVE BEEN HAPPENING...
THE PEOPLE HERE DON'T SEEM TO BELIEVE IN GHOSTS.
I DON'T REALLY BELIEVE IN THEM, EITHER.
BUT IN THE BOOKS COLLECTED ON OUR SHIP, THERE WAS A STORY OF A DEAD LOVER WHO BECOMES A GHOST AND COMES BACK.

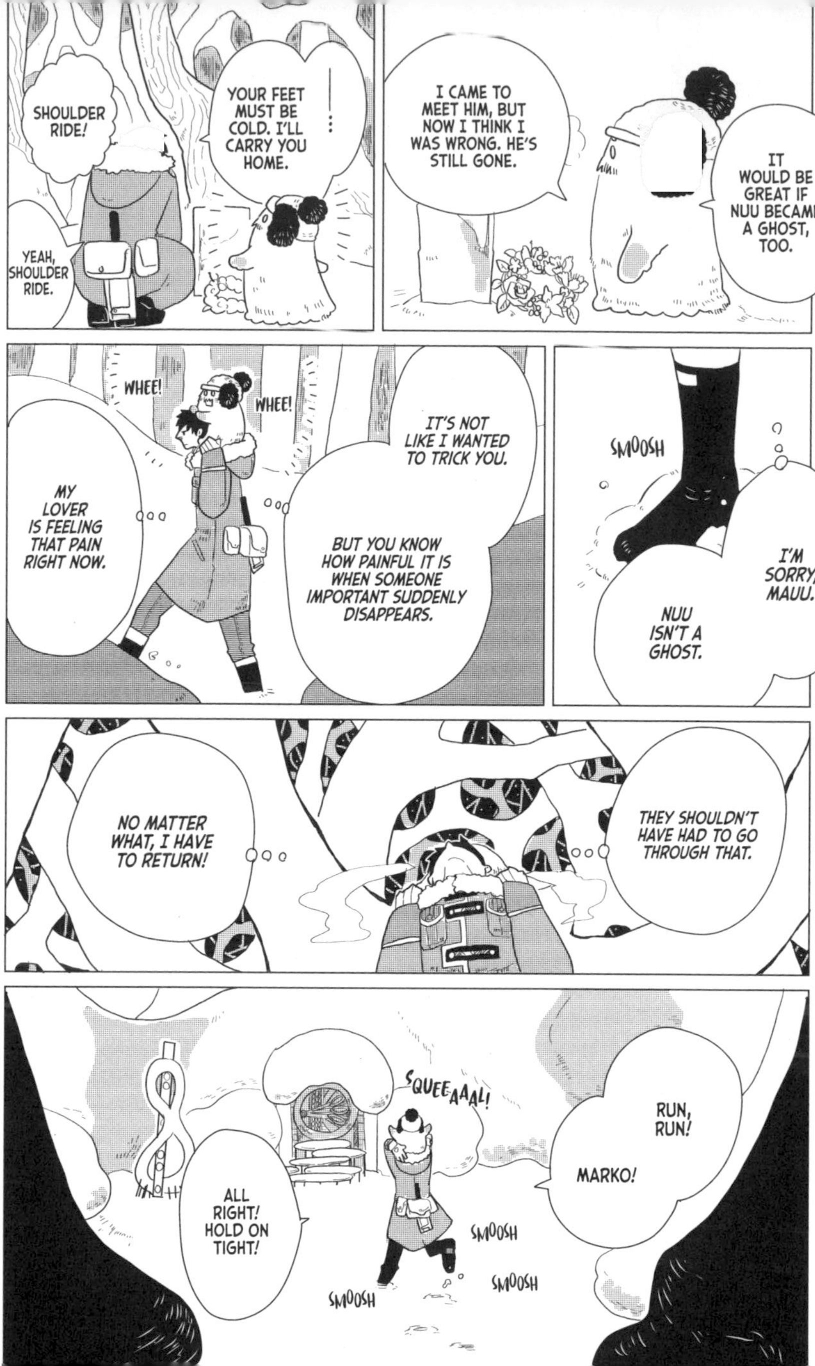
IT WOULD BE GREAT IF NUU BECAME A GHOST, TOO.
I CAME TO MEET HIM, BUT NOW I THINK I WAS WRONG. HE'S STILL GONE.
……
YOUR FEET MUST BE COLD. I'LL CARRY YOU HOME.
SHOULDER RIDE!
YEAH, SHOULDER RIDE.
SMOOSH
I'M SORRY, MAUU.
NUU ISN'T A GHOST.
WHEE!
WHEE!
IT'S NOT LIKE I WANTED TO TRICK YOU.
BUT YOU KNOW HOW PAINFUL IT IS WHEN SOMEONE IMPORTANT SUDDENLY DISAPPEARS.
MY LOVER IS FEELING THAT PAIN RIGHT NOW.
THEY SHOULDN'T HAVE HAD TO GO THROUGH THAT.
NO MATTER WHAT, I HAVE TO RETURN!
RUN, RUN!
MARKO!
SQUEEAAAL!
ALL RIGHT! HOLD ON TIGHT!
SMOOSH
SMOOSH
SMOOSH

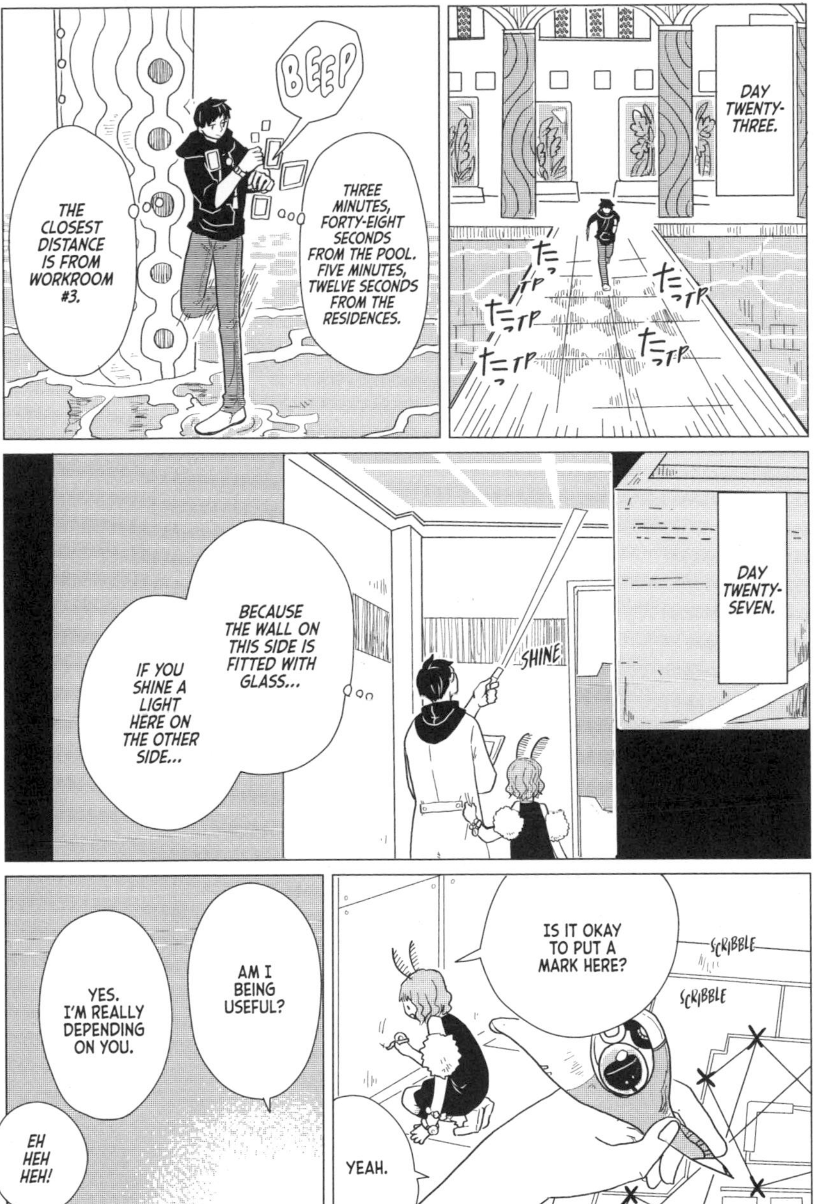
DAY TWENTY-THREE.
たっTP
たっTP
たっTP
たっTP
たっTP
BEEP
THREE MINUTES, FORTY-EIGHT SECONDS FROM THE POOL. FIVE MINUTES, TWELVE SECONDS FROM THE RESIDENCES.
THE CLOSEST DISTANCE IS FROM WORKROOM #3.
DAY TWENTY-SEVEN.
SHINE
BECAUSE THE WALL ON THIS SIDE IS FITTED WITH GLASS...
IF YOU SHINE A LIGHT HERE ON THE OTHER SIDE...
IS IT OKAY TO PUT A MARK HERE?
SCRIBBLE
SCRIBBLE
YEAH.
AM I BEING USEFUL?
YES. I'M REALLY DEPENDING ON YOU.
EH HEH HEH!

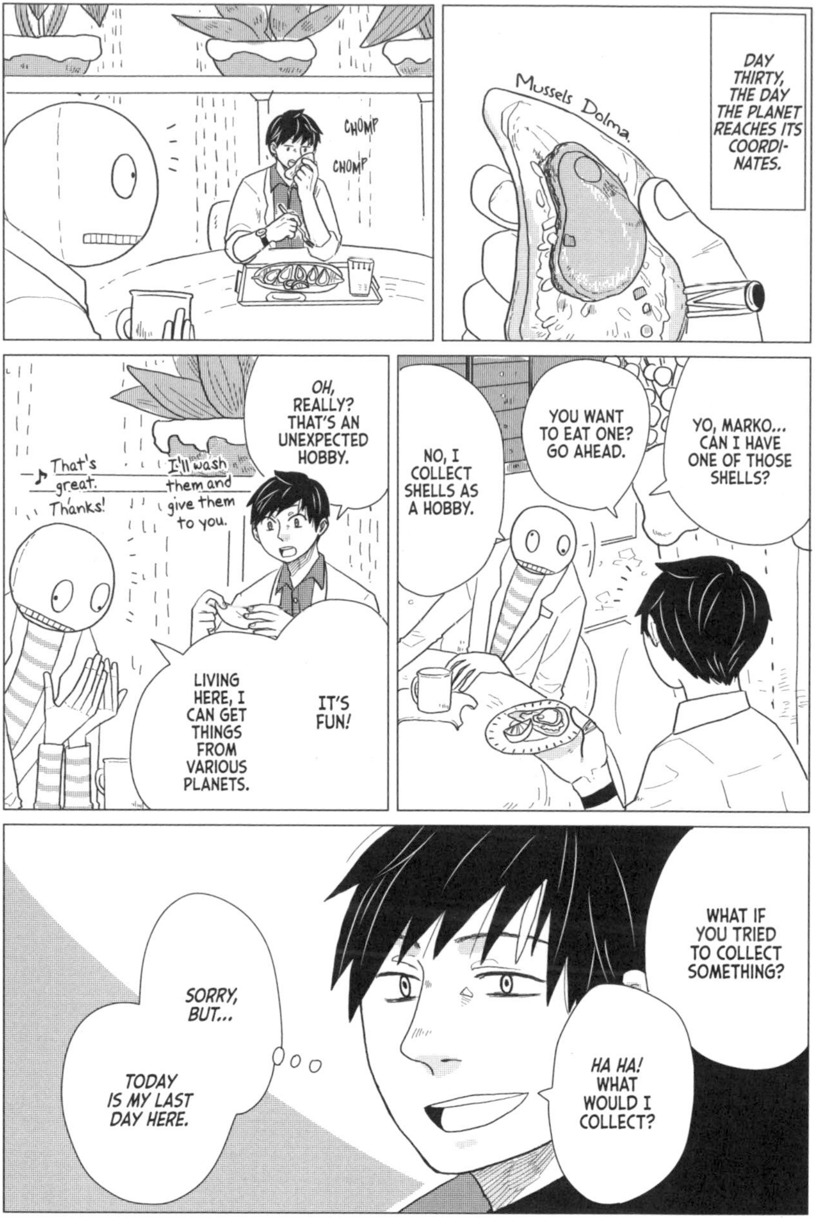
DAY THIRTY, THE DAY THE PLANET REACHES ITS COORDINATES.
Mussels Dolma.
CHOMP
CHOMP
YO, MARKO... CAN I HAVE ONE OF THOSE SHELLS?
YOU WANT TO EAT ONE? GO AHEAD.
NO, I COLLECT SHELLS AS A HOBBY.
OH, REALLY? THAT'S AN UNEXPECTED HOBBY.
I'll wash them and give them to you.
That's great. Thanks!
IT'S FUN!
LIVING HERE, I CAN GET THINGS FROM VARIOUS PLANETS.
WHAT IF YOU TRIED TO COLLECT SOMETHING?
HA HA! WHAT WOULD I COLLECT?
SORRY, BUT...
TODAY IS MY LAST DAY HERE.

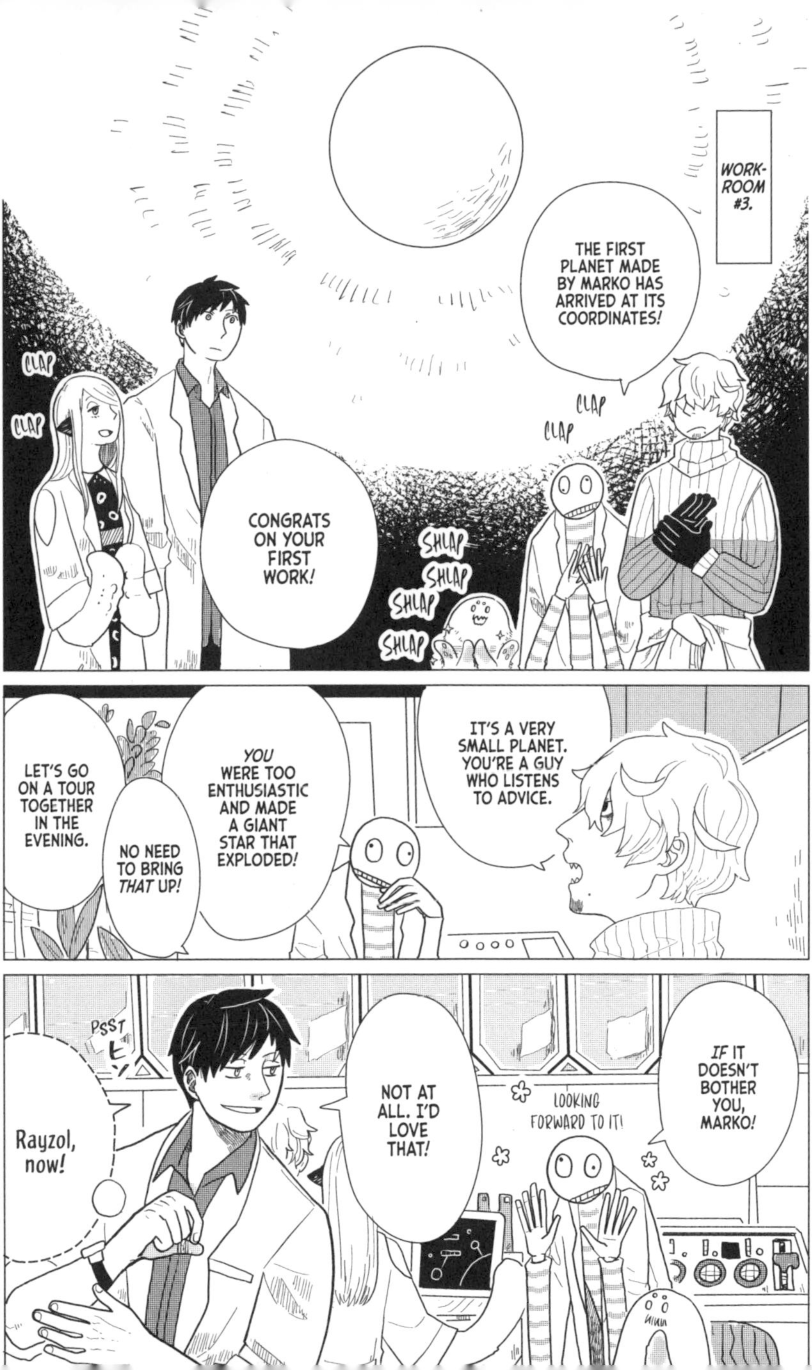
WORK-ROOM #3.
THE FIRST PLANET MADE BY MARKO HAS ARRIVED AT ITS COORDINATES!
CLAP
CLAP
CONGRATS ON YOUR FIRST WORK!
SHLAP
SHLAP
SHLAP
SHLAP
CLAP
CLAP
IT'S A VERY SMALL PLANET. YOU'RE A GUY WHO LISTENS TO ADVICE.
YOU WERE TOO ENTHUSIASTIC AND MADE A GIANT STAR THAT EXPLODED!
NO NEED TO BRING *THAT* UP!
LET'S GO ON A TOUR TOGETHER IN THE EVENING.
IF IT DOESN'T BOTHER YOU, MARKO!
LOOKING FORWARD TO IT!
NOT AT ALL. I'D LOVE THAT!
PSST ヒソ
Rayzol, now!

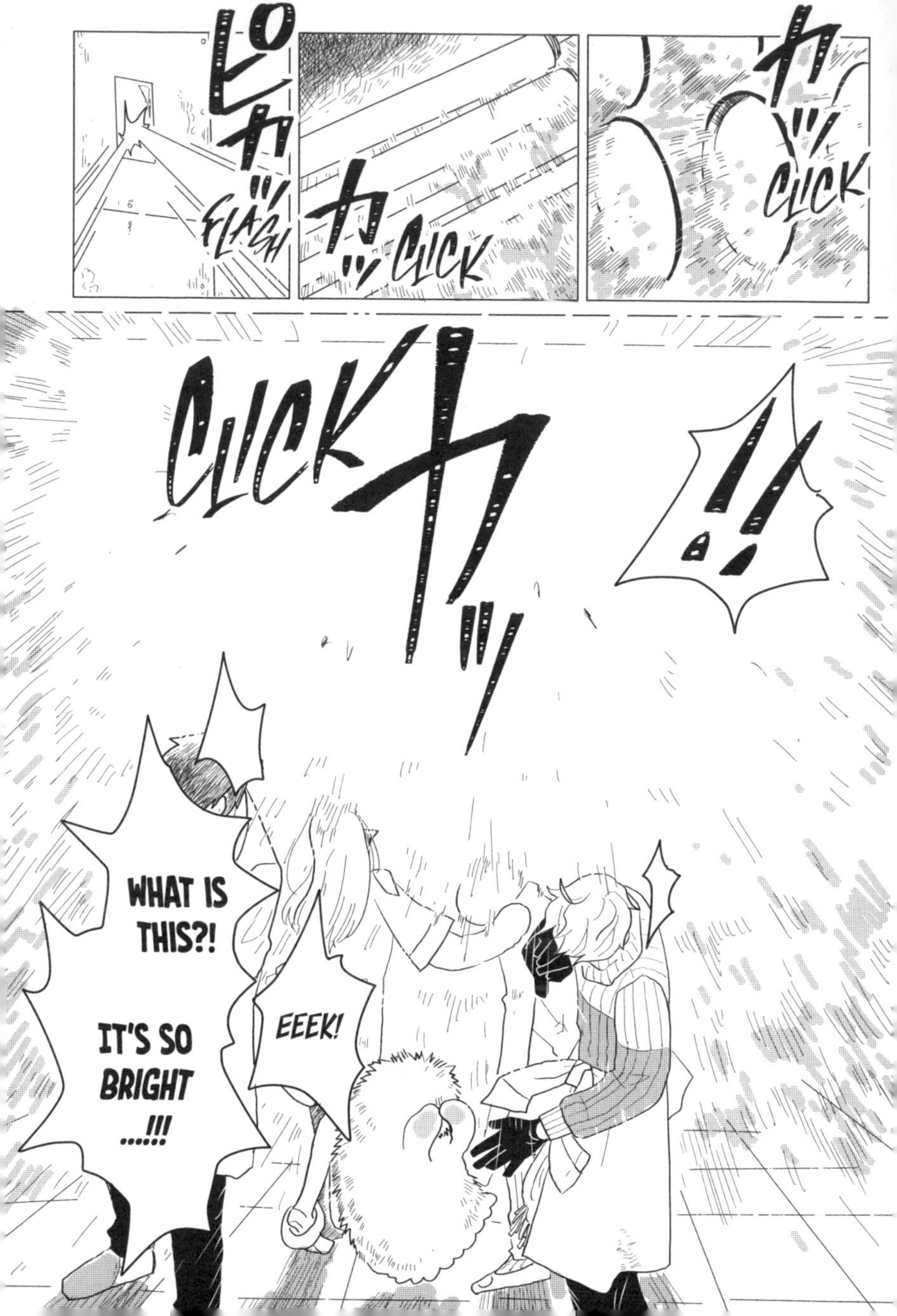
カッ
CLICK
カッ
CLICK
ピカッ
FLASH
カッ
CLICK
!!
EEEK!
WHAT IS THIS?!
IT'S SO BRIGHT ...!!!

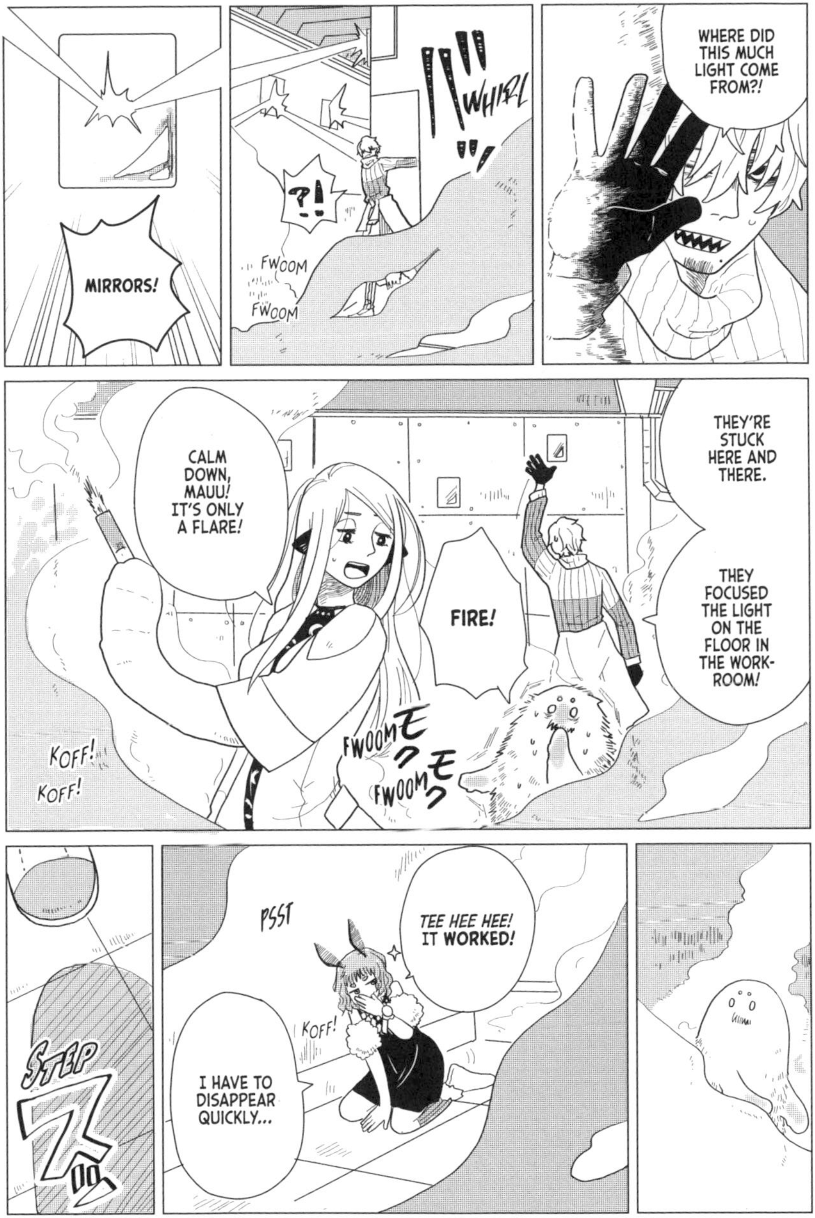
WHERE DID THIS MUCH LIGHT COME FROM?!
WHIRL
?!
FWOOM
FWOOM
MIRRORS!
THEY'RE STUCK HERE AND THERE.
THEY FOCUSED THE LIGHT ON THE FLOOR IN THE WORK-ROOM!
FIRE!
CALM DOWN, MAUU! IT'S ONLY A FLARE!
FWOOM
FWOOM
KOFF!
KOFF!
TEE HEE HEE! IT WORKED!
PSST
KOFF!
I HAVE TO DISAPPEAR QUICKLY...
STEP

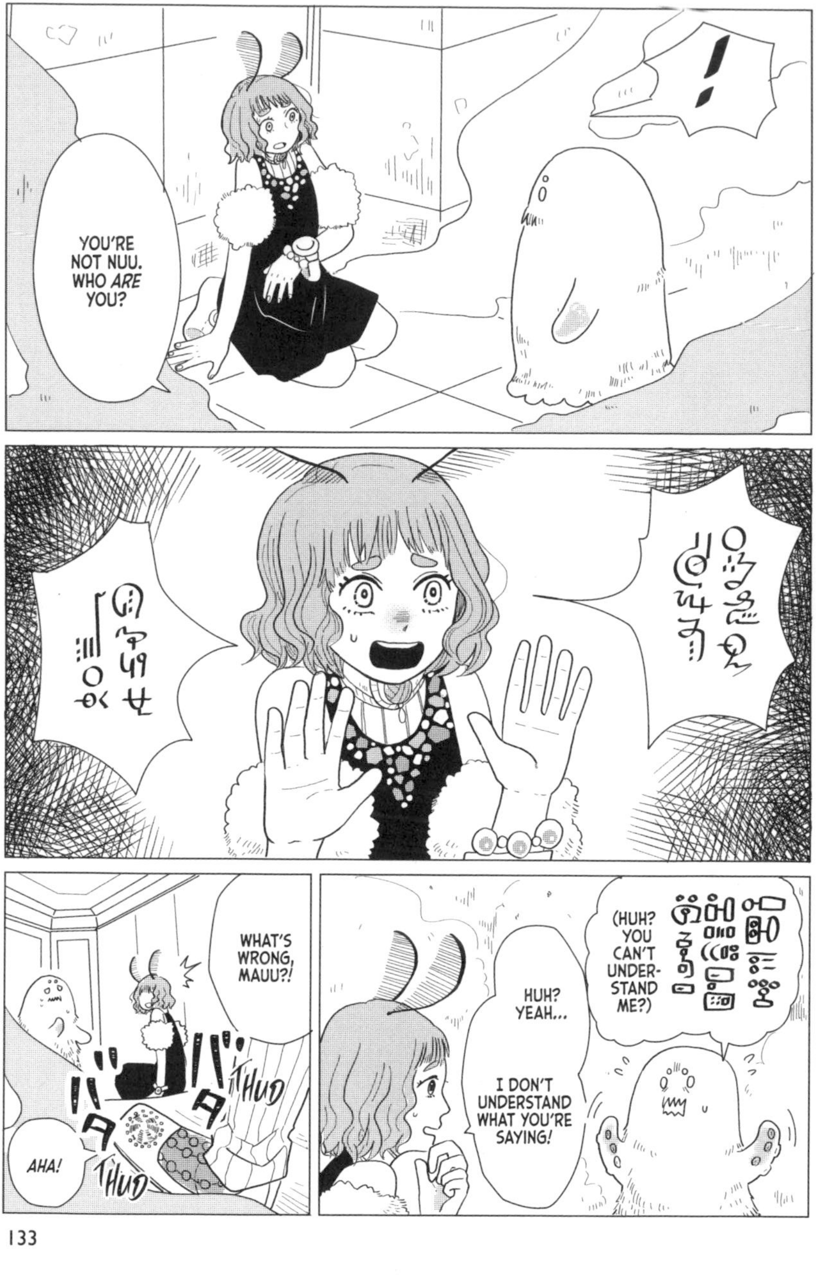
!
YOU'RE NOT NUU. WHO *ARE* YOU?
(HUH? YOU CAN'T UNDER-STAND ME?)
HUH? YEAH...
I DON'T UNDERSTAND WHAT YOU'RE SAYING!
WHAT'S WRONG, MAUU?!
THUD
THUD
AHA!

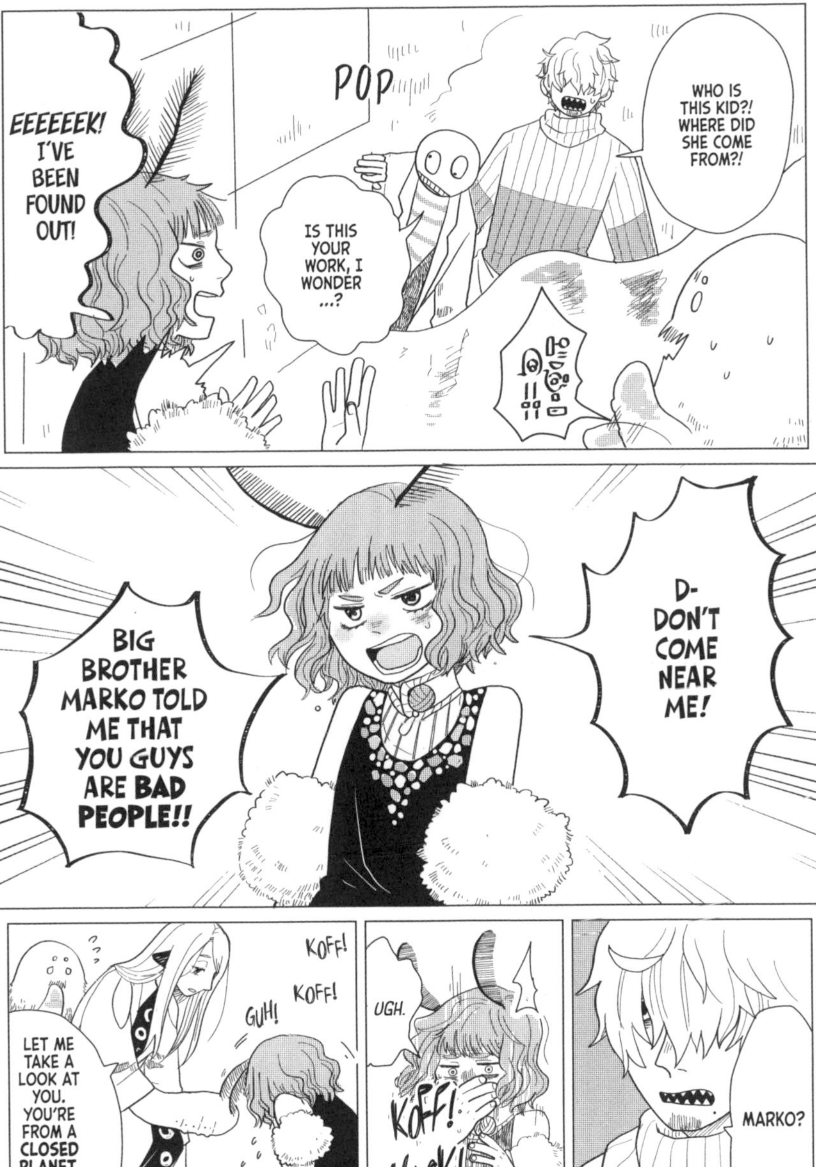
WHO IS THIS KID?! WHERE DID SHE COME FROM?!
POP
IS THIS YOUR WORK, I WONDER ...?
EEEEEEK! I'VE BEEN FOUND OUT!
D-DON'T COME NEAR ME!
BIG BROTHER MARKO TOLD ME THAT YOU GUYS ARE BAD PEOPLE!!
MARKO?
UGH.
KOFF! HACK!
KOFF!
KOFF!
GUH!
LET ME TAKE A LOOK AT YOU. YOU'RE FROM A CLOSED PLANET, AREN'T YOU?

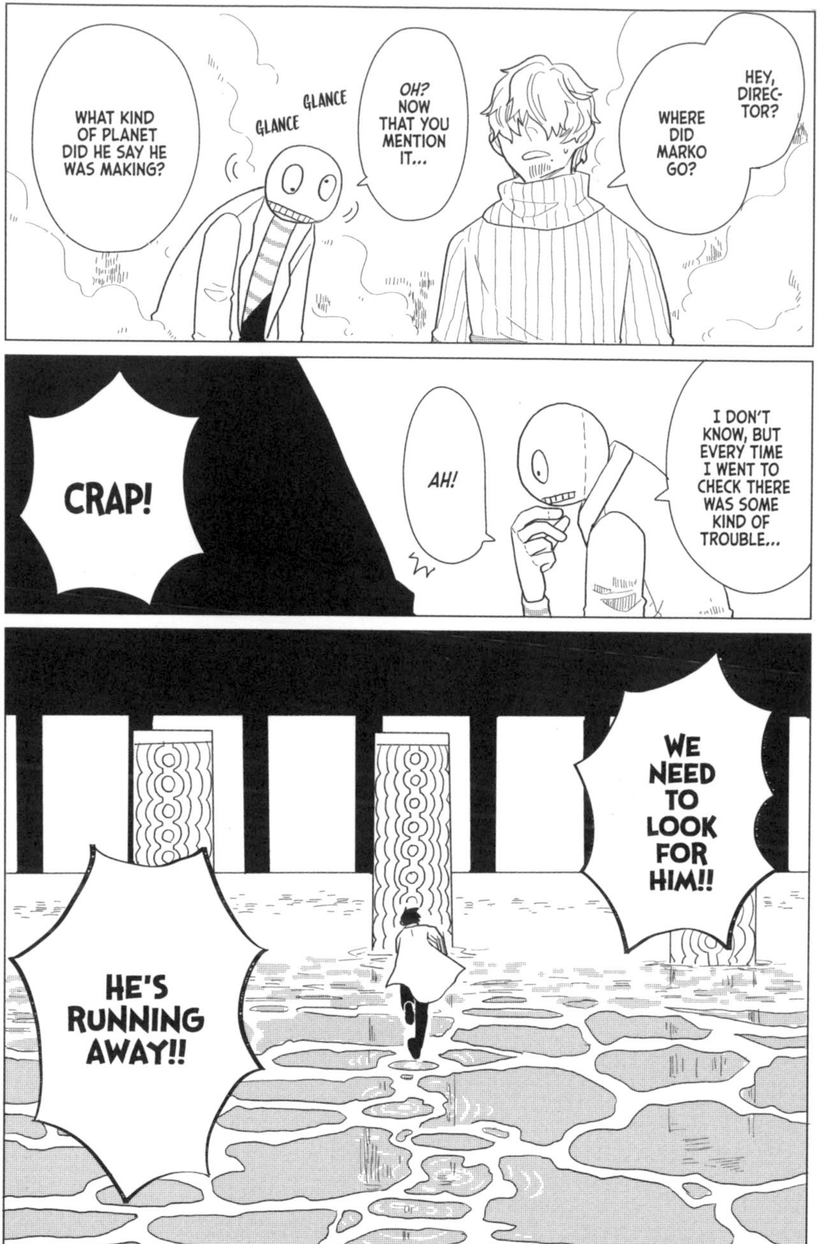
HEY, DIRECTOR?
WHERE DID MARKO GO?
OH? NOW THAT YOU MENTION IT...
GLANCE
GLANCE
WHAT KIND OF PLANET DID HE SAY HE WAS MAKING?
I DON'T KNOW, BUT EVERY TIME I WENT TO CHECK THERE WAS SOME KIND OF TROUBLE...
AH!
CRAP!
WE NEED TO LOOK FOR HIM!!
HE'S RUNNING AWAY!!

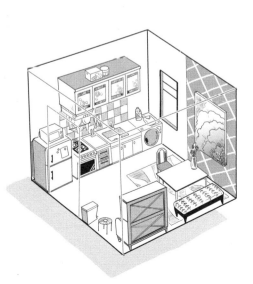

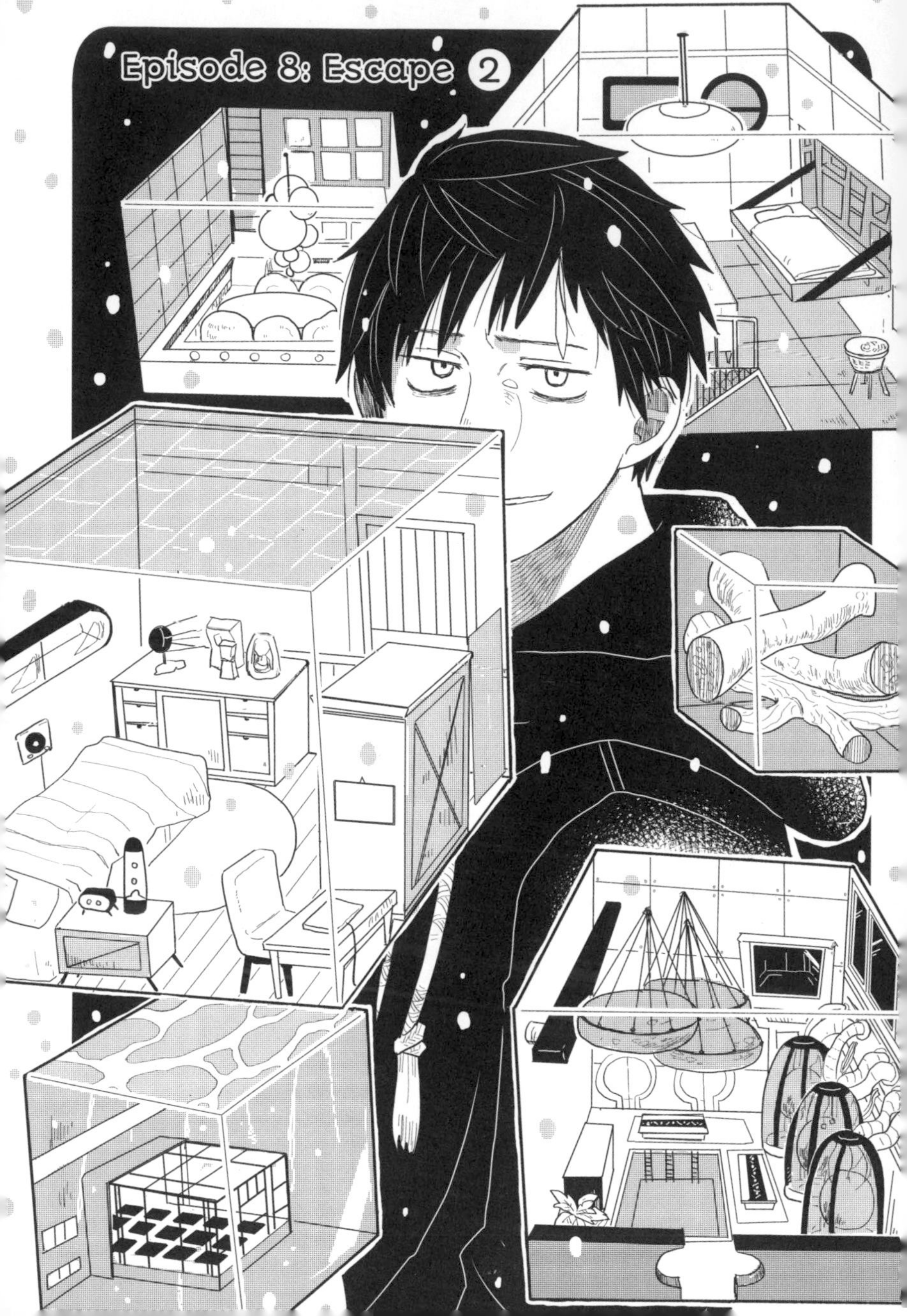
Episode 8: Escape 2

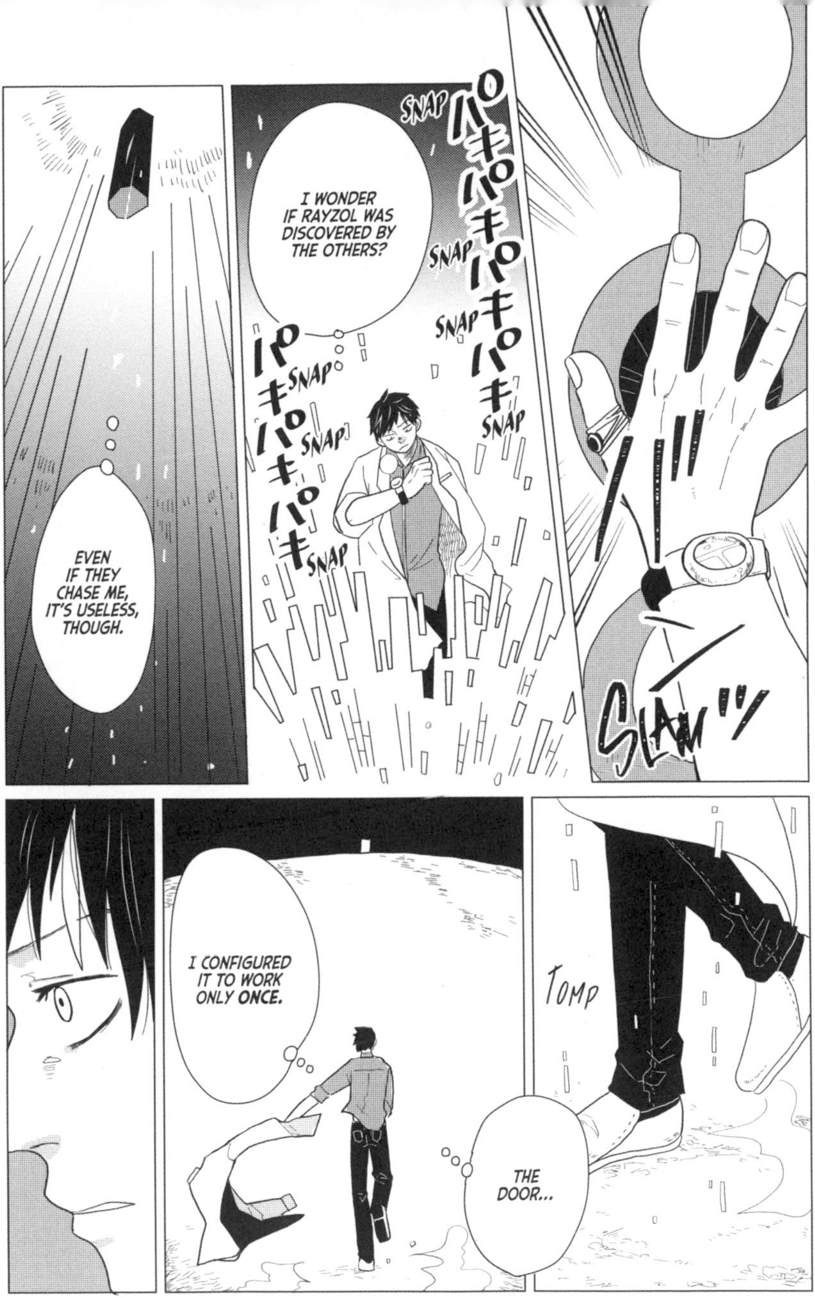
SLAM
SNAP
SNAP
SNAP
SNAP
I WONDER IF RAYZOL WAS DISCOVERED BY THE OTHERS?
SNAP
SNAP
SNAP
EVEN IF THEY CHASE ME, IT'S USELESS, THOUGH.
TOMP
THE DOOR...
I CONFIGURED IT TO WORK ONLY ONCE.

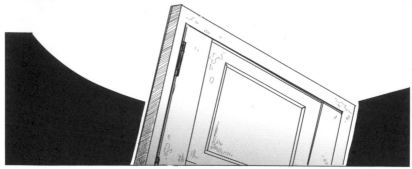

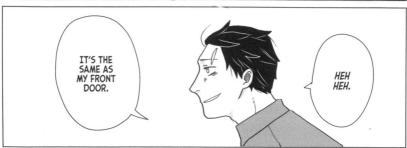

IT'S THE SAME AS MY FRONT DOOR.

HEH HEH.

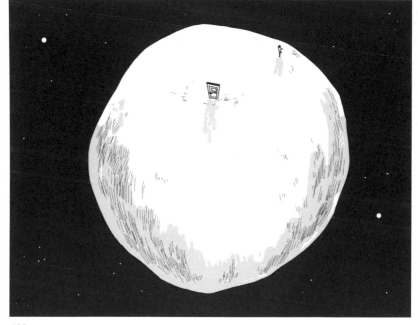

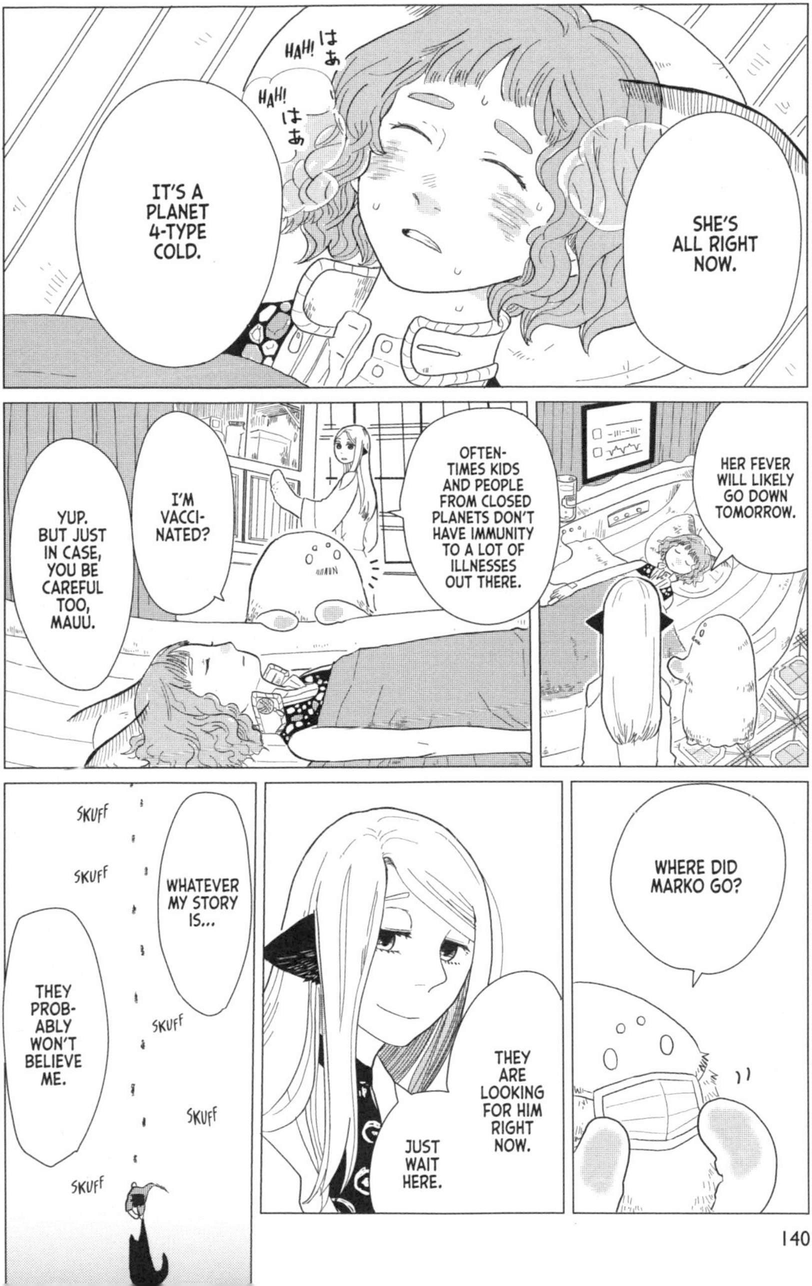
SHE'S ALL RIGHT NOW.
HAH! はあ
HAH! はあ
IT'S A PLANET 4-TYPE COLD.
HER FEVER WILL LIKELY GO DOWN TOMORROW.
OFTEN-TIMES KIDS AND PEOPLE FROM CLOSED PLANETS DON'T HAVE IMMUNITY TO A LOT OF ILLNESSES OUT THERE.
I'M VACCI-NATED?
YUP. BUT JUST IN CASE, YOU BE CAREFUL TOO, MAUU.
WHERE DID MARKO GO?
THEY ARE LOOKING FOR HIM RIGHT NOW.
JUST WAIT HERE.
WHATEVER MY STORY IS...
SKUFF
SKUFF
THEY PROB-ABLY WON'T BELIEVE ME.
SKUFF
SKUFF
SKUFF

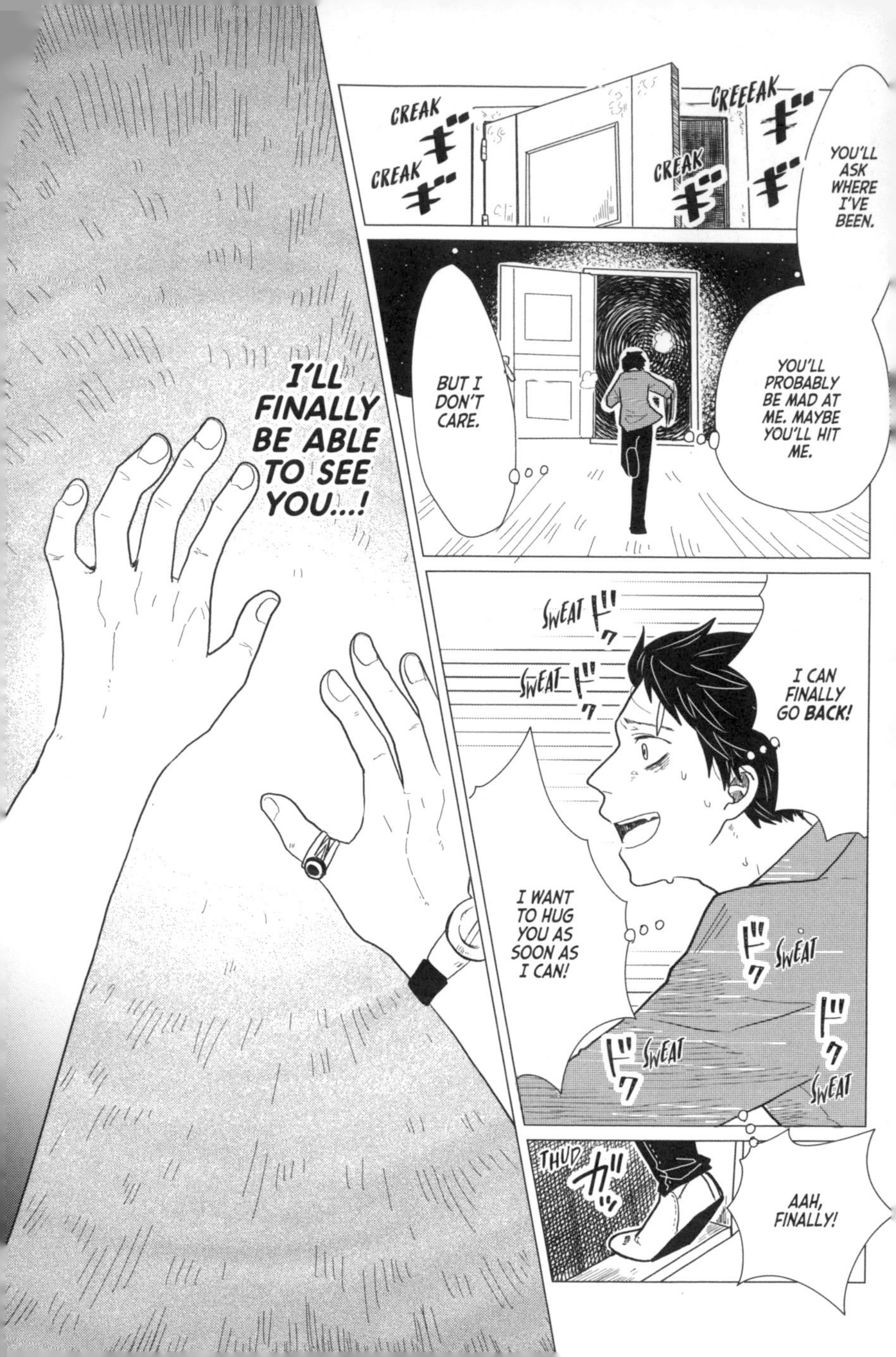
CREEEAK
CREAK
CREAK
CREAK
YOU'LL ASK WHERE I'VE BEEN.
YOU'LL PROBABLY BE MAD AT ME. MAYBE YOU'LL HIT ME.
BUT I DON'T CARE.
SWEAT
SWEAT
I CAN FINALLY GO BACK!
I WANT TO HUG YOU AS SOON AS I CAN!
SWEAT
SWEAT
SWEAT
THUD
AAH, FINALLY!
I'LL FINALLY BE ABLE TO SEE YOU...!

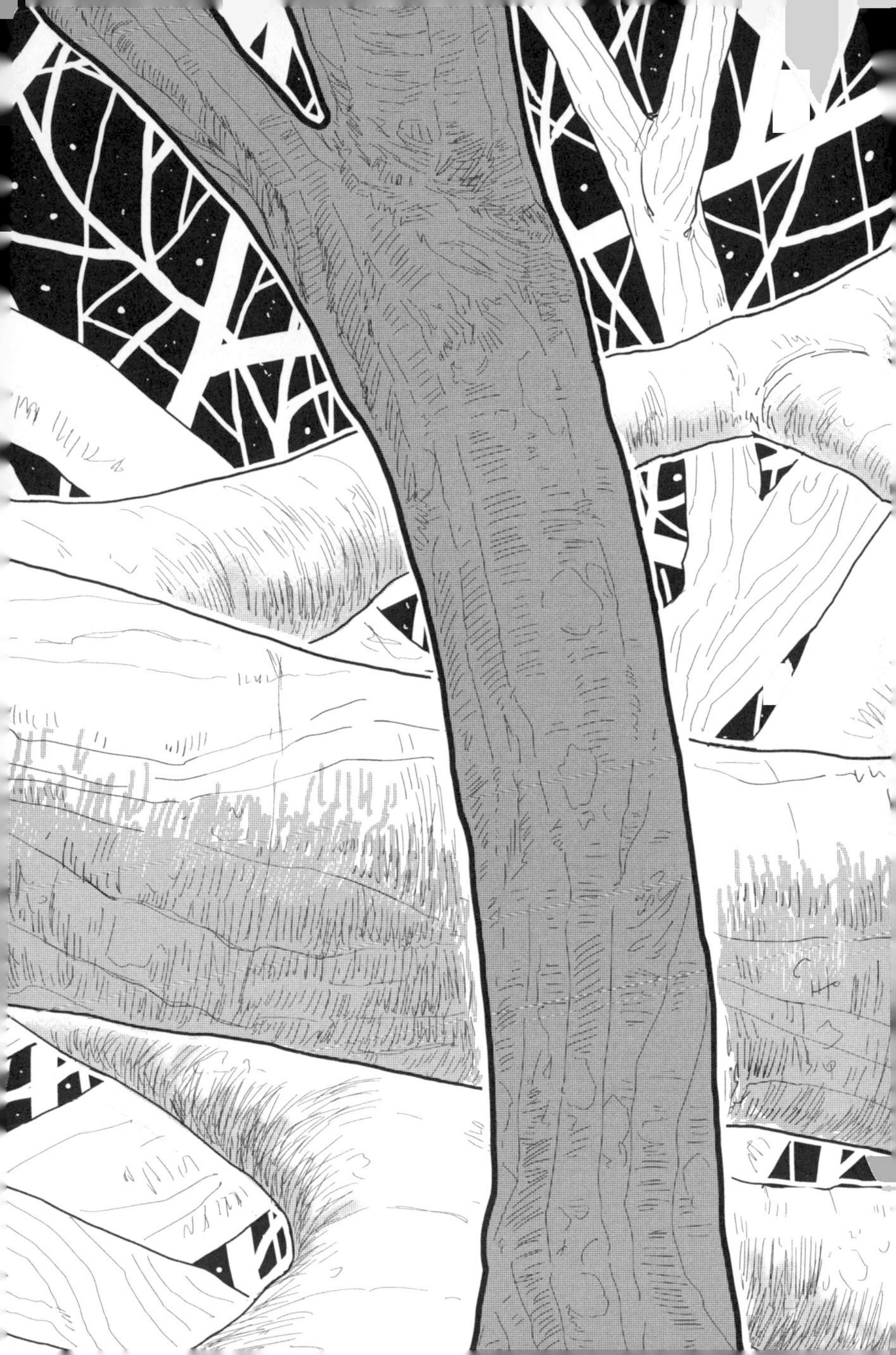

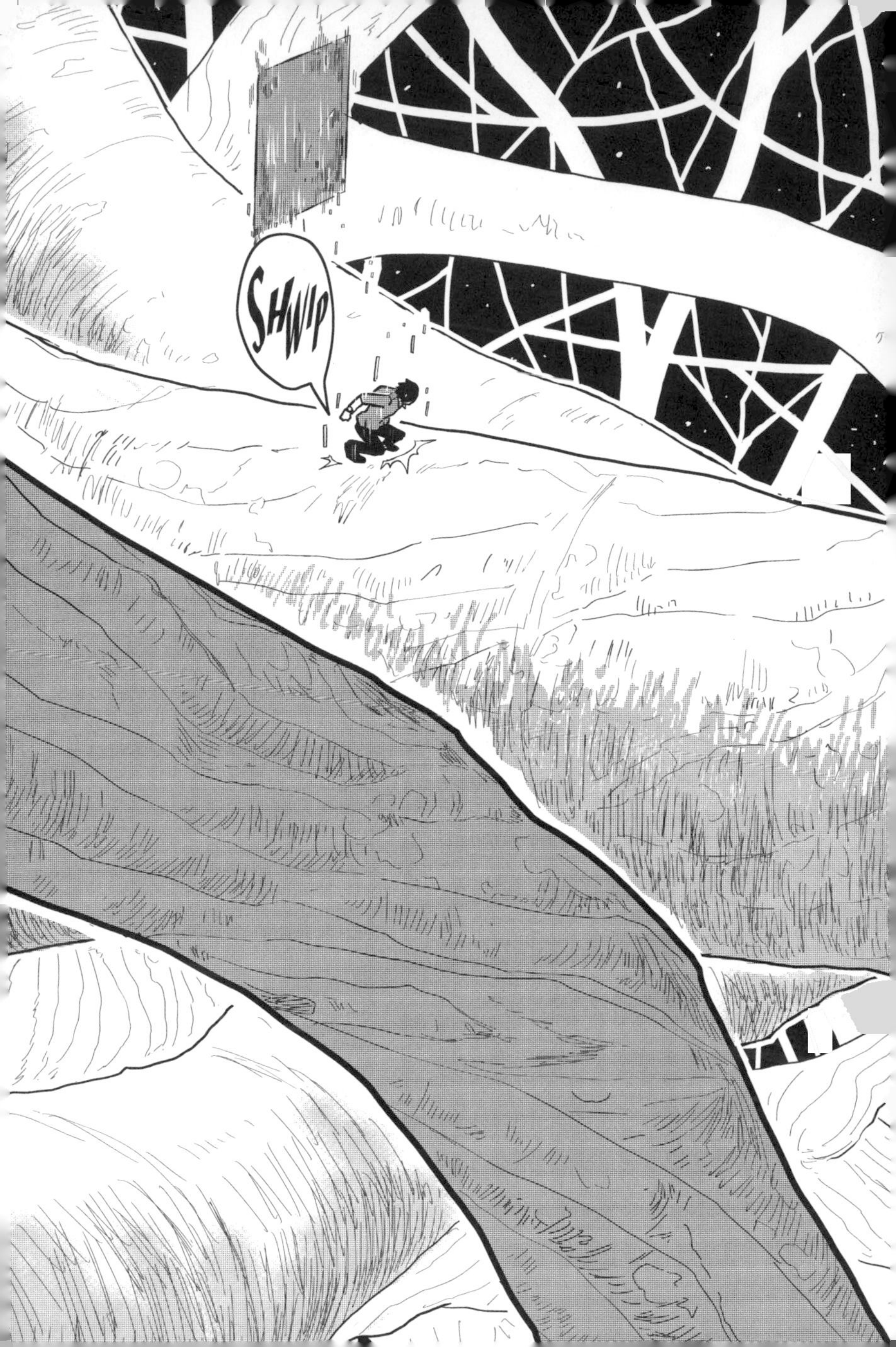
SHWIP

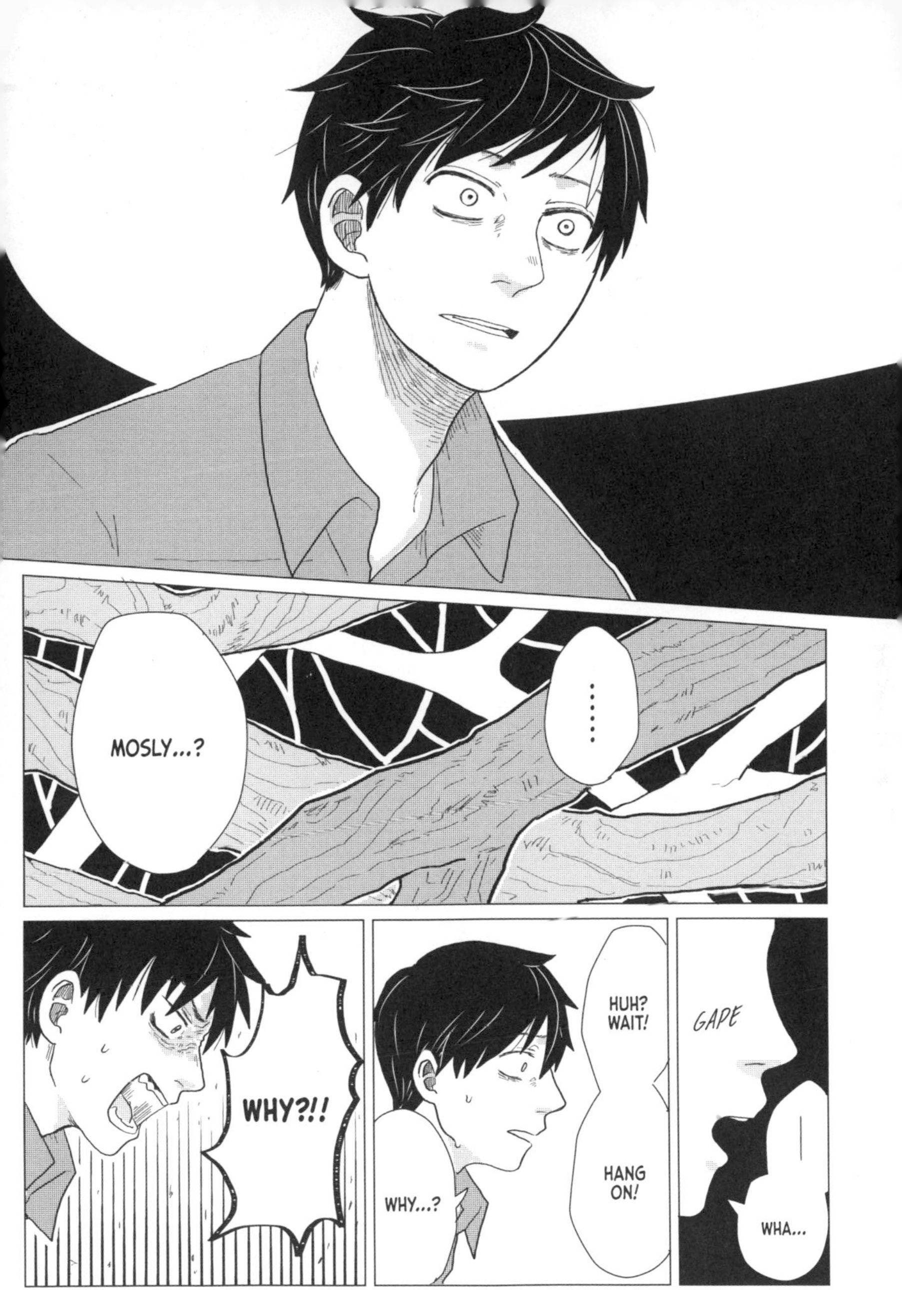

……
MOSLY...?
GAPE
WHA...
HUH? WAIT!
HANG ON!
WHY...?
WHY?!!

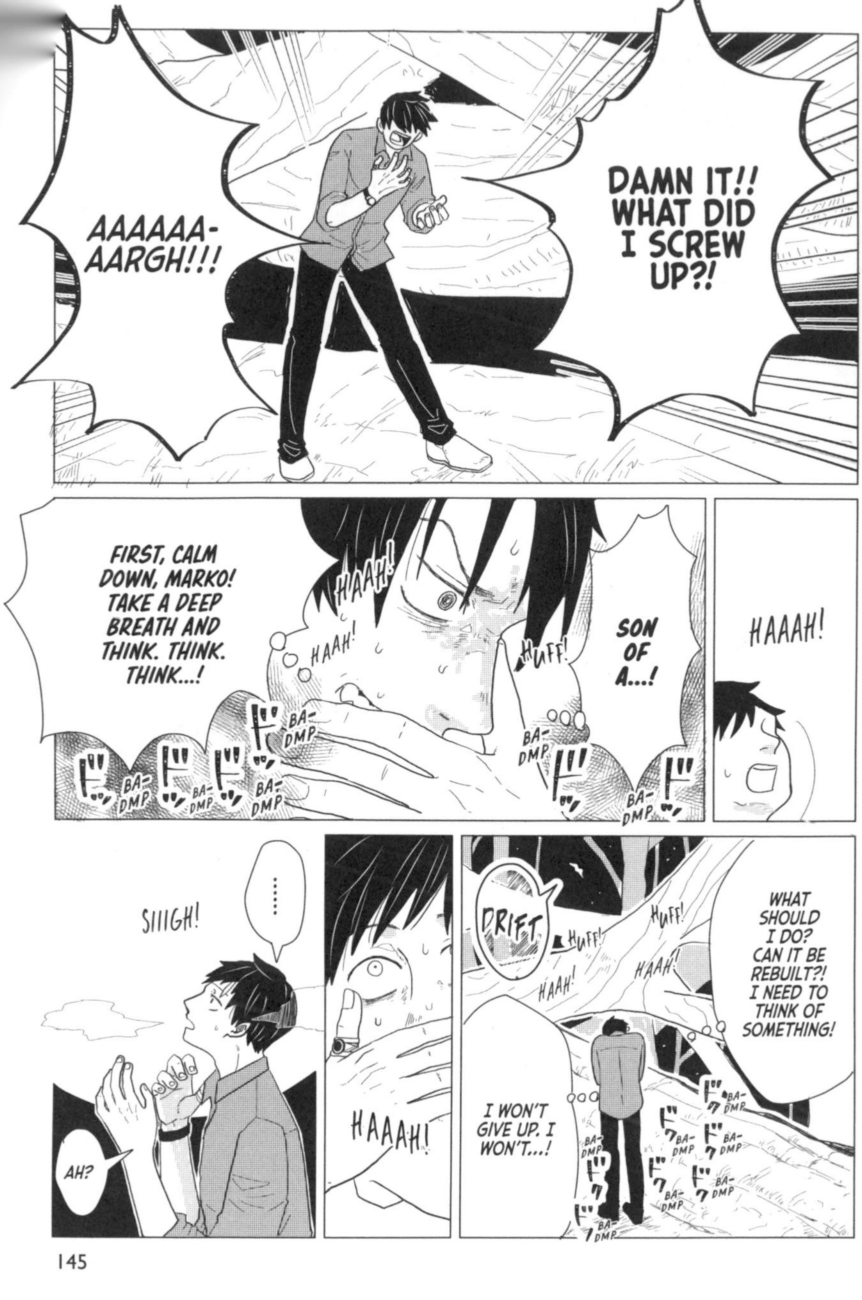
DAMN IT!! WHAT DID I SCREW UP?!
AAAAAA-AARGH!!!
HAAAH!
SON OF A...!
HUFF!
HAAH!
HAAH!
FIRST, CALM DOWN, MARKO! TAKE A DEEP BREATH AND THINK. THINK. THINK...!
BA-DMP
BA-DMP
BA-DMP
BA-DMP
BA-DMP
BA-DMP
BA-DMP
WHAT SHOULD I DO? CAN IT BE REBUILT?! I NEED TO THINK OF SOMETHING!
HUFF!
HUFF!
DRIFT
HAAH!
HAAH!
I WON'T GIVE UP. I WON'T...!
BA-DMP
BA-DMP
BA-DMP
BA-DMP
BA-DMP
BA-DMP
BA-DMP
HAAAH!
......
SIIIGH!
AH?

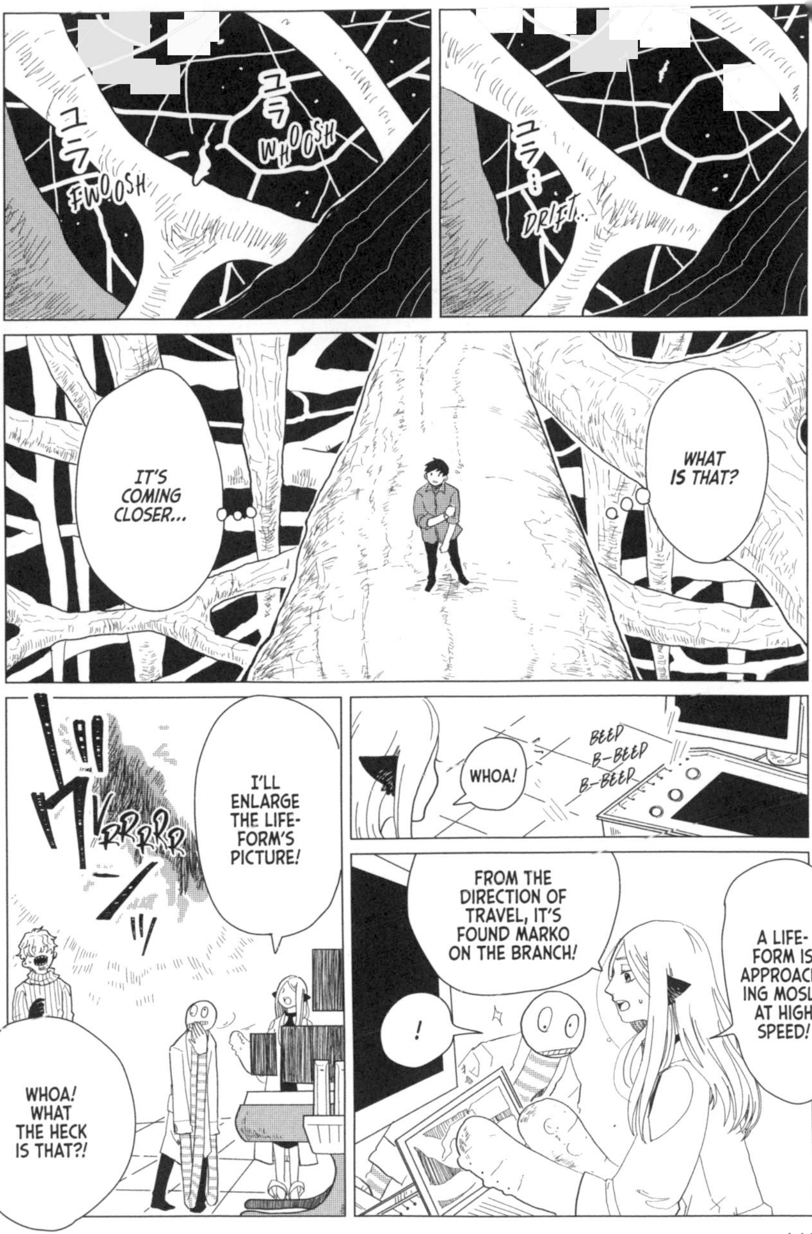
ユラ…
DRIFT…
ユラ
FWOOSH
ユラ
WHOOSH
WHAT IS THAT?
IT'S COMING CLOSER...
BEEP
B-BEEP
B-BEEP
WHOA!
A LIFE-FORM IS APPROACHING MOSLY AT HIGH SPEED!
FROM THE DIRECTION OF TRAVEL, IT'S FOUND MARKO ON THE BRANCH!
!
VRRRRR
I'LL ENLARGE THE LIFE-FORM'S PICTURE!
WHOA! WHAT THE HECK IS THAT?!

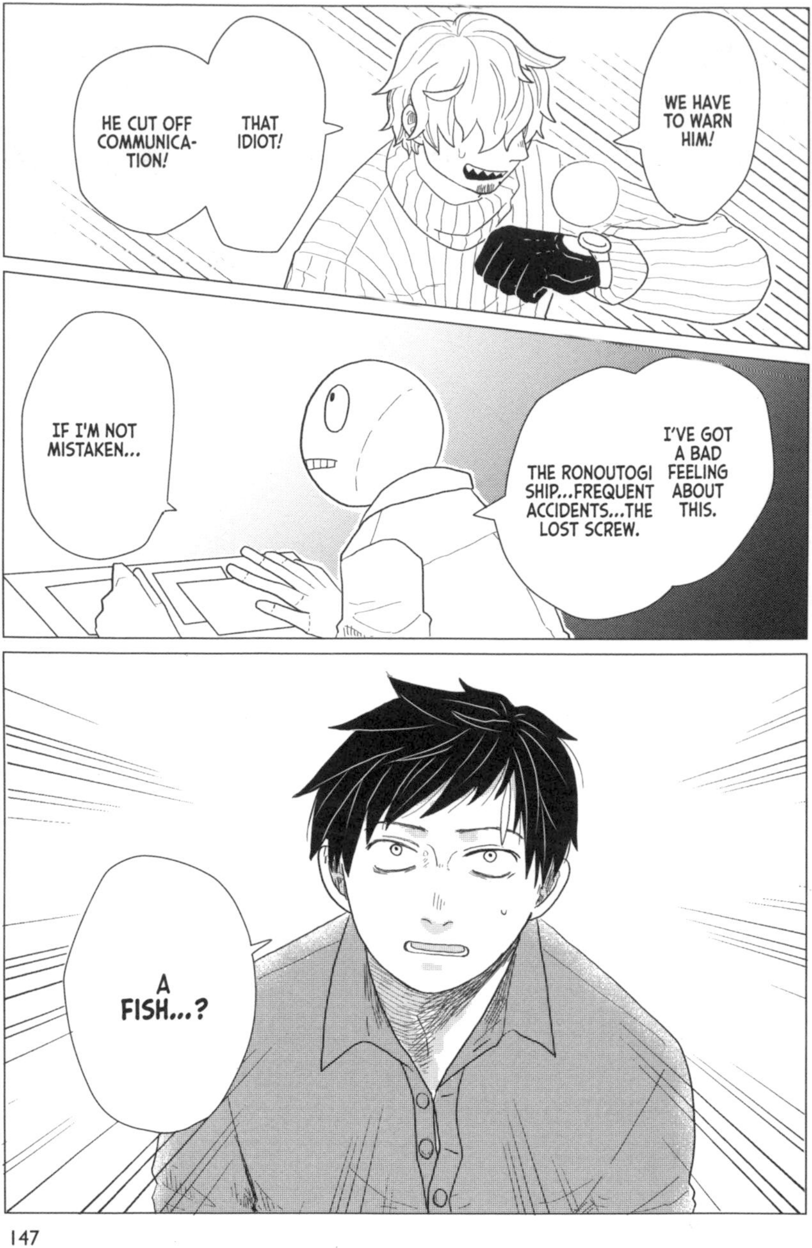
WE HAVE TO WARN HIM!
THAT IDIOT!
HE CUT OFF COMMUNICA-TION!
I'VE GOT A BAD FEELING ABOUT THIS.
THE RONOUTOGI SHIP...FREQUENT ACCIDENTS...THE LOST SCREW.
IF I'M NOT MISTAKEN...
A FISH...?

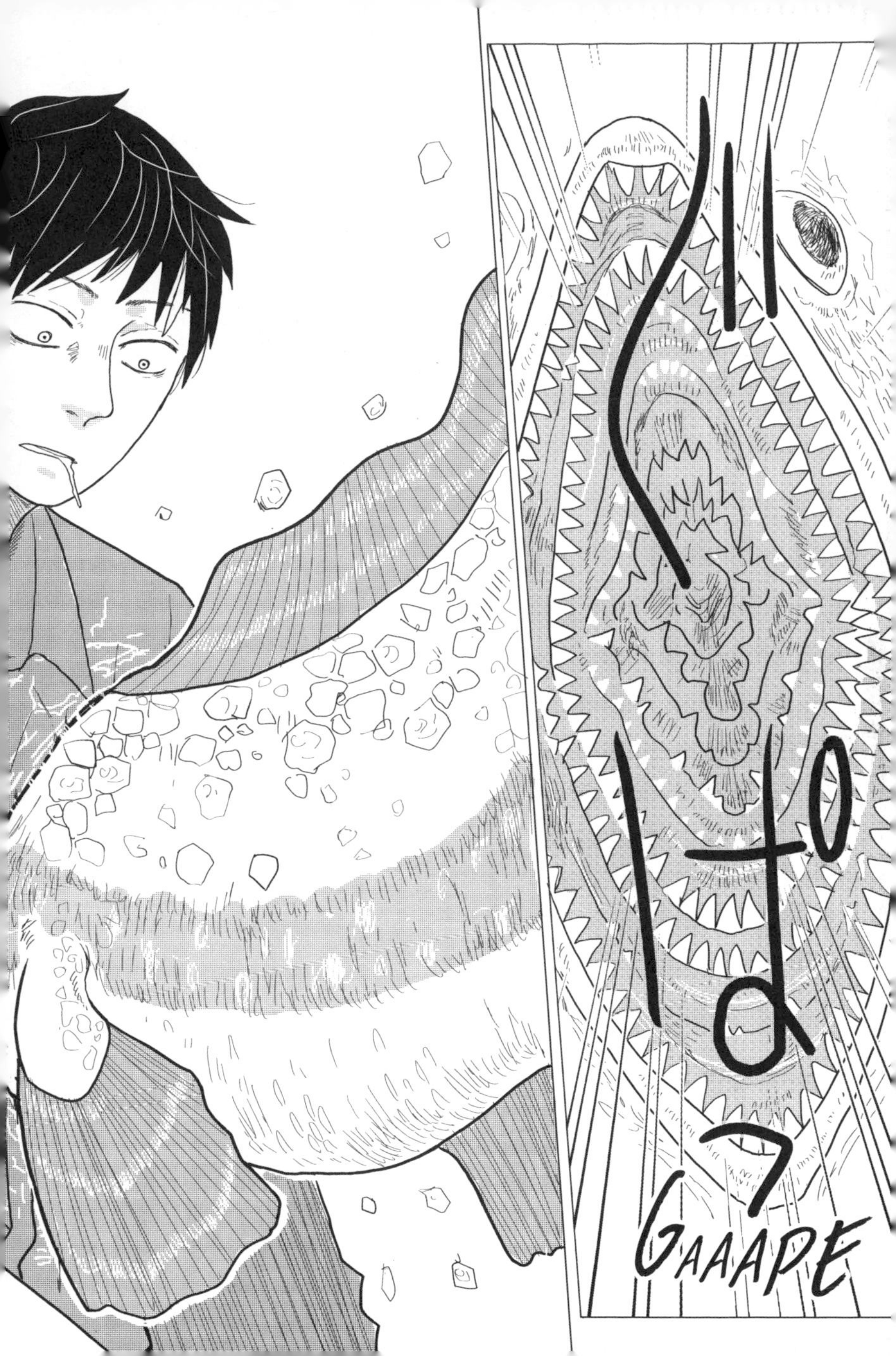
GAAAPE

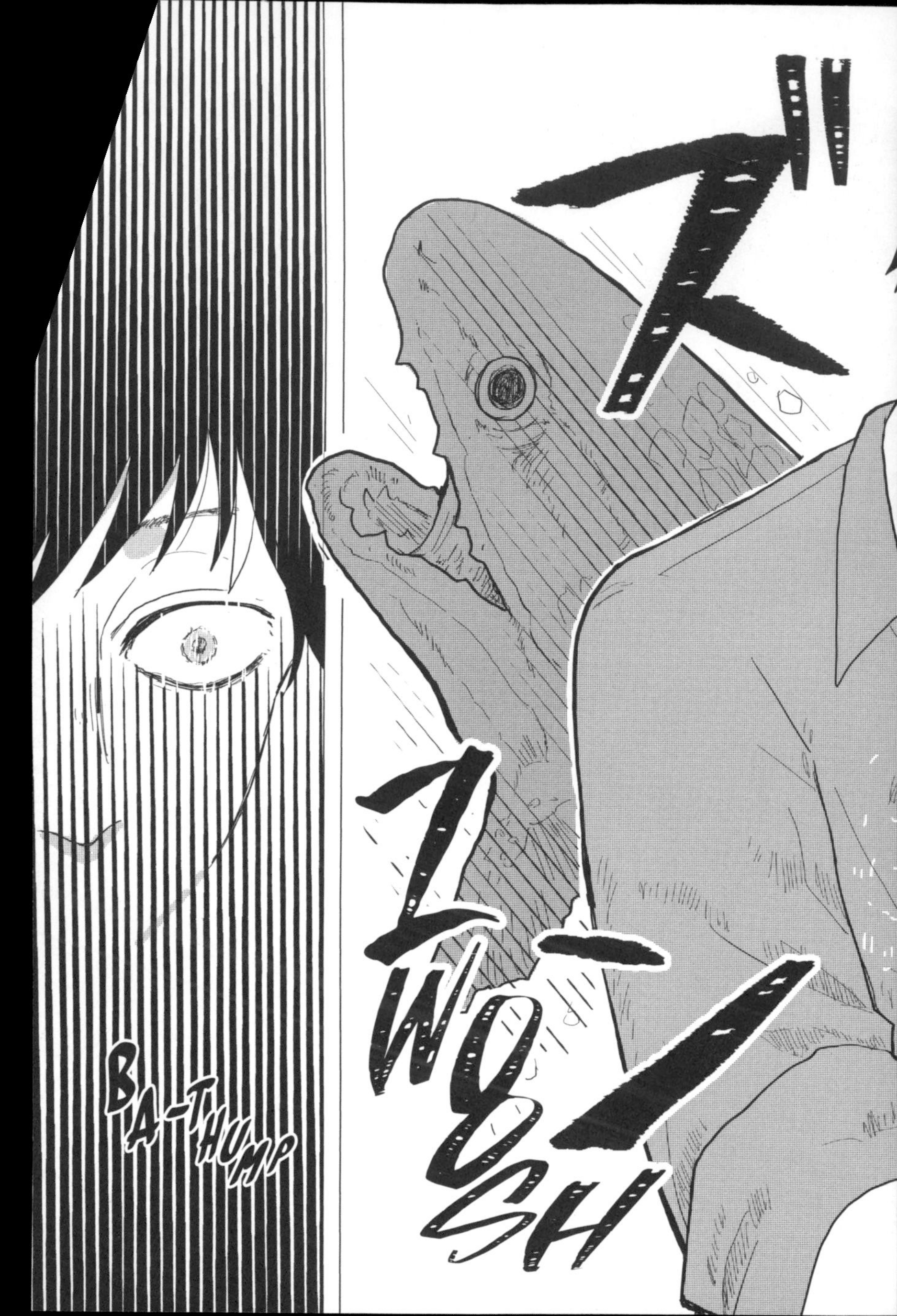
ZWOOSH
BA-THUMP

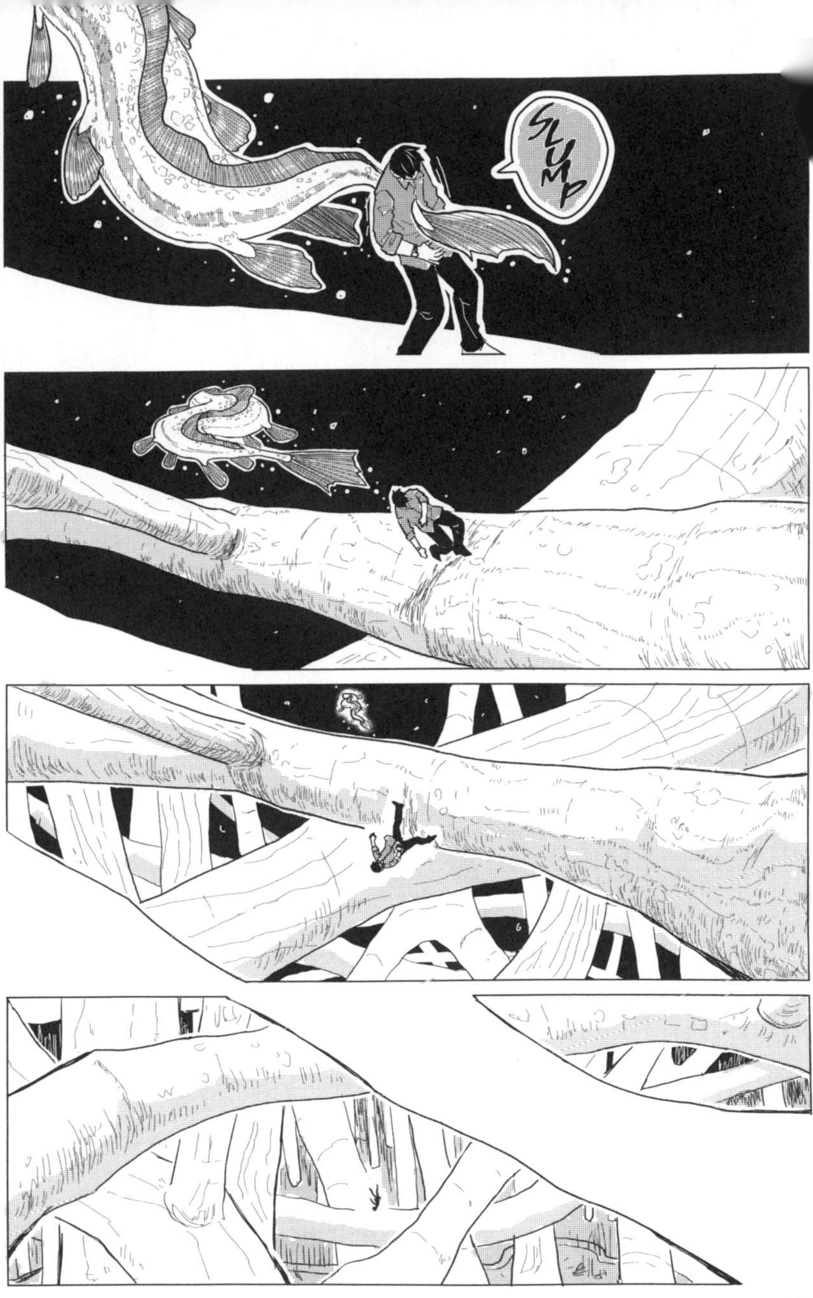
SLUMP

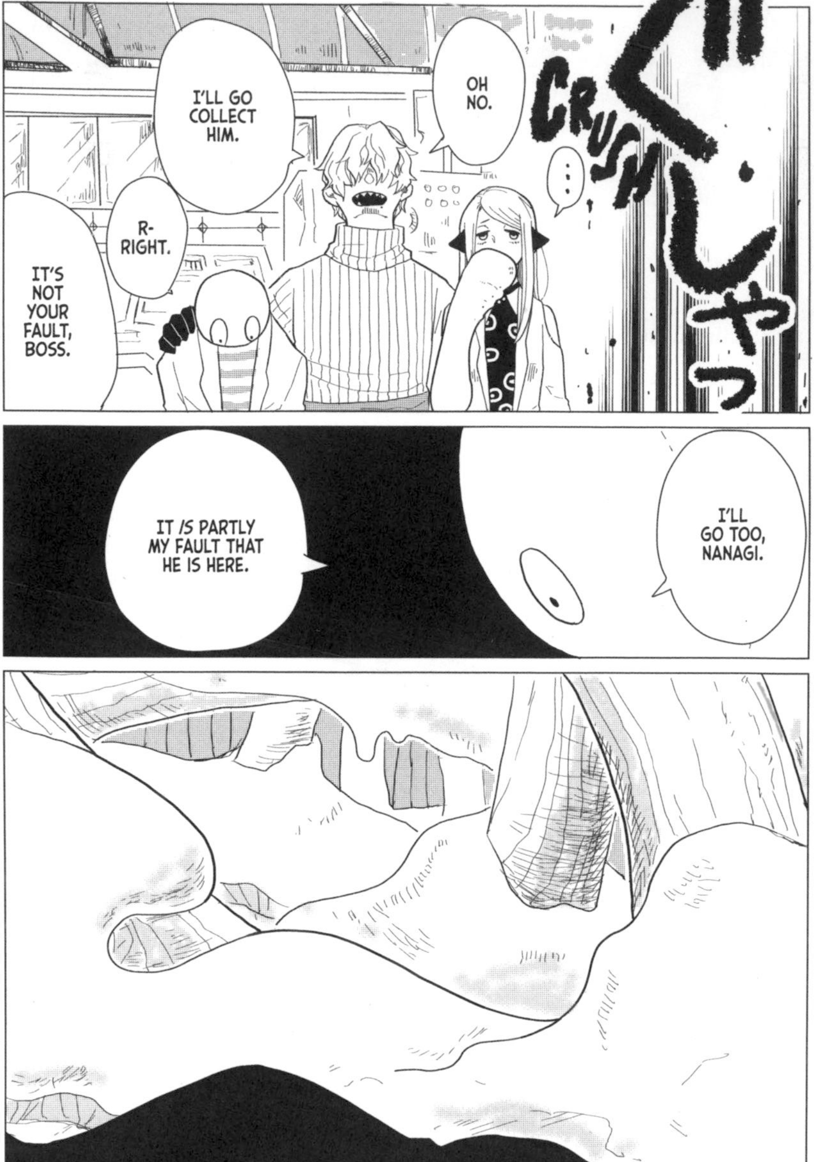
ぐしゃっ
CRUSH
OH NO.
…
I'LL GO COLLECT HIM.
R-RIGHT.
IT'S NOT YOUR FAULT, BOSS.
I'LL GO TOO, NANAGI.
IT *IS* PARTLY MY FAULT THAT HE IS HERE.

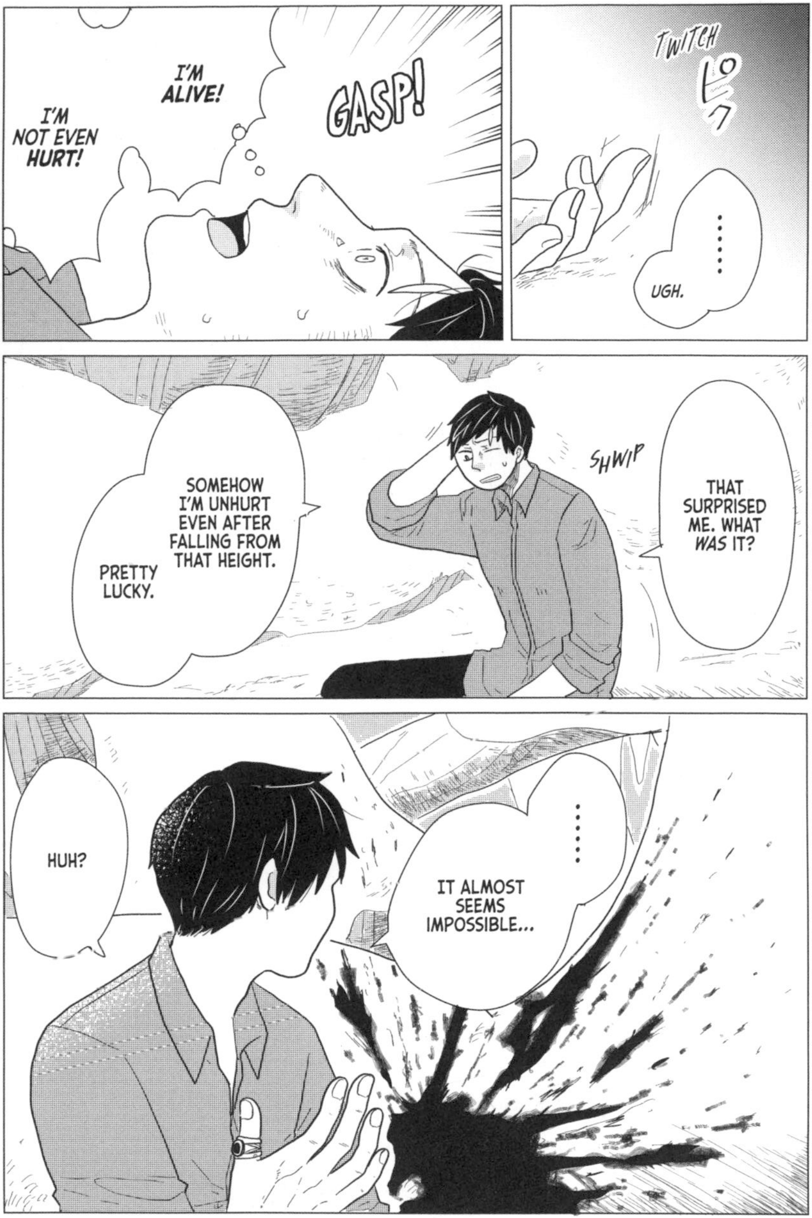
TWITCH
ピク
......
UGH.
GASP!
I'M ALIVE!
I'M NOT EVEN HURT!
THAT SURPRISED ME. WHAT WAS IT?
SHWIP
SOMEHOW I'M UNHURT EVEN AFTER FALLING FROM THAT HEIGHT.
PRETTY LUCKY.
......
IT ALMOST SEEMS IMPOSSIBLE...
HUH?

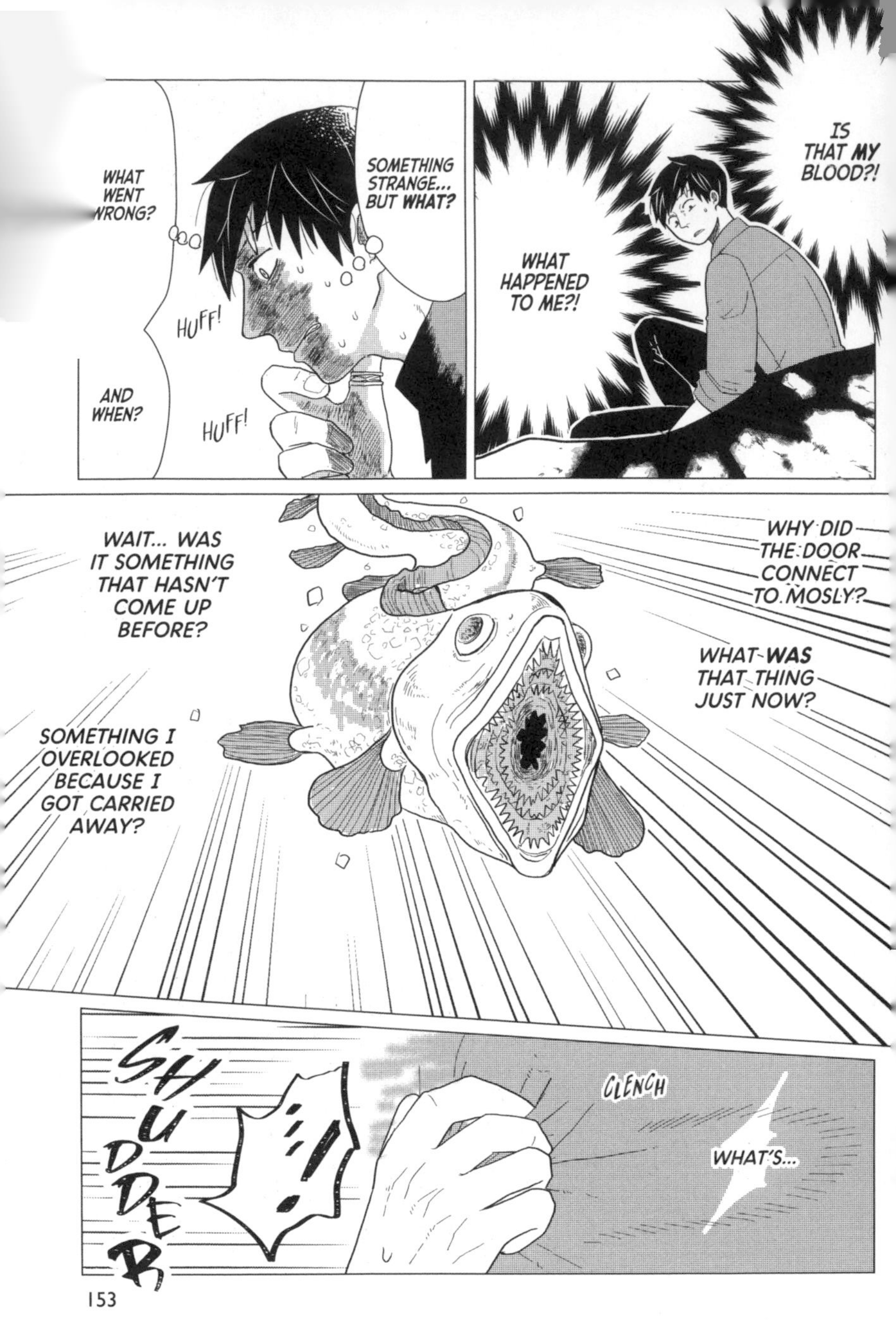
IS THAT MY BLOOD?!
WHAT HAPPENED TO ME?!
SOMETHING STRANGE... BUT WHAT?
WHAT WENT WRONG?
HUFF!
AND WHEN?
HUFF!
WHY DID THE DOOR CONNECT TO MOSLY?
WAIT... WAS IT SOMETHING THAT HASN'T COME UP BEFORE?
WHAT WAS THAT THING JUST NOW?
SOMETHING I OVERLOOKED BECAUSE I GOT CARRIED AWAY?
CLENCH
WHAT'S...
!!
SHUDDER

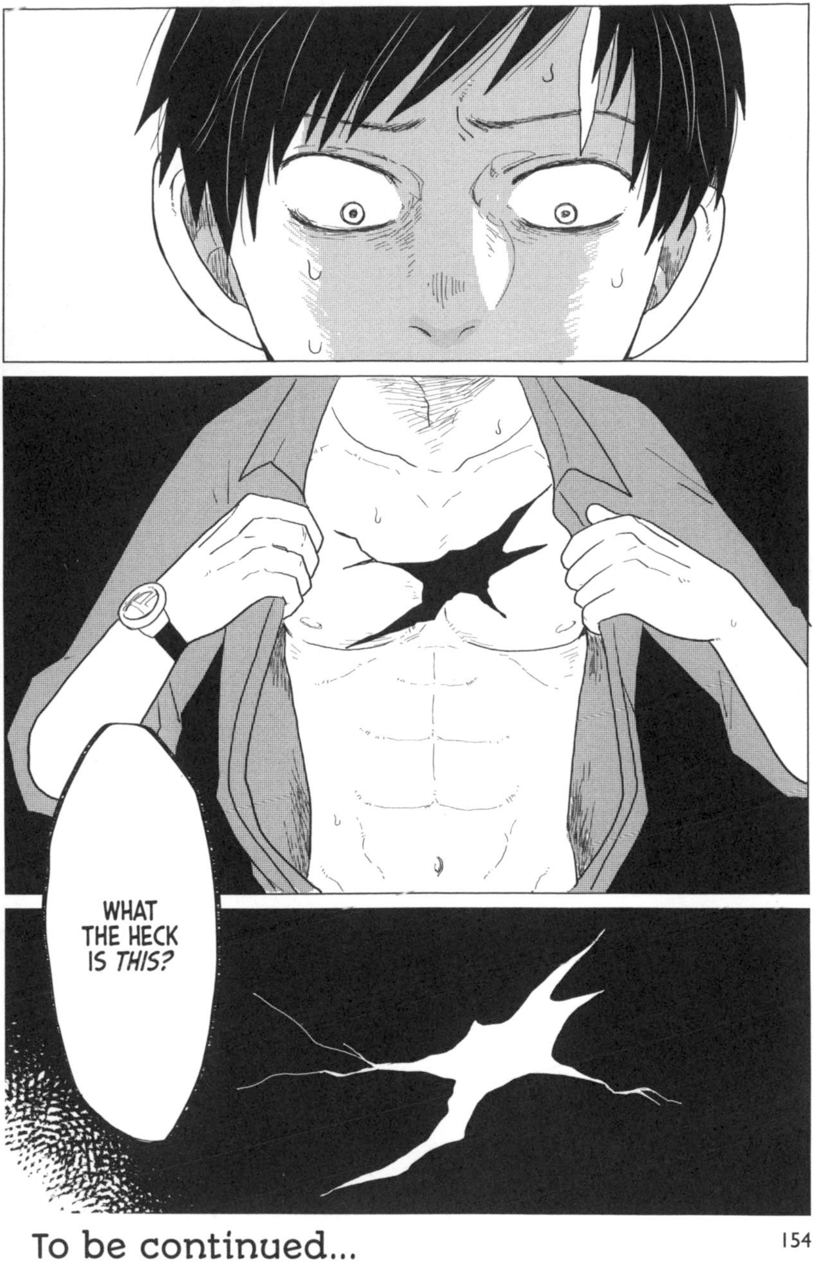
WHAT THE HECK IS *THIS?*

To be continued...

Correspondence from the End of the Universe

Newly Drawn

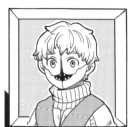

UKUNOARO ALIEN

- [ ] BECAUSE THEIR MOTHER PLANET EXPLODED LONG AGO, THEY ARE NOW LIVING ON THE PLANET MO-SA.
- [ ] THEIR FACE OPENS IN FOUR PARTS AND BECOMES A LARGE MOUTH.
- [ ] COOKED FOOD IS DIFFICULT FOR THEM TO DIGEST.

NUKAAKOKO ALIEN

- [ ] DON'T HAVE MOUTHS, SO THEY ABSORB NUTRIENTS FROM THE SOLES OF THEIR FEET.
- [ ] TELEPATHIZE BETWEEN MEMBERS OF THE SAME FAMILY, AND CONVERSE WITH OTHER ALIENS IN SIGN LANGUAGE.
- [ ] ORIGINALLY A CLOSED PLANET RESIDENT SPECIES. INITIAL ALIEN VISITORS WITNESSED A GROUP BURIED IN THE SOIL AND SLEEPING, AND FOR A LONG TIME THOUGHT THEY WERE PLANTS.

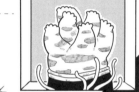

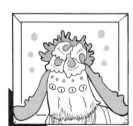

NUKAAKOKOTESSA ALIEN

- [ ] THE PLANET'S NAME MEANS "NUKAAKOKO'S YOUNGER SISTER."
- [ ] MAYBE BECAUSE THEY LOOK DIVINE, THERE ARE STARS THAT ARE SACRED TO THEM.
- [ ] BASICALLY CHEERFUL DANCE LOVERS.
- [ ] IT IS IN FASHION TO MAKE PLANTS INTO LIVING HATS AND PUT THEM ON THEIR HEADS.

MO-SA ALIEN

- [ ] THE PLANET MO-SA HAS MANY ALIENS LIVING ON IT, BUT THESE ARE NATIVE CREATURES.
- [ ] THEIR INTERNAL ORGANS ARE WRAPPED IN HARD GLASS, AND THEY ARE SEE-THROUGH.
- [ ] WELL KNOWN AS THE HOME PLANET OF GALACTIC HONORARY FILM DIRECTOR KAKKALLA. WHEN THEY RECEIVED THE AWARD, A TEN-DAY CELEBRATION WAS HELD THROUGHOUT THE PLANET.

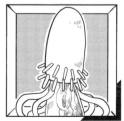

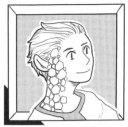

NO. 1086 NONO ALIEN

- [ ] ONE OF THE RACES THAT LIVES ON THE PLANET MO-SA.

- [ ] EVERY TIME THE CALENDAR USED IN THEIR RELIGION REACHES A NEW YEAR, THE NUMBER IN THEIR RACE NAME INCREASES BY ONE.

- [ ] MOST OF THE BODY IS COVERED WITH SCALES. REGARDLESS OF AGE, THEY ARE CONSIDERED AN ADULT AFTER MOLTING FIVE TIMES.

USUUTO ALIEN

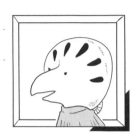

- [ ] A RACE THAT MAKES UP SIXTY PERCENT OF THE POPULATION OF THE EIGHTH GALAXY.

- [ ] MOST BUILDINGS, TOOLS, AND VEHICLES MADE ON THEIR PLANET ARE BASED ON THEIR PHYSIQUE.

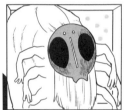

GITEHABA ALIEN

- [ ] ONE OF THE RACES THAT LIVE ON THE PLANET MO-SA.

- [ ] THEY CLIMB INTO ROBOTS TO GO OUT AND ABOUT.

- [ ] THEIR APPEARANCE IS SIMILAR TO EARTH'S HAMSTERS. (THE ILLUSTRATION AT LEFT IS THAT OF THEM RIDING IN A ROBOT.)

KONOE SPRING ALIEN

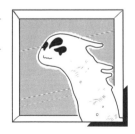

- [ ] A GEL-LIKE CREATURE LIVING ON THE SPRING STAR OF THE SPRING AND AUTUMN STAR BINARY STAR PAIR KONOE.

- [ ] DEPENDING ON THE TEMPERATURE, THEIR BODY CHANGES COLOR.

- [ ] ONE OF THEM WAS A TEACHER THAT WAS LEADING THE CHILDREN ON THEIR EXCURSION TO HORSHE 8.

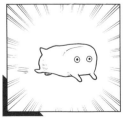

A PLANET MO-SA RABBIT

- [ ] GOT ON A SPACESHIP AND FOLLOWED THE EXCURSION GROUP.

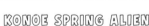

Before Going Far Away

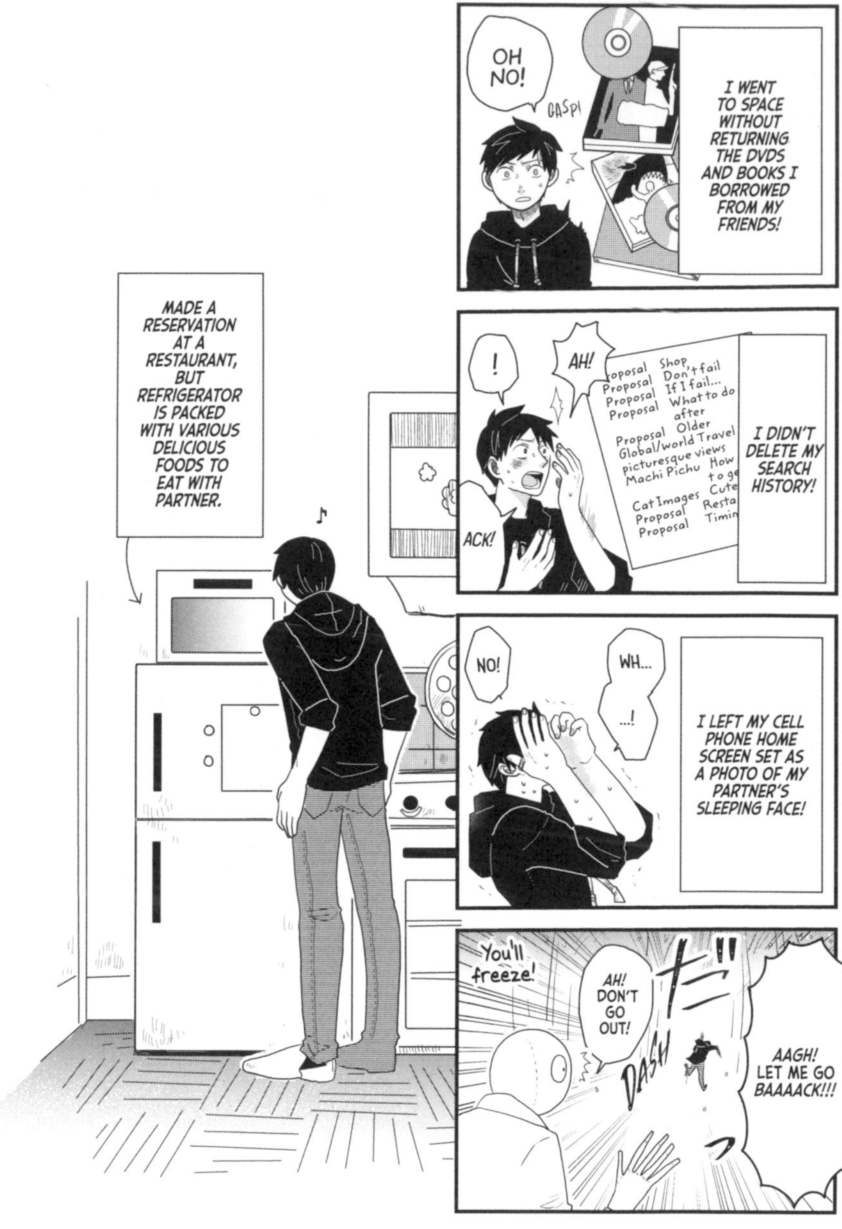
I WENT TO SPACE WITHOUT RETURNING THE DVDS AND BOOKS I BORROWED FROM MY FRIENDS!
OH NO!
GASP!
I DIDN'T DELETE MY SEARCH HISTORY!
roposal Shop
Proposal Don't fail
Proposal If I fail...
Proposal What to do after
Proposal Older
Global/world Travel
picturesque views
Machi Pichu How to ge
Cat Images Cute
Proposal Resta
Proposal Timin
AH!
!
ACK!
I LEFT MY CELL PHONE HOME SCREEN SET AS A PHOTO OF MY PARTNER'S SLEEPING FACE!
WH... ...!
NO!
AAGH! LET ME GO BAAAACK!!!
DASH
AH! DON'T GO OUT!
You'll freeze!
MADE A RESERVATION AT A RESTAURANT, BUT REFRIGERATOR IS PACKED WITH VARIOUS DELICIOUS FOODS TO EAT WITH PARTNER.
♪

Senior Staff Nanagi ①

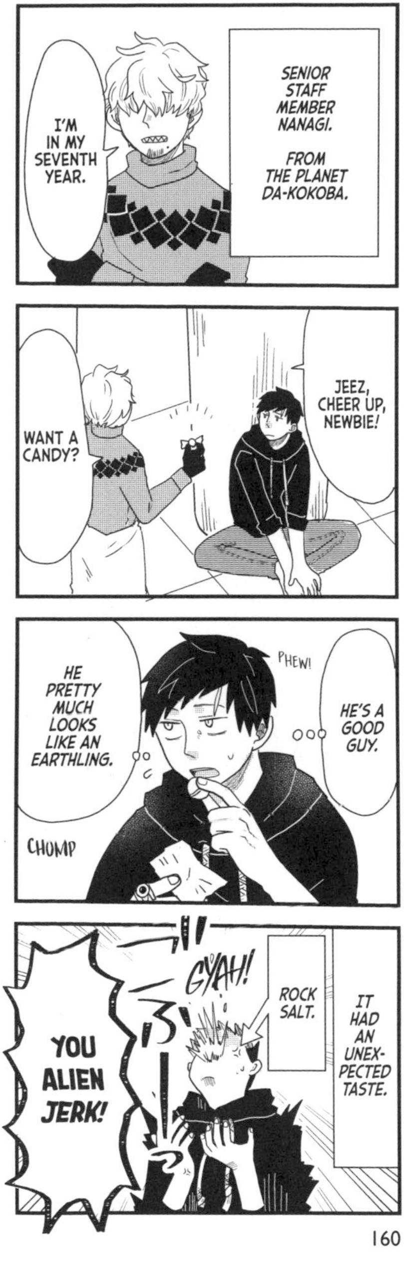
SENIOR STAFF MEMBER NANAGI. FROM THE PLANET DA-KOKOBA.
I'M IN MY SEVENTH YEAR.
JEEZ, CHEER UP, NEWBIE!
WANT A CANDY?
PHEW!
HE'S A GOOD GUY.
HE PRETTY MUCH LOOKS LIKE AN EARTHLING.
CHOMP
IT HAD AN UNEXPECTED TASTE.
ROCK SALT.
GYAH!
YOU ALIEN JERK!

Senior Staff Nanagi ②

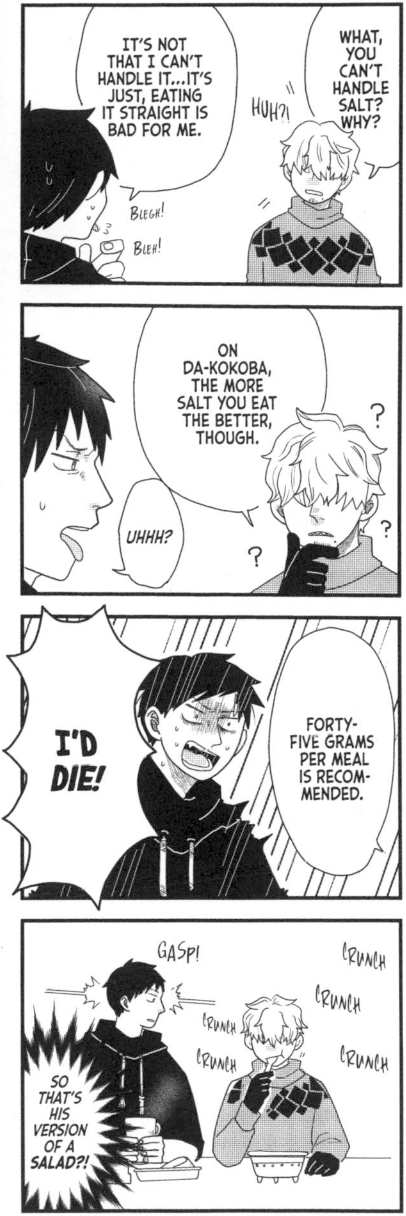
WHAT, YOU CAN'T HANDLE SALT? WHY?
HUH?!
IT'S NOT THAT I CAN'T HANDLE IT...IT'S JUST, EATING IT STRAIGHT IS BAD FOR ME.
BLEGH!
BLEH!
ON DA-KOKOBA, THE MORE SALT YOU EAT THE BETTER, THOUGH.
UHHH?
FORTY-FIVE GRAMS PER MEAL IS RECOMMENDED.
I'D DIE!
CRUNCH
CRUNCH
CRUNCH
CRUNCH
CRUNCH
GASP!
SO THAT'S HIS VERSION OF A SALAD?!

Nickname: Hand-Me-Down Warehouse

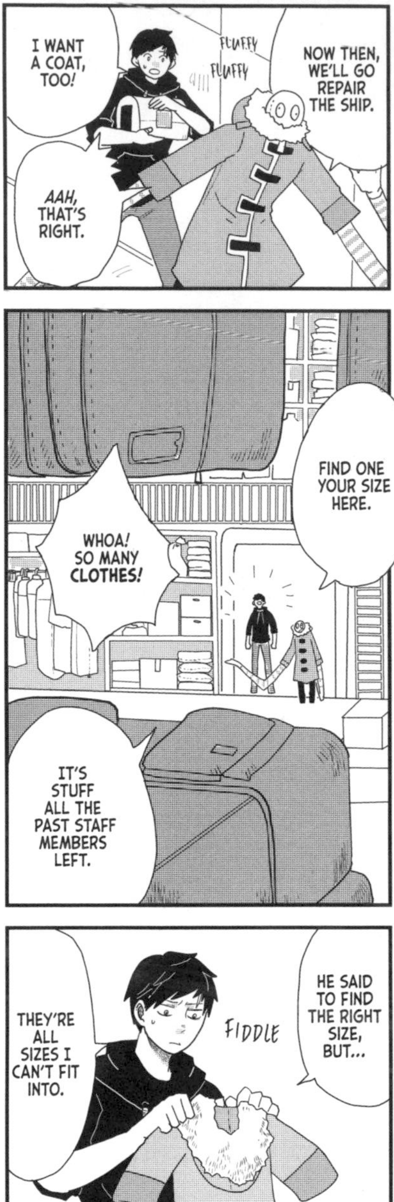
NOW THEN, WE'LL GO REPAIR THE SHIP.
FLUFFY FLUFFY
I WANT A COAT, TOO!
AAH, THAT'S RIGHT.
FIND ONE YOUR SIZE HERE.
WHOA! SO MANY CLOTHES!
IT'S STUFF ALL THE PAST STAFF MEMBERS LEFT.
HE SAID TO FIND THE RIGHT SIZE, BUT...
FIDDLE
THEY'RE ALL SIZES I CAN'T FIT INTO.

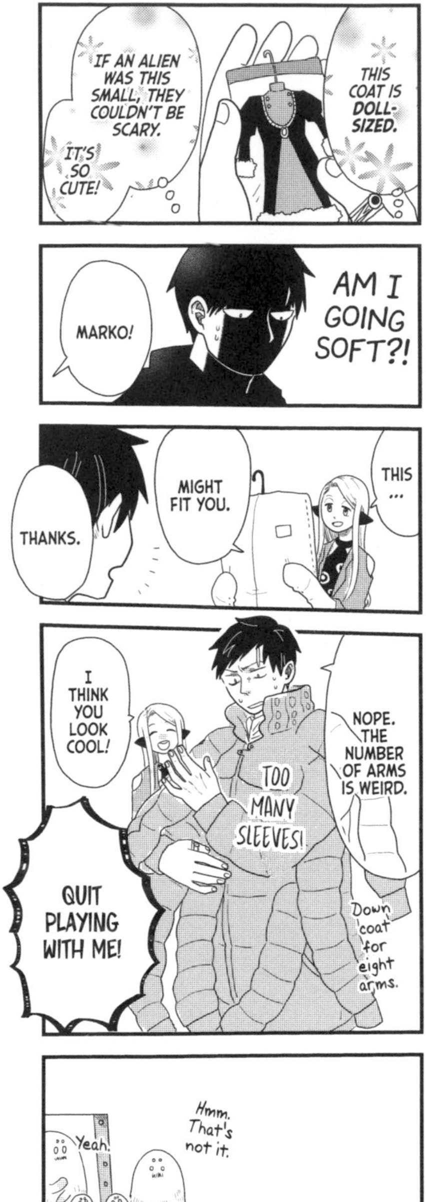
THIS COAT IS DOLL-SIZED.
IF AN ALIEN WAS THIS SMALL, THEY COULDN'T BE SCARY.
IT'S SO CUTE!
AM I GOING SOFT?!
MARKO!
THIS...
MIGHT FIT YOU.
THANKS.
NOPE. THE NUMBER OF ARMS IS WEIRD.
TOO MANY SLEEVES!
I THINK YOU LOOK COOL!
QUIT PLAYING WITH ME!
Down coat for eight arms.
Hmm. That's not it.
Yeah.

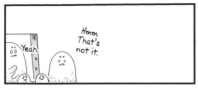

Floor

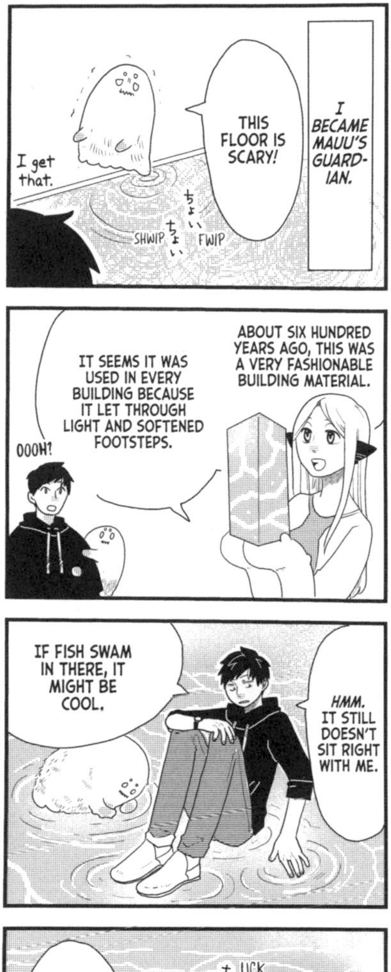
I BECAME MAUU'S GUARDIAN.
THIS FLOOR IS SCARY!
I get that.
ちょい ちょい
FWIP
SHWIP
ABOUT SIX HUNDRED YEARS AGO, THIS WAS A VERY FASHIONABLE BUILDING MATERIAL.
IT SEEMS IT WAS USED IN EVERY BUILDING BECAUSE IT LET THROUGH LIGHT AND SOFTENED FOOTSTEPS.
OOOH?
HMM. IT STILL DOESN'T SIT RIGHT WITH ME.
IF FISH SWAM IN THERE, IT MIGHT BE COOL.
ちる ちる
LICK
LICK
HEY! DON'T LICK IT!

Vast

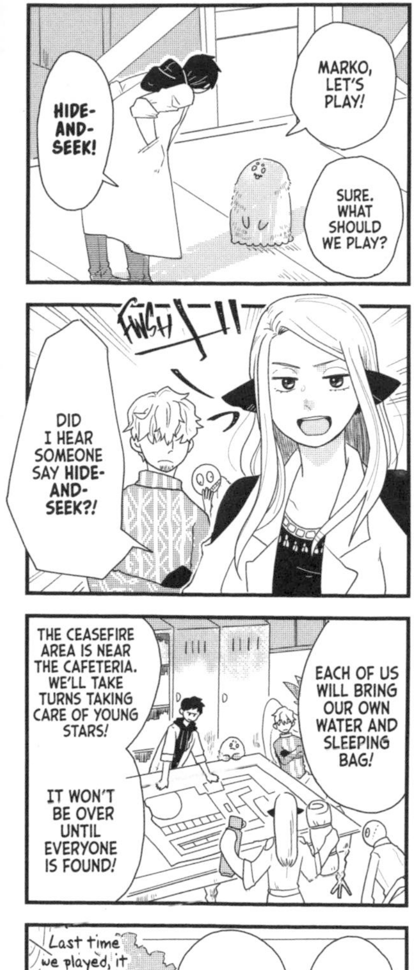
MARKO, LET'S PLAY!
SURE. WHAT SHOULD WE PLAY?
HIDE-AND-SEEK!
FWSH
DID I HEAR SOMEONE SAY HIDE-AND-SEEK?!
EACH OF US WILL BRING OUR OWN WATER AND SLEEPING BAG!
THE CEASEFIRE AREA IS NEAR THE CAFETERIA. WE'LL TAKE TURNS TAKING CARE OF YOUNG STARS!
IT WON'T BE OVER UNTIL EVERYONE IS FOUND!
HOW DID IT ESCALATE SO QUICKLY?
EVERYONE WANTS TO PLAY IT ONCE DURING THEIR TERM.
Last time we played, it took twelve days!

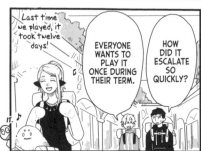

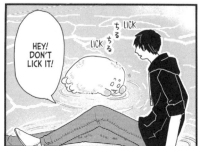

At the Cafeteria ①

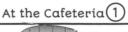

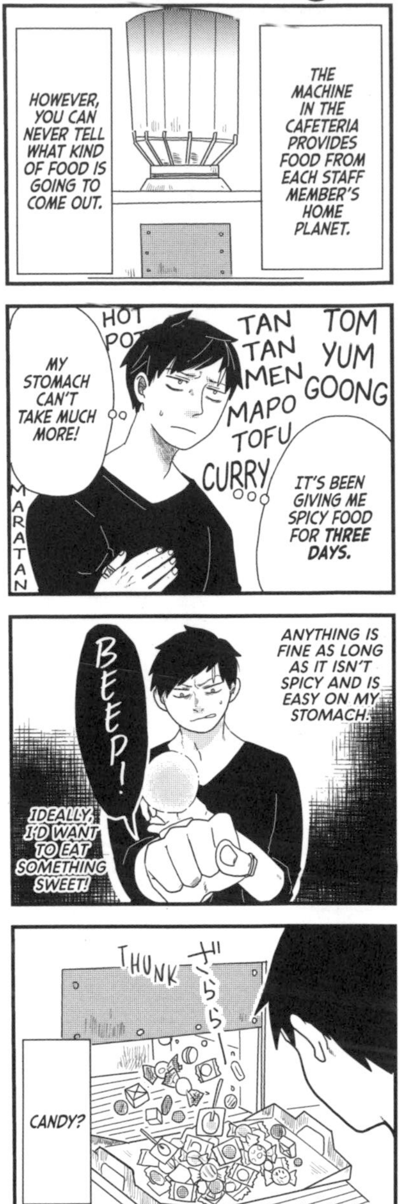
THE MACHINE IN THE CAFETERIA PROVIDES FOOD FROM EACH STAFF MEMBER'S HOME PLANET.
HOWEVER, YOU CAN NEVER TELL WHAT KIND OF FOOD IS GOING TO COME OUT.
TOM YUM GOONG
TAN TAN MEN
HOT POT
MAPO TOFU
CURRY
MARATAN
IT'S BEEN GIVING ME SPICY FOOD FOR **THREE DAYS.**
MY STOMACH CAN'T TAKE MUCH MORE!
ANYTHING IS FINE AS LONG AS IT ISN'T SPICY AND IS EASY ON MY STOMACH.
BEEP!
IDEALLY, I'D WANT TO EAT SOMETHING SWEET!
THUNK
CANDY?

At the Cafeteria ②

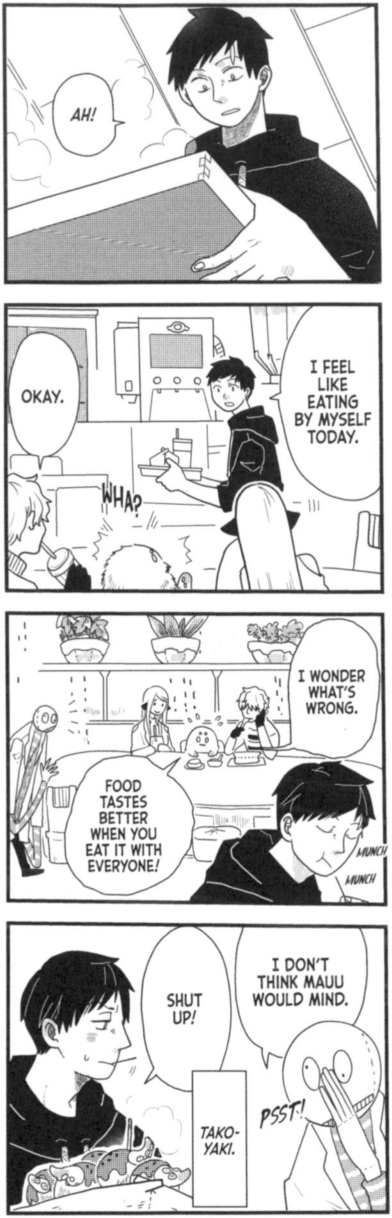
AH!
I FEEL LIKE EATING BY MYSELF TODAY.
WHA?
OKAY.
I WONDER WHAT'S WRONG.
FOOD TASTES BETTER WHEN YOU EAT IT WITH EVERYONE!
MUNCH
MUNCH
I DON'T THINK MAUU WOULD MIND.
SHUT UP!
PSST!
TAKO-YAKI.

※Takoyaki is a fried ball of dough with an octopus filling.

Halfsies

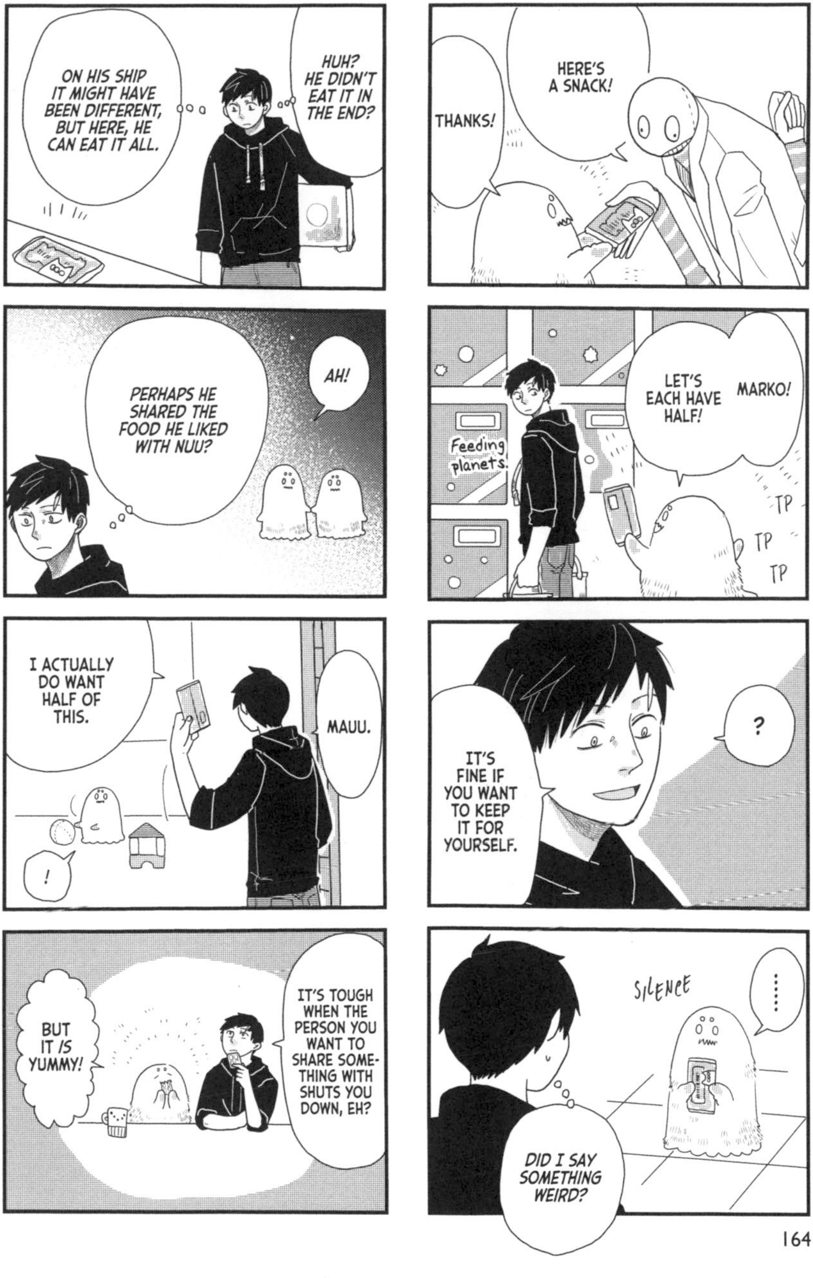
HERE'S A SNACK!
THANKS!
MARKO!
LET'S EACH HAVE HALF!
Feeding planets.
TP
TP
TP
?
IT'S FINE IF YOU WANT TO KEEP IT FOR YOURSELF.
SILENCE
......
DID I SAY SOMETHING WEIRD?
HUH? HE DIDN'T EAT IT IN THE END?
ON HIS SHIP IT MIGHT HAVE BEEN DIFFERENT, BUT HERE, HE CAN EAT IT ALL.
AH!
PERHAPS HE SHARED THE FOOD HE LIKED WITH NUU?
MAUU.
I ACTUALLY DO WANT HALF OF THIS.
!
IT'S TOUGH WHEN THE PERSON YOU WANT TO SHARE SOMETHING WITH SHUTS YOU DOWN, EH?
BUT IT *IS* YUMMY!

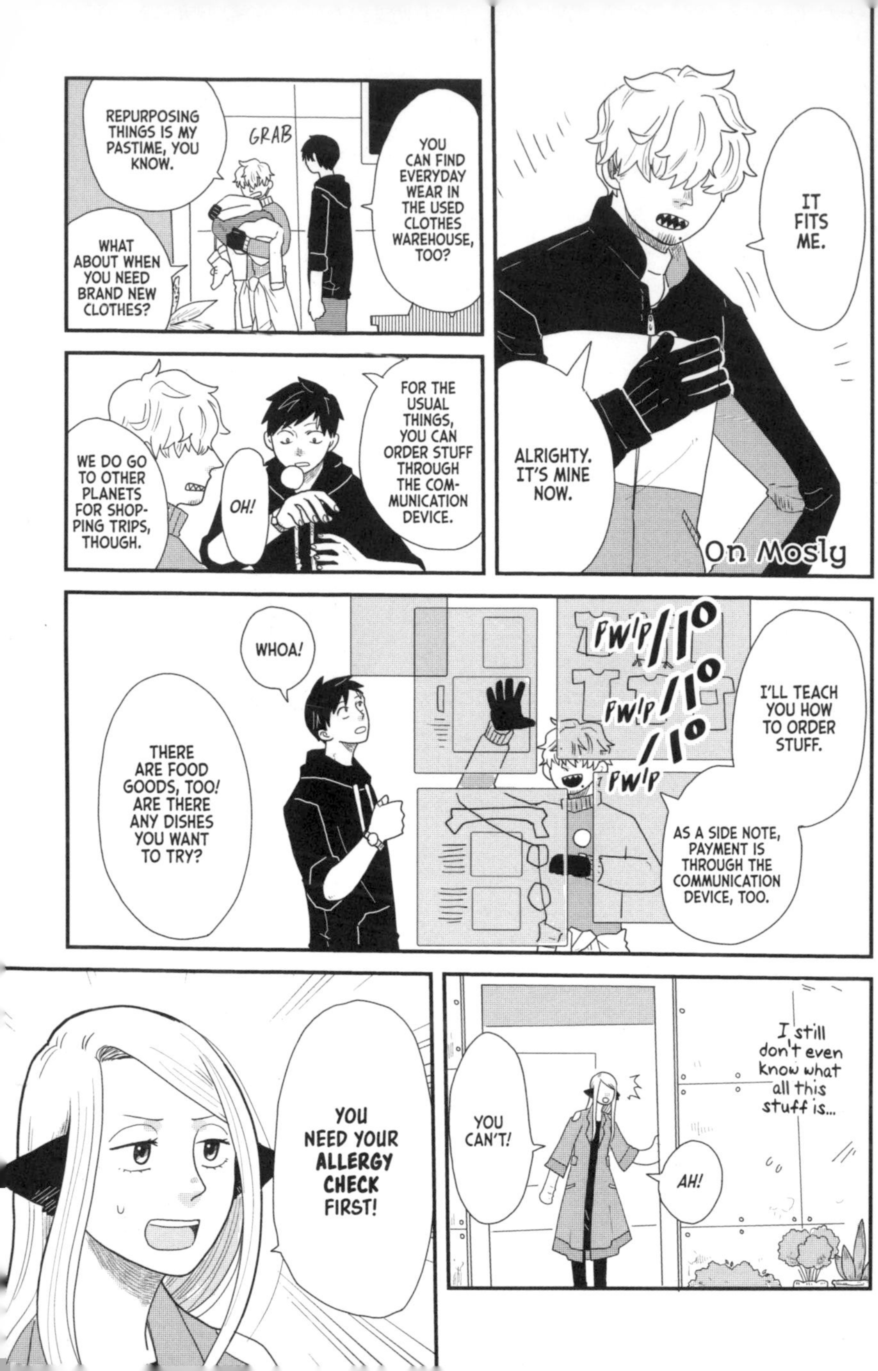
IT FITS ME.
ALRIGHTY. IT'S MINE NOW.
On Mosly
YOU CAN FIND EVERYDAY WEAR IN THE USED CLOTHES WAREHOUSE, TOO?
GRAB
REPURPOSING THINGS IS MY PASTIME, YOU KNOW.
WHAT ABOUT WHEN YOU NEED BRAND NEW CLOTHES?
FOR THE USUAL THINGS, YOU CAN ORDER STUFF THROUGH THE COM-MUNICATION DEVICE.
OH!
WE DO GO TO OTHER PLANETS FOR SHOP-PING TRIPS, THOUGH.
I'LL TEACH YOU HOW TO ORDER STUFF.
PWIP
PWIP
PWIP
AS A SIDE NOTE, PAYMENT IS THROUGH THE COMMUNICATION DEVICE, TOO.
WHOA!
THERE ARE FOOD GOODS, TOO! ARE THERE ANY DISHES YOU WANT TO TRY?
I still don't even know what all this stuff is...
AH!
YOU CAN'T!
YOU NEED YOUR ALLERGY CHECK FIRST!

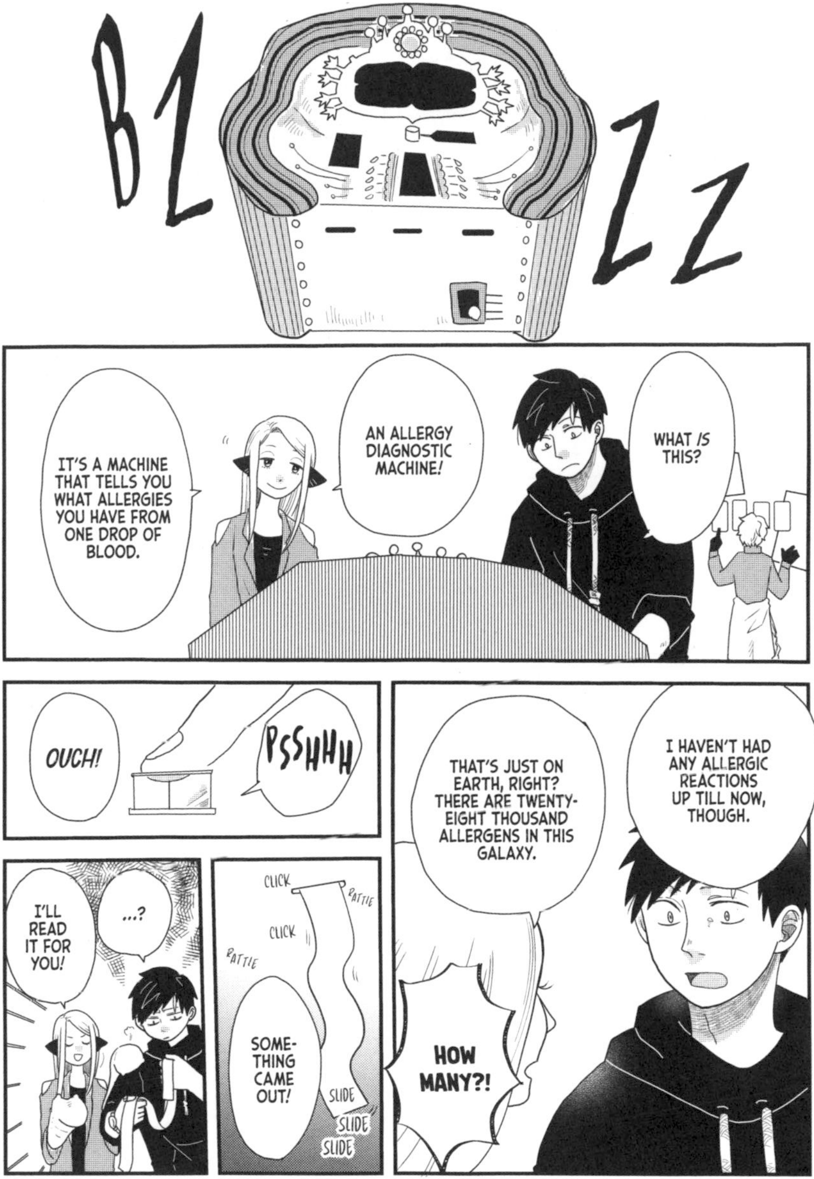
BZZZ
WHAT IS THIS?
AN ALLERGY DIAGNOSTIC MACHINE!
IT'S A MACHINE THAT TELLS YOU WHAT ALLERGIES YOU HAVE FROM ONE DROP OF BLOOD.
I HAVEN'T HAD ANY ALLERGIC REACTIONS UP TILL NOW, THOUGH.
THAT'S JUST ON EARTH, RIGHT? THERE ARE TWENTY-EIGHT THOUSAND ALLERGENS IN THIS GALAXY.
HOW MANY?!
PSSHHH
OUCH!
CLICK
RATTLE
CLICK
RATTLE
SOME-THING CAME OUT!
SLIDE
SLIDE
SLIDE
...?
I'LL READ IT FOR YOU!

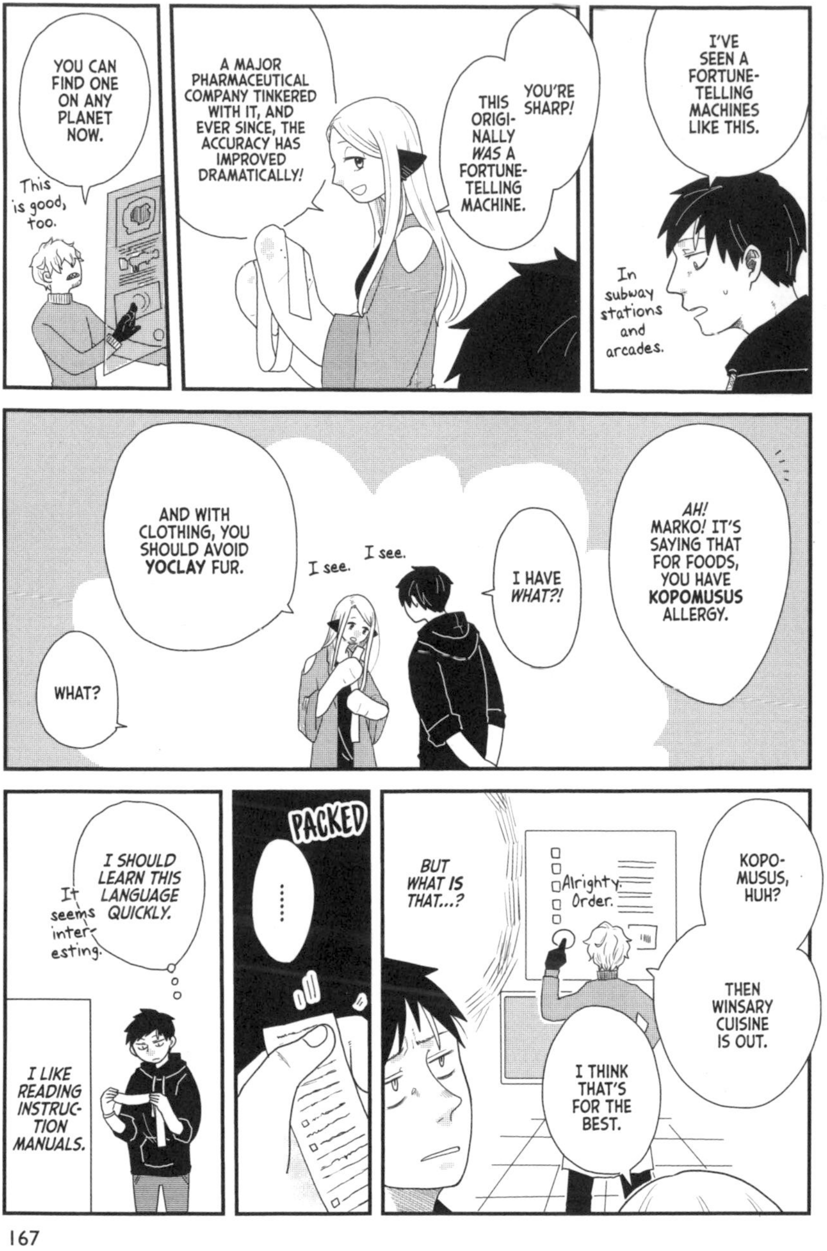
I'VE SEEN A FORTUNE-TELLING MACHINES LIKE THIS.
In subway stations and arcades.
YOU'RE SHARP!
THIS ORIGINALLY WAS A FORTUNE-TELLING MACHINE.
A MAJOR PHARMACEUTICAL COMPANY TINKERED WITH IT, AND EVER SINCE, THE ACCURACY HAS IMPROVED DRAMATICALLY!
YOU CAN FIND ONE ON ANY PLANET NOW.
This is good, too.
AH! MARKO! IT'S SAYING THAT FOR FOODS, YOU HAVE KOPOMUSUS ALLERGY.
I HAVE WHAT?!
I see.
I see.
AND WITH CLOTHING, YOU SHOULD AVOID YOCLAY FUR.
WHAT?
KOPO-MUSUS, HUH?
THEN WINSARY CUISINE IS OUT.
I THINK THAT'S FOR THE BEST.
Alrighty. Order.
BUT WHAT IS THAT...?
PACKED
......
I SHOULD LEARN THIS LANGUAGE QUICKLY.
It seems interesting.
I LIKE READING INSTRUCTION MANUALS.

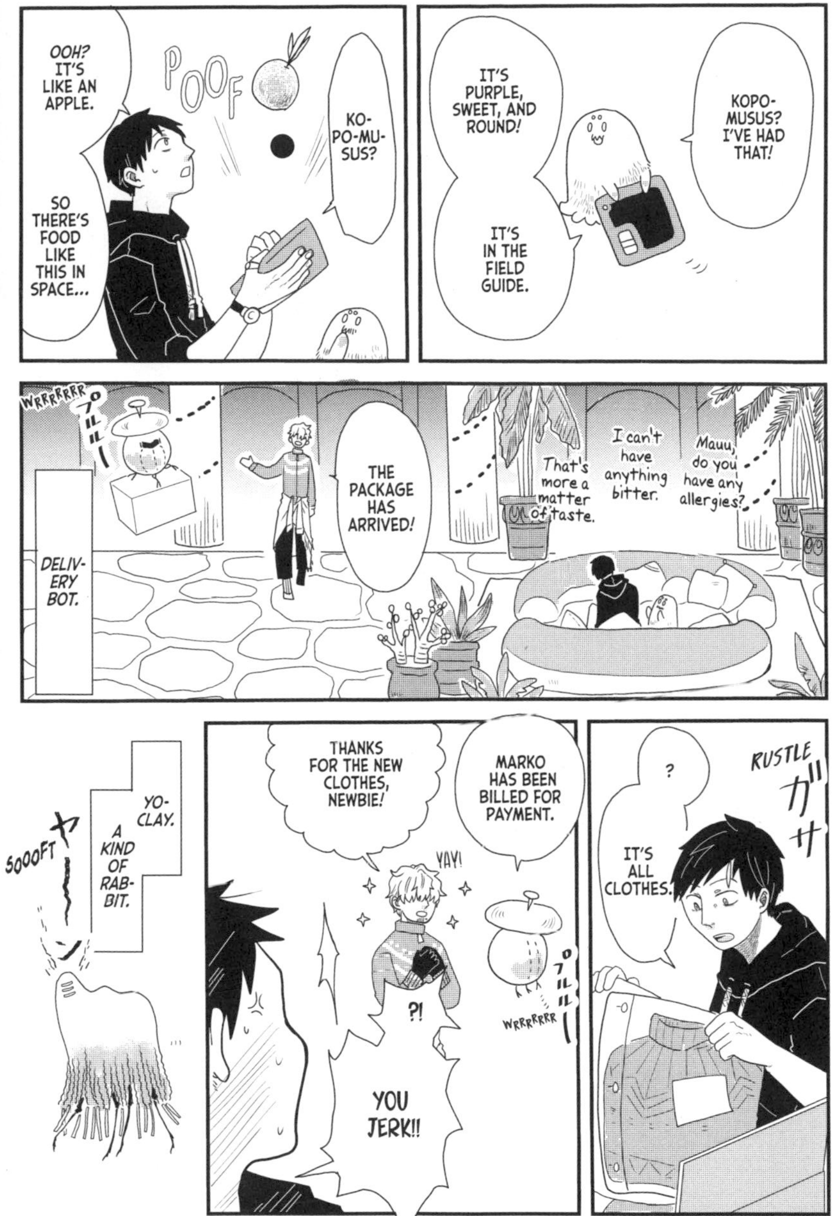
KOPO-MUSUS? I'VE HAD THAT!
IT'S PURPLE, SWEET, AND ROUND!
IT'S IN THE FIELD GUIDE.
KO-PO-MU-SUS?
POOF
OOH? IT'S LIKE AN APPLE.
SO THERE'S FOOD LIKE THIS IN SPACE...
Mauu, do you have any allergies?
I can't have anything bitter.
That's more a matter of taste.
THE PACKAGE HAS ARRIVED!
WRRRRRRR
DELIVERY BOT.
RUSTLE
?
IT'S ALL CLOTHES.
MARKO HAS BEEN BILLED FOR PAYMENT.
THANKS FOR THE NEW CLOTHES, NEWBIE!
YAY!
WRRRRRRR
?!
YOU JERK!!
YO-CLAY.
A KIND OF RABBIT.
SOOOFT

Marko and Rayzol

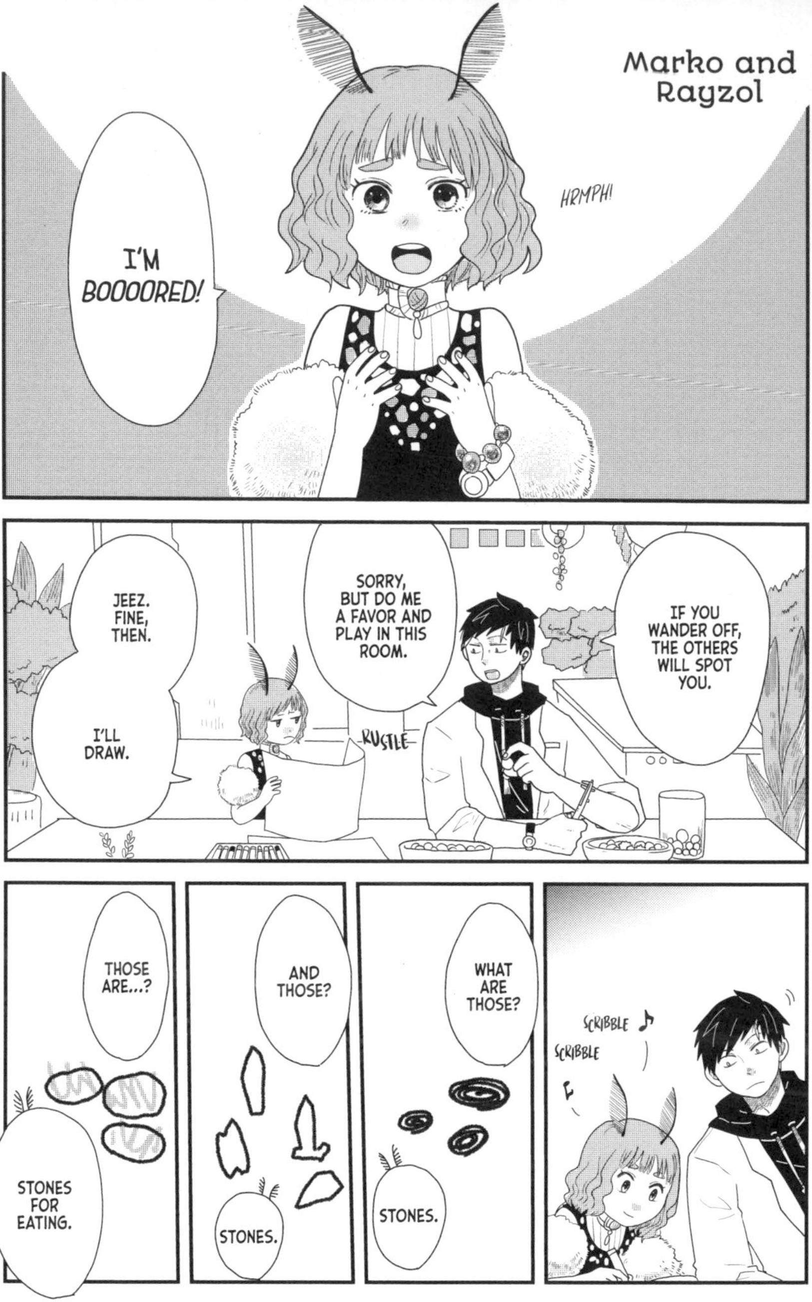

HRMPH!
I'M BOOOORED!
IF YOU WANDER OFF, THE OTHERS WILL SPOT YOU.
SORRY, BUT DO ME A FAVOR AND PLAY IN THIS ROOM.
RUSTLE
JEEZ. FINE, THEN.
I'LL DRAW.
SCRIBBLE ♪
SCRIBBLE
WHAT ARE THOSE?
STONES.
AND THOSE?
STONES.
THOSE ARE...?
STONES FOR EATING.

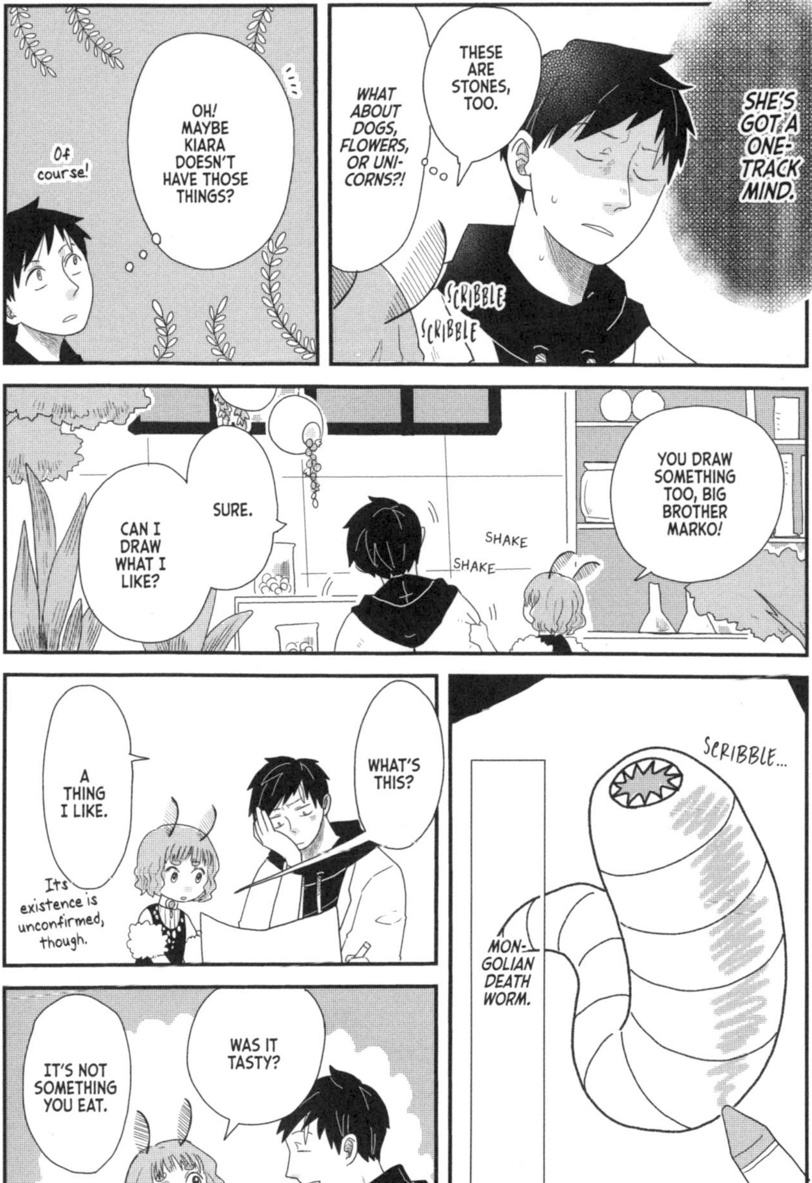
THESE ARE STONES, TOO.
WHAT ABOUT DOGS, FLOWERS, OR UNICORNS?!
SCRIBBLE
SCRIBBLE
SHE'S GOT A ONE-TRACK MIND.
...
OH! MAYBE KIARA DOESN'T HAVE THOSE THINGS?
Of course!
YOU DRAW SOMETHING TOO, BIG BROTHER MARKO!
SHAKE
SHAKE
SURE.
CAN I DRAW WHAT I LIKE?
SCRIBBLE...
MONGOLIAN DEATH WORM.
WHAT'S THIS?
A THING I LIKE.
Its existence is unconfirmed, though.
WAS IT TASTY?
IT'S NOT SOMETHING YOU EAT.

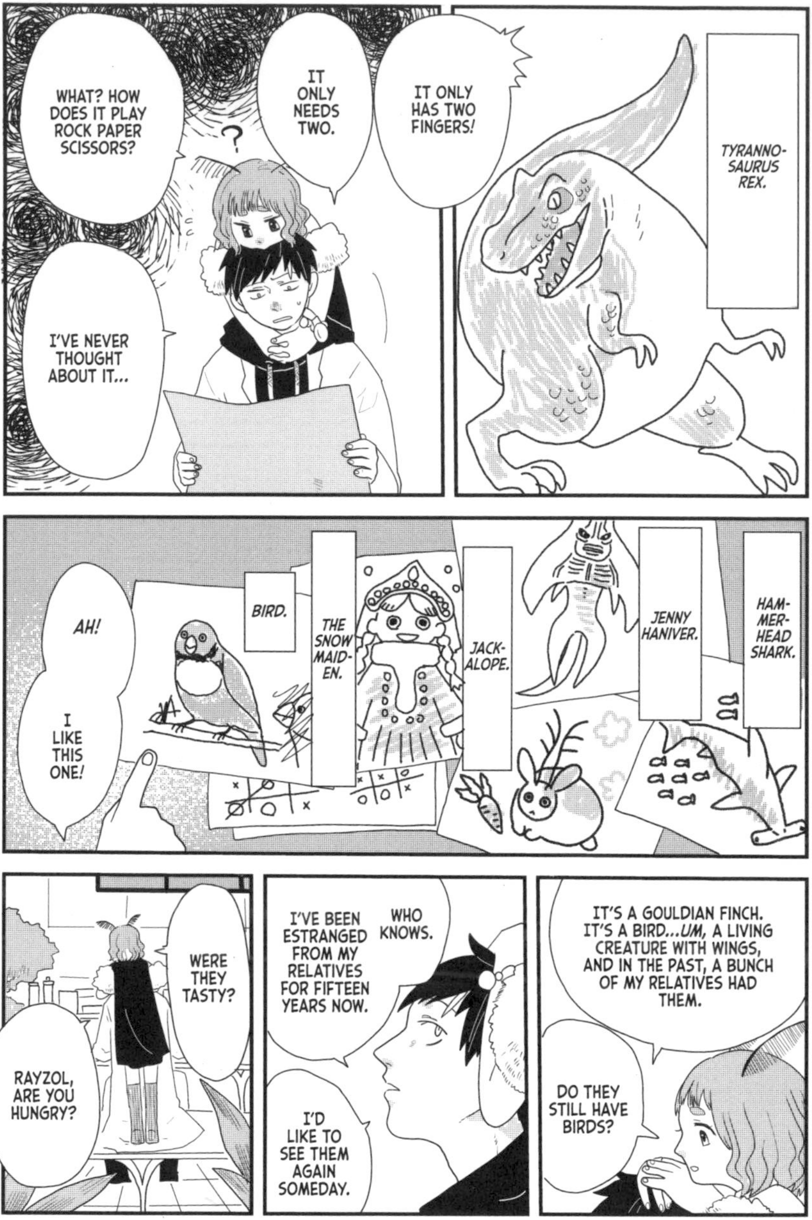
TYRANNOSAURUS REX.
IT ONLY HAS TWO FINGERS!
IT ONLY NEEDS TWO.
WHAT? HOW DOES IT PLAY ROCK PAPER SCISSORS?
I'VE NEVER THOUGHT ABOUT IT...
HAMMERHEAD SHARK.
JENNY HANIVER.
JACKALOPE.
THE SNOW MAIDEN.
BIRD.
AH!
I LIKE THIS ONE!
IT'S A GOULDIAN FINCH. IT'S A BIRD...*UM*, A LIVING CREATURE WITH WINGS, AND IN THE PAST, A BUNCH OF MY RELATIVES HAD THEM.
DO THEY STILL HAVE BIRDS?
WHO KNOWS.
I'VE BEEN ESTRANGED FROM MY RELATIVES FOR FIFTEEN YEARS NOW.
I'D LIKE TO SEE THEM AGAIN SOMEDAY.
WERE THEY TASTY?
RAYZOL, ARE YOU HUNGRY?

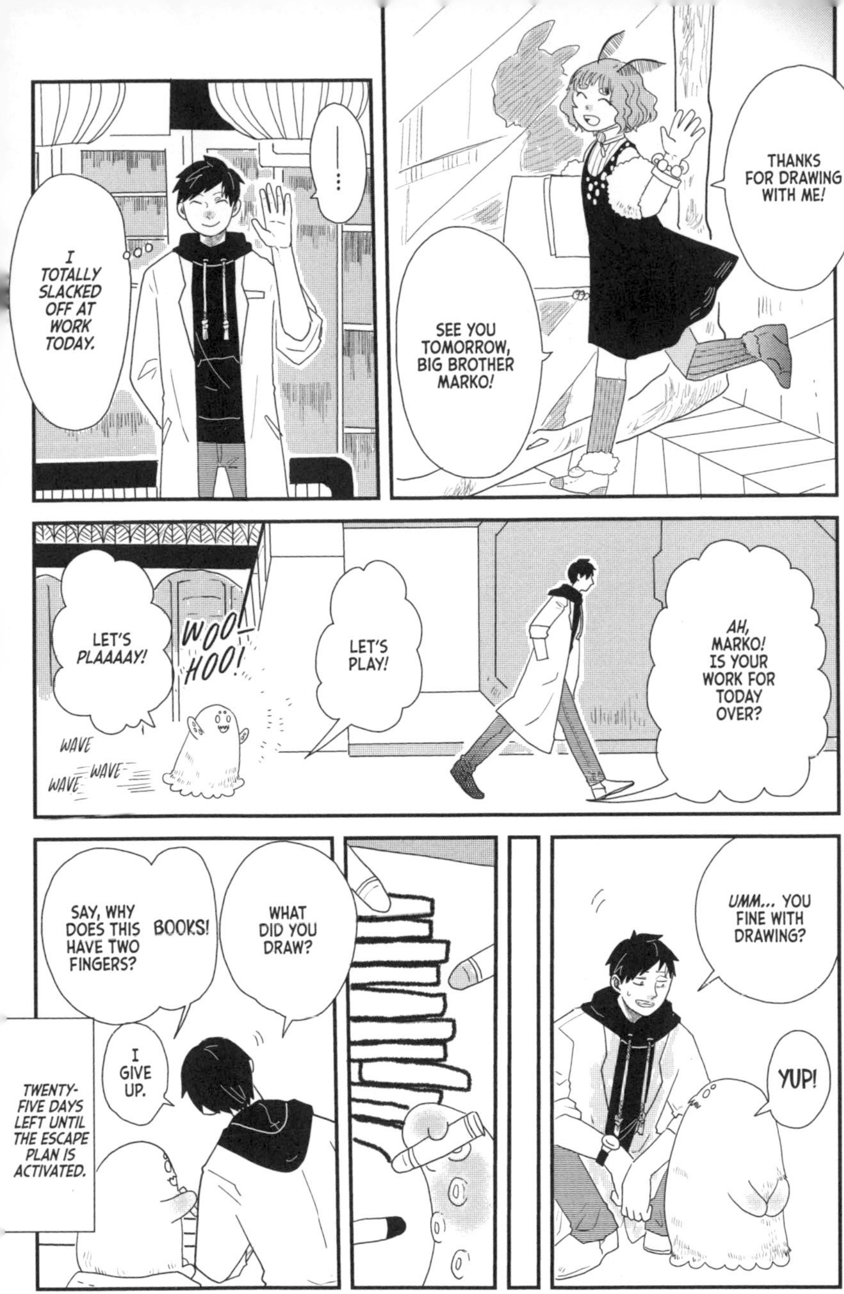
THANKS FOR DRAWING WITH ME!
SEE YOU TOMORROW, BIG BROTHER MARKO!
……
I TOTALLY SLACKED OFF AT WORK TODAY.
AH, MARKO! IS YOUR WORK FOR TODAY OVER?
LET'S PLAY!
WOO-HOO!
LET'S PLAAAAY!
WAVE WAVE WAVE
UMM… YOU FINE WITH DRAWING?
YUP!
WHAT DID YOU DRAW?
BOOKS!
SAY, WHY DOES THIS HAVE TWO FINGERS?
I GIVE UP.
TWENTY-FIVE DAYS LEFT UNTIL THE ESCAPE PLAN IS ACTIVATED.

Correspondence from the End of the Universe

Setting Information

Planet Mosly

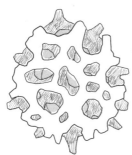

- ONE OF THE END MANAGEMENT BUREAU BRANCH OFFICES, AN ASTEROID OF ABOUT 100 KM². IN THE 8ᵀᴴ GALAXY.

- COVERED WITH A TREE-LIKE SHELL THAT EXTENDS FROM THE SURFACE OF THE GROUND. INSIDE IT IS A WORLD OF EVERLASTING WINTER.

- A HOLLOWED CORE COMPLETELY ACCOMMODATES THE MANAGEMENT STATION FACILITY.

- THERE ARE TWO MOONS.

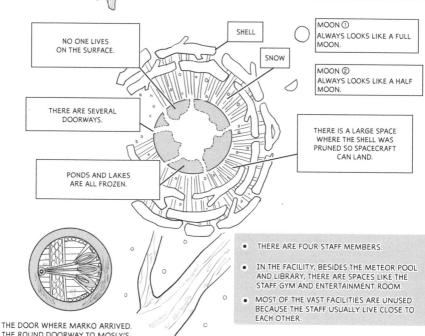

NO ONE LIVES ON THE SURFACE.

SHELL

SNOW

MOON ①
ALWAYS LOOKS LIKE A FULL MOON.

MOON ②
ALWAYS LOOKS LIKE A HALF MOON.

THERE ARE SEVERAL DOORWAYS.

THERE IS A LARGE SPACE WHERE THE SHELL WAS PRUNED SO SPACECRAFT CAN LAND.

PONDS AND LAKES ARE ALL FROZEN.

THE DOOR WHERE MARKO ARRIVED. THE ROUND DOORWAY TO MOSLY'S INTERIOR IS VERY SIMILAR TO THOSE OF THE ETHNIC MINORITY LIVING IN THE NORTHERN LANDS OF ENO PLANET.
FORMER STAFF MAY HAVE COME FROM THERE.

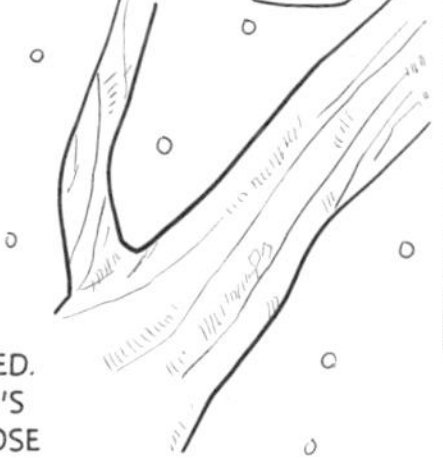

THE SHELL APPEARS SIMILAR TO PLANTS, BUT THE COMPOSITION IS CLOSER TO ANIMAL BONES.

- THERE ARE FOUR STAFF MEMBERS.

- IN THE FACILITY, BESIDES THE METEOR POOL AND LIBRARY, THERE ARE SPACES LIKE THE STAFF GYM AND ENTERTAINMENT ROOM.

- MOST OF THE VAST FACILITIES ARE UNUSED BECAUSE THE STAFF USUALLY LIVE CLOSE TO EACH OTHER.

Staff Residences

· IN THE FACILITY BASEMENT, 8TH FLOOR DOWN (BOTTOM FLOOR)

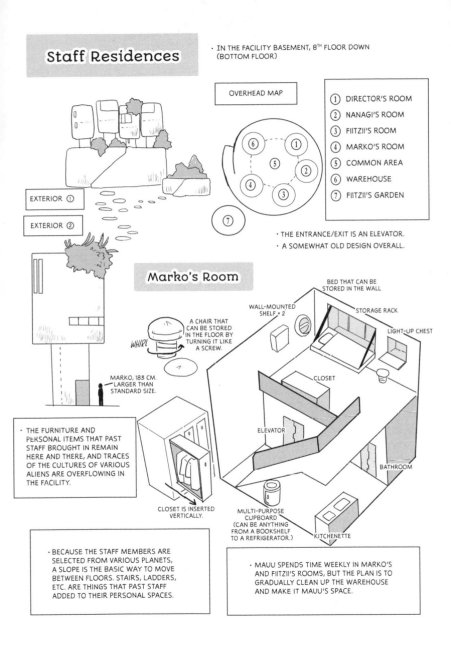

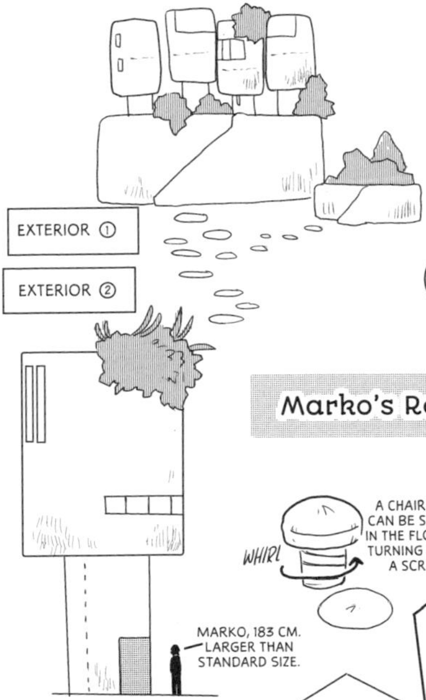
EXTERIOR ①
EXTERIOR ②
MARKO, 183 CM. LARGER THAN STANDARD SIZE.

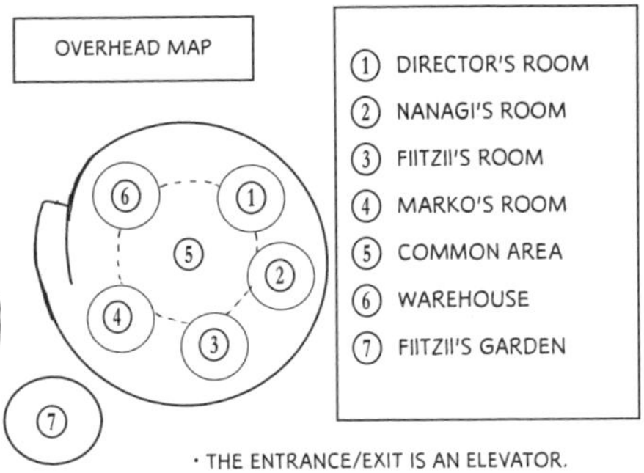
OVERHEAD MAP
① DIRECTOR'S ROOM
② NANAGI'S ROOM
③ FIITZII'S ROOM
④ MARKO'S ROOM
⑤ COMMON AREA
⑥ WAREHOUSE
⑦ FIITZII'S GARDEN

· THE ENTRANCE/EXIT IS AN ELEVATOR.

· A SOMEWHAT OLD DESIGN OVERALL.

· THE FURNITURE AND PERSONAL ITEMS THAT PAST STAFF BROUGHT IN REMAIN HERE AND THERE, AND TRACES OF THE CULTURES OF VARIOUS ALIENS ARE OVERFLOWING IN THE FACILITY.

Marko's Room

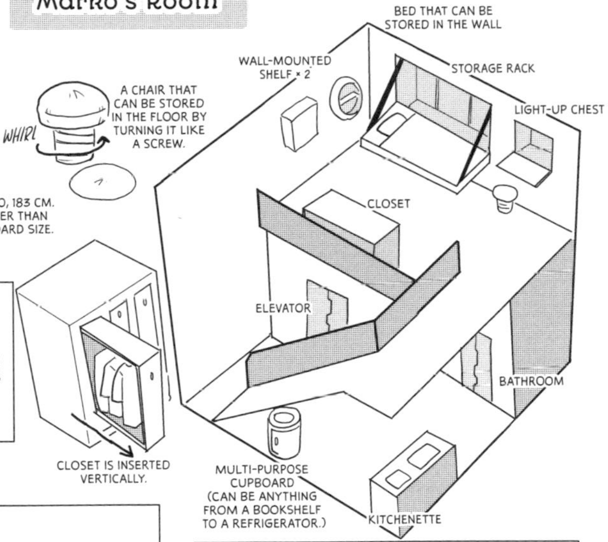
BED THAT CAN BE STORED IN THE WALL
WALL-MOUNTED SHELF × 2
STORAGE RACK
LIGHT-UP CHEST
A CHAIR THAT CAN BE STORED IN THE FLOOR BY TURNING IT LIKE A SCREW.
WHIRL
CLOSET
ELEVATOR
BATHROOM
CLOSET IS INSERTED VERTICALLY.
MULTI-PURPOSE CUPBOARD (CAN BE ANYTHING FROM A BOOKSHELF TO A REFRIGERATOR.)
KITCHENETTE

· BECAUSE THE STAFF MEMBERS ARE SELECTED FROM VARIOUS PLANETS, A SLOPE IS THE BASIC WAY TO MOVE BETWEEN FLOORS. STAIRS, LADDERS, ETC. ARE THINGS THAT PAST STAFF ADDED TO THEIR PERSONAL SPACES.

· MAUU SPENDS TIME WEEKLY IN MARKO'S AND FIITZII'S ROOMS, BUT THE PLAN IS TO GRADUALLY CLEAN UP THE WAREHOUSE AND MAKE IT MAUU'S SPACE.

Horshe 8

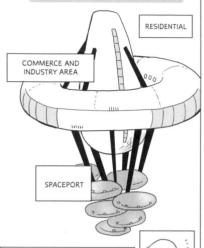

RESIDENTIAL
COMMERCE AND INDUSTRY AREA
SPACEPORT

- A PLANET MADE FOR THE PURPOSE OF PRODUCING AND SUPPLYING NECESSARY SUPPLIES TO END MANAGERS. ON THE FACE OF IT, IT IS A SPACEPORT USED AS A RELAY POINT FOR TRANSPORT OF GOODS. (IT ALSO HAS A HISTORY MUSEUM ABOUT THE CREATION OF PLANETS).

- AMIDST THE OPEN PLANETS OF THE 8TH GALAXY, IT'S COMMON SENSE THAT "PLANETS ARE LIVING THINGS" AND "PLANETS ARE BORN FROM EGGS AND SWIM OUT TO GROW UP IN GALAXIES," ETC., BUT THEY CONSIDER END MANAGERS AND THE SUPERIOR TO JUST BE LEGENDS.

- AS AN EXCEPTION, HORSHE 8 RESIDENTS LEARN FROM AN EARLY AGE ABOUT THE SUPERIOR AND EACH BRANCH OFFICE, AND THEY ADHERE TO OATHS NOT TO TELL ORDINARY ALIENS ABOUT THEM.

- HORSHE 8, ALTHOUGH CERTIFIED AS A PLANET, IS A SPACE COLONY, AND IS DESIGNED TO HAVE THE RESIDENTIAL AREA TURN INTO A GIANT SPACECRAFT BY SEPARATING THE SPACEPORT FROM THE COMMERCIAL AND INDUSTRIAL AREA. (A FEATURE NOT ACTUALLY USED YET.)

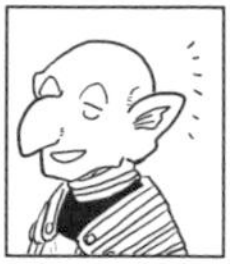

- FROM THE OUTSIDE, HORSHE 8 RESIDENTS APPEAR TO HAVE NO GENDER DIFFERENCE, AND IT IS DIFFICULT FOR OTHER ALIENS TO DISTINGUISH THEIR GENDER. THE ONE WHO GUIDED MARKO AND CREW WAS FEMALE.

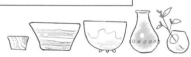

- HORSHE 8 IS LOCATED IN THE SO-CALLED "COUNTRYSIDE" OF THE 8TH GALAXY, BUT IT IS ALSO KNOWN AS A PLACE WHERE THERE ARE A LOT OF GLASS WORKSHOPS. THEY ALSO SHIP TO OUTSIDE PLANETS.

- THE SPACE PIANO HAS NINETY-SEVEN KEYS AND IS A VERTICALLY LONG "GIRAFFE" PIANO.
CURRENTLY DISMANTLED AND ON DISPLAY ON HORSHE 8.
THE STEEL FRAME PART IS IN THE RESIDENTIAL AREA PARK, AND HAS BEEN REMODELED INTO A HUGE JUNGLE GYM FREQUENTLY USED BY CHILDREN.

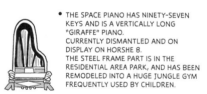

KEY BENCH

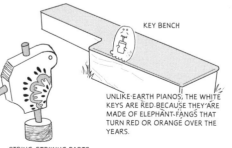

UNLIKE EARTH PIANOS, THE WHITE KEYS ARE RED BECAUSE THEY ARE MADE OF ELEPHANT FANGS THAT TURN RED OR ORANGE OVER THE YEARS.

- AMONG THE ALIENS YOU SEE HERE, SIXTY PERCENT ARE STAFF. THERE ARE ALSO PEOPLE WHO MAINTAIN FRIENDSHIPS OUTSIDE OF THE BRANCH.

STRING-STRIKING PARTS MADE INTO ART.

Marko's House

PIANO IN THE HALLWAY
PARENTS' BEDROOM
KITCHEN
LIVING ROOM
MARKO'S ROOM
BATHROOM
OLDER BROTHER'S ROOM
TOILET
FRONT DOOR (DOUBLE DOOR)

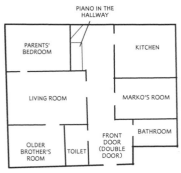

- AN OLD, SOVIET-ERA FAMILY APARTMENT IN ST. PETERSBURG (RENOVATED).
- FAMILY HAS LIVED THERE SINCE MARKO'S GRANDFATHER'S GENERATION.
- LOCATED ON THE 4TH FLOOR OF A FIVE-STORY BUILDING.
- A FLOORPLAN WITH A SEPARATE KITCHEN AND LIVING ROOM.
- IN RUSSIA, YOU CHANGE TO INDOOR SHOES AT THE ENTRANCE. (MARKO WENT TO SPACE WITH HIS INDOOR SHOES ON.)
- PLEASANT ENOUGH IN THE WINTER THANKS TO CENTRAL HEATING.
- PETS ARE BANNED, BUT MARKO KNOWS THAT THE OLD MAN DOWNSTAIRS HAS A CAT.
- THREE CHILDHOOD FRIENDS ALSO LIVE IN THE NEIGHBORHOOD.

DISPLAY CASE NEXT TO THE PIANO. MARKO'S SWIMMING, PIANO, AND COMPOSITION AWARDS ARE ON DISPLAY.

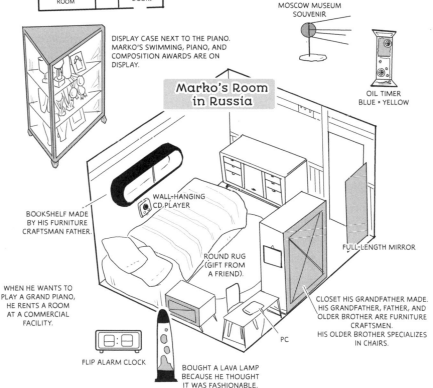

MOSCOW MUSEUM SOUVENIR

OIL TIMER BLUE × YELLOW

Marko's Room in Russia

WALL-HANGING CD PLAYER
ROUND RUG (GIFT FROM A FRIEND).
FULL-LENGTH MIRROR

BOOKSHELF MADE BY HIS FURNITURE CRAFTSMAN FATHER.

CLOSET HIS GRANDFATHER MADE. HIS GRANDFATHER, FATHER, AND OLDER BROTHER ARE FURNITURE CRAFTSMEN. HIS OLDER BROTHER SPECIALIZES IN CHAIRS.

PC

WHEN HE WANTS TO PLAY A GRAND PIANO, HE RENTS A ROOM AT A COMMERCIAL FACILITY.

FLIP ALARM CLOCK

BOUGHT A LAVA LAMP BECAUSE HE THOUGHT IT WAS FASHIONABLE.

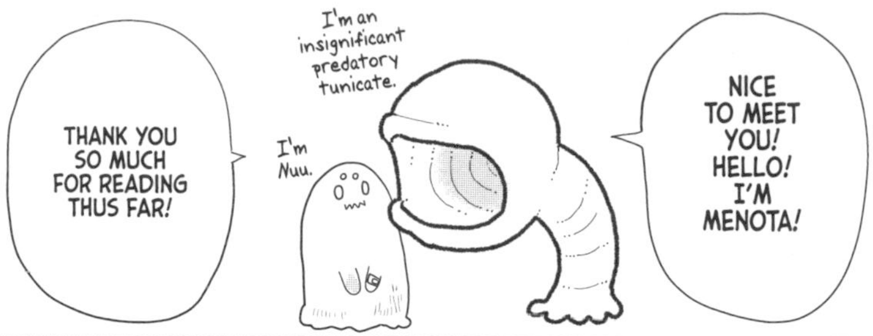
NICE TO MEET YOU! HELLO! I'M MENOTA!
I'm an insignificant predatory tunicate.
I'm Nuu.
THANK YOU SO MUCH FOR READING THUS FAR!

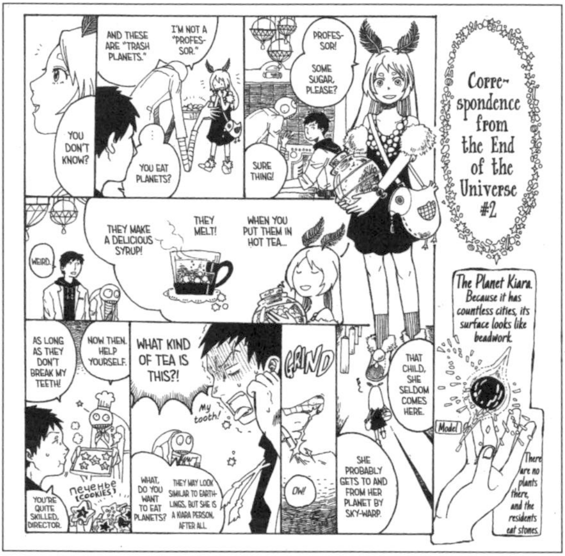
Corre-spondence from the End of the Universe #2
PROFES-SOR!
SOME SUGAR, PLEASE?
SURE THING!
I'M NOT A "PROFES-SOR."
AND THESE ARE "TRASH PLANETS."
YOU EAT PLANETS?
YOU DON'T KNOW?
WHEN YOU PUT THEM IN HOT TEA...
THEY MELT!
THEY MAKE A DELICIOUS SYRUP!
WEIRD.
The Planet Kiara. Because it has countless cities, its surface looks like beadwork.
Model
There are no plants there, and the residents eat stones.
THAT CHILD, SHE SELDOM COMES HERE.
SHE PROBABLY GETS TO AND FROM HER PLANET BY SKY-WARP.
GRIND
OW!
WHAT KIND OF TEA IS THIS?!
My tooth!
THEY MAY LOOK SIMILAR TO EARTH-LINGS, BUT SHE IS A KIARA PERSON, AFTER ALL.
WHAT, DO YOU WANT TO EAT PLANETS?
NOW THEN. HELP YOURSELF.
AS LONG AS THEY DON'T BREAK MY TEETH!
печенье [COOKIES]
YOU'RE QUITE SKILLED, DIRECTOR.

FREE PAPER VERSION

CORRESPONDENCE FROM THE END OF THE UNIVERSE WAS ORIGINALLY PUBLISHED WITH AN ONLINE PRINT SERVICE IN A FREE PAPER DELIVERED ONCE A MONTH.
THE MAIN CHARACTERS WERE JUST MARKO, THE DIRECTOR, AND RAYZOL. I THOUGHT IT WOULD BE INTERESTING IF THE DAILY LIFE OF DISTANT PLANETS WAS PRINTED OUT FROM THE COPY MACHINE IN A CONVENIENCE STORE, AND CONTINUED THE STORY FOR A YEAR AND A HALF.
IN MAKING THE FULL-LENGTH MANGA, MOSLY BECAME LIVELY, AND THE STORY CHANGED A LOT!

THANKS TO ALL MY READERS, EDITORIAL DEPARTMENT STAFF, PEOPLE IN CHARGE WHO I AM ALWAYS INDEBTED TO, AND THE FAMILY THAT CHEERS ME ON, VOLUME ONE HAS BEEN RELEASED. IS IT OKAY THAT I'M JUST ALLOWED DRAW WHAT I LIKE EVERY TIME?! I SOMETIMES WORRY ABOUT IT, BUT IT'S VERY FULFILLING. I'LL BE GLAD IF YOU WILL CONTINUE TO WATCH OVER MARKO'S GROWTH AND THE DAILY LIVES OF ALIENS!

WELL THEN, I HOPE TO SEE YOU AGAIN IN VOLUME TWO!

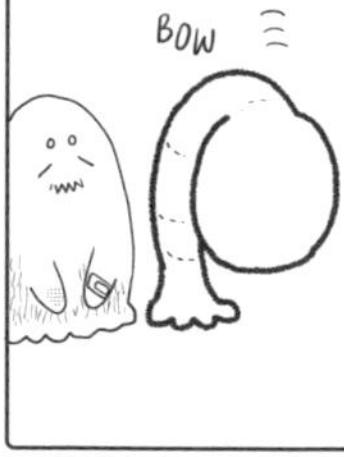
BOW

MENOTA

IN MAKING A PLANET WHERE STONES ARE THE STAPLE FOOD OF THE CREATURES THAT LIVE THERE, WE ORDERED DOCUMENTS FROM ANOTHER BRANCH OFFICE. AMONG THEM, I WAS VERY ATTRACTED TO THE PLANET KIARA'S NATIVE CREATURES, SO I WILL INTRODUCE THEM.

FIRST, THE STONE-EATING CREATURE ITSELF IS NOT UNUSUAL FROM THE PERSPECTIVE OF THE WHOLE UNIVERSE. ON MY MOTHER PLANET, THERE WAS A CULTURAL PASTIME OF WATCHING STONES BE DIGESTED BY MICROORGANISMS.

STONE-EATING CULTURES ARE ONES IN WHICH EITHER THE STRUCTURE OF THE STONE IS DIFFERENT FROM THAT OF A GENERAL PLANET IN THE FIRST PLACE, OR THE NATIVE CREATURES' TEETH AND DIGESTIVE JUICES ARE A SPECIAL TYPE. THE PEOPLE OF THE PLANET KIARA ARE THE LATTER. I WOULDN'T WANT TO GET CLOSE TO THEM. IF ONE CARELESSLY KISSED THEM, ONE WOULD PROBABLY GET MELTED INTO SLUSH.

Stone-Eating Creature Report, According to a Past Staff Member

---

I'VE VEERED OFF FROM THE TOPIC.

ONE TIME ON A CERTAIN PLANET (A PLANET THAT WAS ACCUSED OF INHUMANE EXPERIMENTS BY THE GOVERNMENT AND EVEN HAD TO CHANGE ITS NAME), EXPERIMENTS WERE CONDUCTED TO FEED ANIMALS AND PLANTS TO STONE-EATING CREATURES.

THE RESULTS SHOWED 3 PATTERNS.

1) AFTER A STRONG ALLERGIC REACTION, THEY EXHIBITED DYSPNEA AND DIED.

2) THEY CAN EAT THE PLANT AND ANIMAL MATTER, BUT THEY CAN'T ABSORB ITS NUTRIENTS.

3) THE MATTER CAN BE DIGESTED AND ABSORBED WITHOUT PROBLEMS.

KIARA PEOPLE FIT WITH PATTERN 3.

AFTER ALL, THEY ONLY HAVE STONES ON KIARA, SO THEY WERE ONLY EATING THAT, ALTHOUGH THEY CAN DIGEST ANYTHING. IF A DAY COMES WHEN THEY CAN FREELY MOVE ABOUT THE UNIVERSE, THEY WILL LIKELY ABANDON THEIR MOTHER PLANET AND MOVE TO A PLANET THAT HAS MORE VARIETY.

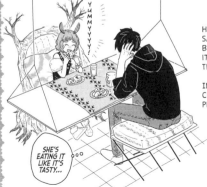

YUMMYYYYY!

SHE'S EATING IT LIKE IT'S TASTY...

HOWEVER, BECAUSE THE COUNTLESS SATELLITES SURROUNDING KIARA ARE BLOCKING THE NAVIGATION OF SPACESHIPS, IT SEEMS LIKE THAT DAY OF REALIZATION FOR THE KIARANS IS STILL FAR OFF.

IN MY PERSONAL OPINION, SUCH A HORRIBLE CREATURE SHOULD BE CONFINED TO ONE PLANET IN PERPETUITY.

Several Memos About the Planet Ronoutogi.

STAFF MEMBER NO. 8733875 WRITES...

The planet Ronoutogi is a planet with just two individuals living on it, male and female. They have a large spacecraft that can withstand long journeys, and the technology to create clones. The clones have copied memories and exceptional scientific talents. Perhaps they were a couple that came (or were exiled?) from another already dead planet to arrive at the paradise Ronoutogi...?

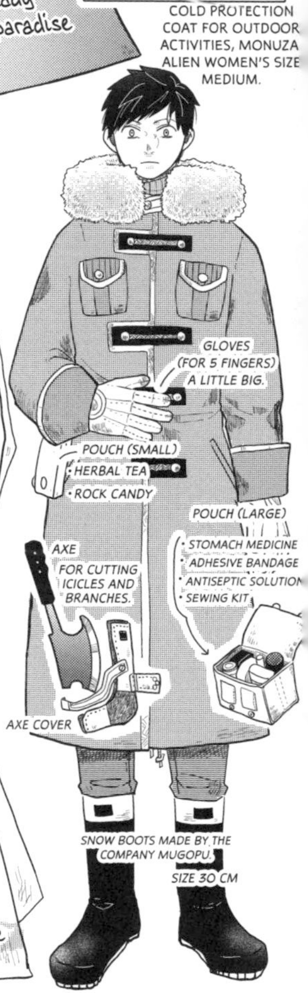

COLD PROTECTION COAT FOR OUTDOOR ACTIVITIES, MONUZA ALIEN WOMEN'S SIZE MEDIUM.
GLOVES (FOR 5 FINGERS) A LITTLE BIG.
POUCH (SMALL)
· HERBAL TEA
· ROCK CANDY
POUCH (LARGE)
· STOMACH MEDICINE
· ADHESIVE BANDAGE
· ANTISEPTIC SOLUTION
· SEWING KIT
AXE
FOR CUTTING ICICLES AND BRANCHES.
AXE COVER
SNOW BOOTS MADE BY THE COMPANY MUGOPU.
SIZE 30 CM

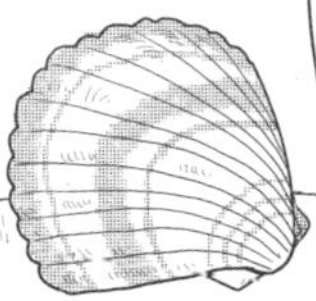

Inside the ship Alcalanca, it was said that fire was strictly prohibited to prevent the collected books from burning.

Inside Mosly's 8th Galaxy, even now, paper books are still mainstream.

This is due to the "eleven planet great power outage accident," which occurred 160 dearu ago, when data conversion of various texts was almost completed (and the data nearly lost). Maybe something similar happened in the Ronoutogi planet's galaxy.

※1 dearu = 20 years in Earth time

About "Mauu," who is a juvenile protected by 8747028 (Marko), and his sibling (?) "Nuu":

Nuu is buried in a hill outside the facility.
Mauu is under Mosly's protection for the time being.

Do not report this to Central.

I saw many clone embryos on board. There are grown clones that take care of newborns, and older ones, too. Nuu and Mauu probably aren't the first case of the "twin bug."

In order to protect, raise, and nurture the "bugged" clones that lack the original's memories, there should have been someone to teach writing systems and history.
Perhaps that was the role of the "bugged" twins in previous generations.
Perhaps it was a mistake to remove Mauu after all...

But now the Ronoutogians are far away, and nothing can be confirmed.

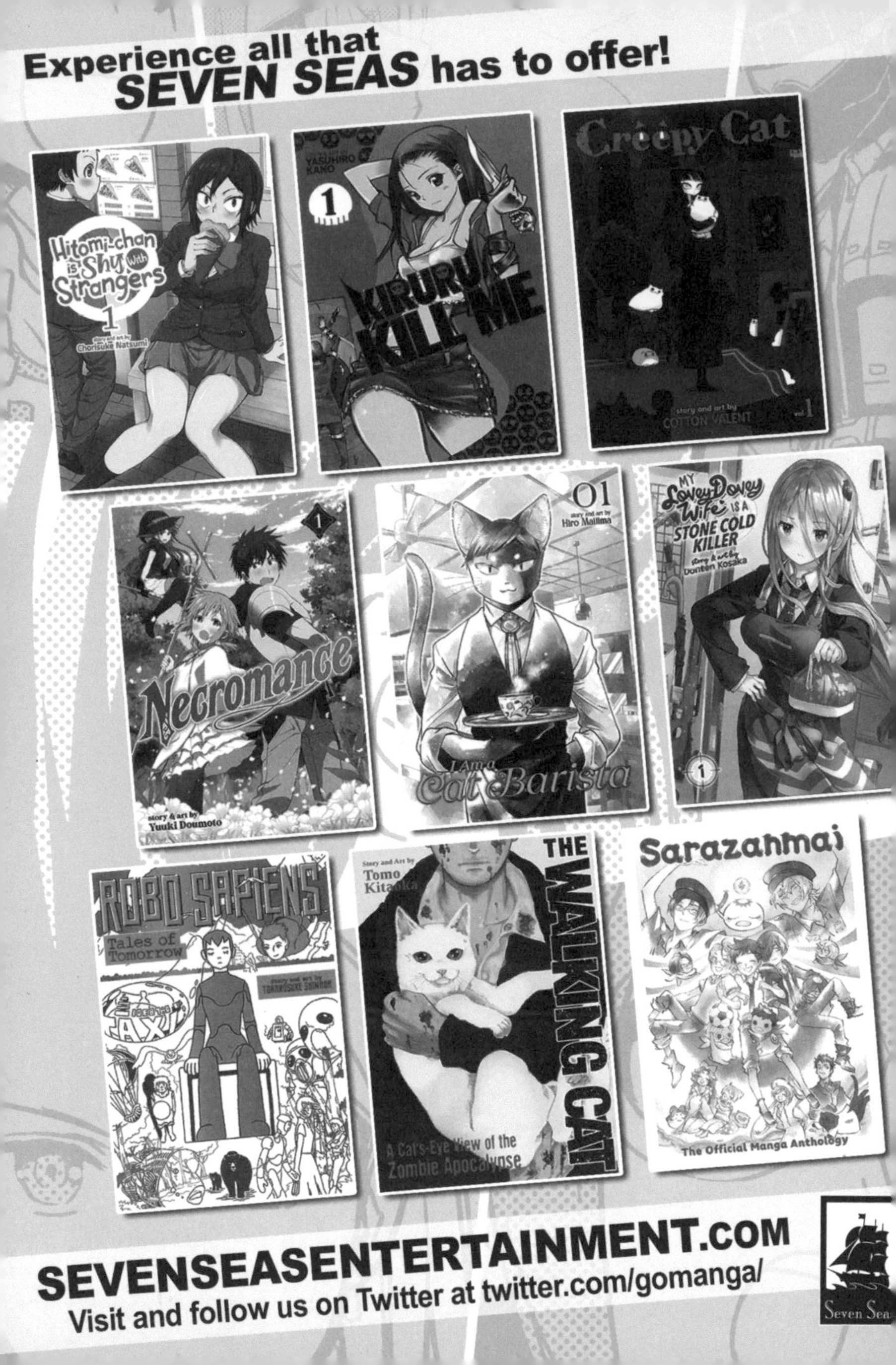

Experience all that
SEVEN SEAS has to offer!
Hitomi-chan is Shy With Strangers
1
Story and art by
Chorisuke Natsumi
YASUHIRO KANO
1
KIRURU KILL ME
Creepy Cat
story and art by
COTTON VALENT
vol 1
1
Necromance
story & art by
Yuuki Doumoto
01
story and art by
Hiro Maijima
I Am a Cat Barista
My Lovey-Dovey Wife is a Stone Cold Killer
story & art by
Donten Kosaka
1
ROBO SAPIENS
Tales of Tomorrow
Story and Art by
Tomo Kitaoka
THE WALKING CAT
A Cat's-Eye View of the Zombie Apocalypse
Sarazanmai
The Official Manga Anthology
SEVENSEASENTERTAINMENT.COM
Visit and follow us on Twitter at twitter.com/gomanga/
Seven Seas

SEVEN SEAS ENTERTAINMENT PRESENTS

Correspondence
from the End of the Universe

story and art by MENOTA

TRANSLATION
Kathryn Henzler

LETTERING
Nicole Roderick

COVER DESIGN
Shi Briggs

PROOFREADER
Krista Grandy
Dawn Davis

SENIOR EDITOR
Shannon Fay

PRODUCTION DESIGNER
Christina McKenzie

PRODUCTION MANAGER
Lissa Pattillo

PREPRESS TECHNICIAN
Melanie Ujimori

PRINT MANAGER
Rhiannon Rasmussen-Silverstein

EDITOR-IN-CHIEF
Julie Davis

ASSOCIATE PUBLISHER
Adam Arnold

PUBLISHER
Jason DeAngelis

HATENO SHOU TSUSHIN
© MENOTA 2019
Originally published in Japa
English translation rights ar
through TOHAN CORPOR/

D1541549

Seven Seas press and purchase enquiries can be sent to Marketing Manager Lianne Sentar at press@gomanga.com. Information regarding the distribution and purchase of digital editions is available from Digital Manager CK Russell at digital@gomanga.com.

Seven Seas and the Seven Seas logo are trademarks of Seven Seas Entertainment. All rights reserved.

ISBN: 978-1-64827-896-9
Printed in USA
First Printing: July 2022
10 9 8 7 6 5 4 3 2 1

READING DIRECTIONS

This book reads from *right to left*, Japanese style. If this is your first time reading manga, you start reading from the top right panel on each page and take it from there. If you get lost, just follow the numbered diagram here. It may seem backwards at first, but you'll get the hang of it! Have fun!!

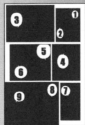

Follow us online: www.SevenSeasEntertainment.com